SUPER AGENT
The One Book the NFL and NCAA Don't Want You to Read

DR. JERRY ARGOVITZ
AND J. DAVID MILLER

SPORTS
PUBLISHING

I want to dedicate this book:

To my beloved mother, Rose, and father, Harry, who taught me life lessons that kept me out of trouble (most of the time) and gave me the confidence and support that all dreams are possible. They placed me on a highwire and told me to walk across, and provided the safety net in case I fell. Their presence, hard work, and total support were the very source of my strength and commitment to succeed in a lifetime of constant challenges.

To my wonderful wife, Loni, who encouraged me to write this book, and for her assistance in helping me every day, in every way. I especially want to thank her for putting up with all of the emotional highs and lows I experienced in writing my memoirs. She has shared all the dramatic memories and experiences, both good and painful, I've been through in the past two years in writing this book.

To my children—Brent, Ricky, Kari Lynn—being a father is the toughest job I ever had—just follow my life lessons—1. "Do the right thing." 2. "Always do the right thing."—3. Repeat steps 1 and 2—teach them to my grandchildren, Jacob and Grayson, and you'll be fine.

To all people who are willing to stand up and fight for the truth and dare the consequences to see justice prevail ....

—Jerry Argovitz

To my dad, Robert V. Miller—Pop, we both know where we've been, and the best is yet to come. I love you. After all these years, we're still standing.

—J. David Miller

Sports Publishing books may be purchased in bulk at special discounts for sales promotion, corporate gifts, fundraising, and for educational purposes. Special editions can also be created to specifications. For details, contact the Special Sales Department, Sports Publishing, 307 West 36th Street, 11th Floor, New York, NY 10018 or sportspubbooks@skyhorsepublishing.com.

Sports Publishing® is a registered trademarks of Skyhorse Publishing, Inc.®, a Delaware corporation.

Visit our website at www.sportspubbooks.com.

10 9 8 7 6 5 4 3 2 1

Library of Congress Cataloging-in-Publication Data is available on file.

ISBN: 978-1-61321-068-0

Printed in the United States of America

Disclaimer

The events in my memoir (*Super Agent*) are described according to my best recollection and understanding of those events. Every effort was made to corroborate memory with fact, and the book expresses the author's sole opinions.

Others might see things differently or have different opinions or memories of the events, but to repeat what Thomas Wolfe said in "Look Homeward, Angel"—this is written from a middle distance and is without rancor or bitter intention." I hope you enjoy reading it as much as I have writing it.

CONTENTS

ACT THREE

ACT FOUR

ACT FIVE

ACKNOWLEDGMENTS

SINCE THIS IS the first book I have ever written, I'm not sure of the proper protocol that I should follow as the author. There are so many people to acknowledge and thank—so I'll give it my best shot. My coauthor, J. David Miller, is an award-winning investigative journalist and has written eleven books, and thousands of sports articles. J. David is a real sports historian, and has assisted me in this journey of words; J. David said, "The problem most writers have with biographies is a shortage of information—but the biggest problem with your story is there is sooo much information that a six-month project turned into two years." Thank you for your passion and research to make my story so relevant, as if my accomplishments and pitfalls occurred last month.

Derek Britt of Derek Britt Entertainment represented me as my literary agent and was always there to support me in telling my story—and thanks to Courtney Williams, Derek's assistant for her help.

Randy Winton was always present, and gave his time and assistance to keep me moving in the right direction. Randy never ceased to amaze me with his timely suggestions. Thanks to my publisher, Skyhorse, for believing in my life's works and to Jay Cassell, my editor, for his dedication and interest he has demonstrated in assisting me to advance the ball over the goal line. Thanks to my executive assistant, Cheryl Davis—who was on call 24/7 to help keep the project on track.

I also want to thank my focus group for reading the manuscript and giving me their feedback—Howard Bernstein, Darryl Burman, Walker Beavers, Eldon Wetsel, Sharon Nugent, Andy Gladstein, Sheila Rosenberg, Maxine Spohn, Tom Weil, Loni Bader-Argovitz, Herb and Donna Weitzman, Patty Andrews, and Stan Glickman.

Last, but not least—I want to recognize and thank all of the young men that believed in me and trusted me with their future as professional athletes and friends for life:

Hugh Green	Vince Courville	Jerry Eckwood
Billy Sims	Gerald McNeil	Kenny Burrough
Curtis Dickey	Kiki DeAyala	Todd Fowler
Jacob Green	Eddie Lee Ivery	Sam Harrell
George Cumby	Jim McMahon	Gary Anderson
Joe Cribbs	Kenny Margerum	Walter Abercrombie
Cleveland Crosby	David Overstreet	Luis S. Sharpe
Perry Herrington	Keith Gary	Scott Boucher
Hosea Taylor	Butch Woolfolk	Curley Culp
James Lofton	Bubba Paris	Clarence Verdin
Ricky Sanders	Stan Edwards	Robert Brazile
	Herschel Walker	

—Dr. Jerry Argovitz

When I first discussed this book in June 2010 with Dr. Jerry Argovitz, I never dreamed it would encompass as much rich history, so many compelling stories, and such powerful proof against the cartels of the NFL and NCAA.

Over the course of nearly two years, there were hundreds of hours of interviews with dozens of sources, hundreds of magazine, newspaper, and website searches; thousands of pages of legal documents carefully poured over, and multiple research trips across the United States.

None of this would have been possible without the kindness of Dr. Argovitz and his lovely wife, Loni Bader, who opened up their homes—and their hearts—to not only me, but also my wife, Laurie Beth, and my children.

Meeting the celebrities with whom Dr. Argovitz is lifelong friends was a gas, especially the backstage get-together after a concert with his longtime buddy Kenny Rogers. Perhaps the most knowledgeable and colorful facts came from Dr. Argovitz's former USFL partner Jay Roulier, who was always spot-on in his humor, timeframes, and facts. USFL executives granted interviews, including Alfred A. Taubman and Carl Peterson. What a treat to see together again with Dr. Argovitz and Mouse Davis, members of the old Houston Gamblers - Jim Kelly, Scott Boucher, Todd Fowler, Scott McGhee, Richard Johnson, Ricky Sanders, Gerald McNeil, and Vince Courville.

Anthony Nunez, a phenomenal source of critical information, is to be commended for his work on Houston-gamblers.com.

The project's representation, Derek Britt, was able to grasp the vision and see this project through every step to completion. Skyhorse Publisher and CEO Tony Lyons and Senior Editor Mark Weinstein both saw that this was a story whose time had arrived. Without their belief in this book, and the passionate efforts of Editorial Director Jay Cassell, it wouldn't have happened.

Editors and researchers Ron Kule and his wife Sherry provided friendship, support, strength, and energy. My old *Sport* magazine editor and best-selling author Curt Pesmen proofed everything I sent his way. The unsung hero, however, had to be personal editor Randy Winton, who spent countless evenings editing and fact-checking the manuscript.

Of course, nobody pays a bigger price over the process of a long book like a writer's family. My mother Jayne Gagliardi and older sister Becki didn't see me for more than a year. My father Bob called often with supporting words.

My daughters Chelsea Rhea, Savannah Bey, Kailey Satsuko, and Madison Elise all offered relentless love, support, dedication, led in their charge by my wife Laurie Beth, whom I love dearly. To all of them, I have nothing but an attitude of gratitude. Finally, I have to express my love and faith in God.

—J. David Miller

FOREWORD

MANY SPORTS FANS know me as the quarterback for the '85 Super Bowl Champions, the Chicago Bears. More probably know me for the "Super Bowl Shuffle" and wild covers on magazines like *Rolling Stone* and *Sports Illustrated*. But only a rare few have heard the unlikely but true story of how a dentist turned football agent took me under his wing and got me the deal that made it all happen.

His name is Dr. Jerry Argovitz, and yes, I let a dentist represent my professional football career. I gravitated toward him immediately. When we met, Argovitz was engulfed in a headline browbeating few would have survived. Yet the players he represented stood up for him like for no other agent I'd ever seen. There's a saying that goes, "If everyone hates you, you must be doing something right!" I could see that was Jerry in a nutshell. He rocked the system, and the system hated him for it. I quickly learned that Jerry was there for me not just as an agent, but as a personal guide. And it wasn't just me; the other players he represented seemed to have an extraordinary trust in him, too. When he promised me that if I signed with him, I would NEVER go to the Baltimore Colts . . . guess what? I didn't . . . and thank God! He fought for his players, and together we won. To this day and for whatever I need, Doc is still just one phone call away.

From page one *Super Agent* took me on an emotional thrill ride like a Hollywood movie. Extremely visual and well-written chapters move you briskly from scene to scene, triggering old memories and opening my eyes to details I never knew existed. It begins powerfully with a nail-biting courtroom thriller, in which Argovitz is branded for life with the title "Egregious Conflict of Interest." The book continues to thrust you into the inner workings of the cutthroat business that is football, a business that few have ever experienced. Even I had never heard stories like these, including private details between Dr. Argovitz and my own head coach Mike Ditka as they negotiated a way for the Bears to play me "my way." I was shocked. I had no idea!

As readers, we walk in his boots—no excuses, rarely an apology. It's the true life story of the one-time "most powerful man in football", and we watch as he changes the face of the game—college and pro—, and launches the careers of legends like Jim Kelly and Herschel Walker. We witness firsthand how Argovitz becomes Donald Trump's business partner in the creation of a pro football team and how together their actions cause the demise of an entire league.

Dr. Argovitz, a former dentist turned self-made super agent, should have been a magician. At the end of every chapter—like David Blaine or Harry Houdini—he escapes another incomprehensible scenario. The return of a former player—his "prodigal son"—will leave you stunned. Yet you will understand why his wild journey was, in his words, "all worth it." Though much of the book spans the life of a sports pioneer, the doctor's modern-day work to reform the flawed NCAA system has you rooting for him to "do it again."

Dr. Jerry Argovitz has spent a lifetime fighting goliath monopolies, organizations, and corporations. He is an underdog who represents underdogs, yet he always seems to come out on top. I loved every moment of this book!

—Jim McMahon

INTRODUCTION—
TIME FOR A CHANGE

MOST OF MY writing and speaking of late on NCAA policies—and the treatment of college athletes in general—stems from the time I shared with my own clients. The travesties and struggles of their youths, and their exploitation by universities, sports, and a failed system, forged my strongly held views. Much of what I saw and fought so vigorously as an agent and team owner continues unabated today. Greed wants no partners. It is up to you and me to modernize the National Collegiate Athletic Association (NCAA). It's time for a rigorous shakeup. It's time for a loud wake-up call.

And I'm not alone.

Let's face it, if college sports were any other business, rational people would have been up in arms decades ago.

In 2011 more than 300 major college football and men's basketball players signed a petition asking for a cut of ever-increasing television revenues, which with each passing year are stunningly astronomical. The petition went nowhere, of course. The NCAA negotiated a nearly $11 billion contract (yes, *billion*) with four television networks to broadcast its annual men's national basketball tournament beginning in 2012.

In 2012, the executive director of the NFL players' union, DeMaurice Smith, and Arne Duncan, the U.S. Secretary of Education, in separate statements, called for sweeping changes to NCAA policies that they felt punished the very people it says it protects—student athletes.

I've led a pretty colorful, exciting life, both inside and outside sports, and I've been told for many years by many people that I should write a book. But just writing a book and telling some wonderful stories and recounting some remarkable history—on the face of it—wasn't enough to fan my internal flame to do so.

That was before Reggie Bush, the former Southern California tailback. Truthfully, this undertaking might not have happened were it not for him. In fact, if not for Bush, there's a good chance you might never have heard the name Jerry Argovitz in football circles again.

It had been a few decades since the sportscaster Brent Musburger had called me "the most powerful man in football," and my advances and contributions to the game had long since either been credited to media hounds or merely forgotten or passed over by the annals of time.

Besides, I'd been fortunate to have a great career outside of sports as an entrepreneur and land developer, reaping annual financial benefits and rewards far beyond my wildest expectations. In fact, I was quite content to just enjoy my semi-retirement and my golf foursomes at my home in Houston and Andy Gladstein and my Redstone Group buddies at Tamarisk Country Club at our vacation home in Rancho Mirage, California.

All this changed however, one Saturday in 2008, when—like most red-blooded American males—I was taking in an afternoon of the NCAA-branded version of so-called amateur football. But like the rest of the nation, I leaned forward in my seat as announcers broke in to explain that Bush, now playing in the NFL, was being accused of taking nearly $300,000 in cash while he was still at USC.

"Based largely on interviews with Lloyd Lake," the announcer said, "a new book alleges that the 2005 Heisman Trophy winner was provided with houses, hotel stays, cash for shopping sprees, and money to buy and customize a car. The book's authors say that USC coaches knew about the arrangements, and if the NCAA determines that USC violated rules, the football program could forfeit victories and vacate a national championship won during that period. Bush will have to retroactively return his Heisman Trophy."

That single broadcast awoke the sleeping giant within me, for immediately I knew what the fallout was going to be. I had predicted this tsunami thirty years ago, first as a sports agent, where I represented and advised some of the biggest names in the game, including several Heisman Trophy winners. Then, as a professional team owner, I had railed against the NCAA and the indentured servitude of its "professional" amateurs in an open letter to then-president Walter Byers, which went ignored. I also called Byers to tell him about agents paying players under the table.

That call, too, went unreturned.

You can't be afraid to take a big step if one is indicated, and you can't climb a mountain in two small jumps. Throughout the late 1970s and early 1980s, I had fought the system of the NCAA as a farce, a fraud, and a hypocritical organization. But today, thanks to the likes of Reggie Bush, the advent of instant information via the Internet, and the inescapable eyes of twenty-four-hour sports news sources, this story wasn't going away this time. Reggie Bush was going to be the tip of the iceberg, and I knew it, and the NCAA was headed for the same fate as the *Titanic*.

If you really want to understand the modern NCAA, look no further than film director Martin Scorsese's very-real movie depictions of the mafia: The Mob, in its heyday, made its own rules, and controlled—among other things—bootleg whiskey, trucking, prostitution, gambling, and insurance. The Mafia answered to no one; it earned billions of dollars, evaded local, state, and federal taxes, and all it offered was protection, muscle, and enforcement.

Likewise, the NCAA makes its own rules, and controls—among other things—every major aspect of collegiate football and basketball: the colleges, the players, the coaches, the college presidents, the conferences, and even the rules on how the game must be played. The NCAA answers to no one, and all it offers is protection to the schools that fall in line, muscles those who resist, and enforcement (penalties) to those who might dare threaten the enterprise (by not abiding by their impossible rules and control). The NCAA earns billions of dollars, refuses to open its books to public audit, and pays its football players little to nothing. It is a non-profit entity and therefore pays no taxes.

Worse, the NCAA allows "needy" players to apply for government grants, thereby using our taxpayer dollars to further subsidize its operation—in what amounts to a legal racketeering enterprise. The biggest difference between the mafia and the NCAA is the mob at least took care of its families and key role players. Each fall, hundreds of new players try out for roster spots at every school in the country, allowing the NCAA to drink from a gushing spring of endless young talent.

Worse yet, a kid who might be academically or scholastically challenged cannot earn a scholarship or get into a major university, and can't even try out for a professional team, under rules adhered to by both the NCAA and National Football League. My friend June Jones, head coach at Southern Methodist University in Texas, told me that when he graduated high school, he had the highest grade-point average of all the student athletes in his school (and the highest SAT score), but today, his grades would not have been good enough to get him into SMU.

These are but a few of the reasons I decided to end my silence, my personal ceasefire, and become an advocate for today's modern college football players, and to fight the criminal elements of the agents—and the NCAA system—that exploit them.

Let's face facts: Agents don't give money to third-string tackles, and of the top blue-chip college players in the nation, the majority are African American who come from single-parent and financially disadvantaged homes. This means virtually every one of these kids has been offered money or something of value by an agent, a booster, or a coach, directly or indirectly, and in violation of the NCAA. Most of the kids who did accept money did so primarily to survive.

There are many people with ideas out there who have hit the airwaves reporting one NCAA travesty after another. Where I differ is that I have a plan, and I'm acting on it. Sports talk shows for years have bantered about the injustices of the NCAA, its endless regulations, inconsistencies in compliance, and discrepancies between the "haves" and the "have-nots." The problems are well-documented, but now, as all the skeletons are being dragged from the closets at Penn State, Baylor, Miami, Notre Dame, Ohio State, Oregon, Georgia Tech, LSU, North Carolina, North Carolina State, Georgia, Auburn, Tennessee, and many others, I made the decision to speak out and enact my plan, because under the NCAA's leadership, our entire collegiate athletic system is in jeopardy.

To combat this problem, I'm using this book and my influence to introduce a structured plan that will put corrupt agents in prison, spread the NCAA wealth, help athletes in need, and punish abusers with legal penalties.

As an aside, I found my real motivation to write this book—to remind people I've been creating change in football for thirty-plus years, and as you'll read, with profound results.

I realize that I risk great criticism as just a media-seeker; one man thinking he can stand up against the NCAA, a billion-dollar empire. But I've already battled another billion-dollar empire called the National Football League and won—on many fronts. I've worked closely with numerous impoverished athletes and made them millionaires. I've changed the way the NFL and NCAA did business in the past. I've been sued by the NFL and have been offered bribes and illegal contracts by NFL owners. My name appears in every sports management law book, quoting the results of the *Sims v. Argovitz* case.

I personally believe with all my heart the NCAA is vulnerable and change must occur now before it's too late. Ultimate success depends a great deal on how the media spins the story: Are they out to make me look like a demented fool who should go back to sniffing nitrous oxide, or will they not shoot the messenger and agree with me and many others that immediate reform of the NCAA is urgent?

So, of course, I know the road ahead will be long and tenuous, but whether it's a protracted contract negotiation, an antitrust suit, or another bloody court battle—nobody loves a fight for justice more than I do. Based on my history, I believe I'm the right man for the job. These young athletes have no advocate looking out for their best interests. I'm willing to stand up because I believe in fighting for the right reasons—even if it makes me unpopular, as nearly every chapter in this book attests.

I'm praying that when you learn the facts about the power, greed, monopoly, self-dealing, and arrogance of the NCAA, you will stand alongside me to change the broken system, whether you're a sports fan or not. This is not a battle I can win alone. This is not about me. It's about kids being grossly exploited, and the NCAA daring the public to do anything about it.

As an agent, I represented some of the game's top draft picks, negotiating what then were the biggest contracts in NFL history. For Heisman Trophy winner Billy Sims, the top pick of the 1980 draft, we demanded—and received—the game's first $1 million cash guarantee. I wrote the language for career-ending insurance policy underwritten by Lloyds of London.

When the NFL refused to budge from its system of "slotting" players in the draft, we withheld services, and in one case, I took two first-round picks to Canada. When the NFL wouldn't sign underclassmen, I negotiated and brokered the deal that brought Heisman Trophy winner Herschel Walker to the United States Football League as a junior, which opened the floodgates for all juniors to soon follow. Billy Sims would later point out that were it not for my ground-breaking deal with Herschel, Sam Bradford would not have received a $50 million guaranteed contract from St. Louis when he elected to leave the University of Oklahoma after his junior year.

My attacks on free agency in the NFL created a groundswell that would eventually dismantle the league's old system, which prevented players from changing teams. I became the first agent to own a professional football team when I became an owner of the Houston Gamblers of the United States Football League. There we signed top collegiate players like Jim Kelly, Steve Young, Reggie White, Doug Flutie, Gary Anderson, Marcus Dupree, and Mike Rozier. We raided NFL rosters for numerous superstars like Brian Sipe, Doug Williams, and Joe Cribbs, and increased player salaries by more than 300 percent in a three-year period. I was a key principal in a lawsuit against the NFL that proved the league was guilty of Sherman Antitrust violations, a verdict that lives on today as the foundation of the current 2011 NFL players' strike.

As the owner of the Gamblers, I gained another perspective from the other side of the bargaining table, and heard the horror stories from dozens of athletes who literally had been mired in poverty prior to signing their contracts. In the last year of the league I became partners with Donald Trump, and it was stunning to see the great disparity between wealth and poverty in this nation.

So I began making phone calls to a few friends whose opinions really matter to me: Texas governor Rick Perry; Donald Trump; former Oklahoma coach Barry Switzer; SMU head coach June Jones; University of Texas athletic director DeLoss Dodds; Texas Tech athletic director Gerald Myers; Jim Kelly; Herschel Walker; Billy Sims; Joe Cribbs; NBC commentator Jim Gray; Eric Dickerson; Hugh Green; Butch Woolfolk; Jacob Green; and Walter Abercrombie, who is now an executive at Baylor University. After discussions with each man, my passion to battle the NCAA sparked into a flame.

One by one, I began to build a formidable team of people who believed in my mission and would join our cause, and together we've set the creaking wheels of reform into motion.

On a gorgeous July day in 2011, I flew to Austin to meet with DeLoss at the University of Texas. He was very pleased when I briefed him on my efforts with the state legislature to enact laws that severely punish sports agents. I was totally surprised to learn that he had already petitioned the NCAA to give $100 per month to players, but was turned down.

"I didn't have a plan as thorough as yours," he said. "But they said 'No.' They want all student-athletes to be treated like all students."

That made me chuckle. How about "all" students be placed under the same demands as "all" athletes?

"But many athletes are not like other students," I said. "They are usually poor and broke."

Dodds readily agreed. "College sports," he said, "is a complicated mess right now."

So complicated, in fact, that I was granted a private meeting with the school's compliance and grant-writing department, in hopes of getting a better understanding of specific issues and some explanation on the 400-plus-page NCAA rules manual given each year to head coaches.

I met with the members of these departments for several hours. They admitted that often, the school's own compliance people are just as baffled as the public when it comes to NCAA rules.

"We live on the edge," the compliance director said. "Many of the rules are so vague and so complicated, we can't even explain them. Every decision we make could have an effect on the entire athletic program."

"If you don't understand the rules, then who does?" I asked.

"We call the NCAA office in Indianapolis and ask for clarifications," he said.

"How long does that take?" I asked.

"Sometimes a few hours, if it's simple," he said. "But if it's complicated, it could take days."

Then I dropped my bombshell, which I had learned from many conversations with coaches from other schools.

"What if a player is broke and has no financial support?"

"Well, we have programs set up for financial aid," he answered. "If a student-athlete was on or below the poverty level, he can apply for a Pell Grant, which the NCAA allows, in which they can receive up to $2,775 a semester. He can also get this if he takes summer classes."

"The NCAA allows this?" I almost laughed out loud. A non-profit, non-tax-paying entity that earns billions of dollars allows athletes to seek help from the taxpayers. Digesting NCAA "rules" is like watching a cat try to crap on a marble floor.

"Of course," the grant-writing officer added, "if the player is above the poverty line, he will get less or nothing, and due to the current economy, Pell Grant money could be drying up."

When I entered the world of professional sports in 1980 as a player agent, the first thing I immediately recognized was the collusion between the NFL and the NCAA. Unlike all other pro sports, the NFL was enjoying a free, amateur, "minor-league" feeder system. America's greatest athletes learned their craft for the mere "price" of a college scholarship and the pride of their school, with only the best—less than 2 percent—winding up in the NFL.

The NCAA was a monopoly and had a sweetheart deal with the NFL, another monopoly; like two crime families cooperating because it increases the take for both parties. The NFL agreed back then to not draft a player until his class graduated, which allowed colleges a four-year lock on talent. This seemed grossly unfair and unreasonable to me: How can you tell a grown man he can't enter his chosen profession, even if it happens to be professional football?

Colleges function very effectively for the NFL, not only for just preparing the players for professional competition, but also setting up the value of a player, because when somebody is playing at the University of Oklahoma or the University of Texas and he is on national television five times a year, all of America now knows about this player. Some of these kids are matinee idols when they enter the draft. These future picks are also the lifeline to resurrecting pro teams who sorely need an infusion of talent.

The second thing that left me stunned was that NCAA rules were flawed, discriminatory, outdated, unfair, unconstitutional, and nearly as old as the organization itself.

The NCAA was originally established as the Intercollegiate Athletic Association of the United States to set rules for amateur athletic sports. Then-U.S. president Theodore Roosevelt initiated what would become the NCAA after his son Ted broke his nose playing rugby. Aware of the growing number of serious injuries and deaths occurring in collegiate rugby football, President Roosevelt brought together the presidents of five major institutions, and the outcome of those meetings in October 1905 evolved into the NCAA.

By 1956 the NCAA had rules in place that said its student-athletes could participate in sports as a vocation while "balancing academic, social, and athletic experiences," and even today lists academics, integrity, sportsmanship, fairness, diversity, inclusion, and amateurism as its core values. NCAA rules prevent a student-athlete from working during the football season. The NCAA rules prevent the student-athlete from accepting any money, gifts, or transportation from an agent or booster.

How does an eighteen-, nineteen-, or twenty-year-old "God-gifted" athlete who is financially disadvantaged exist in a college atmosphere? He can't, unless he breaks the rules.

Herein is the rub: Today the NCAA has 120 Bowl Championship Series (BCS) division teams, in what used to be considered "Division I" schools. It oversees an additional 1,000 schools, organizations, or entities, and runs off an $8 billion overall budget, most of which is generated by television, marketing, and sales revenue from the top BCS schools.

In 2011 the seventy schools in college football's major conferences collectively earned over $1 billion in profit. Only one, Wake Forest, lost money. The University of Texas made $69 million in profit, against $94 million in revenue.

Clearly, the system is grossly out of proportion. Before we can discuss solutions, however, one must weigh the evidence, beginning with the coaches themselves. How do you pay coaches $5 million a year, be tax-exempt, refuse to pay your employees (players), and then enjoy assistance from the taxpayers and federal government (Pell Grants)?

The NCAA is slicker than Capitol Hill, only without any checks and balances.

If the players don't get paid, where does all the money go? For starters, the coaches are routinely paid in the millions of dollars, along with perquisites: free memberships at country clubs, free use of automobiles, and $50,000 of free private jet service whenever they want. Coaches operate in a free market and can change teams at any time. They are permitted to make endorsement deals with companies like Nike and Adidas. They are allowed to be paid for radio and television shows, motivational speeches, and summer camps.

Many easily make or surpass their professional counterparts. Compare a college coach's income to the state governor, a state administrator, or even the university president where he is employed: A college president usually earns between $250,000 and $750,000, where it's not uncommon for the college coach to earn five times as much.

Right out of the gate, the message sent by the NCAA is that football, and basketball, are ten times more important than anything else at the school, including education. College coaches are not rocket scientists. They don't have Ph.Ds. Some of them have M.A.s; some of them just have bachelor's degrees. But due to fair-market value, they are worth whatever the market will bear.

Why are coaches allowed unlimited earning potential? Because the NCAA is a trade association of coaches and athletic directors and conference commissioners, and they're not going to legislate their own reduction in salaries. So in that system, the coach ends up getting paid the money that in a system of free enterprise a portion would otherwise go to the players.

The incomes of BCS head coaches range anywhere from six-figures to over millions; in the Southeastern Conference not a single coach makes less than $1 million annually, with the highest-paid earning $7.5 million a year. So big is the financial "pie" that in 1984, the NCAA lost control of regular-season football television rights when the United States Supreme Court ruled against the association in a landmark antitrust case.

It's no wonder today that among the highest-paid state employees in Alabama, Oklahoma, Kentucky, North Carolina, Texas, California, and Florida, most are college football and basketball coaches. And why not? Their efforts are mainly responsible for generating the income to support the college and all amateur athletic programs provided by the schools.

By 1995 even NCAA architect and former executive director Walter Byers chastised the rules in his book, *Unsportsmanlike Conduct: Exploiting the Student-Athlete*, but still, nobody listened. Byers admits in his own book that the system is broken and must be reformed before it is too late.

The NCAA now exists as a cartel with impossible restrictions that it alone legislates and interprets. The NCAA is the judge, jury, and executioner. It imposes restrictions on the number of scholarships that can be given out. It imposes restrictions on the number of games that can be played and when the games are played. It decides what teams can play for the BCS title. It decides who and when to investigate. It decides unilaterally on what penalties and sanctions to hand out for violations. It imposes restrictions on whether athletes can do endorsement contracting or not, or whether they can receive licensing money or not.

But who oversees the NCAA?

How can a cartel say it exists in the name of amateurism, impose a plethora of restrictions—most of which are consistent with maximizing economic returns to it and member schools—while penalizing its own players, and then call itself a non profit? The NCAA system of "no job, no pay, no money" for its athletes creates the financial desperation that corrupts the kids. For anybody to survive, you must have money.

The NCAA is a non-profit organization, but it operates in a way that benefits the athletic directors and the coaches and the conference commissioners, while leaving nothing for the players, in spite of the bylaws that say it is dedicated to its student-athletes. Personally, such hypocrisy makes me nauseous.

Obviously, this is hardly the NCAA of old. With literally billions in television revenue at stake, young men are being asked to engage their unique skills and talents in a potential career-ending enterprise at virtually no cost to the universities for whom they play. The argument of the value of their scholarship is no longer applicable, for it's impossible to think any of these major schools—with student enrollment often as high as 50,000—are losing anything from allowing eighty football players to attend class for "free" each semester.

Therefore, a star player may rush for 200 yards on a Saturday night in front of 80,000 screaming fans, before a television and radio audience of millions, all of which is profiting from advertising. Thousands of fans can purchase his jersey and other school merchandise on-line and in stadiums, while millions more dollars are reaped in the sale of hotdogs, beer, soft drinks, and parking.

When the stadium lights blink off, the player is asked to return to his dorm, and receives not a cent of this revenue, and is unable to accept a dime from anyone other than immediate family.

Should the player come from a financially disadvantaged home, there is simply no money to be had. This often leaves these superstars in a position where they may be the most popular guys on campus, but can't afford to treat their girlfriends to a hamburger and a movie, or even put gas in their cars, without violating the rules. So, of course, in violation of their scholarships, due to temptation, frustration, and desperation, they find other means, jeopardizing their careers, their coaches, their teammates, and the schools.

And that's where the agents and boosters, who feed off the soft underbelly of the sport, come into play.

This so-called system created the slippery slope that allowed the influx of lying, thieving agents, boosters, and program supporters, thereby allowing them to create a cottage industry of sorts, meaning players and coaches have been paid under the table for decades and playing a game of cat-and-mouse in efforts to not get caught.

Whether it's fake jobs for parents or family, players selling their tickets or game-worn memorabilia for outlandish prices, right down to outright cash handouts and purchases of cars and homes, the system has run amuck.

In one extreme case, a player admitted to me he robbed a pizza delivery guy after a game—not of his money, but because he was hungry and wanted the pizza. Southern players recruited to northern schools have told me recent stories where coaches were "forced" to purchase them cold-weather clothes, simply because they owned none and couldn't afford any. If truth were known, the majority of every single blue-chip athlete is forced by necessity to break the flawed and discriminatory rules that control their young lives.

In theory, the NCAA's "answer" to the problem is to "punish" not just a rules-violating player by suspending him from play, or perhaps withdrawing his scholarship, but the entire team for one player's transgressions. Coaches who violate the rules can be suspended or fired. Universities can lose scholarships and face fines, and athletic directors may be fired as well.

In reality, here's what usually occurs: By the time Reggie Bush's transgressions were revealed, he was already earning millions of dollars in the NFL, and his head coach, Pete Carroll, had moved on to the Seattle Seahawks, where he tripled his salary and appropriately wrote a book called *Win Forever: How to Live, Work and Play like a Pro*. I could only assume that he was teaching his players how to be "pros" long before they left USC, especially those like Bush who had been driving to practice in brand new SUVs and living in posh off-campus homes.

The only penalty to Bush was that he forfeit his Heisman. The agents who paid Bush disappeared back under the rocks from which they originally crawled. At the time, what they did was not a crime. The University of Southern California, its new staff, and remaining players, however, were blasted with NCAA sanctions that hurt the program and its fans for many years to come. The school also was forced to forfeit its national championship, earned while Bush and Carroll were there.

History may have repeated itself during the 2010 season, when Auburn's Cam Newton was believed to have committed similar infractions by his father demanding $180,000 for his son's services. Newton has already moved on to the NFL.

The NCAA waffled throughout the "investigation" process, and since it is allowed to interpret its own rules, it has—to date—penalized USC harder than Auburn for similar infractions. Yet it is still possible Newton, too, will have to give back his Heisman Trophy if found guilty; but not before Auburn earned $20 million for playing in the 2011 BCS Championship game, which it won. On the heels of Newton came Ohio State quarterback Terrelle Pryor and his teammates, who sold memorabilia, jerseys, and signed pictures in exchange for tattoos and other gifts.

Despite these infractions, these players were allowed to play in a bowl game. Pryor left school early rather than admit infractions and refused to answer NCAA inquiries. Head coach Jim Tressell, however, lost his job. Frankly, can you blame Tressell, or Carroll or any other college coach who is forced to exist and win in a system that is crying for reform?

The NCAA admits no complicity to fraudulently inducing eighteen-year-old boys to sign grant-in-aid football scholarships. I don't call them "scholarships"; instead, I refer to them as contracts which many impoverished kids have no chance to honor.

Consider the following:

- The eighteen-year-old student-athlete is not allowed to have an agent and his family can't afford to hire an attorney to advise him before he signs a contract with a college. Many of these kids have been raised by single mothers, aunts, or grandmothers, who often have no college education and, in some cases, not even a high-school diploma. A star player may be recruited by as many as 100-plus adult recruiters or coaches who try to impress and influence him and his family, but the player can seek no outside counsel to advise him on the biggest decision of his life.

- As an unpaid amateur, the average college football player will work forty to fifty hours a week at his sport in practice, film study, and weight lifting. In addition, he must miss classes to travel to road games, while carrying the same number of minimum hours as any other student. A single road game alone carves out forty-eight hours of a player's week.

- By signing a scholarship, the player signs away all rights to the use of his name, image, and likeness, thereby allowing the NCAA and the school to use both for commercial promotion—and profit.

- In normal business, it is unfair and illegal to induce someone (especially a seventeen- or eighteen-year-old kid) to sign a contract wherein one knows the person will default and forfeit his gains; especially since the organization's rules and regulations would not allow him to get independent advice or counsel. Remember that while these are talented athletes, they often have minimal, if any, business experience.

- The NCAA system forces complicity by the coaches. It's not money that attracts the player to a school; it's the coach's salesmanship, reputation, and charisma. So in the present system, the coach ends up getting the "big bucks" by recruiting, confusing, over-promising, and convincing these blue-chip athletes to sign with them and to continue the school's "winning tradition." (The pressure is steep: A Hall-of-Fame running back told me that in one case, a blue-chip high school player was told that if he didn't attend his state university, he would never get a job in that state.)

- For the athletes in the high-profile sports—for instance, football—about 60 percent of them never get a degree, and those who do get a degree are getting it often under false pretenses, because they're not doing a normal course of study, and they're not doing a lot of the work themselves.

- Earnings from basketball and football subsidize 90 percent of the scholarships in other sports.

- Since 1973 an NCAA "scholarship" really consists of four one-year, "renewable" scholarships. The NCAA says its rules are clear, and that athletic scholarships are one-year, "merit-based" awards that require both demonstrated academic performance and "participation expectations" on the playing field. This couldn't be more unclear.

- College sport watchdogs—and, occasionally, athletes themselves—tell a different story. They see unkept promises and bottom-line decisions at odds with the definition of a student-athlete, to the point that now the U.S. Justice Department is looking into the matter.

- A star football player at a Division I school can be worth anywhere from $800,000 to $3 million in earned revenue, against the $30,000 value of his average scholarship.

What's at stake for the college football player is serious business: NFL Commissioner Roger Goodell said recently he believes that by 2015 the league will be generating $25 billion in annual revenue, an average of roughly $15 million annually for every single player on an NFL team. Every college football player is vying to earn a living at his trade, which ultimately is a shot at that professional money.

Major media outlets are having no issue with reporting the grotesquely sick corruption incubated by the lie of amateurism, but none are mounting a serious, consistent call for overhaul of the NCAA rules. Why should they? ESPN—the self-proclaimed "World-Wide Leader in Sports," built a multi-billion-dollar network from the foundation of broadcasting tape-delayed college football games, and NCAA tournament basketball games. CBS, ABC, and NBC earn billions in advertising from its college football programming, not to mention March Madness in basketball.

Nobody's going to shoot the goose that's laying the golden eggs.

So a major college football player earns a scholarship as an athlete, not a student. But he can lose it if he struggles at either. He has no job security. And let's face facts: Approximately 80 percent of the top players in the nation each year are black, and of that percentage, 75 percent are raised in single-parent households that are financially disadvantaged.

Throughout my life—as you'll read about in greater detail in the pages to come—I've been inside many of these homes, from those of Herschel Walker, Billy Sims, Curtis Dickey, and Joe Cribbs, to Gary Anderson, to name a few. Many of these kids are poor, with no financial support, and virtually every one of them—to a kid—chase the dream of one day buying their mom, aunt, or grandmother a home. But to do so, they will have to somehow survive the rigors of being a student-athlete.

This is where "amateurism" implodes: (a) the fallacy of Title IX; (b) the tremendous overhead of the NCAA and the schools; (c) the frustration of each school's respective "compliance departments"; (d) the abuse of government programs that shouldn't be spent on athletes; (e) the once amateur Olympic basketball competition now being played by our professional NBA players, who earn millions of dollars in salaries.

- The NCAA claims it is non-discriminatory, but take a quick peek behind the smokescreen of Title IX, wherein monies earned by member schools must be shared with all of the school's athletic programs; that is, women's volleyball, golf, and lesser sports. But the only two sports that really give a major university national notoriety is football or basketball, and most of these kids are minorities whose only currency is the sport they play.
- The performances of these world-class football and basketball players earn 90 percent of the revenue, open the wallets of alums and other individuals to make donations to the athletic program, and reap millions more in donations to the general fund.
- The fact is there is a vicious and competitive process for each college and coach to establish a winning program and tradition. This means money, money, and more money to everyone involved, except the players. Great players make great coaches stay great. A few blue-chippers or impact players add tremendous value to the school and increase the competitive advantages to every facet of the school. This taxes compliance departments as coaches look for constant loopholes to procure such players.
- Players are left desperately searching for any means of income, and abuse occurs; that is, Pell Grants. Why should government money (taxpayers) be given to a poor athlete who is earning his school millions and the NCAA billions?

Follow the results of our country's greatest coaches in recent memory—Nick Saban, Mack Brown, Urban Meyer, Bob Stoops. Bobby Bowden, and it is evident that success begets success. A winning school plays in major bowl games and gets national television presence and exposure, and many of the players become high NFL draft choices. These accomplishments give these coaches a distinct advantage to sign the most talented collegiate football players every year.

At the University of Oregon alone, Nike co-founder Phil Knight has single-handedly donated so much money that the Ducks are perennial contenders each year. T. Boone Pickens at Oklahoma State has changed the face of the university's football fortunes—and inadvertently, school administration and its resources. Every major school has wealthy benefactors who contribute on the basis of the popularity of the school's major sport, which is predominantly football. Unfortunately, the popularity is directly proportionate to the school's win/loss record and how it fares against its major rivals—for example, Texas versus Oklahoma, or Ohio State versus Michigan. Coaches realize that two consecutive bad years might leave you job hunting by the third year.

So there's a certain irony to the fact that so-called institutions of higher learning are exploiting the most exploited of all and using them to subsidize other sports. Poor African American kids are producing a surplus which gets transferred to support scholarships for the golf team, the swimming team, and the ice hockey team—sports that are staffed by people who are primarily middle-class whites, often upper-middle-class whites.

Title IX is like a "reverse" Robin Hood transfer of funds: from poor minority kids to relatively wealthy white kids, often playing elite sports. This raises serious racial, discrimination, and ethical issues, further ignored by the NCAA.

Think about this: You're better off being an actor or a band member than an NCAA athlete if you intend to survive financially during four years at a major university. For example, at the Loeb Theater at Harvard University, which is owned by the Harvard Faculty of Arts and Sciences, students perform their own plays in the main theater, as does a professional company, the American Repertory Theater.

Harvard graduate students, and occasionally undergraduates, have been able to act or otherwise assist in the professionals' productions. The American Repertory Theater has run theater workshops with the students, and many of them get paid for it.

But athletes are not allowed to use their athletic skills or name recognition for financial gain. You can't work during the season, and now many schools demand they have non- mandatory, wink, wink, mandatory workouts during the summer. However, if you're a chemistry student on an academic scholarship, you can work for pay at a nearby lab.

A trombone player on a band scholarship can play any instrument he chooses for money at any time. He also gets his notoriety from marching on the same football field where many players get crippled for life. The examples go on, and on, and on.

However, if you're a football player or basketball player, the NCAA says "no" to any money in its sacrilegious protection of amateurism.

Recently, I drafted this letter to current NCAA president Mark Emmert:

Mr. Mark Emmert, President
National Collegiate Athletic Association
700 W. Washington Street
Post Office Box 6222
Indianapolis, Indiana 46206

Mr. Emmert:

Congratulations on your appointment to president of the NCAA. Your new leadership and wisdom will give you the opportunity to correct an age-old problem—agents and boosters paying money to undergraduate student-athletes.

I certainly understand the problem, and I have a solution that won't require a dime from the budget of the NCAA. Thirty years ago I notified the NCAA on multiple occasions that—as a routine business practice—many agents were paying undergraduate football players, while thumbing their noses at your organization. I never once paid an undergraduate player a nickel to sign with me, and I usually represented some of the nation's top picks.

As you're well aware, however, there are many who have and still do attempt to coerce and violate players with cash. But the problem remains: There are many scholarship athletes who come from pure poverty and have no means of financial support from any family member. My question is and has always been: How do these gifted but financially-distraught athletes put two dollars in their pocket legally? What are their options? There are none.

Mark, I can help you and the NCAA resolve the ongoing problem. The Reggie Bush situation isn't isolated—he just got caught. If the truth were known, I know a dozen more Heisman winners who did the same thing as Reggie Bush. It's the system, not the kids. With that said, I can provide solutions that will eliminate this egregious problem and it would not come out of the NCAA or a college budget. Can we sit down together to discuss this, and take positive strides toward resolving the problem?

Sincerely,
Dr. Jerry A. Argovitz

How did Emmert respond? He didn't. Nothing has changed in thirty years, except for the players. They still get crumbs while everyone else is stuffing their pockets with money.

What a shame.

So here, in summary, is my ten-point plan for NCAA reform:

1. I propose the formation of the CPAA—the Collegiate Players Athletic Association. It would be an independent, non-profit association that can legally negotiate for players' collective bargaining rights with the NCAA and its associates, and ensure that players' rights are protected. The NFL has the NFLPA, the NBA has the NBAPA, and it is essential that Division I collegiate football and basketball have their own association to protect the players from the egregious conflicts of interest and antitrust violations being committed by the NCAA.

    The CPAA will reinforce the severe penalties to the player if he breaks the rules. This, to me, is the most important facet of anything we're doing. Any agreements players make with the NCAA would be negotiated, and both rules and penalties would be agreed upon by the CPAA.

2. Proactively begin by offering amnesty for every single NCAA football or basketball player. By amnesty, I propose we allow all athletes a thirty-day period in which they can come forward and disclose any violation, without penalty to themselves and their school. This would include who paid them, the amounts, and the approximate dates on which these infractions occurred. If they took money they wouldn't have to pay it back, and if they signed any agreement for representation, it would be null and void.

    This brief period of amnesty will allow us to start with a clean slate and end the witch hunts. I promise that if the NCAA were to dig deep enough, most of the Heisman Trophies would have to be returned and most all of the major college conference championships—including BCS victories—would have to be forfeited. Georgia Tech, for instance, had to forfeit its conference championship when it was revealed that a player had received $312 worth of clothes. Under amnesty, nothing would be returned or forfeited, and no penalties or punishment would be meted out.

3. We must stop the deception. Tell the truth: Division I—the "super powers"—are professional amateurs. Stop the nonsense and pay the players. I propose that players earn an allowance (stipend), paid out in bi-monthly payments. This eliminates the need to go to outside agents for help. During my tenure in the United States Football League, I had the pleasure of working with Steve Spurrier, now the head coach at the University of South Carolina. I was hardly surprised when at the 2011

annual meeting of coaches, athletic directors, and university presidents of the Southeastern Conference, Spurrier proposed a $300 per game stipend, a direct-cash payment that student-athletes could use for food, gas, or tickets, or travel expenses so their families could see them play.

And I loved Steve's idea—let the coaches foot the bill. "A bunch of us coaches felt so strongly about it that we would be willing to pay it—seventy guys, $300 bucks a game, that's only about $21,000 a game," Spurrier said. I agree. But the NCAA will never agree that these players are employees because it would kill their real reasons—no workman's compensation and no money in addition to scholarships in order to protect their tax-free status.

When the players are receiving legal stipends there is no longer any reason or incentive to take money illegally from agents or boosters and put the entire program in jeopardy. The players should also be required to take special courses in money management and fiscal responsibilities. Schools should also provide emergency financial crisis management to assist its athletes.

4. Severe punishment would then begin with agents and marketers. Some coaches, such as Alabama's Nick Saban, have at least attempted to address the issue, but directed their angst in the wrong direction. Coach Saban correctly pointed out that the practice should stop, but admonished the NFL to "control its agents." The agents, understand, are not under control by the NFL. They act alone, particularly the rogue agents. Again, the problem does not lie within the athletes themselves—or even the NFL—but the antiquated system of the NCAA.

So among my top goals was to go after the unscrupulous agents with severe penalties. During my tenure as an agent, I had never paid a player a nickel, and I felt like attacking the agents first was a logical place to begin. So I wrote and proposed "zero-tolerance" legislation in Texas, wherein any agent who pays a college-eligible player directly or indirectly would be guilty of a third-degree felony, and if found guilty, could receive two to ten years in prison and also be liable for recovery of the financial damages caused to the plaintiff, including court costs and attorney fees.

I approached my close friend Harold Dutton, a Texas state representative, and he agreed to sponsor House Bill 1123, entitled "Don't Mess with Texas Football." We took it before the state legislature, and the bill was subsequently passed and signed into law by Governor Perry, and now allows recourse for universities to prosecute rogue agents to the fullest extent of the law, while also seeking damages, penalties, and court costs.

Second, I sought and received the same penalties for any college or university employee who paid an agent or third party to help recruit an athlete. Third, I sought and received legislation that the agent would be decertified in Texas for life.

Currently, I'm working within my circle of influence to get this same legislation passed in every state, and with the National Football League Players Association (NFLPA) and the National Basketball Association Players Association (NBA-PA) to decertify an agent for life for breaking these rules.

5. If found guilty, players may be held legally and financially responsible for the damages caused to the school by illegally taking money or anything of value for themselves or their families (I estimate the damages to the school caused by Reggie Bush in the USC debacle at $50,000,000).

6. Next, players should have the constitutional right to enter the NFL draft after two years of college—and even attend the NFL Combine—and reserve the right to withdraw and return to their university and continue on scholarship without penalty if it is determined by NFL scouts they aren't yet ready for professional football.

7. Players should have the rights to own their likenesses and receive monetary benefits from the sale of their jerseys and/or likenesses on school memorabilia. Players should be allowed to sign endorsement deals and collect royalties. If the NCAA is really concerned about amateurism, then it could insist that such monies are placed in an escrow account that is available to the athlete after his eligibility has expired, for his post-college career.

    This allows the athletes to have more flexibility and more freedom, and to be less exploited. Currently, this is a very clear violation of the publicity rights of the athletes. From an antitrust point of view, it's a conspiracy among the various schools and the NCAA that come together and allows this to happen. It's also called restraint of trade.

8. If players can get jobs based on their athletic notoriety, more power to them. They're earning that right. If Herschel Walker can get a job at a car dealership signing autographs on his day off, he should be allowed to do so. Every eighteen-year-old man has a constitutional right to work; who is the NCAA to deny him this right and dictate how much he can earn?

9. Restrictions between players and local alumni who are successful businessmen and community leaders should be loosened. The players need educated and professional friends to prepare them for life outside of football in the event of injury, or if they simply aren't good enough to play at the next level. To ensure efficacy, participating alumni could easily be approved and monitored through a pre-screening

process that weeds out those who might have ulterior motives. Any alumni participating in such a mentor program which violates a code of ethics could and should be given a lifetime ban from the university.

10. Use a different curriculum for those who want to major in professional athletics. The proposal would call for this curriculum to include English, as well as classes focused on finance, psychology, speech, and economics (with emphasis placed on bookkeeping, banking, and investments). This department of study would also provide guest speakers whose experience would greatly benefit these athletes.

I've spent months researching and talking to players, coaches, athletic directors, school presidents, and politicians—enough to learn they all want a system that works. All with whom I spoke are privately, and some publicly, outraged with the NCAA.

With your help, our voices will be heard for the thousands of student-athletes who have become victims of the NCAA's broken system, which creates financial despair. The NCAA has refused to address the real problem for decades, but now in light of the outpouring of allegations and subsequent media fallout, the time has finally arrived to shine the national spotlight onto this age-old issue.

If you love your college football team, and never want to open a newspaper or turn on the news and discover a Reggie Bush situation in your own back yard, then jump on the bandwagon by merely lending your "voice" and participate in this opportunity to change sports history.

If we all work together and lend our voices to those who can't speak for themselves, we can help those in financial hardship legally; and hope that the NCAA will join us on the side of truth and justice and work amicably to create mutual solutions.

I won't slow down until the system is changed.

In my lifetime, I've always been ambitious, unfailingly competitive, and driven by an urge to succeed at whatever I undertook. No autobiography can portray a man exactly as he was. The best that can be hoped for is an approximation, from which all that is false has been expunged and in which most of what is true has been set forth.

In the stories that follow, you will find examples that are almost contradictory in nature. I've led many lives, but no reader would want to hear every detail or every story, so I've chosen the ones that had the greatest impact on me and the people around me. My father always said, "if you're telling the truth, you're not bragging." I've been overbearing in my youth, and even used my anger like a club, only to mellow into a warm and generous friend. I've been a non-hero longing for heroic status, and achieved it, only to fail in relationships that should have been simple.

Yet I am proud of my staying and recuperative powers, my reputation, and my ability to size up the terrain. My whole life, others have been telling me I bit off more than I could chew, and perhaps they'll say the same about this book . . . and now my ensuing, pending battle with the NCAA.

But in the words of John Wayne, tomorrow is the most important thing in life. It comes to us at midnight very clean. It's perfect when it arrives, and it puts itself in our hands. It hopes we've learned something from all of our yesterdays.

While I hope you enjoy my yesterdays, I'm thrilled that—together—we can bring about change for many exciting, new tomorrows!

Enjoy the book!

ACT ONE

One should rather die than be betrayed. There is no deceit in death. It delivers precisely what it has promised. Betrayal, though, is the willful slaughter of hope.
— American Playwright Steven Deitz

1

TREASON FOR DIAMONDS

NOTHING PIERCES THE human spirit like the pain of betrayal, because its heart-beat is deceit. Betrayal relies on the sacrifice of another's trust—a lover, a spouse, a par-ent, a child, a friend, and when discovered, the lingering pain can leave a lifetime of scars.

Nothing can prepare you for betrayal, and certainly not my upbringing. I didn't grow up rich, powerful, or dangerous. I shared no blood pacts with the Mob, and my last name is Argovitz, not Soprano. The odds of a Jewish boy with big ears from dusty Borger, Texas, winding up with his back to the wall in a saloon fight with the invinci-ble National Football League—in one of the biggest landmark court cases in sports history—are about the same as a Houston dentist becoming a power broker in the world of professional sports.

How this happened to me is a miracle, because I was an average kid with average grades who seemed destined for an average life. I grew up selling nails in my dad's hard-ware store, which was little more than a shotgun shack on a two-lane road on Borger's Main Street, which could have easily passed for a Norman Rockwell painting. This was about as far away from the NFL's glistening New York offices—amid the skyscrapers in midtown Manhattan—as one would get.

My mom and dad raised me with simple, basic beliefs: Hard work, patience, trust, and devil-be-damned perseverance can defy conventional wisdom and beat all odds. We believed in underdogs like the shepherd boy David, who in the scriptures protected his flock from bears and lions, before defending his countrymen against the giant Goliath.

This served me well through a whirlwind career that wound its way through dentistry, land development, and—in the most unlikely twist of fate—as a sports agent to the nation's most prominent football players. Fame, or infamy, came quickly as my opinions and negotiations were splashed across America's sports pages. This was heady stuff for a country boy; admittedly, I reveled in the fame of the "big time."

Deceit, however, is a serpent. It lies in wait, striking at your most susceptible moment. I never saw it coming. When it hit, the blow dropped me to my knees, sucked the wind from my lungs, and left me gasping for air as I publicly fell from grace.

Worse, it came from a friend whom I considered a son, who chose treason over diamonds.

When you're Public Enemy No. 1—not to mention the most hated man in all of football—the last place a Texas boy wants to find himself is walking up a frigid Detroit sidewalk with his wife and mother toward a shootout in a federal courtroom.

Yet, that's exactly where we were January 25, 1984; and ominous storm clouds made the 32-degree morning seem nastier than it actually was. Dirty snow lined the slick, black streets as I made my way to the United States District Court, Eastern District of Michigan. My tie and hair blew wildly in the biting 29-mile-per-hour gusts of wind, and the weather reflected my mood. I felt intermittently angry, frustrated, lonely, betrayed, and even downright saddened about the series of events that had led to this moment, and I had a pretty good idea it was about to get worse.

The local media and fans of the Detroit Lions were treating me like I was a member of the Purple Gang, the Jewish hoodlums of the Detroit criminal syndicate that had been a major bootleg supplier to outlaw Al Capone.

"Jerry Argovitz is a scumbag!" a local sports radio jock had screamed earlier that morning. "I'm telling you, this man is dirt. He is spineless. He's a pig. He's a pimp. He is a crook who takes advantage of his players for money! I hope he gets killed in court today!"

Such was the so-called grandeur life of being one of the first major player agents during an era when they weren't glorified, but instead vilified, and uninformed fans—for the most part—felt the words "agent" and "asshole" were synonymous. During that time period, few, if anybody, even understood the role of a player agent; what an agent did, how he did it, and why he was a necessity to protect the rights of players.

I strode up the courthouse steps with unwavering courage and my head up; I had no reason not to, frankly, and I was looking forward to telling the world why. People were scurrying into the courthouse from all directions, and staring at me like a leper as I made my way past the huge white columns and ducked inside, just as a television van squealed to a stop behind me, nearly killing a pedestrian. The reporters chased me up the steps. I just kept moving.

"There he is! That's him! That's the guy!" people whispered, pointing, as if I were deaf. This is a joke, I thought. Absolutely ridiculous. But my father back in Borger, Texas, used to tell me that you don't know who you are until you get a little blood in your mouth. I'd never backed down from a fight, and no way was I going to start now.

"You gonna be OK, son?" my mother asked. With self-control, I put my arm around her waist.

"Mom, I believe in the justice system. I hope I can get a fair trial in Detroit, but I've done nothing wrong."

"I can't believe Billy turned on you!" Mom replied. "The two of you were so close."

"Money and greed make some people vulnerable," I replied, out of breath.

"Son, money has no home!" she replied. "It comes and it goes! Hopefully, the judge will see the truth."

I sure as hell hoped so.

The definition of a pioneer is a man with arrows in his back. And on this day, I was wearing a bulls-eye. My mind raced. After all the time and effort and money and fear and doubt, would we win a Divine victory, or face humiliation, ruin, or some other evil? We walked through the thick, heavy glass doors onto the marble floors of the building. Cops seemed to be everywhere, while lawyers scampered about in penny loafers like dark-suited spies.

How in the hell did I get here? I wondered. Putting a Texas boy in a Michigan courtroom is like sticking a milk bucket under a bull, and I was snorting to be done with this.

The hardened East Coast media had reveled in making a mockery of my Texas drawl, my cowboy hats, and shoot-from-the-hip quips. I was young and flamboyant, and my act didn't play well in the Motor City, so much so the entire state had galvanized itself against me. This never concerned me, however, because I've always tried to do the right thing, even when others wouldn't. I never took shortcuts and stood up for what was right, even if it meant being controversial; and in my book, leaders don't always grade highly on a pleasing personality.

The walk to the federal courtroom of the Honorable Judge Robert DeMascio seemed to take forever, and when we got there, it was clear this was not going to be the average trial. The only thing missing were the gallows. The energy around the courtroom was more frenetic than a Times Square Starbucks. There were photographers, paralegals, and jury experts.

Everyone was on high alert, buzzing around outside, drinking coffee or soft drinks, scribbling in notebooks, and chatting nervously. A layer of cigarette smoke wafted from the "designated" smoking area. To me, everything in Detroit reeked of smoke. It was mayhem. Inside the courtroom, people were jockeying for position and arguing over seats.

Then I saw the plaintiff, and my opponent: Detroit Lions' running back Billy Sims.

Yes, that Billy Sims, who was my client and my friend. Billy Sims, the football prodigy from Hooks, Texas, where he set the Texas high school record (that still stands) for most 100-yard games in a career, with 38. Billy Sims, the Heisman Trophy winner from the University of Oklahoma. Billy Sims, the best running back in the National Football League.

And, sadly, Billy Sims, the new darling of Detroit.

Attorneys surrounded him like a covey of quail. Billy wouldn't look at me, choosing instead to huddle with his subordinates. His face revealed nothing. He merely nodded as they spoke. One way or another, this was going to be a day of infamy—one with life-long repercussions.

As I flipped open a clean legal pad and took my seat at the defendant's table, I turned to the gallery and winked at my wife and mom, who were sitting just behind me in the front row. Inside, however, I was so sick to my stomach I wanted to puke. Billy had deceived me, but because of the might and muscle of the Detroit Lions and the NFL, it wasn't Billy who was on trial. It was me.

Deceit and disloyalty never sat well with me, and today I would be supremely tested in both departments. To put it simply, I was accused of ripping off Sims, the most prominent professional player of our time, by breaching my fiduciary duties as an agent, and acting for my own personal gain.

I'm not exactly sure what death feels like, but this had to be close.

2

ADVOCATE FOR THE UNDERDOG

THE HEISMAN TROPHY is notably awarded annually to the most outstanding college football player whose performance best exhibits the pursuit of excellence with integrity. Sims was a three-time All American who won the Heisman Trophy playing for the University of Oklahoma in 1978. The kid was quicker than a Texas jackrabbit; he sliced and danced through defenses with stabbing fakes and pirouettes that left defenders grasping at air. And he was dirt tough: Give him the ball near the goal line, and—with a single leap—he would elevate 5 yards over the line of scrimmage before tumbling in for the score.

His countless accomplishments while playing for Sooners' head coach Barry Switzer earned him not only the most prominent individual honor in college football, but also the right to a reasonable portion of the enormous monetary value he would bring to any professional team in the league. Predictably, Billy was the number-one draft pick of the Detroit Lions.

I'd spent years negotiating all phases of real-estate deals: buying, selling, leasing, developing, financing, and syndicating. I was quite proficient—I understood two $5 cats for one $10 dog, and that everything was always negotiable. I learned decision making from my father, and how he treated the locals and tended the store. He was always fair and just, never wavered, and relied on the facts. I was taught that patience is power, and that in any negotiation, both sides had to feel like they came away a victor. "Son," he used to say, "this occurs as you develop mastery over the details, when you're willing to assume full responsibility, and you make a habit of doing more than you're getting paid to do."

His philosophy was spot-on until I found myself dealing with the NFL, where negotiations can be particularly filthy. There is no business acumen. To be sure, the NFL is a hierarchy, and it holds all the cards. In Billy's case, I spent months locked in brutal negotiations with the Lions and Russ Thomas, their imposing general manager, whom some people said had the same build, dashing good looks, and electric personality of Herman Munster.

The Lions' brass was the antithesis of leadership. Thomas was incapable of organizing details, much less arguing them. I was raised believing that "the greatest among ye shall be the servant of all," but Thomas didn't have a humble bone in his body. The outright arrogance of the organization created an unforgettable stench. Every session lacked imagination, choked by the Lions' self-interests.

And the lies—damn, the frigging lies!—would drive you outright insane. I am a creature of habit. I write everything down, then and now. If you said it, then I've got it, so the next time you see me and tell me you didn't say it, you're lying, and I'll prove it. When I got there, many people said that the Lions led the league in deceit and disloyalty with their existing players, and it only took a few meetings to understand why.

Thomas was caught up in the authority of his leadership, and would flex his title and position whenever possible—as if I cared. Thomas's intemperance destroyed my endurance and vitality every time we met. So disgusting were these sessions that every time I met with Russ, I couldn't wait to get home and take a shower and scrape off the crap. The truth is there was nothing fair about Thomas's so-called negotiations, because there were no negotiations. He was merely another face on the NFL's system designed to control player movements, salaries, and signing bonuses for draft choices.

Lions' owner William Clay Ford—yes, as in Ford Motor Company—used to call Russ Thomas "my very dear personal friend." In that capacity, anyone might assume that Thomas was doing the bidding of his employer, or friend, but when push came to shove it was strictly up to Bill Ford to bypass Thomas entirely if Sims was to earn even close to the value he brought Ford's team.

When Billy became the first overall pick in the NFL draft, by all accounts, he was the best player in the nation, yet it still took the Lions six months to sign him. But at the end of the day, we prevailed: As a rookie Billy signed a three-year contract that was the most lucrative in history, and he became football's first recipient of a $1 million cash signing bonus, which was tax-free. Furthermore, injured football players aren't worth much to the NFL, so we also made Billy the beneficiary of a Lloyd's of London insurance policy, which guaranteed him a multi-million-dollar settlement in the event of a career-ending injury, a settlement that would have also been tax-free.

Sure, Billy trusted me for whatever aid, advice, or protection I could give him in several professional, financial, and personal matters. A lawyer isn't supposed to become friends with his clients, but I wasn't a lawyer. I was an agent, and I only followed one master—my client. I never represented a player that I couldn't treat as family. Loyalty and connection were inherent in my Jewish upbringing. It's in our blood, dating back to my own family's historic fight for survival.

I've always been an advocate for the underdog, and my father and mother raised me that way and taught me the strength of being a winner, not a good loser. In our family, a good loser was just that—a loser. Dad always impressed on me that if I really believed in something to stand up and take the lead in the fight against it. Of course, he added, with your eyes wide open, and your chin tucked in.

At that time, there were no greater underdogs than the players in the NFL, who were receiving but a fraction of the revenue being earned by its member teams.

My critics were always quick to remind the press that I was little more than a "retired ex-dentist," with no knowledge of football and certainly no experience as an agent. My Houston swagger, cowboy boots, and lifestyle—He must be raping his players!—was always a subject of great debate.

Of course, overlooked were a few "minor" details, such as how much money I earned outside of football, which was virtually all of it. Through the years after I left my dental practice, I was fortunate enough to have earned a nice living by helping other medical professionals with their exit strategies upon retirement. I say "fortunate," because I had to fight for every dollar I gained.

Stories about long hours of tedious work with rooms full of accountants poring over spreadsheets don't sell newspapers. Nobody was interested in the fact that I was a self-confident, energetic leader who sold my six-figure dental practice in 1973, then worked tirelessly at pursuing real-estate and business opportunities.

One of the penalties of leadership is the necessity of being willing to do more than you require of those who follow you. In just a single instance, we turned property that once sold for $3,500 an acre into plots that sold for $3 per square foot, or $130,000 an acre. Buying land on the corners of major freeways worked out well.

I was blessed that what I earned in my twenties and thirties alone in land speculation and development enabled me to buy more than a few extra cowboy hats, boots, and Texas-sized belt buckles.

3

THE FOLLY OF FOOLS

IN 1922, WHEN Henry Ford decided to produce his famous V-8, he chose to build an engine with the entire eight cylinders cast in one block, and instructed his engineers to produce a design that would. The design was placed on paper, but the engineers agreed, to a man, that it was simply impossible to cast an eight-cylinder engine-block in one piece.

Produce it anyway, Ford told them, I don't care what it costs. "I know what the people want," he said. "And we are going to give it to them." The engineers followed direction, and if by a stroke of genius, it happened, and it made Henry Ford very rich. Ford built an empire with little schooling, without a dollar, and with no influential friends. His word was his bond, and his handshake was as iron-clad as his automobiles.

The Ford family seemed to be following the same formula in 1980, when it made Billy Sims the NFL's first-overall pick. The Detroit offense sorely needed a new engine, and the best wheels in football were the powerful legs of Sims, the pride of Hooks, Texas. Judging from the overnight flood of new season-ticket sales, Sims was exactly what the people wanted.

But the enthusiasm and similarities stopped there. When I entered negotiations with Henry's great-grandson William Clay Ford and his "ace," GM Russ Thomas, I quickly came to my senses. At that time, the highest-paid player on the team was quarterback Gary Danielson, who was earning a whopping $165,000, about $2 million less than what I was asking for their new rookie sensation.

It took me six months of bloody negotiations to convince Thomas and Ford that having the flashy Heisman Trophy winner meant not only yards, points, and total offense, but also excitement in a cold, drab industrial city where there wasn't any. This, in turn, meant sales—ticket sales, parking sales, concession sales, merchandise sales, and advertising sales.

If Detroit had to pay a couple of million dollars for that, it would be money well spent; money that would swiftly turn to profit every time the Lions filled the 80,000 seats in the Pontiac Silverdome—with half the crowd wearing freshly minted Billy Sims jerseys, eating hot dogs, and drinking beer.

But the same Ford stubbornness once demonstrated by Henry to make a deal was now being flipped to break a deal. We wanted a short deal, to let Billy prove his worth. The Lions insisted on a four-year deal; three years, plus an "option" year.

"Get rid of your dentist," Bill Ford told Billy at one point, "and we'll get this deal done."

"Tell you what," Billy countered, "you get rid of Russ Thomas, and I'll get rid of Doc."

To break the impasse, I suggested to Thomas and Ford that the contract be drawn for three years; and by the fourth year (the option year)—and any subsequent year—we would negotiate monetary amounts based on Billy's performance on the field

I was shocked the day Thomas and Ford quickly agreed. "You have my word, Jerry," Thomas said, shaking hands with Billy and me like a piston. "If Billy does his job, we'll do ours." Later, Ford would look me right in the eyes and echo Thomas, and shake hands with both Billy and me.

We walked out of that meeting with Billy as the highest-paid rookie in NFL history, and a handshake that he would remain that way if he held up his end on the field.

Over three seasons, Billy packed the Superdome, earned Rookie of the Year and Pro Bowl honors, broke every franchise record possible within that timeframe, and carried the Lions to the playoffs. Billy's performance had been exhilarating, and now I was thrilled to talk to Russ about years four, five, and six, pursuant to our original agreement. The Lions were showering Billy with praise in the locker room, and I couldn't wait to carry that to the boardroom. I reached Thomas by phone, and excitedly asked when we could make good on our handshake.

"What handshake?" Thomas asked. I thought he was kidding, and I played along for a second before I realized he was serious.

"Whoa, Jerry," he said again. "What handshake?"

In Texas, we have names for the likes of Russ Thomas.

But, wow, did the plot thicken when my application was approved to become an owner of the Houston Gamblers of the new United States Football League, a fledgling venture of spring professional football that would be broadcast on ABC and ESPN.

There, I joined some deep-pocketed owners who were committed to competing with the monolithic monopoly known as the NFL for talented college players, as well as NFL free agents.

I certainly didn't have the kind of cash that some of the other owners had, but regardless, for me, this was a negotiator's dream come true. If Ford didn't want his new V-8 engine, the USFL sure did. I had created leverage. The Lions were about to learn just what a handshake meant in the great state of Texas, where one's word is his bond.

Sitting down one by one with each of my clients, I explained to them individually that I could no longer represent them due to the conflict of interest of now being a team owner in a competing league. Most of them understood, but three of my players refused to pass the torch—and Sims was the most vocal in his staunch insistence that I remain his agent through his next deal.

After a protracted series of stalled discussions with the Lions, I presented Billy's situation to my Gamblers co-owners. After several trips to Houston, the Gamblers signed Billy—on July 1, 1983—to a "futures" contract with the Gamblers that would come into effect at midnight on February 1, 1984, the moment his Lions' contract expired. At the time, there was no legal precedent to a futures contract, because it had never been done before.

The Gamblers would pay Billy a record, guaranteed $3.5 million over five years, including a $500,000 loan at an interest rate of 1 percent over prime, including skill and injury guarantees for three years. At signing, Billy was handed an additional check for $300,000 cash. It was the most lucrative contract for any player in the NFL. By making the $500,000 a loan, it was effectively tax-free.

Throughout the entire negotiating process with the Lions every detail, every step, was painstakingly disclosed to Billy. His distrust and dislike for the Lions, Thomas, Ford, and the entire organization had risen to the point that he no longer wanted to play in Detroit, even if the front office met our demands. Billy was so insulted by the Lions' initial offer of $1.5 million for five years that he asked that I tell Russ Thomas to "kiss my black ass goodbye!"

The $1.5 million offer was less than they paid Billy his rookie year. I thought Thomas and Ford were delusional.

Understand, gifted football players are especially proud, confident men, and if you cross that very thin line of disrespect and distrust, money can be secondary to playing for a team that appreciates and respects your efforts. A player wants to play for an organization that is committed to winning and paying its players fairly. The Lions? Their actions spoke for themselves.

"Why do the Lions have to treat me like this?" Billy said as he stared out the window in my Houston office, which overlooked the Galleria. "I can't wait to be a Gambler. Screw the Lions."

I was sitting in my office a few days after Billy signed with the Gamblers, and my private fax machine suddenly stirred to life. The cover sheet read DETROIT LIONS FOOTBALL CLUB, and the pages that followed contained a plain vanilla, five-year, $2.5 million offer, with no guarantees, annuities, or insurance. I immediately called Billy.

"Billy, they just sent us another offer," I said.

"But I already signed with the Gamblers, Doc," he said. "I'm confused."

"Billy, the Lions don't know you signed with us. If you want me to keep negotiating this, I will."

"What are the numbers?"

Other than the math, it was a standard NFL contract, but I went through the financial terms, line by line.

"I want nothing to do with them, Doc," Billy said. "I'm a Gambler."

Because Billy would have to fulfill his final season in Detroit in the fall of 1984, we had included a confidentiality clause in his Gamblers contract—namely, for his own protection as a "lame duck." But when the story leaked, it hit the newspapers like a Michigan snowstorm. As expected, the city, and then the state, revolted.

With no knowledge of the actual facts, the public treated me like a pariah overnight; I had become a sleight-of-hand horse dealer who somehow had plucked a beloved sports icon from the hearts of the people. The silver and Honolulu blue-clad Detroit fans hadn't been this upset since heavyweight champion Joe Louis had defected to New York to fight for the title.

And this time, they were determined not to lose another hero.

I never imagined I'd wake up one day in the middle of an Aesop fable. Remember Androcles? Well, I had my own Texas version, and it went like this: I had silenced the roaring Lions by taking a thorn—the Gamblers—and sticking it up their paw.

The general public will never believe this, but I never intended for Billy to play a down for the Gamblers. My motive and strategy all along had been to leverage the Lions, to get Detroit to pay him fair present-day value, with skill and injury guarantees, and a signing bonus worthy of his value to the team.

I knew the Lions could not afford to lose Billy Sims. I had them between the proverbial rock and a hard place. Billy loved the Lions fans, and it was mutual. If the Lions lost Sims to the Gamblers, it is unlikely either Ford or Thomas could show their faces in public. My goal was to negotiate a $4.5 million contract with the Lions for five years, including a million-dollar signing bonus and injury protection and performance bonuses.

Behind closed doors, meanwhile, the Lions were springing a trap of their own.

4

TRIAL BY FIRE

AT BILLY'S INVITATION, Gene Burrough, my partner and the brother of the Houston Oilers' wide receiver Kenny Burrough, and I spent the weekend of December 18, 1984, with him in Detroit. That Sunday, the Lions were playing the Tampa Bay Buccaneers and another of my clients, All-Pro linebacker Hugh Green, in what would be Billy's final game as a Lion.

We enjoyed dinners and social time with Billy and his wife, Brenda, and Billy told us that at the end of Sunday's game, he would hold a press conference to thank the great fans of Detroit, but announce that he was moving on to the USFL and the Houston Gamblers. We all agreed this would send shockwaves through the Silverdome, and I assured him we were ready to handle the fallout and support him and his family in his move back to Texas.

Frankly, as Gene and I headed to Sunday's game, we both believed that Billy's future had never been brighter. Just before halftime, we were enjoying the game and eating hot dogs in the press box at the Silverdome when a stranger opened the door.

"Jerry Argovitz?" he asked politely. I smiled, and nodded yes.

"This is for you." With that, he tossed a lawsuit in front of me. When I read "Billy Sims, Detroit Lions versus Jerry Argovitz," I dropped my hot dog in my lap. A quick glance through the paperwork revealed the lawsuit had been filed on the sixteenth, two days earlier, and the day Gene and I had arrived in town. Worse, Billy had known about the suit the entire time we'd been there.

"We've been set up," Gene growled, pounding his fist in disgust.

Stunned, I frantically tried to reach Billy after the game, but he had vanished like a puff of smoke. I wept silently on the flight back to Houston. Billy had been a son to me. I remembered when he had come to me after the Hula Bowl in Honolulu after his senior season, where he broke down and admitted he had not only taken money from Mike Trope, a Southern California agent with a vast empire of players, but also boxing promoter Don King. He was broke again, he owed some very powerful people money, and he needed help.

Gene and I embraced Billy, and one by one, we worked him out of each dilemma. When the Lions wouldn't negotiate a fair contract with us prior to the draft, or even have him attend the draft in New York (they actually refused to buy him a plane ticket), I paid for Billy and Brenda to be there. Over the years, our families had stayed together, vacationed together, and broken bread together. Countless times we had talked until the wee hours of the morning, and I just listened as he described the misfortunes of his youth. I genuinely loved this kid. Now he had been deceived, manipulated, and now sequestered, by the very men who were accusing me of doing the same.

My shock and dismay didn't end with the lawsuit. On Monday morning, I discovered the Lions had cornered Billy and that he had signed a five-year, $3.5 million contract, complete with a $1 million signing bonus. The $4.5 million deal was exactly what I had been asking for the past six months, with no movement on their part. The fact that Billy had signed the agreement the day before I arrived to see him was bad enough, but worse still was that he did it without any representation, and the money wasn't guaranteed.

The great Billy Sims now had two contracts, with two teams in two different leagues.

"Honk if you have a contract with Billy Sims!" was one of the most popular bumper stickers in Detroit leading up to the trial. Newspaper headlines around the country, from New York to Hollywood, and up and down Woodward Avenue in Detroit, had already convicted me: "Dentist Engages in Blood Feud with Lions!" "Cowboy or Crook?" And my personal favorite, "Would You Buy a Used Horse from this Man?"

Sports radio- and television-talk shows were peppered with insults, exaggerations, and half-truths, and had done a stellar job shaping the opinions of fans around the country.

I will swear to my grave that I believe the Lions made Billy's signing bonus contingent upon him joining the lawsuit against me, which gave him a million reasons to do what he did, and frankly, it was no different than bribing the star witness. The powerful gears of the NFL's public-relations machine immediately whirred into action, and instantly, the Lions were trying their case in the court of public opinion; poisoning the media with stories of how "poor" Billy Sims had been hijacked—misled and duped by his thieving agent—into signing with the Gamblers.

It was clear from the outset that the Lions and the NFL were sending a message to not only me, but also the entire United States Football League.

Here's the rub: The allegations were false, and now it would be up to a federal judge to decipher the truth. Not just any judge, but a judge in Detroit. I can't prove this, but I was told that Judge Robert Edward DeMascio was also a season-ticket holder of the Lions, and a personal friend of Bill Ford's.

Now our family name and business reputation were at stake. Prior to even meeting Billy Ray Sims, I had been a general partner in at least sixty different business ventures worth more than $100,000,000, and not only survived, but thrived. Attracted by my love for sports and total self-confidence in my own business acumen, I honestly believed I had entered an arena where I could stimulate change, offer solutions, and create a better opportunity for NFL players.

Instead, I had fallen through a carefully choreographed trapdoor, and found myself as a pawn in a much larger game that was far bigger than I was. The Gamblers didn't need Billy, but the USFL—an exciting spring league seeking attention—needed him. The NFL, on the other hand, needed to make an example of someone to stop the exodus of its best players. I had no idea this courtroom drama would lead to events that would change the professional game forever, with lifelong ramifications of my own.

This was trial by fire in far, far more ways than one.

5

THROWN TO THE LIONS

"WHAT IN GOD'S name happened here, Jerry? If Billy Sims was your 'son,' why didn't this kid just pick up the phone and call you and just tell you that the Lions had agreed to pay him more?"

The booming voice belonged to attorney Stephen D. Susman, a tall, imposing man with the same look and intensity of an American bald eagle. I had never worked with him before, but I sure had heard of him. Just a few years earlier, Susman had won several landmark victories as a plaintiff's attorney, including one award of more than $550 million to the victims of a nationwide price-fixing conspiracy.

Word in Texas was that if you stepped in something or something stepped on you, the Houston born-and-bred, Yale-educated Susman was a pretty good guy to have on your side of the aisle. My partners with the Houston Gamblers all agreed: He gave us the best chance to beat the Lions and the NFL and to do something no defender could ever do—tackle Billy Sims in the open field.

Susman could not have cared less if you didn't appreciate his arrogance. You could just feel that he always believed he was the smartest, most talented steer in the ring, and he'd staked his career on proving it every time out of the chute. The word "settle" didn't exist in his vocabulary; he lived for the battle. The bloodier, the better. Like me, Susman loved the underdog, and loved fighting for the little guy.

This was no Bible story now; we were modern-day Davids fighting a contemporary Goliath, and this time, a single stone wouldn't be enough. The thought made me chuckle.

As an agent, I'd already whipped the Giants (Butch Woolfolk) and the Bears (Jim McMahon), and frankly, I couldn't wait to add the Lions to the list.

"What other players have you represented?" Susman asked.

"Curtis Dickey, Jacob Green, George Cumby, Robert Brazile, James Lofton, Butch Woolfok, Gary Anderson, Curley Culp, Jim McMahon, Herschel Walker, Hugh Green, Bubba Paris—that's just a few," I replied.

"Would they be willing to testify to the veracity and satisfaction of you as an agent?"

"Every one of them," I said. "They'd all sit for a deposition, or appear in court, if necessary. Hugh Green even asked me if Billy had lost his mind."

We prepared for trial at Steve's pristine, fifth-floor office at 1000 Louisiana Street in bustling downtown Houston. Because the USFL season was literally days away, we were eager to get into court, and in our minds there was no chance we would lose. Gene Burrough often accompanied me to help us go through all the details.

Stacks of files sat piled atop a long, shiny mahogany table in his conference room. Always impeccably dressed, Susman paced around like a caged animal, stopping occasionally like a symphony conductor to scribble notes on legal pads that were laid out in front of him like sheets of music. He'd sit, write, stand, and pace, then start the process all over again.

"I know you think Billy Sims is your son, Jerry, but he's not," Susman said, almost sneering. He held up copies of the *Houston Chronicle* and *Detroit Free-Press*. "Sons, I believe, don't talk about their dads like this in the papers. I know you like to help people, buddy, but when you're playing with chips this big, you underestimated greed. Quick riches always make a guy like Billy Sims far more dangerous than when he was in poverty. Essentially, the Lions bought his trust and loyalty for a million dollars.

"Billy grew up dirt poor," Susman added. "He's been punching his football ticket his whole life, from high school, to Oklahoma, and now the pros. He's used to special privileges, and a kid from Hooks, Texas, thinks a million bucks is a helluva lot more than your 'fatherly love.' You got played, Jerry. But damn, you'd think he'd have the decency to just call you."

Rays of sun pierced through the windows and cast odd shadows in the room. Outside it was a balmy 74 degrees, but inside, it was a little chilly. Susman rolled up the sleeves on his starched light blue button-down, unbuttoned his collar, and loosened his red-striped tie.

"Listen, I know you're a busy man with a lot of obligations outside of football," Susman said. "And I read these papers. I know you're not the most patient guy in the world. But you are going to have to fall on the sword to win this case.

"They are going to come after your morals, and if I were them, I'd try to make this a case of you neglecting your fiduciary duties and obligations to your clients. So let's start at the top. When did you apply to be an owner of the Houston franchise of the USFL?"

"Sometime in February or March of 1983," I said. "Why does that matter?"

"Let me ask the questions," Susman replied. "I want to know why an agent would want to be an owner in a competing league, and I'm sure the other side wants to know, too. When was your first offer to the Lions, and when were you awarded the Houston franchise?"

"In April of 1983, I believe on the fifth, I told the Lions that Billy wanted $6 million for four years, including a $1 million interest-free loan, to be repaid over ten years, and skill and injury guarantees for three years. The Lions countered a couple days later with a $1.5 million deal for five years."

"That's when Billy told them to kiss his black ass," chortled Gene.

Susman smirked. "And then you got the franchise?" he probed.

"Yes. Then on May 3, 1983, we had a press conference in Houston announcing that our application had been approved," I answered. "A lot of the players I represent were there for the announcement."

"Sims, too?"

"Of course. Billy was there, along with Hugh Green, Joe Cribbs, Curtis Dickey, Jacob Green, Keith Gary, Robert Brazile, and a lot of other members of the Argovitz family."

"Why do you insist on calling them 'family'? You do realize that to the outside world, this sounds a little condescending, a little controlling, even manipulative?"

"I really don't give a damn, Steve, what it sounds like to the outside world. It's a fact. A lot of my guys had no father figure, no mentor, and very few of the right kind of friends. I was there for all of them, on and off the field, even if I had to do some unorthodox things."

"Dammit, Jerry, you don't get it! This is exactly what the other side is going to say," Susman railed. "They aren't going to use the word 'unorthodox.' They are going to say you broke every protocol known to man as an agent, they are going to call you a liar, and they are going to say you broke the rules for your own selfish interests!"

"My best interests?" I argued. "How in hell could someone misconstrue me negotiating the best contract in the history of the game—twice—for Billy as acting in my own best interest? Especially if I were responsible for paying one-third of his salary. I worked my ass off for Billy and actually put him in a position to do what he's done."

Susman stared at me, and the silence between questions was uncomfortable. I was having trouble convincing my own attorney of the bond Gene and I both had felt with Billy.

"What, exactly, was your obligation to the Gamblers?"

"I received 29 percent of the franchise for $1.5 million."

Susman scribbled notes in his legal pads, flipping sheets back and forth.

"Was that hard cash?"

"No," I said, "bank letter of credit."

"You are also the team's president, correct?"

"Yes, and managing general partner."

"How much is the team paying you?"

"My contract calls for about $275 grand annually, plus 5 percent of the yearly positive cash flow. Obviously, these numbers are flexible, based on our cash position."

"Do you have any criminal history?"

I bristled, but couldn't help but laugh out loud. "Are you kidding me?" I huffed. "I have perfect credit, no criminal history. In fact, in Billy's case, I showed him my actual financial statements proving my net worth outside of football before he ever signed with me. Ask Mike Trope if he ever did *that*!"

"Mike Trope's not on trial here," Susman replied.

"I understand, but I've got to be the only agent in the history of the sport to do that. Billy, in fact, acknowledged and waived any conflicts regarding my being a part owner and his agent. He told me that I would be the only person to ever represent him, and that I was the only person he trusted. The Gamblers contract was the richest contract at the time in pro football, period."

"I understand, Jerry, but the validity of those waivers is going to be called into question. Bear with me," Susman said, pen scratching away liberally. "And didn't the USFL have bylaws that forbade owners from acting as agents ... " He flipped open documents he had acquired from the league office, and ran his finger down the page.

"It says here in the USFL constitution that ... gimme a sec ... here it is ... 'a holder of any interest in a member club is prohibited from acting as the contracting agent or representative for any player.' "

The hair on my neck stood up.

"But I went to Chet Simmons, our commissioner, and asked for a special waiver in regard to three of my players who insisted that I stay with them through current negotiations! Gary Anderson, Billy Sims, and Joe Cribbs all wanted me to continue to represent them. Chet approved it, but insisted they be the last ones. I sat down with the rest of my clients and told them I could no longer represent them, it was a conflict of interest."

"You actually used the words conflict of interest?"

"Yes! And I sold my sports agency business and signed over all of my other clients! And Billy, of all people, was informed of every single phone call, every detail, every step that was taken on his behalf."

Susman smiled at my red-faced intensity, and sipped from a perspiring glass of water.

"Wanna take a break?"

I exhaled in frustration. "Hell no," I said, slumping in my chair. "Just keep going."

"So you had permission from Simmons to keep negotiating, and you did, and then you countered the Lions on May 3 with a significantly smaller deal, right?"

"Well, I knew that Nash was hung up on the skill guarantees. Since I had never negotiated with him, only Russ Thomas, I told Nash anything we agreed upon had to be approved by Billy. So I asked for $3 million over four years, including a $1 million signing bonus, plus incentives, a $50,000 annual annuity, and a $2.5 million Lloyd's of London career-ending insurance. This was a test run to see Nash's response, and for me to discover how much authority he actually had to make a deal."

"Who's Nash? What happened to Russ Thomas?"

Gene interrupted. "Steve, Billy was so pissed off and insulted after the first offer of $1.5 million that Jerry had to get rid of Russ Thomas. He called Bill Ford and told him about the $1.5 million offer, and Ford said he was 'unaware' of it. Jerry made it clear that he would only negotiate with him or Billy would play out his options. So Mr. Ford removed Thomas and replaced him with a lawyer who, as far as I know, had never done a player contract in his life."

"Frederick Nash?"

"Correct."

"So, Jerry, on May 30, 1983, you submitted a third offer to Nash, right?"

"They wanted a longer contract, so I talked to Billy, and we decided to go with $4.5 million for five years, including a million-dollar, interest-free loan; also, there were incentive bonuses, plus a $50,000 annual annuity for five years, and injury protection insurance, with no demands for skill guarantees."

"And how did the Lions respond?"

Gene nearly jumped out of his chair. "They didn't!" he said. "They told the media, though, that we were only about $500 grand apart, which was absolute horseshit. We were still over a couple of million dollars apart, and Nash wanted nothing to do with the annuity or skill and injury guarantees. I told Billy, and at that point, he was just fed up with the Lions. He point-blank said to me, 'What about the USFL?'"

"So Billy asked you first, Gene?"

"Absolutely! And I told him that Jerry was only one of three owners, and he would have to consult with his partners, Bernard Lerner and Alvin Lubetkin. But this is where it gets interesting."

"How so?"

"Well, Billy wanted out of Detroit altogether, because he felt he never got the respect he deserved. Jerry, on the other hand, wanted to use the Gamblers as leverage to force the Lions hand at the table. To be honest, Mouse Davis, our offensive coordinator in Houston, had already told us that our Run 'n' Shoot offense didn't need Billy Sims. He told us to go buy an offensive line to protect Jimmy."

"Who's Jimmy?"

"Jim Kelly," I shot back. "He's our franchise quarterback with the Gamblers."

"What does he earn?"

"A little over $3 million for five years, but what does that have to do with Billy Sims?"

"Let me ask the questions, Jerry. You have to trust me, OK? Now tell me about the trips Sims made to Houston."

"It was the last two or three days in June for sure," I said. "His first night there, we didn't discuss the contract. He was pretty upset over the Lions, so Gene and I just visited with Billy and his wife Brenda and went to dinner."

Susman paused, and pulled out a copy of Billy's agreement with the Gamblers. "Is this a correct copy of the contract Sims saw the next morning?"

I read it carefully. It was dated June 30. "Yes. This is what I negotiated on his behalf with Bernard Lerner and Alvin Lubetkin. I wasn't acting as an owner, but as Billy's agent. Billy, Gene, Brenda, and me went into a separate room to discuss it. Billy was pretty thrilled because this contract had all of the guarantees he had asked for with the Lions. I told him that if we called the Lions, there would be a good chance they'd match the Gamblers' offer, or better it—except for the guarantees."

"So you actually gave Sims the option of calling Detroit?"

"Absolutely. Both he and Gene didn't think the Lions would match it. Ironically, Nash did call sometime during the day and left a message."

"Did you call him back?"

"Yes. He had left for the weekend."

Susman sighed deeply. Steve could be arrogant, bullish or dogmatic, but the twists and turns of this complicated case were making him earn every penny of his $500 hourly rate.

"So now, we're late in the day, and Sims is holding a guaranteed, five-year contract for $3.5 million, with skill and injury guarantees, a $500,000 loan, with $300 grand right there on the spot?"

"Yes," I said.

"What were you getting out of this?"

"My standard agent fee," which was 6 percent.

"That doesn't look so good, Jerry, I gotta tell you," Susman replied, rubbing his eyes. There was a slight dip in his shoulders. "It looks like you were getting paid to negotiate with your own team."

"Listen, Steve, I understand the dilemma. Gene and I also discussed this. When I sat down to negotiate Billy's contract with the Gamblers, I was representing Billy. I had zero, zilch, to do with anything Bernard and Alvin did in representing the Gamblers. I was working for Billy, and his best interest only. Looking back, I could understand how that could be misconstrued. But I took no fees at that time. I was still planning to spring this on Detroit, and honestly, I thought I'd get my money out of the Lions. My only regret was not having a third-party attorney present with Billy while this played out, but he was given the opportunity to do so. We went over the contract in detail and Gene and I both asked Billy and Brenda if they understood every word, and they both said, multiple times, yes."

"What happened next?"

"We all went back to Bernard's office, and Billy agreed to the terms offered."

"When did he sign the contract?"

"I told Billy to sleep on it. Then Billy, Brenda, Gene, and me all went to dinner that night. The next day, July 1, 1983, I left to go out of town, and Billy, before heading back to Detroit, met Gene at the office to sign his contract. And, by the way, without me present, Bernard Lerner reiterated everything I'd told Billy already—that my position with the Gamblers did create a conflict of interest, and that Billy had the right to call an attorney right then, or even hire another agent, to read the contract one last time before he signed it. Billy declined, in the presence of his wife, Gene, and Bernard, and he signed the contract."

And so it went, deep into the night, for several weeks, as Susman deposed witnesses and conducted interviews with dozens of others. Finally, he felt ready for battle.

"There's a few sticky spots," Susman said in our final pre-trial meeting, "but nothing we can't overcome. They had over a year to sign Sims, and they didn't. You accomplished more in forty-eight hours in Houston than the Lions did in fourteen months. Everything was out on the table, and Sims acknowledged that he was given everything. Facts are facts, and we should win this case on those merits alone."

Not one person who truly understood the case could disagree.

6

"THESE BOOTS WERE MADE FOR WALKIN'"

THE COURTROOM WAS as intimidating as the charges against me.

High oak-lined walls surrounded three sections of seats that would only hold about 150 people: one each to the left and right of the judge's stately bench, and another behind the long L-shaped litigants table set parallel to the bench. The witness stand was on the judge's right and near to the front and left-center attorney's podium. A uniformed bailiff stood to the left of the judge's bench, picking his nails. A large American flag hung behind the bench.

My mom and wife were struggling to maintain composure as looks of discontent and disapproval were lobbed their way. I could see the pain on my mother's face, and frankly, it was heartbreaking. My biggest concern was that I somehow—despite my good intentions—might have ruined our family's good name.

In front of me was the court reporter, a defense paralegal, and an attorney to my left. Steve Susman sat to my right. Across the way, Billy sat with Frederick C. Nash, Michael Lewiston, another Lions attorney, two assistant attorneys, and a paralegal. Lead attorney Elbert L. Hatchett appeared, lugging a huge briefcase.

Susman's nattily tailored attire was nothing compared to Hatchett, who looked like Johnny Cochran and was color-coordinated down to his tie, scarves, and fedora; he would've been as comfortable in a jazz club as a court room. The two of them stared each other down like gladiators.

Does the guy with the most lawyers win by default? I wondered. I quickly realized, too, that I was the only guy in the room wearing cowboy boots—not a good sign.

That was another bizarre twist. I had wanted the case tried in Houston. After all, the fact of the matter is that I was from Texas, Billy was from Texas, the Gamblers were from Texas, and the contract was signed in Texas.

However, because I had been served in Michigan, it had wound up here, yet all parties had stipulated that the trial would be heard under Texas law. Go figure. But Steve was confident we would win in any courtroom, and he had a two-week window to do it. A change of venue to Texas would have pushed the case into summer. "Let's just kick their ass and get it over with," Susman told me.

Hatchett was firing salvos of his own to the national media. "They scheduled this trial for five days," he told the *New York Times*, "but it could last five minutes, based on the facts."

This all seemed like wasted effort to me, unless you're into cockfights, car wrecks, or sumo wrestling. The dull courtroom lights cast a yellow pall over the throng that had taken up residence for the duration of the trial. There were fans, media, and members of management, waiting like vultures.

At the start of the trial, two things were immediately evident: First, that even in a packed courtroom, Thomas still occupied half a row by himself, and was about a biscuit away from tipping the pew. Second, that Susman had grossly underestimated the pressure on a Michigan judge in a case involving the beloved Detroit Lions.

Stepping into a major trial is like jumping off a pier with all your clothes on: You might fight your way to the surface for air, but the rest of the world doesn't care. You always think you're drowning.

"All rise," announced the bailiff.

My heart was pounding through my chest, and yes, I was nervous as hell. As the charges were read in the case of the Detroit Lions, Inc., a corporation, and Billy Sims plaintiffs, versus Jerry A. Argovitz, individually, and as president of the Houston Gamblers, Inc., corporation, defendants, I could almost hear my dad saying, "Son, I just hope you can get a fair trial in Detroit."

In upper-case letters, the heading alone for the trial was nineteen single-spaced lines long. This was particularly tough, because of the broken bond of love and deep trust that Billy and I had built together. We had worked with two minds, but a single heart. Now, with Billy on that side, I felt like a displaced father; it was no longer about money, at least not for me. Betrayal leaves deep, deep wounds; and it couldn't have been worse had he spit in my face, turned, and walked away.

The Lions and Billy's lawyers were looking to destroy my good name, reputation, and integrity in the process.

Too bad the Lions aren't as fierce and serious about winning games as I thought.

"Take your seats," said Judge DeMascio, a former naval reservist who had been nominated for his position by President Richard Nixon. "Good morning. I expect decorum at all times. No outbursts."

Exchanging paperwork with court clerks, Judge DeMascio frowned, pinching the bridge of his nose as he scanned them, his forehead burrowed with heavy wrinkles. From his mannerisms alone, I could only assume he was a persecuted Lions fan, because he just looked like one.

Just as Susman had surmised in pretrial discovery, the case was going to hinge on the definition of fiduciary duty. A court reporter read the definition. "Fiduciary duty," she said, "is a legal or ethical relationship of confidence or trust regarding the management of money or property between two or more parties, most commonly a fiduciary and a principal."

Therefore, by definition, the pivotal deal in this case would be my ethical relationship toward Billy; in other words, to do what is right for him, as opposed to a letter-of-the law, legal relationship. If you read the papers, you would've thought "sleazy" was my first name, but the press all neglected to report that prior to even meeting Billy Ray Sims, I had been a general partner in many business ventures worth millions.

To suggest I didn't understand fiduciary duty, or fiduciary obligation, was an insult. Had Billy just placed a single phone call to me, this mess could've been avoided. I referred to Billy as a son, and I wanted what was best for him not only as a client, but also as a friend, as family. One phone call, one discussion, and I gladly would have approached the other Gamblers owners to release Billy, and he knew it.

In fact, three months before the trial, when the Lions played the Houston Oilers on November 12—and prior to the public's knowledge of Billy's Gambler contract—Gene and I met with him and asked him again if he had any second thoughts about playing for the Gamblers. "Hell no," had been Billy's reply. If that's not fiduciary duty, what is?

My relationship with Billy would turn into hearsay in court, leaving little wiggle room. I could see this coming like a Santa Fe freight train. I wanted to stand up and scream that this was a matter of principle, that Billy was a liar, and that had he told the truth to people who had done everything he had asked, every anguished moment of this could have been avoided.

Meanwhile, the lawyers were hell-bent on teaching me a lesson in fiduciary duty, when the NFL had been running a monopoly for sixty-two years in outright violation of the Sherman Anti-Trust? Are you kidding me? Listen, if fiduciary duty requires me to act at all times for the sole benefit and interests of someone, with loyalty to those interests alone, above mine, well you just described me.

My initial interest in the USFL had been to break the stranglehold the NFL had on its players. I had become a one-man wrecking ball to the NFL, and I didn't give a damn if they hated me for giving players and coaches new options and opportunities they had earned and rightfully deserved.

7

"I THINK WE GOT THIS"

"NEVER PICK AN argument with men who buy their ink in barrels" is a common joke among old newspaper pundits, and it's true. The media couldn't get enough of the trial, and it had escalated into one of the largest sports stories of the year, including coverage in *Sports Illustrated*. There were more media at my trial than there had been at the press conference announcing the Houston Gamblers.

After opening statements, Billy's attorneys went to work like surgeons, dissecting me into pieces on the argument that I breached my fiduciary duties brought on by my "blatant conflict of interests." I was described in great detail as a low-end hustler, the ambulance-chaser of agents, preying on the ignorance of my uneducated clients.

There wasn't a single mention of the rest of the players we represented. Conveniently omitted were the record-breaking windfalls of cash I had brought my clients or the manner in which I had viciously protected them, on and off the field. No discussion whatsoever of how happy Billy had been, right up until the day I had been served with the lawsuit, or that he planned to keep the $300,000 he pocketed when he signed with the Gamblers.

I'd been pretty reserved to this point, but pure anger and disdain began to boil inside me.

Who else had a better deal going for players? I thought. Do you think Lions' quarterback Gary Danielson, if given the chance, would've traded Billy's original $2 million for his $165,000 salary? Billy's signing bonus with the Gamblers was more than Danielson earned outright.

If my contracts for Billy had the highest monetary value of any in the game, if I had made full and complete disclosures, if Billy waived any conflicts I have, then where are his damages?

Billy Sims was a horrible witness. I couldn't help but feel sorry for him. He was sweating profusely. His mouth was dry. He couldn't put words together. He shuffled. He squirmed. He repositioned his chair so he could look everywhere in the courtroom except at me. He was so confused by the questions being fired by his own attorneys that he probably wouldn't have remembered his mother's name if asked.

Hatchett, Billy's "personal" attorney, spent more time ranting, raving, and pontificating than he did questioning; none of it with a legal basis. Pointing at me again and again and again, he ridiculously played the race card, over and over and over.

"This man right here," he bellowed, stabbing his finger in the air in my direction, "took a poor black kid—who won a Heisman Trophy—and took advantage of him.

"This man right there sold himself as a father figure!

"This man cheated a kid he calls his son!

"This man never told him he owned a football team!

"This man lied and swindled this poor black kid to fill his own pockets!

"This man treated Billy Sims like he had just fallen off the watermelon truck!"

Answering one simple question at a time, Billy managed to stammer out enough "yes" and "no" answers to satisfy Hatchett that he had never been given proper counsel; had never been told that the Lions might match the Gamblers offer; didn't realize the extent of the fees I was pocketing; had suffered emotionally and financially due to my "questionable" conduct; and, finally misled him into believing the Lions had no real interest in signing him.

Are you kidding me?

When Billy did answer in complete sentences, they were so painstakingly stilted that it seemed evident they were rehearsed. Nevertheless, when the star witness repeatedly said he "did not know about all this stuff," the damage was done.

On cross-examination, however, Susman spun Billy silly. He refused to make eye contact with me or Steve; he'd glance at the judge, then his own counsel, after each pertinent question; he'd ask for the questions to be repeated or, simply, with a quivering voice, reply, "I don't remember" or "I don't recall." His reluctance on each and every question Susman asked him was like stabbing me with a knife.

This disaster had been looming for months, but it still crushed me. I believe if you tell the truth, it will set you free, but I knew that Billy was brainwashed, essentially coerced with a million dollars, and they were delivering a message to me and the rest of my owners in the USFL.

Billy was unsophisticated, scared, and passive, the opposite of the dominance he exuded on the playing field. Still, watching Susman work him over on cross-examination was like watching my own child get run over by the ice-cream truck. I was downright bitter at what the Lions had done to my kid—I felt like I was in a family custody case that had gone horribly wrong, and that the oppressive parent had intimidated his way to victory.

Just when I thought this circus couldn't get worse, the plaintiffs brought out Boston-based agent Bob Woolf, one of my competitors, as their expert witness.

When he was called to the stand, I literally laughed. At this juncture, this probably did me no good in front of the judge, but this had gone too far.

Woolf was a long-time Boston attorney who morphed his legal representation into a sports agency in the 1970s, representing mostly basketball and baseball stars. At the time Billy signed his first contract, the cherubic Woolf had no football clients, but due to high-profile stars like Julius Erving, Jim Craig, Larry Bird, Larry King, and Carl Yastrzemski, had become widely known. Current Heisman Trophy winner Doug Flutie was represented by Woolf, and they had just signed with Donald Trump and the New Jersey Generals of the USFL.

Woolf had agreed to testify for the plaintiffs, and quickly summarized how I had breached my fiduciary responsibilities by not immediately pitting the Gamblers offer against the Lions to create a bidding war. "An offer from another team is probably the most important thing in negotiating the best deal for the client," he said.

Susman could hardly hold back his glee on cross-examination, nearly bounding over the defendant's table.

"Mr. Woolf," he said, "you know a lot about fiduciary duty, don't you?"

Woolf nodded. "Of course," he said, "I have to. I'm both an agent and an attorney."

"I wasn't referring to that, Mr. Woolf," Susman replied. With one David Copperfield-like sweep of his right hand, Susman seemed to produce a document from thin air, and showed it to the judge.

"May I?" he asked.

"Objection," interrupted Lions' attorney Lewiston. "Why were we not aware. . . . "

"Overruled," Judge DeMascio told the plaintiffs. "You put the witness on."

Susman cleared his throat, and continued.

"I'm referring to the lawsuit between you and Andrew Brown of the National Hockey League. Apparently, you negotiated an $800,000 contract for Mr. Brown, of which he only received $150,000 when the team got into financial trouble, correct?"

"Yes," replied Woolf.

"Yet," continued Susman, "you still charged him fees against the entire $800,000 value of his contract, including money he never received. Correct?"

The courtroom fell silent. Woolf looked just like actor Bob Hoskins feigning a heart attack in *Who Framed Roger Rabbit?*

"Correct, Mr. Woolf?" Susman pressed. "In fact, you were found guilty of constructive fraud and breach of fiduciary duty, right, sir, so that would make you a real expert in this field, correct? And your guilty verdict hasn't prevented you from continuing your career, either as an agent, or attorney, has it?"

Susman couldn't hide his smirk. He turned to the judge. "No further questions, your Honor."

Greg Lustig, who had represented the Gamblers star quarterback Jim Kelly, was our expert witness. Nash and Hatchett did their best to twist his testimony, but he delivered the facts just as Susman predicted. While Greg did testify that he felt it was only "prudent" to contact the NFL's Buffalo Bills to report the offer he had received from the Houston Gamblers, he was quick to add that he believed he had already received Buffalo's best offer.

Our offer to Kelly was about $60,000 less per year than what we were offering Billy, but we had given him a clause that would ensure that he would always be among the top-three highest paid quarterbacks in the USFL—if he was in the top three of USFL quarterback passing ratings. When asked if, at the end of the day, the phone call to Buffalo had made a difference, Lustig said no. "They refused to match Houston's offer," he said, "and I don't believe they ever had any intention of doing so."

Nash made an issue out of the discrepancy in the clauses offered to Kelly, an unproven rookie, and Billy, an established NFL star; a point Susman was quick to discredit. "Mr. Kelly might be among the highest-paid USFL quarterbacks," Susman argued. "But Mr. Sims' contract at the time was the biggest for a running back in either league, and it was guaranteed.

"There was no way the Lions were ever going to guarantee Mr. Sims' contract," Susman argued in closing. "They wouldn't do it then, and they didn't do it now, with the new agreement. It makes the Gamblers' deal a far better deal for the client."

Susman was confident when he sat down next to me. He leaned to my ear. "I think we got this," he said.

On January 28, 1984, both sides rested. Judge DeMascio thanked everyone for their time and testimony. "We will take a brief recess," the judge said, "and I will render my decision."

Nobody could have predicted what happened next.

8

BRANDS DON'T COME OUT IN THE WASH

I WAS ELEVEN YEARS old the first time I saw a calf get branded on a nearby ranch. See it once, and you'll never forget the look of sheer terror and disbelief in the calf's wide-open eyes; the unmistakable smell of its burning flesh permanently sears your nostrils and memory forever.

Your natural instinct at that age is to go rescue the calf from the rugged cowboy foreman who is applying the pressure, but before you can, quick as a wink, the little calf is up and off to the races. Regardless of sex, they all run bawling right back to their mothers. It's an amazing phenomenon.

Branding is not for the tender-hearted. The branding iron must go deep enough to burn the hair and outer layer of skin. When the branding iron is lifted, the brand is typically the color of saddle leather, and the foreman works as slowly as necessary, because the brand must last a lifetime.

A cowpoke's motto is that "brands don't come out in the wash." Any cowboy will tell you there is no more defining mark of ownership and deterrent as a brand. "Trust your neighbors," they say in Texas, "but brand your stock."

One would think my Texas upbringing would have triggered a fight or flight response when I entered Judge DeMascio's courtroom for the verdict on the afternoon of January 28—or at least smelled the smoke from the campfire heating the branding irons.

Truthfully, I never saw it coming.

It was my understanding that a federal judge, before rendering a verdict, takes his or her time building a foundation based on fact, precedents, and expert opinions. Judges rely on clerks for detailed research, while spending hours weighing the oral arguments that had been presented by both sides.

All I wanted was fairness, so we had reason to hope. Judge DeMascio had earned a conservative reputation of fairness in the thirteen years since he replaced Theodore Levin on the bench at the U.S. Courthouse at 231 West Lafayette Boulevard in Detroit, which now had been named after Judge Levin.

After serving in the military, the Wayne State graduate had worked his way through the court system from the ground up, first in private practice before permanently switching to the public sector in 1961. He had ruled on the desegregation of Detroit schools in 1977, but refused to overturn another landmark case on appeal that involved the National Labor Relations Board.

Susman was contagiously confident, evident by the little extra skip in his giddy-up as we headed to the courtroom. I must admit, however, that the negative energy radiating from the Lions' side of the courtroom could have made a pessimist out of Pope John Paul II.

"All rise, the Court of the Honorable Judge Robert Edward DeMascio is now in session," barked the bailiff.

Shuffling papers, the judge took his seat, adjusted his glasses, cleared his throat, and began to read from his notes.

"The relationship between a principal and agent is fiduciary in nature, and as such imposes a duty of loyalty, good faith, and fair and honest dealing on the agent," Judge DeMascio said. "A fiduciary relationship arises not only from a formal principal-agent relationship, but also from informal relationships of trust and confidence.

"In light of the express agency agreement, and the relationship between Sims and Argovitz, Argovitz clearly owed Sims the fiduciary duties of an agent at all times relevant to this lawsuit.

"The law denies the right of an agent to assume any relationship that is antagonistic to his duty to his principal, and it has many times been held that the agent cannot be both buyer and seller at the same time nor connect his own interests with property involved in his dealings as an agent for another.

"It is not sufficient for the agent merely to inform the principal that he has an interest that conflicts with the principal's interest. Rather, he must inform the principal of all facts that come to his knowledge that are or may be material or which might affect his principal's rights or interests or influence the action he takes."

"The evidence," Judge DeMascio continued, "persuades us that Sims did not know the extent of Argovitz's interest in the Gamblers. He did not know the amount of Argovitz's original investment. The defendants could not expect Sims to comprehend the ramifications of Argovitz's interest in the Gamblers or the manner in which that interest would create an untenable conflict of interest, a conflict that would inevitably breach Argovitz's fiduciary duty to Sims.

"For the reasons that follow, we have concluded that Argovitz's breach of his fiduciary duty during negotiations for the Gamblers' contract was so pronounced, so egregious, that to deny recision would be unconscionable."

I leaned over to Susman and whispered in his ear. "What in the hell does egregious mean? Isn't that a bird?"

Susman scowled. "It means as bad as it gets," he said, gritting his teeth.

"We conclude," Judge DeMascio said, "as a court sitting in equity, recision is the appropriate remedy. We are dismayed by Argovitz's egregious conduct. The careless fashion in which Argovitz went about ascertaining the highest price for Sims' service convinces us of the wisdom of the maxim: No man can faithfully serve two masters whose interests are in conflict.

"Judgment will be entered for the plaintiffs rescinding the Gamblers' contract with Sims. *It is so ordered.*"

With a sharp clack of his gavel, Judge DeMascio ended the trial, and disappeared to his chambers.

"What just happened?" I asked Susman.

"They won," he said. Reporters raced for the exits to file the story. In the time it took to gather my belongings, pack my briefcase, and face the courtroom, Billy Sims was long gone, like a 60 Pitch Sweep to the open field.

I turned around and embraced my mother.

"I'm sorry, son," she said. "You have the rest of your life to prove them wrong."

The verdict was a life sentence for me. Judge DeMascio had branded me forever. The case never went away, instead standing the test of time as it was repeated, referenced, and taught again and again, decade after decade, in law journals, classrooms, and courtrooms across America. It would leave me ostracized in sports circles, cost me millions in future business outside of sports, and make me the subject of ridicule from friends and peers alike.

It would be my name, not that of Billy Sims, that would become synonymous forever with deceit, greed, and betrayal. The verdict, not the arguments or facts, would be all that attorneys, judges, and the rest of the world would ever see.

Egregious conflict of interest.

It would be seventeen years before Billy and I spoke again. But the NFL had not heard the last of me. They might have won the battle, but I walked out of that courtroom chin down, shoulders upright, and back stiffened, determined to win the war.

The NFL was a monopoly, and I swore I would prove it once and for all before I died.

ACT TWO

Fear makes us instruments of Power. When we are afraid, we obey those who would persecute us.

—Matthew 10:28

9

"I WILL WAIT
FOR YOU"

Please, Max. I pray you don't leave me and our baby son Louie, though
I know you must. Facing these nights alone is almost more than I can bear.
I will wait for you to send for us.
—From the diary of my grandmother Dora

FOR ME, FIGHTING fear and overcoming oppression was a birthright, one that made the National Football League pale by comparison, and on a playing field where neither Ford, Sims, nor the Detroit Lions could ever achieve. Mine was a heritage formed in the bitter winters of Lodz, Poland, where my maternal grandparents, Max and Dora Weitzman, were living proof that endearing love, faith, trust, and courage will, indeed, conquer all fears.

These were not mere words, but a repeated prayer my grandparents, who by the turn of the twentieth century were facing insurmountable odds as Eastern European Jews. Hundreds of thousands of emigrants had already taken appointed paths through the German Empire to reach the giant steamer ships in Hamburg and Bremen. For the 7 million Jews fleeing poverty, hatred, danger, and discrimination and the soon-to-be-realized potential of organized massacres, the United States was beckoning with the prospects of hope for a better life.

Like 2 million others between 1881 and 1914, my grandparents—as a last resort—chose emigration to America in the early 1900s. The German government, in a collaborative effort with the shipping companies "Hamburg-Amerikanische

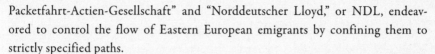

Packetfahrt-Actien-Gesellschaft" and "Norddeutscher Lloyd," or NDL, endeavored to control the flow of Eastern European emigrants by confining them to strictly specified paths.

The biggest questions for my grandparents had been first whether to flee, and second where to go. While most chose Ellis Island and New York, the Galveston Plan offered the diversion of immigration from the poor, congested cities of the American East Coast to sparsely populated towns in the western United States, via the port of tiny Galveston, Texas.

Only 7,000 people chose the latter. My grandparents weren't just numbers among them. They had names. They were Max and Dora, not identification numbers, they were people; they fought through circumstances you and I will never appreciate or understand, or should.

Based on the diaries of my grandmother, I'm grateful we never will. They never lost hope for freedom to work, worship, and raise their son, Louie.

If the unknown eleven-day journey across unknown seas to an unknown world wasn't daunting enough, my grandparents also had to meet strict criteria: They couldn't be more than forty years of age. They had to be strong, healthy, and able to satisfy the requirements of the immigration laws of the United States. They would have to scrape together $41 apiece for fare as "steerage class" passengers. They had to agree to work on the Sabbath, due to economic conditions.

To all of this, they willingly agreed. But when they reached the port of Bremen, next to the Weser River in frostbitten northwestern Germany, they were given heart-shattering news: Husbands must go first, alone, to prepare for the arrival of their families.

That was nearly a deal-breaker. It was an "*ah-ha*" moment of sorts. My grandmother had tremendous wisdom. She was so good at teaching others that if they weren't so busy agonizing over all the little things, she could bring the parts into the whole, and show not only me, but also others, where everything fits. But this wasn't just a little thing, and it was agonizing for them both.

Grandpa Max was reluctant to go.

According to her writings, he sought details. Would she and her baby son be safe without him? Could they possibly be captured in his absence? Was he capable of sailing to a completely foreign country with little money and a language barrier, find work, and somehow be able to reconnect with his bride?

She worried, too, about her mother and father, and her brothers Fischel and Morris Rosenstein, who were refusing to leave their beloved country. "Am I brave because I am not afraid?" she wrote.

The only thing that was certain was that persecution was coming, and this out-weighed any fear of the unknown. It was a time when nothing was safe, and had my grandfather stayed, they both eventually no doubt would be killed like the rest of their families by the Nazis.

In 1909 the Norddeutscher Lloyd had ninety-three vessels, and Grandpa Max would make his trip to Galveston on the *Köln*, a single-stack steamer transport. Roughly half the size of the *Titanic*, the *Köln* was 446 feet long, with a displacement tonnage of 8,850 tons. She could accommodate 50 cabin passengers and 1,600 steerage passengers.

The "steerage," or between-deck, was the deck immediately below the main deck, and primarily built for carrying cargo. Like cattle, my grandfather and the other emi-grants would be herded here. Temporary partitions were usually erected and used for the steerage accommodation.

My grandmother Dora's diary described their tearful goodbye.

"I pray to God this craziness stops. Please Lord, protect our families and keep them safe. My Max is leaving for somewhere, and as I kissed him I wondered if that would be our last. He hugged me tight, and said, 'I will send for you! I will send for you!' I must believe! And I will wait for him!"

Incredibly, a short time later, he sent for her. Grandma Dora and my Uncle Louie indeed would make the long sail to America, where my grandparents were successfully reunited, joining the handful of just a few thousand Jewish families in the state of Texas, where they would build new lives.

In the coming years following their journey, the city of Lodz was captured by the Wehrmacht after the start of Operation Barbarossa in 1941. Thousands of Polish and Ukrainian prisoners were shot. Upon Nazi occupation, most of the Jewish inhabitants of the city were forced into ghettos and then murdered at the Polanka hill near the city.

I remember my grandmother telling me that the rest of her and Max's family were taken to concentration camps and eventually killed. She would read us letters from her brothers describing the eventual Nazi occupation of Poland: The air raids, the bomb-ings, and the utter destruction were unfathomable.

Of all my great ancestors, only Grandpa Max, Grandma Dora, and Uncle Louie escaped. Their courage, influence, and persistence would have a profound impact on everything else that would follow in my life. Their determination to overcome all fears and even the most impossible odds would be something handed down through our family for generations to come.

I never realized I had been born an underdog. My heritage and survival instincts were inbred in me at birth.

After escaping Poland, my mother's side of the family would eventually migrate to the Texas panhandle and the town that would eventually become Borger, Texas, where no one had seen a Jew before, and only a couple of Jewish families would settle into a town of 20,000 people. My grandfather Max opened the Metropolitan Hotel and Café when my mother was ten years old, and Uncle Louie was nineteen.

Eventually, this would be the place where I would cut my first deal.

10

IF YOU DON'T BELIEVE IN YOURSELF, THE VOTE'S UNANIMOUS

BORGER, TEXAS, DURING the "Dirty Thirties," could easily have been a Norman Rockwell painting set in a wild West Boom Town. Tucked in between New Mexico to the west and Oklahoma to the east, the Texas panhandle is comprised of twenty-six Texas counties, and it had only been in existence a little more than a decade when I was born on July 31, 1938, in North Plains Hospital.

There was little reason for the development of early Borger, if you didn't count its untold millions of dollars' worth of rich natural resources of oil and gas that lay in vast pools under the earth, invisible to the naked eye. This, of course, attracted exactly the kind of characters made famous in Hollywood westerns—oilmen, prospectors, roughnecks, panhandlers, fortune seekers, card sharks, bootleggers, and prostitutes. They all descended on Borger, and in its early years, it also was a refuge for criminals and fugitives from the law.

Main Street was a three-mile strip that housed a post office, a jail, several stores, and the city's first hamburger joint, opened by J. D. "Big Heart" Williams. As the city grew, streets improved, boom shacks were replaced by permanent buildings, and families like ours would eventually become part of the Borger business landscape.

My father, Harry, had learned a trade as a skilled carpenter. By day, he worked for the J. M. Huber Company; by night, he fixed clothing irons, waffle irons, and other appliances. There always seemed to be spare parts around our house, which led to my dad opening his own shop on Main Street called Popular Supply & Appliance. Whatever one needed, chances are he'd find it there, and if he didn't, Dad would find a way to get it for you. And always at a fair price.

Dad had rented a 25-by-50-foot space in town and used his skills to build a dividing wall. The store was in front, and we lived in the back. A lot has been made about our living conditions, or lack of them, because most of my family crowded into this tiny, primitive space. But to us, these weren't hard times; they were the best of times, and that was all we knew. My mom and dad were a testament to the power of love and the courage and sacrifice we are capable of when our loved ones are at stake. Though my dad never fought a single round in his life, he was constantly in the ring against the age-old opponents of hunger, poverty, and self-pity, and his ability to face his silent fears resonated inside of me.

Harry Argovitz was a self-made man. He worked hard, told the truth, was fair to his family and friends, and saved every penny. To me, he was Sam Walton before the world ever knew who Sam Walton was.

I was a second-grader in Borger when I started negotiating deals—I shined shoes, and I'd offer a shine for a nickel or a spit shine for a dime. I could pop that rag with authority, too. By the time I was eight, I was selling newspapers; and at age nine, I graduated to running the cash register and waiting on customers at the hardware store as I earned my father's trust. Behind the register, I learned to develop rapport with people of all ages and races, even those who were critical, rude, or unfair. My dad taught me to have a firm handshake, to look people in the eyes, and that the customer was always right.

During the Great Depression, America was in a financial tailspin. Grandpa Max had been a baker, and when the bakery failed, he did whatever necessary to earn a living. I followed his lead, and I wasn't short on entrepreneurial ideas. During the Christmas holidays, I ran the Lionel train display in the store window, and I'd let customers handle the speed generator for the going rate of a nickel for five minutes.

My paternal grandfather, Izzy Argovitz, was a tailor. My beloved grandmother Rose was a homemaker—a tremendous cook who ran a strict kosher household in their Dallas home. I never understood why I couldn't mix meat and milk on the same plate. And bacon, to be sure, was always out of the question.

My grandmother Dora stood merely 4 feet, 10 inches, and she spoke only broken English and mostly Yiddish to me, which I never really learned as my own. We both suffered verbal abuses from other kids, which bonded us into a close-knit, personal relationship based on mutual trust. It taught me not only to be tough, but also to be able to trust my judgment when it came to other people.

We weren't rich, but we weren't poor, either, because Dad could turn nickels into dollars. He refused to cast blame for any situation, instead expressing gratitude for what we had and reminding us that others had it much worse. My dad was as big a hero to me as Babe Ruth, and in my eyes, easily could've been played on the big screen by Jimmy Stewart or Gary Cooper.

"To live a healthy, successful life," he'd say, "follow these three rules: First, do the right thing. Second, always do the right thing. And third, repeat rules one and two."

That's something I tell my own grown kids to this day. Dad would love to tell us his stories, including those of my mother, Rose, the matriarch of our home and the love of his life. He used to call her the admiral of our ship. They had been teenagers—just eighteen years old—when they had taken a trip to nearby Oklahoma with another young couple to witness their wedding. The other couple got cold feet, but Mom and Dad obliged the preacher by getting married themselves, and they would stay married for the rest of their natural lives. That was my first lesson in commitment.

"If what you say and what you do don't match," he would say, "you're going to have problems for the rest of your life."

I loved listening to the stories of his childhood. When he was ten, he sold football programs for the Cotton Bowl, and he ran a lemonade stand. He worked odd jobs for nickels and dimes and saved most of what he earned—except on the occasions when his older brother Abe would raid his coffers. Along the way, there was that common theme that one needs a burning desire to succeed in order to overachieve.

"If you don't believe in yourself," Dad taught often, "the vote is unanimous. Whatever the mind of man can conceive and believe, he can achieve."

My parents, especially my dad, didn't just give lessons, they lived them. When I was nine years old, my younger sister, Merna—at nine months old—had to be transported to the Mayo Clinic in Minnesota, where a tumor the size of a grapefruit was removed from her stomach. Her ordeal would be reported in contemporary medical books; she would be considered a miracle child for having survived it.

My parents exemplified their own parents, and they were always stoic. Life situations such as little Merna's might have sunk other families. It only strengthened ours, because it became a teaching example in our home on how fragile life can be. It taught us how to overcome fears, and when one battles life's obstacles, he will wake up each day in a tighter family, and as a better human being, too.

Belief in one's self is a priority, he said. Sometimes the only person you can really count on is you.

The more I learned about the deep roots of racism, discrimination, and hatred, it took little time to realize I was going to need every lesson I'd been taught.

11

JEW BASTARD

WHEN YOU'RE A kid in Texas and your last name is Argovitz, you know right off the bat you're different; you just don't understand how different. Kids don't understand anti-Semitism, they are merely repeating racial slurs that have been handed down in their own families forever, and it represents the ignorance of the people who raised them. Borger probably wasn't the easiest place to learn about racial prejudice, which is why I grew up thinking "Jew Bastard" was actually one word.

"Jews are here, Jews are there, stupid Jews are everywhere!" the kids taunted me. Of course, this ignited a powder keg inside me, and by the fifth grade, I was getting into two fights a day—one on the way to school, and another coming home. Torn shirts, bloody noses, split lips and dirt baths all became part of the normal routine. I was tiny, only about 80 pounds, and the born-and-bred Texas kids had a distinct advantage, especially one, Jimmy, the school bully, who sought me out at Weatherly Grade School. It finally boiled to a head one day during recess, and Jimmy was in for the surprise of his life.

Instinctively, the second I smelled a fight, I simply stepped forward and fired the first punch, and it was a shot I'd remember for a lifetime. Jimmy's eye took the full force of my looping right hand, and the look of shock on his face is frozen in my memory forever. The fight raged until Coach Gilcrest broke it up.

"Argie," Coach Gilcrest said, "Way to stand up to Jimmy. You landed first, and you got up every time he knocked you down. I like your spunk Argie, and next year, I'm gonna make you a nose tackle for the Weatherly Eagles, all eighty pounds of you!"

That day, I discovered a fury inside that shocked even me. I was tired of being pushed around, I was tired of the snickering and the jokes, and with a single punch and by taking the fight to him, I had neutralized the bully. Bullies usually start off with attitude problems, but when faced, end up with a perception problem.

Jimmy wore that shiner for days.

When you find something you're good at, by all means, keep doing it. I was good at fighting, but Dad—while pleased at my ability and willingness to fight—wasn't without cautious instruction. When I got home, we discussed what had transpired.

"Son, listen, I'm proud of you, but you might want to develop a new plan," he said. "Let's think about this. You always have three options. One, you can walk away, even run if you have to. Or two, you can learn how to negotiate and talk your way out of a fight. Or three, you can learn how to fight and really protect yourself."

I had tasted blood, so of course, I instantly chose the last option.

The Golden Gloves and I were made for each other: I loved pugilism, and it embraced me. The discipline, training, strategy, and sheer violence thrilled me, and it gave me the unique opportunity to display skills I didn't know I had—while venting anger against opponents who all represented "Jimmy" to me, and frankly made me proud to fight for my family.

There is something about the idea of you and me alone in the ring—your strength versus mine, your best against my best—throwing and landing our best shots against each other to see just who is the best man inside the ropes on that night. More often than not I was the best, and so I quickly and easily won the 80-pound championship. As I grew older, my skills and technique became reflexive. As a result, I won the regional championship in the lightweight, welterweight, and middleweight classes and in 1958 would fight at 168 pounds for the title in the light-heavyweight championship in the state tournament in Fort Worth. Golden Gloves in Texas during this time was wildly popular, and each city sponsored its own matches, with winners meeting in the regionals.

I fought in dimly lit gymnasiums using brown leather gloves and wearing trunks bearing a yellow Jewish star in fights all over the Texas panhandle. I fought before empty stands, and packed bleachers. I fought kids faster, taller, stronger, and more experienced, and beat them. Most of all, I just fought. Frankly, once I was taped and the gloves were on, it didn't matter to me who was in front of me. My mantra was simple: Put in my mouthpiece, ring the damn bell, and let's go to work. I loved the simplicity: There would be no negotiating; my fists wrote the contracts.

I did have one superstition: I wore a gold Jewish star around my neck, and once I stepped between the ropes and took off my robe, my coach would remove my star just prior to the fight. I guess it worked—I only lost twice in my boxing career.

Sugar Ray Robinson became a boyhood idol. He was flamboyant, sleek, fast, fluid, and had power in both hands. He could throw bolo hooks and create moves on the spur of the moment. He also had a chip on his shoulder, and he was fighting for more than belts; he was fighting for his people, too.

No question: I wanted to be Sugar Ray. With every jab I landed, I felt like asking, "Who's the Jew Bastard now?" Dad never missed a fight, and he beamed with pride every time the referee would raise my hand in victory. To hear the sound of his voice, or simply see him in the audience between rounds, fueled me to even higher excellence. And the same kids who once mocked me? It wasn't long before they were ringside, too, cheering raucously as I piled up victories. It was an early lesson, however superficial, that would ring true throughout my career.

Everybody loves a winner.

I loved sports, I loved to compete, and I loved to win. My life would become as simple as that, but not necessarily in that order.

Unfortunately, my boxing skills meant little on the gridiron. In boxing, my small size was irrelevant. In football, it was a glaring weakness. I trained harder for football than anything in my life, and played quarterback for the "C" team—The Rovers—when my coaches discovered I had a great arm and could accurately deliver a football. However, arm strength is only part of the equation when a coach blatantly discriminates against you and purposely attempts to hold you back; but regardless, I was still able to earn scholarship offers in boxing, baseball, and football.

In the classroom, I was an average student, but managed to earn the respect of enough teachers to keep good grades coming and pass classes. I had become popular with the girls as a boxer, and believe it or not, a dancer. My Uncle Louie and Aunt Sadie and their three children—Herb, Suzanne, and Maxine—lived in Dallas, and I'd spend my summers with Herb. He and I were like brothers, and we'd learn all the new dances in Dallas, then I'd come back to Borger and be "big man on campus." Somehow, I attracted the eye of Ramona McCharon, the most beautiful and popular girl at Borger High.

I'll never forget Ramona. Even though she left for college before I did, she left an indelible mark on my life, because that feeling of first love is so sizzling, it is safeguarded for life by memory.

I honestly believe that because she loved me, it rounded out my courage and confidence in a way that even sports could not. Simply because of Ramona, there was a brief period when, just for her, I improved my grades, did my homework, and worked even harder on my football skills.

Two of the greatest fears in life are rejection and surprise, and I got both in a single dose when I fell in love with Mary Jane Chandler. Mary Jane and I had discovered one another at a dance in Phillips, Texas, five miles away. It was love at first sight, and she wore my letter jacket with pride. Imagine my shock that, after dating for four months, when I went to get her on a routine date, only to be told she wasn't coming.

"I can't go," she said, standing partly in her front door. Tears ran down her cheeks. She was shaking. She reached out with her other hand, which held my letter jacket.

"Take it," she said. I couldn't believe what I was seeing. "Take it! Just please take it and go!"

"Is it your dad?" I asked. "Let me talk to him."

"You don't want to do that," she answered. "He says I can't see you because . . . you're a Jew."

"I was Jewish when we met." I argued. In my opinion, it wasn't a Jewish boy who wasn't good enough for his daughter; it was the bigoted father who wasn't good enough for his daughter.

With her crying in the doorway, I took my letter jacket and drove away. The sting would linger longer than any punch I'd ever taken in the ring. Mary Jane and I would create alternative ways to see one another, but the lesson was much larger.

There are vicious, bigoted people in the world who will stop at nothing to suppress others for no good reason, other than they can. That single incident fueled my internal engine. I was fearless now, and ready to fight. I would go to college, find a profession, and prove to the world once and for all that this "Jew Bastard" could and would be whoever he chose to be, and that I would spend my life fighting for the little guy, starting with me.

Dad and I had a serious talk before I left for college.

"Son, do you know right from wrong?" I paused, and he pounced.

"If ever you're not sure about something you're about to do and you have to think about it for five seconds—about whether it's right or wrong—it's wrong. Never, ever have to justify your actions!"

I graduated high school in 1956, and headed off to college, with a major score to settle.

Ominously, it was the very same year that 1,600 miles away, Boston attorney Bob Woolf was just becoming the first so-called agent in professional sports.

12

LOW BLOWS

THERE'S NOTHING LIKE being pissed off and charging off into the world to do something about it, only to fail miserably on the grandest stage in the state: The University of Texas. While all the eyes of Texas weren't quite yet upon me, the scrutinizing eyes of my mom and dad certainly were, and they didn't like what they were seeing, because what they had taught me and what I was doing didn't match.

My freshman year at the University of Texas I was a pre-dental major. I walked on to the freshman football team, and was sponsored by Alpha Epsilon Pi fraternity, where instead of studying, I wound up spending most of my time playing football and flat-out partying. I was eighteen years old; everything I owned was in a suitcase and a brown sack. My focus, self-discipline, and grade-point average plummeted as one, to the point that it caught the eye of my own mother, who thought her son had gone stark raving mad.

I was disappointed in myself. I had really screwed up, but I had a damn good time; in the process, I'd developed some relationships that would last a lifetime. I realized that my "best thinking" had put me in this predicament.

If there were only two people left in the world I feared, my mom was one, and I'll let you guess the second. So instead of changing the world, I wound up with my mother in front of the school psychologist. I'm not crazy, I thought, as they debated my future. I just like girls. Besides, I already knew what I wanted to do with my life, and it caught a lot of people flat-footed, because dentistry is probably the last career anyone might have guessed for me.

I had wanted to be a dentist since the tenth grade. Dr. Waldo Beckley, our family dentist, had a beautiful daughter, lived in a beautiful home, and drove sparkling new cars. He explained to me once that even an average dentist could earn a good living; and on top of that, I was good with my hands—I built model airplanes, and whittled constantly with my pocket knife.

So my mother's inquiry, and my interest in dentistry, resulted in a meeting with Dean Michael D. McKinney of the UT Dental School. I was told in no uncertain terms that with my grades, dental school was out of the question, and I best start thinking about another career or buckle down and make my grades.

When school was out I went back to Borger. My father didn't say much. His look said it all. I had never felt so disgusted with myself in my life. I was going to become a dentist if my life depended on it, and judging by the look on my dad's face, it did.

"Until you have a son of your own, you will never know the joy, the love beyond feeling that resonates in the heart of a father as he looks upon his son," Dad said. "You will never know the sense of pride that makes a man want his son to be more successful than he is, and to pass something good and hopeful into the hands of his son. And you will never know the heartbreak of a father whose son isn't living up to the man he can be. Son, it's up to you. We can't do it for you. So what are your plans now?"

I told him to give me a few days, and we'd discuss it. After careful thought, I met with Mom and Dad and laid out my plan.

I was too embarrassed to ask my folks for money to repeat the freshman courses I'd failed. I realized that my best thinking had put me in this predicament, so my "new" best thinking would have to be radically different. First, I proposed that I accept the athletic scholarship that I'd been offered for boxing and baseball from Frank Phillips Junior College in Borger. Second, I would get a job working with Dr. Beckley and Dr. Logan and begin learning my desired craft. Finally, I would live at home.

"My plan," I explained to my mom and dad, "will allow me to make up my poor grades, and you can bet the house I won't fail again. I'll be working for two great dentists, earning money and gaining expertise. Living at home and playing sports will keep me focused during my spare time. And it won't cost you guys a dime. And then I can go back to the University of Texas and apply to dental school after I complete my junior year."

Mom and Dad agreed.

It would take many more years, another failed attempt at the University of Texas dental school, and a move to Missouri to complete my mission. Dr. Fred Elliott at the UT Health Sciences Center, a champion for dental excellence from Pittsburg, Kansas, had recommended me for another chance at the University of Missouri–Kansas City School of Dentistry in 1962, but only on a probationary status.

I had married the former Elaine Laviage the summer before dental school, a beautiful girl. Flowing hair, very popular, great personality, and always smiling. It had been love at first sight. We were a perfect match, and had much in common—both of us were from very close-knit families, and she was a gamer. We would go to Galveston and hang out at the beach, go dancing on Friday nights, and watch football together. It was her dream to marry a doctor, have children, and live in a house with the proverbial white picket fence. Potentially, I was her solution on every front.

However, when Elaine couldn't get pregnant, we visited doctors, who delivered the cruelest blow of all: That trauma and accidents—such as low blows—can lead to infertility in men, and—are you kidding me?—I was the (not so) lucky candidate. Doctors asked if I had ever suffered any such trauma, and I shook my head in disbelief. I didn't believe what I was hearing. Immediately, I knew when it happened—during a light-heavyweight fight that I never should have taken.

In 1957, when I was nineteen, I had returned from college, and went to the fights in Amarillo to watch "Scooter" Darden, who was fighting for the regional welterweight championship. He had nearly won the state championship in a different weight class the same year I was runner-up champion as a light-heavyweight for the state of Texas. That night, the opponent slated to face Duke Ward in a preliminary light heavyweight fight didn't show.

"Hey, Argovitz, you wanna fight Duke?" The question came from the head of the Amarillo Golden Gloves commission, and I couldn't help but grin. Stupid question: If there were girls in the crowd, the answer was always yes, and I could win another trophy. There's a fine line between courage and stupidity, and when you're that age, it's hard to tell the difference. I couldn't resist. In one of my more (not so) brilliant life choices, I went to the locker room, borrowed some trunks, a cup, and shoes. They wrapped my hands and laced on the gloves.

The very beginning of the first round wasn't spectacular. We traded casual punches, testing each other, almost goofing off. Then someone in the crowd booed, and bam, it was on. Everything's funny until you get a little blood in your mouth, and I hit big Duke with an overhand right that forced him to step back. Duke countered, then he went low and away with a left hook to my nuts that nearly crippled me. He outweighed me by fifteen pounds. After a timeout, I battled through it, and in the second round, I beat him senseless, and upset him by TKO.

I refused to let it show, but I was seriously hurt. Days later, the pain would dissipate, but unbeknownst to me, the damage was done.

Four years later, however, as Elaine stood in the doctor's office, she didn't give a rat's ass about a tough night in Amarillo with a guy named Duke, booing crowds, my machismo, or anything else. All she knew was that I didn't have any bullets left in the gun, and we were going to have to do something about it. We both wanted children.

I was struggling on my own. For a boy as close to his mother and father as I was, my greatest dream was to have a son of my own. I wanted to be the mythical and infinitely important protector my family had been—the guy who, in the words of Tom Wolfe, would keep a lid on all the chaotic and catastrophic possibilities of life. I wanted my own son to teach the difference between love and fear, just as my mom and dad did. Now a doctor was telling me that not only was it unlikely, it was downright improbable.

It was a terrible discovery. I held Elaine as she cried. She didn't notice that I was crying, too.

Elaine and I were bowed, but not beaten. My mother had taught me that when one door closes, another one opens. Quickly, we realized that adoption can be the ultimate expression of love: to embrace another person's child as your own. The more research we did, the more we realized how many children needed stable homes.

"When you think about it, in God's eyes, we're all adopted," Elaine said. Our decision was quickly made, and we adopted Brent when he was three days old, and in coming years, we would adopt Ricky, and Kari, too. Our three children, each two years apart, were all from different biological parents. Had Elaine and I had three children of our own, we couldn't have loved them any more than our three adopted children.

My uphill struggle to become a dentist finally ended when I graduated in 1964. Against all odds, I had fought my way around, over, and through years of hurdles and hardships.

I was now Dr. Jerry A. Argovitz, D.D.S.

13

THE WIZARDRY
OF DENTISTRY

A DENTIST'S DRILL HAS three separate parts: there's the dental "engine," or power source, the dental hand piece, and the burr, which is what actually comes into contact with the tooth. Whereas the earliest dental drill dates back to 7000 B.C., drill speeds of 3,000 rpm in 1914 matched those of automobile engines today, and modern drills accomplish as much as 800,000 rpm. Dental enamel is the hardest substance in the human body, and a burr revolving around 600,000 to 800,000 rpm will cut through enamel like a hot knife through a stick of butter. Being a dentist isn't for the faint of heart; nor is it for one with shaky nerves and, especially, shaky hands.

On top of it all, half the time a dentist is plying his trade while looking in a mirror, where everything is backward. The summer prior to enrolling at Texas, I had worked on a jack hammer, and I chuckled at the irony every time I put a drill in a patient's mouth. A good dentist has to be a perfectionist, develop good chair-side manners, understand research, have great discipline and patience, be painless and have a light touch, examine all possibilities, and be able to make quick decisions. I was blessed to have those skills. You have to remember at all times that there's a person attached to those teeth.

My first patient was a guy named Mr. Green, who had an abscessed tooth. It took me about three minutes to extract. Afterward, he addressed me in my office. "It only took you three minutes, and you charged me $40." I said, "I didn't bill you for my time, I billed you for my expertise. Would you feel better if I put your tooth back in and spent another twenty minutes removing it? Or would you feel better about paying me the $40 fee for being quick and painless?"

He paid the bill.

Most people judge a dentist not by his skill and workmanship, but by the measure of pain. Does it hurt? Many times, my patients would open their mouths, and I would see shoddy, defective work done by other dentists that I would have to overcome. The joke in dental school had been that the "A" students made the best instructors; the "B" students made the best dentists; and the "C" students made the most money.

The irony is that it was no joke. I had worked for Dr. Beckley, and took away many life lessons from him. He always taught that "if it's not perfect, then it's not worth a damn," and there were many times I told my dad I wanted to quit. "Dr. B" was all about precision, and dad would say that "if you can please Dr. B, you can satisfy anyone. But you must master his teachings." And eventually, I did.

What they didn't teach me in dental school, however, is that dentists have the highest rate of divorce among any other medical profession, and shockingly, the highest rate of suicide, as well. A dentist is 6.64 times more likely to commit suicide than the rest of the working population, according to researchers, and common disorders among dentists are rapid burnout, anxiety, and depression. Let's face it, few people enjoy going to the dentist—most hate it—and when they get there, you're sticking something in their mouth that, with a single slip, could slash through a cheek or tongue.

If I thought dental school had been stressful, having my own practice multiplied it by a hundred. There were a myriad of practice management and financial issues that I had to learn, and I did. But I loved being a dentist, and in little time my Houston practice was thriving. I had a light touch, did beautiful cosmetic dentistry, and I developed great relationships with my patients, many of whom were prominent local citizens.

Relieving excruciating pain, alleviating fear, and practicing painless dentistry became my identity. My patients rarely felt the shot or saw the needle. My theory was that the most important patient was the one in the chair. I believed every procedure or restoration had to be perfect, or I would end up doing it again.

I loved taking everyone from adults to crying kids in emergency situations and making them feel better. To have people trust and respect you for your diagnosis and treatment and pay you for your services is a wonderful feeling. It was in my blood: Take a bad situation and make it comfortable. I was making a great living through my chosen profession for my wife and three kids, and that success led to my being selected president of the Houston Academy of General Dentistry.

Still, the stress and long, long hours were taking their toll at home. Elaine's family was a bit unusual to begin with. There were two brothers and a sister married to two sisters and a brother. Thus the Laviage and Nathan family were all intermarried, and when things turned bad between the wives and husbands, brothers and sisters—sheesh, to be at a gun battle at OK Corral would have been safer.

Cracks were starting to show in my marriage to Elaine, but—sadly—I was so driven, that I hardly noticed. What I did notice, however, was that to build real wealth, I would have to take the money I was earning and do something else with it.

When I discovered that 90 percent of dentists are still practicing at age sixty-five, I decided this was not for me, and that one could not rely on his own practice alone to acquire wealth. I was paying a tremendous amount of money in taxes, and while I believed in paying my fair share, there were tax rules that provided for tax breaks—not evasion, mind you, but tax avoidance—and the options in real estate attracted me.

Every new beginning comes from a former beginning's end, and my newest beginning led me to enroll in real estate classes, where I quickly earned a license.

It wasn't long before I was only practicing dentistry two-and-a-half days a week. Dentistry had gone from my first love to my hobby, but still represented a tremendous source of income to fund my rapidly mounting number of real-estate deals. My money, however, wasn't enough. Houston had become a booming equivalent of the California gold rush of the 1850s. To say the least, the economy was fantastic, and I needed cash. So I did the most logical thing: syndication. I used my time and expertise to put the deal together, and other investors would supply the money.

Syndication is where two or more property investors form a partnership and take part ownership of a real estate asset; the asset is then divided up into two or more investment units. I was seeking out real-estate opportunities, specifically land and income properties, and I made a special deal with the top real-estate brokers in Houston: I would give them all of the commission if I got first shot at their listings.

I had a God-given talent for negotiating deals. I was a swashbuckler who preferred boots and jeans and open-collar shirts over suits and ties. I was informal enough that I was always approachable, which drew people to me. Most of all, the work was fun. I could drive around on weekends, look at properties—like an Indian who walks over a piece of land—and discover water under the surface. My game plan was to identify properties in the paths of growth on the corners of major intersections that were ten or fifteen years away from being developed. I used common sense to acquire prime future commercial sites where gas stations would go. I had a great nose for real estate, especially for raw land. I bought land by the acre and sold it by the square foot.

The old adage that "timing is everything" is absolutely true. Houston was exploding with opportunity, and so was my knowledge as I learned another business. I formed these limited partnerships, and I was the general partner with professionals and other high-income individuals, and we just kept buying and selling properties.

Using public records, we were able to find properties along proposed economic development paths. Here's an easy example: I would go to the Texas Department of Transportation to look at the property records to identify the land owners and where the corners and intersections would be and where the right-of-ways for the freeways would be set. I met with land planners, attorneys, and engineers. I met the politicians. In fact, I met everyone involved, and I learned to hate surprises. In each case, we had to know about the drainage, flood plain, utilities, easements, and pipelines to get clear title to the property.

A successful land speculator must have vision, do his homework, and be prepared to hold the property until the time is right. One can't wait until there's a Phillips 66 gas station and a shopping center on the property. By then, it's too late, and too expensive to speculate. I liked buying land on corners, with good frontage-to-depth ratios, accessibility, and of course, location, location, location. Always remember that patience is power: If you control a strategic piece of land, knowing when to buy and when to sell is the key to major profits.

I would put up the earnest money, negotiate the contracts to buy the land, and enjoy a ninety-day due diligence period to check everything out; if everything was in order to our satisfaction, I would close the transaction.

There was no inside information; it was all public record and common sense. This was nothing different from the hardware store back in Borger with my dad: Give customers what they need, at a cost-effective price. Nothing comes for free, do the leg work, make it a good deal for everyone involved, and then get after it. I was only doing what I'd been taught all my life, just in a larger arena.

I was buying major tracts of land which in time would front major freeways to be built. The federal government was giving me five years prepaid interest as tax deductions. In the meantime, I was learning how to get deductions from my dental practice. I could prepay interest and get a 50 percent write-off, which meant I was working with 50-cent dollars. I always bought land using great leverage and owner financing, with no personal liability.

We were buying land ahead of the growth patterns and selling them for huge profits. Later on, some of the land we developed for shopping centers and other business development. People talk about luck, but truth is luck had little to do with it. It was Harry Argovitz all the way: Find an exploding market, isolate problems, create solutions, and discover what the people need, or might need. Then deliver it, on time. Be honest. Be a man of your word. Make it a good deal for everyone involved. Be humble; take your fair share, and then put every penny in the bank so you'll have money for the next deal.

Dad's teaching and example was reflected in all I did . . . only on a bigger scale. Had my dad been there doing business, he'd have provided shovels to people who needed shovels. And he would have provided them at a fair price, all the while reminding me that timing is everything.

"Son," he would say, "this is how fortunes are built, or lost."

His best advice, however, came in regard to the amount of money I was borrowing. "Son, you're borrowing money for your investments. What happens if times get tough and you don't pay the bank or the holder of the note?" I said, "Well, I guess they'd foreclose on the property."

"Well, that's something I never have to worry about, because all my property is paid for."

That really hit home. Keep in mind, this was a process. I was learning on my feet, and learning as fast as I could. It was like drinking from a fire hydrant. My mother always told me a smart man doesn't know all the answers, but he surrounds himself with people who do. She would say, "don't work harder—work smarter." Truer words were never spoken.

I have been blessed to have Darryl Burman and Walker Beavers as my attorneys to advise me for over twenty years and Lenny Teninbaum, my accountant, for over thirty years. These men not only are my trusted advisers, but have become my close personal friends.

During an interview with Burman, a corporate business attorney, I asked a simple question: "Darryl, you are a young guy, I feel good about you and I have a question out of left field. When you walk into a movie theater, what is the first thing you look for?" He smiled. "I look for the best seats." I smiled back. "I look for the exit signs, period; I want to know how to get out of there in case a fire breaks out." We both laughed out loud. He got it, I got it, and I hired him immediately.

Prolific deal-making became the nature of the day. I was finding unbelievable deals and apartment complexes and developing shopping centers. I was negotiating contracts and syndicating deal after deal. My clients now included professional athletes, entertainers, physicians, dentists, attorneys, and other high-end professionals, and at any given time, we could have millions of dollars changing hands.

I'd use the money from the investors, market and manage the property; and when it sold, I got a real-estate commission and a 25 percent return of the net profits after the investors got all of their money back, plus interest, and 75 percent of the net profits. We would create a single-purpose limited partnership or an LLC that owned the asset. We signed agreements, and none of the partners had any liability.

I turned some land purchases over quickly, and all of my partners got significant returns. Word traveled swiftly, and I had so many people calling me and meeting me because they wanted to invest with me that I wound up with more investors than I had deals—a good problem to have.

To me, real estate was never good or bad. It's either a buyer's market or a seller's market. Our deals would make the Houston newspapers, and my business reputation grew in leaps and bounds. I amassed thousands of acres of land. I was making so much more money in real estate that I branched into banking, too.

These deals were complicated, far more so than any NFL contract I would ever negotiate in the future. Virtually overnight, I had multiple companies—the Argovitz Financial Clinic and Land Baron Investments. I was invited to join the boards of several associations and banks in my community, and my investments by now had grown to encompass other major cities in the state of Texas. In some cases I was the youngest member of bank boards and other committees.

Just as my parents had coached for so many years, my word and my signature became my bond in every transaction. The freedom to negotiate was only one side of a very large coin. The other side was a reminder to never forget the immortal words of my friend Kenny Rogers: "You've got to know when to hold 'em, know when to fold 'em, know when to walk away, and know when to run."

One day I had a patient in the chair when I was right in the middle of another real-estate deal. I put some impression material in the patient's mouth, and then went back to quickly talk to Kenny Margolis, my real estate broker. I got distracted talking to Kenny, to the point that three times the nurse came in to tell me to hurry, the material in the patient's mouth was hardening. By the time I got back to the chair, the material had—sure enough—totally hardened. I had to chip out the extra, and ended up giving this woman two crowns for free. The time had come to sell my dental practice.

My real-estate syndication work and public lectures allowed me to share my knowledge on the national Professional Lecture Series circuit with other physicians and dentists. I also shared a stage on positive-thinking rallies of influence with such renowned orators as Dr. Norman Vincent Peale, Zig Ziglar, Art Linkletter, Paul Harvey, and Earl Nightingale. It was fun to get up in front of a huge crowd and inspire confidence and motivation in thousands of others. I would show my parents letters from audiences indicating that some of the things I taught played a small part in bringing something positive to their lives.

At home, things weren't so good. My long hours on the job had isolated Elaine, and divorce seemed inevitable. Elaine loved the lifestyle my hard work had provided for her and the children. She didn't want a divorce, but was willing to accept a separation. Our marriage, however, was in a rut, and while Elaine preferred the status quo, she was afraid of change if we got divorced. To me, though, it was time to move on with our lives.

Still, I had so many questions and answers swirling in my head. I knew Elaine and the kids would be set financially. I also suspected Elaine might eventually remarry, because she was sweet, charming, and very beautiful. Did I want to keep doing syndications or just invest for my own personal account? What do I want to do with the rest of my life? I was concerned about my three children and always—always—wondered where was I going to find more than twenty-four hours in a day?

My meteoric rise to wealth and prominence in the Houston business climate was as breathtaking as the ride in my private elevator to my posh twentieth floor office at the Houston Galleria. I was pretty proud of my achievements, and my parents were, too. I loved the feeling of knowing how many lives had been affected for the better through my many deals.

But even with imagination and ambition as large as mine, I could not have guessed what lay in store for me, just around the next bend.

14

ALL THAT GLITTERS
ISN'T GOLD

THE LOUDEST MAN at a party is not always drunk. In fact, one Houston evening, at a private social party in a condominium high above the city, I heard a boastful shout above the din of the music, clinking of glasses, pouring of drinks, and the heightened conversations among a crowd of businessmen, professional athletes, and beautiful women.

"My boss, Mike Trope, just completed the best contract in the NFL for Earl Campbell, the great running back from the University of Texas, to play for the Houston Oilers."

Fascinated, I broke off my conversations to walk around the corner and see who the speaker might be. I came face-to-face with a large black man who stood well over six feet tall and was built like an NFL player. He explained how "great" the deal was for Earl. "But a lot of the money was deferred," I interjected, to which he replied, "So what?"

The next words out of my mouth took him aback.

"My grandmother could've negotiated a better contract," I told him with a certain degree of smugness, "and she's been dead ten years."

The man introduced himself as Gene Burrough, brother of the Houston Oilers' wide receiver Kenny Burrough. He curiously asked me what I thought my grandmother would have done differently.

Fair question, I thought. "Gene, my name is Dr. Jerry Argovitz and Kenny is a good friend of mine," I said as I reached out to shake his hand. "Let's find a quiet place to talk."

"Gene, my grandmother would have known about not deferring payments out for so many years, due to the loss of present-day value. It would be better for Mr. Campbell's future in the long run," I said. "She would have asked for an up-front, tax-free loan against his signing bonus and also get the team, and possibly its owners, to guarantee all the payments." Gene listened intently as I explained the concept of present value. A signing bonus of $1 million, I explained, when deferred over forty years at 5 percent interest, was worth only $145,000 in present-day value.

Being a sports fan, of course, I had heard of Mike Trope, the player-agent. At the time I met Gene, Trope was just twenty-seven years old, yet he had represented some sixty-plus NFL players in the previous five years, including three out of the past four Heisman Trophy winners. Trope had become an agent during the summer before his senior year at the University of Southern California, where he majored in history.

Gene loved to talk, and I enjoyed listening. He was flamboyant and entertaining as he described how he and Trope, his boss, had signed and represented household NFL names like Ricky Bell, Tony Dorsett, and Archie Griffin. I couldn't believe some of what I was hearing. As I understood it, sports agents went to campuses and signed college kids to undated contracts . . . and paid them. Obviously, when you show money to a college kid who—despite his athletic gifts—is living hand-to-mouth, it's betraying: The player doesn't know if the deal is good or bad, he just needs money, and that's an immediate way to get it. I wasn't too surprised to learn that most of these kids came from poverty.

Still, paying players can't possibly be ethical, I thought.

"How many guys did you personally recruit this season?" I asked him.

"Twenty-two, bro, between this season and last season," Gene replied. "Twenty-two."

"Are you and Mike Trope partners?" I asked.

Gene paused. "Nope," he said. "I just recruit for him."

"Sounds to me like you're doing all the work, and this Trope character is getting all the credit," I said. Gene, for the first time all night, grew quiet. He couldn't disagree, and I could tell he was processing my words.

"If you really want to be serious about this business, call me, and we'll talk," I said. "I'll make you a partner, not an employee. Think about it." I really liked Gene right away—he was smooth, full of energy, well dressed, and enthusiastic. We spent the rest of the party talking football, finance, real estate, and contracts; but to be honest, I really didn't think I'd be hearing from Gene any time soon.

Imagine my surprise when—a few weeks later—I received a phone call from Gene, and we scheduled a meeting at my office in Houston. From the moment Gene strode into the building, it was evident he was impressed at its luxurious surroundings. We rode the elevator up to my office, where we sat down at my polished cherrywood conference table. Gene took in the Houston skyline through the picture window behind me.

Quickly, I got down to business, and Gene pulled no punches explaining how the business worked: He would develop relationships with budding college stars, fly out to meet them regularly, and induce them to sign by offering cash, rental cars, or whatever was necessary. Immediately, I saw the fallacy in what Trope was doing. He was signing players to what appeared to be "big" multi-million-dollar contracts, but as Gene had explained at the party, most of the money was deferred.

Trope, however, would charge his whopping commission on the stated value of the contract. He wasn't providing any other services, either, such as financial planning, business management, or skill development outside of football. Just from the Earl Campbell contract alone, I could see there was tremendous room for improvement in this business, and I was intrigued at the challenge of negotiating against the general managers of the National Football League.

"Gene, here's what I'm willing to do," I told him. "Obviously, I've worked hard to have one of the most prestigious offices in Houston, and I'll give you an office here, which will considerably raise your profile with the kids and the teams that draft them. I'll make you a 40 percent partner, and I'll pay you a salary. But I'm concerned about this issue of paying players. Isn't paying the players illegal?"

"Hell no," he said. "It's against the NCAA rules, but it's not against any laws. They can't put you in jail. And every agent in the business does it."

"Well, we're not going to," I said. "I'm not breaking any rules. I'm not going to put a kid's college career in jeopardy. I'm not going to endanger the universities, either. I don't believe in breaking the rules. Rules are meant to be changed, not broken. The end doesn't justify the means."

"But we won't get any players," Gene argued. "Jerry, everyone in this business pays the players!"

"Gene, if you can't sign players without giving them money, we'll be out of business in a short time," I answered. "Here's the deal: Write down ten players for us to focus on in this first year together. Let's only focus on those guys. Go back and tell each of them the truth; that you're no longer with Trope, and explain why. Tell them who I am. You're going to have to get each of them to come here individually to Houston. You get the players, and I promise you, I'll close them."

I devised a plan: As soon as a player's college eligibility had ended, I would take them down to the bank and co-sign a note with them that could be repaid when they signed their NFL contract. Right out of the gate, our players would have the cash they needed, and they would have a line of credit with a major bank. I would set them up with accountants and financial advisors so they would be protected long-term, they would live on a budget, all of their investments and business deals would be scrutinized, and we would sit down and do tax planning for them as well as file their tax returns. And we wouldn't charge more than 6 percent commission for our negotiating services and 1 percent per year for management.

"Our job, Gene, is to give our players options," I said. "I'm aware that most of them will have already taken money from another agent. They don't have to pay that money back if they choose not to, because it was wrong for the other agents to do it in the first place. The kids need to realize they are in charge. Our role is to protect them, protect their skills, and create contracts that give our guys every option available to them."

Unlike other agents, money wasn't the reason I decided to do this. I had plenty of money. I loved sports, I loved doing deals, and I loved teaching and motivating. I saw an opportunity to help athletes, their families, and their careers. I wanted to see these guys get better deals for themselves, and in the process, reach a better understanding of business. I told Gene we would make each client a legitimate businessman off the field, and give him every resource he needed to accomplish that goal.

Gene and I worked out our operating basis for working together and agreed we would build an agency that was totally transparent and open with the clients we were sure would come our way. We also decided that what we would create together was a "family" of clients, because we were going to do more than represent them as agents; we were going to manage their lives with the same care and responsibility parents would with their own offspring.

I also loved the fact that it was high-profile, intense, and challenging. For a dentist to take on the NFL might have seemed like a leap of faith for some; but to me it was no different than a dentist becoming a successful land speculator.

Gene was still a little reluctant on the issue of not paying the players, but he finally agreed. We shook hands, and we were in business. With that, I loaned Gene my dog-eared copy of *Think and Grow Rich*, by Napoleon Hill. "Read this Gene," I said. "It will change your life."

We talked about where to begin, and immediately, Gene brought up the name Eddie Lee Ivery, running back for the Green Bay Packers.

My trial by fire was under way.

15

EDDIE LEE IVERY AND THE FROZEN TUNDRA

FOR ME TO understand the plight of the contemporary athlete in 1979, Gene couldn't have picked a better first candidate with whom I could work than Eddie Lee Ivery, the pride of Thomson High School, thirty-five miles west of Augusta, Georgia. Eddie Lee had grown up in outright poverty in a dirt-floor shack with a firewood stove. He never knew his father. He was raised by his mother and grandmother, both of whom were unable to work and lived on welfare.

"My mother was determined that when I grew up I wouldn't be on welfare," Eddie Lee told me. "My mom was a first-grade dropout. She never went back. She used to come in my room in the morning and say, 'Boy, you better get your butt out of bed, get dressed, and go to school.' Those words still ring in my ears. She had my clothes laid out, firewood in the stove, and a hot biscuit on the table. And then she pushed me out the door. She and my grandmother were special. I have often looked back and drawn strength from what they endured."

In high school, Eddie Lee played football, basketball, and baseball, and ran track. In his senior football season, he gained 1,710 yards and averaged nearly 10 yards a carry. He was named to All-State, All-Southern, and prep All-America teams. When more than ninety football scholarship offers came pouring in from around the country, his mother swiftly sat him down and told him how blessed he was to even have the opportunity to get a college education.

"She reminded me that when she and her brothers were growing up, there was no chance for blacks to have an opportunity like this," he said. Of course, I was immediately reminded of the similarities to my own upbringing in Borger, and the anti-Semitism I had encountered all my life.

I felt an immediate bond with Eddie Lee, one which I eventually would share with all my players. Hearing his story was both heartbreaking and heartwarming at the same time, and I was overwhelmed by the feeling of this new relationship and my new undertaking. It was a feeling I hadn't had since my early days of dentistry, when I realized that with some effort, I could take away another person's pain. Hearing what Eddie Lee had been through in his young life, I couldn't help but admire his courage.

At Georgia Tech, the 200-pound Eddie Lee was a spectacular running back. He scored 22 touchdowns for 158 points, and set the university's single-season rushing record with 1,562 yards. In his Tech career, he broke seven Yellow Jacket rushing records, and totaled 3,517 yards, the third-highest total in history. In all, he piled up 4,325 all-purpose yards, also third-best in Jacket history.

Pepper Rodgers, his college coach, called him "the greatest player I've ever coached. Although he was the greatest college football player in America his senior year, he practiced every day like he was trying to make the team."

His most memorable game came in 1978, when Tech visited the Air Force Academy. In a blinding storm, with a wind-chill factor of zero and an accumulation of 3 inches of snow that made it difficult to walk, much less run, Ivery set the NCAA single-game rushing record with 356 yards. With the stadium turf frozen, the game should have been cancelled. Instead Eddie Lee "rambled" and "wrecked" his way to touchdown runs of 80, 73, and 57 yards.

In that game, he caught the eyes of scouts for the Green Bay Packers, who wanted a reliable back who could flourish in the extreme Wisconsin weather conditions. The Packers had found their man, and drafted Eddie Lee in the first round of the 1979 draft, making for a promising first step to a bright NFL future. But on the third play of his professional debut, he tore the ligaments in his left knee, finishing his season before it started.

His knee wasn't the only thing that was a mess. The Iverys obviously had never dealt with large sums of money, and he was ill-equipped to handle his first professional contract. Virtually overnight, he was already upside down. To say there was no financial planning is an understatement: His first move had been to take care of his mother and buy her a house, and he blazed through his $250,000 signing bonus. Before he knew it, he also owed $90,000 in tax liabilities.

By the time I got involved, Eddie Lee had—literally—about $33,000 left in cash, and he needed help. Frankly, he was scared to death, and I had a long talk with him and his wife over dinner. I shared my background, and we discussed the many similarities in our lives. We also talked deep into the night about overcoming fears. I told him that what he had suffered growing up was far tougher than working something out with the Green Bay Packers. So with his approval, I got on a plane and flew to Green Bay to meet with Bob Harlan, the Packers' general manager and chief executive.

Green Bay is an industrial city with several meatpacking and paper plants and a port on the bay of Green Bay, an arm of Lake Michigan. It is home to the National Railroad Museum, the Neville Public Museum—and its exhibitions of art, history, and science—and the University of Wisconsin-Green Bay. It is also steeped in professional football tradition.

The Green Bay Packers professional football team was formed in 1919 and joined the National Football League in 1921. Green Bay is by far the smallest market with a North American major-league sports team, although the Packers are avidly supported in the larger Milwaukee market, throughout Wisconsin, and in Michigan's Upper Peninsula. Green Bay's unofficial nickname is "Titletown, USA" for the record number of NFL world titles the Packers have won, including several Super Bowls. "Titletown" appears on the city seal, is used by the Green Bay Chamber of Commerce for its web address, and appears in the name of more than two dozen local businesses.

As the plane touched down in Green Bay, I found irony that the beginning of my career as a sports agent would be here, the most famous of all NFL cities—the frozen tundra—and it would be with Bob Harlan, one of the league's most respected executives.

The Packers offices seemed to be about as old as the team, but the people working there were friendly and down to earth, and I immediately found Mr. Harlan to be likeable and affable. We made small talk, then I got right down to brass tacks.

"Is Eddie Lee important to your football team?" I asked.

"You bet, Jerry," he replied. "He's a great kid, and a heckuva talent. We hope to have him around here for a long time."

"Well, let me explain," I said. "Eddie Lee has found himself in quite a bind. He didn't understand anything about taxes, and he's stuck with a pretty big tax burden. He took care of his mom and bought her a house. He paid his agent and bought a car. He took care of his family. But he had no guidance after he signed his contract, and he needs some help. It's one thing to grow up with no money, then another thing to get some, and blow it because you didn't know what to do with it. I'm here to help the young man."

"What do you propose?" Bob asked.

"To me, the easiest deal would be to give him a $70,000 "reporting" bonus when he reports for training camp, and take it off the back end of his contract," I said. "He gets relief, he stays happy, the team benefits, and it's not any additional money."

Bob nodded his head in agreement. On the spot, we negotiated a new deal for Eddie Lee Ivery; just like that, my first NFL deal was done, and it had gone flawlessly. When I called Gene, he couldn't believe it—he thought I was magic. It wasn't magic, but logic.

Eddie Lee and his wife were ecstatic; they had tears in their eyes when I told them the news. The respect and appreciation they gave me was a wonderful reward. I felt like I had just uncovered a worthwhile profession that I could embrace and, in the process, help a lot of people.

16

FEAR OF THE UNKNOWN

IN SHORT ORDER, I'd learned a powerful lesson through Eddie Lee Ivery that would lend itself to my future dealings involving our athletes. For all the courage these great athletes display on the football field, they are scared to death off the field, and it usually involves fear of failure, fear of financial dealings, and fear of the unknown.

Traveling around the nation during the course of my public speaking tours, I met many people who were unhappy with their jobs, their marriages, their circumstances, or their situations. I would listen carefully, and almost every time the reason people fell short of their goals boiled down to that four-letter word that is both ugly and crippling at the same time—"fear"—and usually it is the darkest of all fears . . . fear of the unknown. We all get caught up in ruts, and most people just accept and tolerate their unhappiness; they simply resign themselves to the status quo.

My grandparents, Max and Dora, didn't. They were willing to put everything on the line to seek a better life for their future. They were fearless. They spit in fear's eye, and were willing to take a chance in a strange country, with a language barrier, and very few worldly possessions.

I told Gene: I don't want to be *just* an agent.

I wanted to be an agent of life change. I wanted to give stability to each player; I wanted to keep fear in his rear view mirror; I wanted to give him the confidence to perform at his highest level; and I wanted to create a family where he could learn how to enjoy, embrace, and grow his wealth.

We would do more than just negotiate contracts. We would teach them how to be young, responsible businessmen who, through hard work, could determine their own futures far beyond the playing field.

Together, Gene and I sat down and looked at his targeted list of players. At the very top was a single name: Oklahoma Heisman Trophy winner Billy Sims, who, Gene told me, was already signed illegally by agent Mike Trope.

Gene said, "Billy has already taken money from Trope."

Things were about to get fast and furious.

ACT THREE

Let us never negotiate out of fear. But let us never fear to negotiate. Freedom is never negotiable. We cannot negotiate with those who say, "What's mine is mine, and what's yours is negotiable." It doesn't work that way.

—John F. Kennedy

17

COLLISION COURSE
WITH THE NFL

BY 1979 THE business climate in the National Football League was hotter than ever for each of its twenty-eight owners and markets, largely due to the influence of Alvin Ray "Pete" Rozelle, the league's upstart commissioner, who had been on the job for nineteen years since the ripe age of thirty-three.

Rozelle's influence on the game had been swift, fearless, and ruthless. I had watched him—with great interest and flat-out fascination—navigate through the shark-filled waters of professional football, and for a number of reasons.

For starters, when Rozelle became commissioner in 1960, the combined revenue for every team in the league was slightly less than $20 million. But Rozelle immediately went to work. He moved the league's offices to 1 Rockefeller Plaza in New York City. He dealt with the challenge of the rival American Football League, which had robbed the NFL of current players, pirated away star college players, tied up valuable network television time, and escalated football salaries exponentially.

Eventually, to end the threat and stabilize salaries, Rozelle would tactfully negotiate a cease-fire merger and realignment between the ego-driven owners of both leagues. Rozelle then invented the Super Bowl, though he disliked the name, which had been the idea of the son of Kansas City owner Lamar Hunt (who got the idea after bouncing a "Super Ball" against the garage door). He implemented rule changes to make the game higher-scoring and far more entertaining to fans. But he had an even bigger agenda, one that would make the NFL the most powerful business in sports.

Outsiders were stunned when Rozelle traveled to Washington, D.C., where he actually persuaded Congress to grant the NFL the first of two exemptions to the Sherman Antitrust Act, which enabled him to fold the two leagues into a single, albeit fragmented, business. He then welded the owners of the newly expanded league into a coalition, which required another exemption from the antitrust laws, which Congress granted in 1966.

The result created overwhelming bargaining power. The new revenues went into promoting the game and grabbing an ever-greater slice of the entertainment business. Rozelle had recognized that the greatest contribution to the game came in a single word: television. As black-and-white television sets gave way to color, Rozelle realized the value of the sport on TV: It wasn't just a game anymore, it was programming, and his bold moves to unite the league and negotiate league-wide contracts with the biggest networks—ABC, NBC, and CBS—entirely changed the sport. His brilliant brainchild and execution of Monday Night Football put his sport in millions of living rooms during a primetime weeknight, which became a financial boon for the league.

Essentially, one morning executives from the three major television networks woke up and found not a collection of individual NFL teams competing with one another to sell their respective broadcast rights, but a single entity, with a sense of value that would explode exponentially.

Rozelle was an iron-willed tycoon who had created a business model for all of professional sports to follow. "He figured out a way to make the NFL far more valuable than other sports, including baseball, the national pastime," wrote *Time* magazine. In years to come, his influence would soon spawn other media moguls like Ted Turner and Rupert Murdoch, who recognized the genius in his ideals and soon would build entire networks around sports.

The structure of Pete Rozelle's National Football League was suddenly responsible for the soaring popularity of the league, and created millions of new television, merchandise, and marketing dollars for league owners. Though some owners had enjoyed business success outside of football, they all became very, very wealthy virtually overnight.

I was impressed, because through my own syndication deals, I had witnessed firsthand how consortiums with total command over bargaining power and price could yield great dividends, especially when one could control supply and demand. I had created wealth through syndication; Rozelle, on the other hand, had created an outright monopolistic cartel. The NFL was a closed, tightly regulated system, operating without competition, and benefitting everyone . . . except the players.

In hindsight and in reality, Rozelle was running a business that operated in seemingly outrageous violation of American free-market principles. As I ventured eyes wide open into the world of professional football, I had no idea that very soon, my concept of negotiation—the classic diplomatic sense that assumes parties are more anxious to agree than disagree, and that two parties could start out to strike a fair deal and end up with a deal—would clash head-on with the NFL.

Pete Rozelle and I were on a collision course, in many more ways than one.

18

RUN, BILLY, RUN

BILLY RAY SIMS was at the top of Gene's prospective client list, and prior to the 1979 season, we set our sights on the great Sooner back, but catching him was going to prove harder than running down a prairie rabbit with your bare hands.

Billy was twelve years old and in the eighth grade when he moved from St. Louis to Hooks, 428 miles from my old hometown of Borger. Born on September 18, 1955, in Missouri, he had spent the early years of his life in sheer poverty in one of St. Louis's toughest neighborhoods. His decision to live with his grandmother Sadie—among the other 2,000 residents of this tiny northeast Texas town—paid dividends the first time he picked up a football. "I have just seen," said his ninth-grade coach, "one of the best backfield runners ever." The people in Hooks paid homage to Billy by naming the dirt road that led to Miss Sadie's house, "Billy Sims Road."

"They called me Crazy Legs," Billy would later tell me. "I ran like a chicken with its head cut off." At tiny Hooks High School, he scored 516 points and gained 7,738 yards in three years. Not once did he gain fewer than 123 yards in a game, and he twice topped 300. The first time Oklahoma head coach Barry Switzer saw game film of the Hooks Hornets, his jaw dropped. "It was a playoff game," Switzer remembers. "Billy must've rushed for around 300 yards. I knew Hooks had to be a small school, because I'd never heard of it. I called up his coach—Jack Coleman—and said, 'What's the possibility of my talking to Billy Sims?' He said, 'Pretty good. He's sitting right here in my office.'"

Switzer believed so much in Sims' potential that he sent assistant coach Bill Shimek to Hooks with a simple suggestion: Live there until Billy Sims signs with

Oklahoma, which is exactly what happened. Shimek had been told that Billy was a country boy, and that's where he found him, working on a farm, helping cows give birth, chopping cotton, and hauling hay. After football games, Billy helped clean the stadium. After basketball games, he cleaned the gym. He worked as a janitor at a local hospital, pumped gas at the local service station, and even sold televisions to help support his grandma. His girlfriend, Brenda, was a cross-town cheerleader.

Coach Shimek was shocked the first time he actually saw Billy. "He was carrying two big buckets of cow feed like they were water glasses," he says. "From the waist up, he looked like a Greek god. He weighed 179 pounds. I said, 'Good Lord.'"

On Saturdays, Billy worked at Pat James' Conoco service station, and Switzer made it a point to call him there, just prior to Oklahoma's games—and often from the locker room. "Once, they were playing Colorado in Boulder," Billy says, "and Coach Switzer called me at halftime from the locker room. I said, 'Coach, don't you guys have a game?' And he said, 'Billy, we're winning 35-0, so I've got the whole halftime to talk. How's your grandma?' I knew right then if he was talking to me, then he wouldn't be talking to anybody else."

Like most freshmen under Switzer in Norman, Oklahoma, Billy had a quiet first season. As a sophomore, he injured his right shoulder in the season's third game and missed the season, but was given an extra year of eligibility by the NCAA. The next year, Grandma Sadie passed away, Billy injured his right ankle, and he didn't see much action; fans and coaches began to wonder if he would turn into a bust.

"I knew she was sick," Billy shared with me, "but I didn't know how bad. She was dying from cancer when I was in high school, but she kept it hidden from me. I almost gave it up. I thought about joining the Army. I was crazy about my grandmother. I was more like a son to her than to my mother. She was a lovely person, and it seemed like the whole world collapsed when she passed.

"You know, people always talk about pressure in football, but that's nothing compared to growing up without a father. When I was growing up, I always wished I had an older brother I could talk to. I never wanted to go to my mother and ask for anything, because I thought it was a thing a man should deal with. It troubled me when I was growing up. But people have no idea how close I was to just walking away from the game."

But his junior year at Oklahoma, everything changed overnight.

Running out of the right halfback position in the Oklahoma wishbone, Billy broke 100 yards against Stanford and West Virginia. At 6 feet and 210 pounds, he worked his bench press up to 400 pounds. Billy was now built for power, too, not just speed and explosiveness. This was evident two games later, when he rolled through arch-rival Texas for 131 yards and two scores on national television. For the first time, the names Billy Sims and John Heisman were being mentioned in the same sentence.

Billy delighted crowds with his acrobatics and nearly had people convinced he could fly. Switzer would close his eyes when Sims would daringly leap over huge piles at the line for touchdowns, and his athleticism was overwhelming. "We were losing one game," says Switzer, "and Billy did two hurdling acts that saved us. On a critical fourth-and-one, he went airborne for 5 yards. Then we're down on their seven-yard line, and he hurled himself into the end zone. It was the damndest thing I'd ever seen. The seven-yard line was where his feet left the ground, and he landed in the end zone. Ran wide open, full speed, and just leapt. Came down for six. No one ever touched him . . . he cleared everybody."

By season's end, Billy had become the only Big Eight player to ever rush for 200 yards in three straight games, and finished the season with 1,762, averaging 7.6 yards every time he touched the football. Both his 20 touchdowns and 160.2 yards per game led the nation. He was rewarded with the Heisman Trophy and was selected as a football All-America. He also claimed the Walter Camp Trophy and the Davy O'Brien Award, both of which honor collegiate football's player of the year. The next year, as a senior, he was a Heisman runner-up to Charles White of USC, and ended his college career as the nation's leading rusher with 1,896 yards.

Gene Burrough had blossomed before my eyes. The man was literally like a piece of clay, and the more I taught him, the more aggressively he learned. I grew very fond of his energy, insight, and passion for the business. We had become very close friends, and I enjoyed watching him grow every day as a man. He was bright and trustworthy, and I also enjoyed the company of his wife, Toni.

As I developed Gene on the business side, he equally educated me on the agent side. I really studied Gene during the 1979 college season. His technique was smooth; he was a brazen cold-caller. He'd network through other players and coaches he already knew well and gather top-flight information on the players we had on the list. Then he'd just show up on a campus and ask questions to strangers—like, "Do you know where Billy Sims stays?"—until he found a player's apartment. He'd then boldly knock on the door and introduce himself, state his reason for being there, and ask if he could step inside.

"When I get inside their apartment, Jerry," he said, "I like to work on their girl-friends. If I can get the girlfriend or their wife to listen, I know their pillow talk later on will be the strongest form of recruiting there is. And if not their girlfriends or wives, then I want to talk to their moms. Those are the greatest influences in their lives."

That's where Gene found Billy, in a modern apartment complex that rose up from a dusty lot, just a mile past Owen Field, home of the Sooners. I was informed that Sims spent most of his free time lounging in front of the television set. He didn't like the sun or the heat, and while he appreciated the Sooners' diehard fans, he shied away from constantly being "great." He enjoyed being low-profile, even to the point of not telling his closest friends when he married Brenda before his senior year.

"Jerry, he keeps his Heisman Trophy up on a bookshelf over his television!" Gene said. "He's got some trophies, some game balls, and a couple pictures. They're just non-chalantly thrown up there, like, 'no big deal.' And get this—he works out with another running back named David Overstreet, who I think will be another first-round pick in a few years."

True to form, Gene charmed Brenda, who spent hours showing him scrapbooks of fan mail, including some from children as young as ten, describing her husband as their hero.

After the Sooners finished the 1979 season with a 24-7 victory over Florida State in the Orange Bowl, Billy headed west to appear in Hawaii's Hula Bowl, an All-Star game at Aloha Stadium featuring outstanding college seniors from around the country.

I told Gene to pack his bags. "Let's get our wives," I said, "we're going to Hawaii."

The truth was that players—and people in general—just liked Gene. He was funny, good-natured, and polite. Using the same techniques he'd already honed for years, he had built a relationship of trust with Billy, David Overstreet, defensive end Keith Gary, and linebacker George Cumby at Oklahoma; two-sport star and running back Curtis Dickey and defensive end Jacob Green, both from Texas A&M; Auburn running back Joe Cribbs; University of Arizona defensive end Cleveland Crosby; and Jackson State running back Perry Harrington.

The best part is that he was getting it done without paying a single one of them. Gene was succeeding at convincing the draft-eligible players they needed to come see me in Houston. In the meantime, Gene continued to fill the pipeline with future poten-tial clients. Sims, however, was being just as elusive off the field as he was on it, which Gene attributed directly to pressure from agent Mike Trope.

When we arrived in Hawaii, Trope already had one of his minions camped out with Sims at Hula Bowl practice. We went to practice the first night we were there, and Billy stalled Gene with half-hearted explanations of previous plans.

"We're going to have to outsmart them," Gene said.

"Gene, do you remember the old American Football League?" I said. "There was a coach in the old AFL who climbed a wall and stood on the ledge to knock on the win-dow in order to sign a player. Well, it's time to climb that wall."

"We'll get him," Gene insisted. "Trust me, Jerry, we'll get him. Just be ready."

Like any true Boy Scout, I was always prepared.

Two days later, Gene called my room. He had plucked Billy out from under the nose of Trope's scout, and literally was hiding him in another hotel room across the street while the other guy searched frantically—in all the wrong places. I grabbed my briefcase and headed in that direction. This was fun, like spy versus spy. I knew I would get just one shot at this deal, but I had a bold plan, and I was ready to play jacks like aces.

Sims' afro was just as big as his athletic reputation. I was amazed at his physique, but beyond that, he seemed like just a shy, country college kid. I asked him what was next on his agenda.

"Well, I'm going to play in the Senior Bowl in Mobile, Alabama," he said.

"Why would you do that?" I asked. "You've got nothing left to prove."

"I've got 20,000 reasons," he said, flashing a megawatt smile. Obviously, he was getting paid $20 grand to play in the game.

"That's chump change next to your talent," I told him. "If you go there and you get hurt, you have no insurance or assurance that you will ever make another dime. You need to come see me in Houston. I'll take you to a bank and we can get you that much money on your signature."

Now he was listening. "Billy, here's the deal," I explained. "I'm a businessman. And I'm looking for a job. To tell you the truth, I've never negotiated an NFL contract from start to finish before. But I've negotiated contracts worth hundreds of millions of dollars. I want you to know that I'm not just an agent; I'm your business manager, too. We're building a family, and we'll treat you like family. We're going to change every aspect of your life."

Billy leaned forward, elbows on his knees. I played my ace in the hole: I pulled my personal financial statement out of my briefcase. "Billy, I'm not lying to you," I said. "This is my personal financial statement. I'm not looking to get rich off of you." Pointing to the various columns, I explained. "Here are my assets," I said. "Here are my liabilities. Here's my cash in the bank. And this line right there shows you my net worth."

Billy's eyes got large. "Well, we have a problem," he said. "I've already taken money from two people."

That was a bombshell.

"Billy, I want you to come back to Houston with me when the Hula Bowl's over," I said.

When the game ended, he came to us, bags packed. "We're going to Texas, right?" he said. "When do we leave?"

Billy was awestruck when we got back to Houston, and we treated him like a son. We spent quality time with Billy and Brenda, and they got to see how we worked, lived, and enjoyed everyday life. There was no phony put-on presentation, no false promises, only complete transparency. Billy had grown up without his father, so we connected instantly at a very deep level. He enjoyed hearing stories of my mom and dad, my grandparents, and how a family functions.

He asked lots of great questions, and so did I.

When Billy started telling me the plight of the major college athlete, I was shocked. Never before had I realized just how overtly wrong the NCAA system really is. As a fan, I'd never paid close attention to it, but now that I could peer inside the belly of the beast, I was repulsed. The system was designed to fail: It exploited athletes at every turn, from the very time they were recruited. It put all the liability and pressure on the player, from making the team to making the grades to staying eligible; from making ends meet to finding a way to eat.

The schools were reaping all the benefits in television exposure and revenue, ticket and merchandise sales. However, if the player failed or got caught accepting money, he was summarily replaced like cattle, and in most cases, lost his scholarship, too.

What I'd learned from Eddie Lee Ivery barely scratched the surface. Billy was telling me stories that made my skin crawl. Virtually all these kids came from poverty, or near-poverty, and many of them were fatherless. It dawned on me that these kids arrive on campus with a scholarship-contract that they can't possibly fulfill, because they're broke. NCAA rules don't allow them to work or take money from anyone.

It was incredible to think that an Eddie Lee Ivery or Billy Sims literally could dazzle 80,000 fans and a television audience of millions on a Saturday afternoon, only to return to their dorms without enough money to go get hamburgers and a milkshake with their girlfriend.

To a kid, a scholarship is essentially a four-year commitment to the college, but in reality, the college only makes a one-year-at-a-time commitment to the athlete. After each school year, it's the option of the college to renew or cancel the scholarship. Any contract that is tendered with the prior knowledge that it would be impossible to fulfill, in my book, is devious. The kids were set up to fail. Clearly, the universities held all the leverage: They made the rules, controlled the product, dominated the "employees," fixed the prices, kept all the money, and monopolized the market. Players could not work or take outside gifts of any kind—both were rules violations. They could not sell their own game tickets, even at face value.

This is hardly free enterprise or capitalism, I thought. This is modern-day slavery, hidden behind the thin veil of a college education.

I asked Billy how he survived.

"If I told you Doc, you wouldn't believe it," he said, giggling. He described how he "sold" ads for the *Oklahoma Sooner* weekly magazine, and in one afternoon had generated a whopping $6,500 in sales. He winked at me, and I got it. Unless he was selling for *Sports Illustrated*, no ad space was worth $6,500. And Billy wasn't done yet. He also "sold" t-shirts, ballpoint pens, snuff-can lids and ashtrays that fit atop beer cans, all featuring the crimson and cream "OU" logo.

I was catching on. "My favorite, Doc, were these lighters that played the 'Boomer Sooner' fight song when you flick them!" he said, roaring with infectious laughter. "There was another one that played 'Smoke Gets in Your Eyes.' The people who bought this crap used to tell me, 'Whatever it is you're selling Billy, I'm buying.'"

"Doc, you know the problem with the Heisman Trophy? I took it to the store, and I couldn't buy groceries with it!" He was on a roll now. "If you offered me money to do anything, I took it. And anybody who says they didn't, well, they're lying." Billy told me he'd been embarrassed and humiliated by the need to take money and lived with the constant fear he might be "discovered," and lose everything. "But I couldn't work. With no food and no money, what were my choices?" he asked.

I just shook my head. I'm looking at the best player in all of college football, I thought, and the NCAA has done nothing but turn this kid into a two-bit hustler.

"Billy," I said, "I want you to make more money off the field than on it. I want you to live a clean life. Have you ever seen the O. J. Simpson commercial for Avis? Well, that's corporate life. If you can become an All-Pro on the field, it is my goal to make you just as much money—or more—off the field."

Billy got serious. "Doc," he said, "I'm going to put all my trust in you." "You will never regret it," I told him. "I will get you paid fairly, and support you in all you do."

We made a pact: I would help him live up to the dreams that he'd promised his late Grandma Sadie. We'd get him the money to pay back his debts. Most of all, this was the beginning of a new life for Billy, one he had never before known.

The next morning, we were preparing for the press conference to announce Billy Sims as our first client. Around 11 AM, Billy walked in, and we didn't recognize him. He had cut off his Afro and was dressed like a business professional. "Doc, is this what you meant by corporate America?" he said, grinning like a kid in a candy store and rubbing his freshly cut hair.

Moments later, Gene took the podium in my Galleria office in front of a dozen or more reporters holding pens, microphones, and cameras. "Dr. Jerry Argovitz has been managing people's money—and his own—since 1973," he said. "When we got together, he said that 'we would operate with integrity, or we would not operate at all.' With his help and ability to do more than negotiate contracts, like build wealth and security, we have captured the interest of the nation's top collegiate players. Today, we are proud to announce our first signee—Oklahoma Heisman Trophy winner Billy Sims."

There was clapping from the small gathering as Billy stepped up. I'd never been more proud in my life. The first question was to be expected. "Hey Billy!" yelled one writer. "Why would you pick a dentist over other agents?"

Billy flashed his trademark smile. "Well, because I want good teeth."

The room broke up with laughter.

We had convinced Billy to turn down $20,000 to play in the Senior Bowl, which to that point would have been more money than he'd ever seen in his life. We'd convinced him to cut his hair. We were taking the steps necessary to make him a professional.

In our first deal, Gene and I had landed the best running back in the game. In my book, Billy's worst days were behind him: The neglect he'd suffered from his father, the poverty he and Sadie had endured, the exploitation he'd experienced in college—was all finally over. He was going to the National Football League, where he would finally be treated with the respect he had earned and be paid the money he deserved, and if my brief negotiations with the Packers' Bob Harlan were any indication, this was going to be fun.

I assumed that every team in the NFL would have the best lawyers, the best negotiators, and the most pedigreed, talented executives in the country. I couldn't wait to lock horns and test wits with the best of the best.

Wow, was I naive.

19

PRIDE OF THE LIONS

HAD I BRIDLED my excitement and taken more than just a cursory glance at the history of the Detroit Lions, I would have realized I was walking straight into a jungle of bizarre dysfunction that spanned decades: from losing to lies to totally illogical business dealings. The Lions had been created in 1934 by George Richards, the owner of Detroit's powerful WJR radio station, who had purchased the Portsmouth (Ohio) Spartans and moved them to Detroit.

Out of respect to the Tigers baseball club, he renamed his team the Lions, stating that the Lion was a "monarch of the jungle," and he intended for his team to become the "monarch of the NFL." Due to Richards' broadcasting ties, the Lions began playing on Thanksgiving Day, a long-standing "tradition" that would bring the team's haplessness into the nation's living rooms for decades to come.

Two years before I was born, quarterback Dutch Clark led the Lions to the first NFL championship. Through the 1940s, they averaged three wins a season, including an 0-11 mark in 1942, in which they never scored more than seven points in a single game. In 1943 the Lions and New York Giants played to a 0-0 tie at Detroit—the last time an NFL game ended in a scoreless tie.

All this briefly changed, however, during the 1950s, when a rebel quarterback named Bobby Layne directed the team to NFL championships in 1952, 1953, and 1957, and lost to the Cleveland Browns in the 1954 championship. But the Lions—setting a trend that would continue long after Layne—inexplicably traded the future

Hall of Famer to Pittsburgh. As the stunned Layne was leaving town, he predicted to the media that "this team will not win for another fifty years."

In 1959 minority owner Ralph Wilson bolted to upstate New York, where he became owner of the American Football League's Buffalo Bills. On November 22, 1963, William Clay Ford Sr.—great grandson of famed automaker Henry Ford—purchased a controlling interest in the Lions for a paltry $4.5 million.

Before it was over, history would set up opportunities for me to battle both men.

Griffithsville, West Virginia, is an unincorporated community in eastern Lincoln County, West Virginia, with a population of 929 people, about one-third the size of Hooks, Texas. It lies along Route 3, southeast of the town of Hamlin, and has a single post office, one middle school, and two greenhouses, and is best known for its Christmas tree farm owned by Larry and Syble Wilkerson and Jeff and Landin Harper. Three-fourths of its residents have a high-school education equivalent or less.

In 1924 Russ Thomas was born in Griffithsville, where there were two stores, one movie theater, and a single Pennzoil pumping station. "We grew up dirt poor," Thomas would later say. "But everybody was poor. I learned that you didn't need money to be happy. Money has hurt more people than it has ever helped. My family was resourceful. I was taught that money is the root of all evil."

On the football field, Thomas was an absolute beast: He grew to the imposing stature of 6-foot-4-inches tall and weighed nearly 300 pounds. His chest was bigger than a barrel and his neck looked like an oak tree stump. He became such a dominant offensive and defensive tackle that he caught the eye of Ohio State head coach Wes Fesler and earned a scholarship as a Buckeye. Four years later, in 1946, he was drafted in the second round by the Detroit Lions.

A severe knee injury limited Thomas to just twenty-seven starts in forty-four games, and he was forced to retire after three years, during which the Lions won a total of ten games. Thomas bounced around, toiling as a scout, a broadcaster, an assistant coach, controller, and personnel director. During this span, the Lions drafted some Hall of Fame, legendary players, such as receiver Fred Biletnikoff, safety Johnny Robinson, and quarterback John Hadl. Trouble was, each of them chose the other league, the American Football League, rather than play for the Lions.

Biletnikoff chose to play with the Oakland Raiders, where he won a Super Bowl (and was the game's MVP) and was chosen to six Pro Bowls. Robinson played with the Dallas Texans his first two years, but made his mark with the Kansas City Chiefs, where he set the modern-day standard for safeties. His fifty-eight interceptions is still a team record, and his play helped lead the Chiefs to a Super Bowl IV title over the Minnesota Vikings in 1970. Robinson is a seven-time Pro Bowl selection and a member of the LSU, Kansas City Chiefs, and Missouri Sports Halls of Fame. Hadl's notoriety came with the San Diego Chargers—for whom he played eleven seasons before moving on to three other teams. Hadl threw for 33,503 yards and 244 touchdown passes and was chosen All-AFL three times, was an AFL All-Star game selection four times (and was MVP of the 1969 AFL All-Star game) before moving on to become a two-time Pro Bowl selection and team MVP for the L.A. Rams.

In 1967, less than twenty years after his last game, Thomas was appointed to Detroit's general manager post by Lions' owner Bill Ford. It was an odd move on many levels. For starters, Thomas never graduated from college. He had little to no business experience, other than what he'd been taught as he worked his way through the Lions' system. Just like Billy and me, Thomas somehow had made the unlikely leap from humble beginnings to the grand stage of the NFL. But I never dreamed I'd end up negotiating with someone from a town smaller than either Borger or Hooks.

Thomas seldom talked about winning, because the Lions seldom won. The burly GM did, however, brag often about how Detroit was a picture of fiscal responsibility, and the team was guaranteed at least one annual chance—Thanksgiving—to hold court on national television, win or lose. Bill Ford never uttered a word. The Lions didn't have to win to make money, and hordes of it. By 1970 Commissioner Pete Rozelle was masterfully directing the merger between the American Football League and the National Football League, realigning the league's conferences and divisions, and money was flush from burgeoning new television contracts.

Suddenly, being an NFL owner was akin to winning the lotto.

Thomas's role was to rule the financial roost with an iron fist and to ensure that not a single penny escape the miserly Lions without notice. The average life span of a real lion in the wild is ten to fourteen years. In Detroit, not so much. Thomas made it clear he would rather cut or trade a player—or fire a coach—than pay fair-market value. He took his job seriously, and soon word spread like wildfire: Players and coaches would rather die than play in Detroit, and two did—Chuck Hughes and head coach Don McCafferty. Hughes, a wide receiver, became the first NFL player to die on the field when he collapsed of a massive heart attack in 1971. The very next year, McCafferty died of heart disease just before training camp.

The Lions were so bad that even singer Marvin Gaye tried out for the club. Gaye became friends with legendary Lion defensive backs Mel Farr and Lem Barney, and—true story—they actually sang background vocals in his classic single, "What's Going On?" which for all practical purposes should have become the Lions' fight song—to this day.

The mediocrity, inconsistency, and utter disasters didn't quell Detroit's success off the field. The Lions played their final game in Tiger Stadium on Thanksgiving Day, 1974, and then moved to their new suburban headquarters in Pontiac at the Silverdome, a glistening, temperature-controlled, multi-million-dollar facility with 85,000 seats, no snow, and exponential profit-earning potential.

Back on the field, the budgets stayed status quo, and so did the team. In their first three years in their new digs, the Lions went 7-7, 6-8, and 6-8. Rozelle expanded the schedule to sixteen games in 1978, and they responded by promptly losing nine. The 1979 team refused to be outdone, and lost fourteen. Losing had its upside, however; Rozelle had introduced a word to sports called parity, wherein the league's teams would draft college players in the order they finished in the league the previous season, worst to first.

On the surface, it seemed a good idea, one that would allow the NFL to maintain competitive efficacy among its member teams. In 1980 the best player on the draft board was none other than University of Oklahoma Heisman Trophy winner Billy Sims, and the dead-last team in the league was the hapless Lions, who made him the first player taken overall. After Billy was chosen, I had six more of my clients go in the first and second rounds in the first draft ever covered start-to-finish by ESPN.

For the Lions to land Billy, however, was akin to a wannabe pilot who couldn't get a Cessna off the ground in a headwind becoming the proud owner of an F-16, with a cockpit chock full of fancy buttons and a deadly armament of toys. Thomas, who had proven time and again he could screw up a one-car funeral, was now staring at the sleek, beautiful, and magical Sims the way a kid with a penny left in his pocket stares at a gumball machine that costs a quarter. Disaster was imminent, but I was too new myself to pack a parachute.

Adventure defined is a difficult endeavor in which the outcome is unknown, but the possibility of great reward exists, and that's what was lurking in upcoming negotiations with Thomas. My flight from Houston to Detroit screeched down at Wayne County Metro Airport, and I jumped in a cab headed for the Silverdome and marched right into the Lions' den and the jowls of Russ Thomas, where I was about to brazenly ask for more money for a single player than Bill Ford had paid to own the entire team.

The average lion eats sixteen pounds of meat a day, or roughly 500 pounds a month. At the time, Thomas weighed 300 pounds and I weighed 200.

I should've done the math.

20

AN NFL HANDSHAKE IS A PROFESSIONAL HAND JOB

BY HIS OWN accord, Russ Thomas had grown up dirt poor, and he wanted to make damn sure everyone else had the same opportunity. And while no one will accuse Thomas of being racist, there wasn't a single African American living in his home town until after he died in 1991. So it was more than a little ironic that he would find himself in the racially charged town of the Motor City, where his primary job was dealing with black athletes, which put him in a position to largely control their incomes and manipulate the media who managed their fame.

Now, however, he had a problem: Billy Sims was no run-of-the-mill athlete, and I wasn't a card-carrying member of the NFL's good ol' boy network. Thomas had to be wondering, Who in the hell is this dentist representing the top player in the draft? No one in football had ever heard my name. I wasn't new at negotiating contracts, but I also wasn't part of the brat pack of new agents who had appeared on the scene. Mike Trope was a kid. Bob Woolf was a Boston attorney, as were two other California agents, Howard Slusher and Leigh Steinberg. Leigh was a good one, but had stumbled into the business when his friend and college classmate Steve Bartkowski had been drafted by the Atlanta Falcons.

Being a player agent in 1980 was unchartered territory: a wide-open frontier with few rules or standards at the time—many agents operated out of the trunks of their cars. I didn't see myself as an agent, per se. I was an accomplished dentist, a skilled business negotiator, and a successful land developer. I saw myself as a business coach and a mentor to my young players. When I looked at what information I had gathered regarding NFL salaries, particularly the Lions, it was obvious there were huge discrepancies between revenue being earned by owners and compensation being made by the players who created it. My goal was to decrease that gap, but in a fair and satisfactory manner to both sides.

"Mr. Thomas will see you now," said the secretary. I grabbed my briefcase and followed her back through the serpentine hallway, honestly believing with each step that what was about to occur would be swift, fair, and professional. I turned the corner and saw Thomas, whose giant frame was as wide as his office doorway. I began having second thoughts when we shook hands, because he nearly dismembered my arm with a grip so crushing and enormous I felt like I'd inserted my forearm into a fifteen-pound baked ham.

"Welcome to the NFL," he growled.

We made small talk, like two boxers circling each other in the first round. Finally, Russ let out a sigh and opened his desk drawer. "I've taken the liberty," he said, "of preparing a contract for your review and approval from Billy Sims. Here is our offer. It's more than fair, and Billy will be an instant Detroit hero. The Lions want to get this wrapped up and make an announcement to our fans."

I took the contract and reviewed it: A $300,000 signing bonus, deferred over ten years; a three-year contract at $100,000 per, with a one-year option season at $110,000. It didn't take a mathematical genius to realize we were planets apart. Inwardly, I was insulted and incredulous. Outwardly, I kept a poker face. Without hesitation, I opened my own leather attaché and pulled out a copy of *Sports Illustrated*, with a cover photo of Boston Celtics' first-round pick Larry Bird, who had just received a $1 million signing bonus.

"Russ, before the draft, I urged you not even to pick Billy before we could work out a deal. . . ."

"Why in hell would I listen to any agent, much less a dentist, telling *me* not to draft a player until we negotiate a contract?" he bellowed. Thomas wasn't used to being challenged, that was obvious. "The rules are simple," he continued. "You begin negotiations after the draft. The salaries are slotted, based on the last year's draft, plus inflation. This deal is better than what last year's first-overall pick received, plus some."

You couldn't "slot" Sims—as the first overall pick, he had already been determined by the whole league to be the best player in the draft. "If you aren't going to pay him his value, you should trade him to one of the twenty-seven teams that are interested in him." I tossed the *Sports Illustrated* on his desk.

"What's this?" he asked.

"It's Larry Bird, the number-one player taken in the NBA," I said. "He just got a million-dollar signing bonus. I want a million-dollar cash signing bonus for Billy guaranteed, plus another $3.5 million for four years, and no option."

Thomas pushed away from his desk, stood up, and towered over me.

"Football and basketball are two different sports!" he roared.

"I know!" I said, smiling softly. Thomas grabbed the so-called contract he'd prepared for Billy, opened his bottom desk drawer, threw it inside, and slammed it shut. "When you're ready to sign," he snapped, "and when Billy's ready to play football, his contract—this very same one—will be right here waiting for you. The only place in the world Billy Sims is going to play football is right here in Detroit, and if he doesn't like it, he can get a job sweeping floors. You really need to get an experienced agent to help you because you don't understand football contracts and your expectations are totally unrealistic."

My hand was still smarting from the last handshake. I just got up, looked Russ squarely in his eyes and said, "You drafted him—now let's see if you can get him signed." Then I left. When I got back to Houston, reporters told me that owner Bill Ford had told the Detroit media: "Jerry Argovitz is a Machiavellian idiot."

I laughed. "I'm not sure what that means," I told them, "but tell him I said, 'You too, buddy!'"

Thomas harped on my "inexperience," in spite of the fact that I'd negotiated more contracts for far greater money than he ever did or would in his career. "Argovitz is unreasonable," he told reporters. "I'd much rather deal with someone who knows what he's doing."

Me, too, I thought.

The Lions, like most NFL teams, had for years engaged in what is called position-based negotiations, which tend to view the "pie" as fixed, such that a greater share for one means a lesser share for the other. Thomas had become the de facto king of the jungle by "winning" hard-ball negotiations over the agents and some players who were typically inexperienced at negotiations and often not represented by an agent or attorney at all. All contracts contain issues over money, years, tax structures, skill-and-injury guarantees, bonuses and no-trade clauses, property, benefits, and obligations; and doing business with Detroit usually meant you surrendered all of the above or you picked another profession.

I had been brought up by my father, teachers, and mentors to embrace "win-win" scenarios, wherein everyone walks away from the table feeling as if they had been heard and respected, with mutual goals attained as a result. "Win-win" negotiations adhere to a certain set of principles, but right out of the gate, I realized this was going to be a challenge.

But patience is power.

Usually, the first step is to separate people from the problem. Misperceptions, emotions, and communication problems place themselves in the way of resolution. Thomas made sure he was both the person and the problem. He was confrontational and cantankerous. He did his best to manipulate the media with distasteful comments about Billy being represented by a "dentist," or that the Lions had "offered Sims more money than they have in all of Hooks, Texas," or that if he didn't like it, he should "go find another job outside of football . . . or get another agent."

Thomas infuriated Gene, who didn't hold back his disgust. "The man is an idiot," he said, "and the way he's treating Billy is proof. The players we represent in this draft alone could beat the Lions. Billy Sims will put them in the playoffs. What's that worth to the Lions and the city of Detroit?"

"Obviously, not much to Russ and Ford," I said. "I can't imagine the star power Billy would have had in New York or Los Angeles, or even San Francisco, but because of the NFL's closed system, which is a total and complete monopoly, we have no choice but to deal with Detroit."

The truth was that I had promised more than I could deliver to Billy and six other young athletes who had invested their trust in me. I had promised they would be paid fairly, and there is nothing fair about the NFL. To me, the draft is wrong and unconstitutional.

Russ made these negotiations adversarial and personal. I was baffled; how, in America, could someone own your rights? Every time Russ and I would speak, I would reframe the deal to emphasize that both the Lions and Billy would benefit from a sold-out Silverdome, that the team would benefit from Billy's talents, and that Billy's worth couldn't possibly be based on a closed system of slotting, but on his overall contribution to the club, at fair-market value. After all, they had picked Sims, and for all of those reasons. One of the enduring myths of pro football contends that you win by filling your weaknesses. Another myth counters that you should draft the best athlete available, and that great athlete would immediately help your team, regardless.

Billy was all of the above.

Another way of creating a win-win negotiation was to explore options for mutual gain, such as incentive bonuses and insurance policies. For instance, if a player performs well—makes the Pro Bowl, or rushes for 1,000 yards, say, he earns more. I had many ideas to this end, not the least of which would be a Lloyd's of London insurance policy in the event that Billy suffered a catastrophic injury. Billy—get this—wanted some of his bonus money divided among his teammates—like his offensive linemen and his blocking back—so they could share in his success.

The NFL's system stunk and was a one-way street, which was all in favor of the league and its rich and powerful owners. It's impossible to negotiate a fair deal when a team owns your rights and no one else can bid for your services. Obviously, slavery wasn't abolished—but in fact, alive and well.

Regrets are hard to live with, and other than wishing Detroit had never drafted Billy, I had two: The first was mentioning the Canadian Football League as a possibility during another heated exchange with Thomas, and the second was thinking I could ever trust him.

During one argument with Thomas, I made the mistake of suggesting that if the Lions didn't want Billy, we'd go north, to the Canadian Football League. The previous year—in 1979—Ohio State linebacker Tom Cousineau had been drafted by Buffalo, but shocked everyone by signing for twice the money with Montreal and becoming the Most Valuable Player of the Grey Cup.

I'd barely hung up the phone with Thomas when I was informed that Sims' CFL rights had been picked up by Saskatchewan, coached by—you guessed it!—a friend of Thomas named Ron Lancaster, who had grown up in Pennsylvania. Thomas had "suggested" that Lancaster claim Sims and offer him $30,000 a year; in return, Thomas would give him first dibs on the Lions early cuts of the season. It was tit for tat, and any leverage using the CFL had just gone up in smoke.

Thomas was using totally different tactics to force my hand: eliminate leverage, work under the table with cronies and media, throw out false deadlines, and repeatedly offer less and ask for more.

But we had the ultimate leverage: Sims himself. While the negotiations raged and waged forward, Billy and I agreed he should attend rookie camp, and he wowed the media, coaches, and fans. He ran 4.5 in the 40, bench-pressed 390 pounds, and dazzled everyone with open-field running and pass-catching skills. "I don't know if you saw (Billy) out there," head coach Monte Clark told the press, "but what he did on the field is probably some of the best negotiating I've ever seen. He reminds you of Gale Sayers, or Walter Payton." When we were alone, Billy would just laugh. "I don't run like those guys Doc! I run like me!"

When regular training camp with the veterans finally arrived, we decided that Billy would hold out until the deal was done. The media, which Thomas had used against me as an "outsider," slowly began to flip: Detroit was desperate for a winner, and everyone wanted to see the flashy new rookie. Thomas and I fought openly in the local and national media, and we sold a lot of newspapers. "Getting a dollar out the Lions," I told the press, "is harder than pulling teeth."

The breakthrough came when I finally received a call from Bill Ford himself, who said, in so many words, they wanted the impasse to end. He explained that his friend Russ wasn't a bad man, just loyal to those who wrote his paychecks. I tried to explain things to Mr. Ford in a manner he, too, could understand: If you were buying a T-Bird, fully loaded, don't expect to get it for the price of a go-kart.

Ford explained to me that he was having heart surgery in a week, and that he would meet with Thomas himself to get the deal done. The next day, Thomas shockingly declared to the press—as if this was his idea—that "we want to pay Billy what he's worth. We're just working with his dentist to determine what he's worth."

Russ and I were close to a verbal agreement, subject to Billy's approval. Thomas wanted a three-year deal, with a one-year "option." NFL teams love the "option" year, because it's their option whether to keep you, and they take your final year, add 10 percent, and that's your option year. The team has no real contractual or financial obligation to the player, but the player's rights are owned by that team through that so-called option year. The player can be cut at any time. In fact, the only part of an NFL contract that is guaranteed is the signing bonus—each year the player has to make the team and pass the physical exam.

On June 6, 1980, at 1:46 AM Houston time and 2:46 AM Detroit time, I called Thomas at home. I told Russ that Billy would accept a three-year deal, no more. He insisted that we fly to Detroit and meet and we could close the show.

When we arrived, I kept it simple and wanted Billy to be present in these final negotiations.

"Russ, let's do this," I said. "We want the $1 million cash bonus to sign. We insist on the Lloyd's of London policy, the incentive clauses, and the annual salaries. Let's settle on three years. When Billy proves himself on the field, then let's all agree that we'll 'fill in' the fourth-, fifth-, and sixth-year figures after the 1982 season based on Billy's performance."

I pointed at Billy. "Does this work for you?" I asked. "Yes," Billy nodded.

"That's a good idea," said Russ. I stuck out my hand, and Thomas grabbed it. "Deal, Jerry," he said, then he shook hands with Billy. "Welcome to the Lions!" A Russ Thomas handshake is a lot like being shot; you don't enjoy it, and you'll never forget it.

I was relieved, and Billy's deal came with a lot of "firsts": It was the first multi-million dollar career-ending insurance policy. It was the largest rookie contract in NFL history. It was the first million-dollar, tax-free signing bonus. It was more than three times the amount than any other Detroit player was currently being paid. "Doc, I never doubted you," Billy said. "Together, we can make things happen."

It was vintage Billy when he reported for camp, driving a 1979 Blazer truck he had brought with him from Oklahoma. "Nice to meet everybody," Billy told his new teammates. Laughing, he broke the ice. "Looks like I'm gonna be the reason none of you guys get a raise this year," he said. In reality, Billy and I were going to be the mitigating reasons why the entire salary structure and free agency system of the National Football League were about to radically change, resulting in a raise for everybody.

Two games into the season, Billy was having a banner year, leading the Lions in rushing and scoring. "We knew he was good," said Bill Ford, "but he is more than we ever hoped for."

Most people would rather act stupid than think, and Thomas never disappointed—continuing to talk about how Billy was "one guy in a team sport, and the entire team is improved." Right. The proof was in the pudding: The same guys who couldn't win a year before were now far better than they could have ever dreamed to be; not the least of which was quarterback and future big-time broadcaster Gary Danielson. Danielson came to the Lions after the team had discovered him working in a Detroit sheet-metal plant after his pro football aspirations faltered. Now he was leading the Lions to the playoffs.

"The biggest motor in the Motor City," Gary told me one afternoon at practice, "is Billy Sims." We signed Billy to additional endorsement contracts with Adidas and Wilson, and charged $1,250 an hour for his personal appearances—at a four-hour minimum. His countless visits to hospitals, however, he did for free, especially the children at Henry Ford Hospital.

During one promotion at a nearby Detroit shopping mall, more than 4,000 parents with an additional 5,000 kids—in spite of freezing weather outside—packed in like sardines for a glimpse of Billy, his Heisman Trophy, and a possible autograph. We all donned cowboy hats and blue jeans, and Billy was nothing short of phenomenal. One by one, hour after hour, he reached out and touched every one of them. Billy connected with the poor and the powerless, to the mighty and the wealthy, sharing his mega-watt smile and friendly conversation while tirelessly signing black-and-white glossy action photos.

More than 27,000 jerseys bearing his name and number had sold at that mall alone since the day he signed his contract; heady stuff for the once-obscure little boy who had been born into poverty. Yet Billy kept a snapshot in his pocket of a 39-acre ranch back in Hooks, Texas, near the home of his departed grandma. It was a home owned by Bob White, a boyhood mentor for whom Billy had worked as a kid. He had dreamed about this house since he was a teenager, when—as a day laborer—he had helped install the swimming pool and tennis court. Behind the house was a large lake for fishing, lots of trees, and spacious living quarters. I worked out a deal with Bob White, and now Billy owned it. Dreams do come true.

"Doc, if it all ended right now, I'd be OK," he said that afternoon. "I'd go back to my fishing hole in Hooks and just toss me a line in the water. As long as I can stay this happy and have enough to eat, I'll be just fine." I cared deeply for Billy Sims. It hurt me when he talked of growing up fatherless. My new career as an NFL agent had placed me in daily contact with men who had lived through precarious economic conditions; I was determined to defend them and fight for them. These were 21- and 22-year-old kids coming into serious money. Many of them had never even owned a car. They were getting too much too quick and they were ill-prepared to deal with it; most guys earning $100,000 a year were spending $120,000 a year. No one ever taught them about Uncle Sam's share. I put all of my players on a budget and did their financial and tax planning.

The image of football players as idiots was a notion that needed to be laid to rest. The game itself is so complex that if they didn't have brains, they wouldn't have been drafted. They realize they need tax shelters, real estate, and ways to meet the needs of their mothers, brothers, or sisters. They just didn't know how, and I was thrilled to be in a role where I could ensure them that when it's over, nobody's going to take away the house, the car, or the lifestyle they'd worked so hard to attain.

Sims, while not overly educated or particularly genteel, had a practical wisdom far beyond that of the ordinary man. I don't care what anybody says, humility is tougher when you're a star, and I couldn't decide at that time which was Billy's best trait—humility or integrity. Watching him interact with the public made me earn an instant respect for the common sense of people, a factor routinely ignored by intellectuals, or underestimated by those chasing front-office promotions. Billy's word was his bond, and his handshake, his currency.

As for Thomas—God bless him—he was child's play compared to what happened in Baltimore, where the Colts had drafted my client Curtis Dickey, the fastest running back in the history of Texas A&M.

Without help, Dickey was about to be stomped like hay in the stall of maverick Baltimore owner Robert Irsay, who had done likewise with Johnny Unitas, the NFL, and the once-proud Colts.

21

A FOOL
EVEN A MOTHER
COULDN'T LOVE

IN TEXAS, IF your own mother doesn't love you, well, you're just a fool. When it comes to Robert "Bob" Irsay, former owner of the Baltimore/Indianapolis Colts, there is no other explanation. Irsay is portrayed in a 1986 *Sports Illustrated* article as a drunken, incompetent owner who single-handedly destroyed one of the greatest dynasties in sports history.

"He's the devil on Earth," his mother, Elaine, would say before she died. "He was a bad boy. I don't want to talk about him."

Bert Jones, the man who quarterbacked the Colts under Irsay, had this to say about him: "Irsay lied, cheated, and he was rude and crude. He doesn't have any morals. It is a sad statement for the NFL to be associated with him."[*]

To get your own mother and your players to hate you takes hard work. We would learn what she meant when the Colts took Curtis Dickey with the fifth pick of the 1980 draft. It was impossible then to grasp the long-term ramifications of my grappling with Irsay, or how my battles with him would influence this draft, future drafts, the outcome of Super Bowl XX, and future owner selection in the NFL.

At the outset, I was giddy with excitement to learn that I'd be working with the Baltimore organization, because any boy who ever laced up a pair of cleats spoke of the Colts with awe and reverence, and rightfully so. Prior to Irsay's purchase of the Colts in 1972, the team had never suffered a losing season. The team was a dynasty: three NFL

---

[*] *Sports Illustrated*, December 15, 1986.

championships, two Super Bowls, and legends like Johnny Unitas, Tom Matte, Raymond Berry, Art Donovan, and Don Shula.

Under Irsay, losing took less than twelve months. Joe Thomas, Irsay's first general manager, benched the great Unitas, traded away thirteen players in one fell swoop, fired coach Don McCafferty (who had won the 1971 Super Bowl), and sunk Baltimore to the NFL basement in a single season. They settled there with pitiful mediocrity. By 1980 only three teams had finished with a worse record than the Colts, and I now had clients on two of those clubs.

"Gene, I gotta warn you," Jerry told me after Dickey was drafted, "I heard Bob Irsay doesn't like Jews. If there is a single human being on this planet that I can't handle, it's Bob Irsay. In my opinion, he is a poster boy for why innocent young kids need agents, they need representation. This is a guy who drops a grand on drinks at night and screws a minimum-wage carpenter out of a nickel the next morning."

What? A glance at the Colts press guide said he was Catholic. In fact, the press guide said a great deal: Irsay had been raised in the "Bucktown" section of Chicago, the Near Northwest Side, historically an ethnically diverse area with a large Eastern European population. He had been raised in poverty; his father died when he was very young; he washed dishes and did odd jobs to support himself and his mother through graduation at the University of Illinois; he played in the 1946 Rose Bowl with the Fighting Illini; he served with the Marines in World War II before being hit by a live grenade in New Guinea; he built his heating and ventilation empire with an $800 loan from his wife.

By all accounts, I was about to be dealing with one super-human, indestructible, self-made man. In fact, most of these accomplishments had been well documented in wild stories in the *Baltimore Sun*, including his incredible overseas heroics as a member of the Army, Marines, and Navy, where he was hand-picked by the Seabees.

Trouble was, none of this was true. I had no idea who, or what, I was dealing with.

For starters, Irsay was as Jewish as me. In fact, his grandparents escaped Eastern Europe just as mine did, only they had been shipped to Ellis Island, not Galveston, as Max and Dora had. His birth name wasn't Irsay, it was Israel. He and his younger brother had been raised in an upper-middle-class home by both Jewish parents in Chicago's West Rogers Park.

Irsay's father—still very much alive—was a sheet-metal contractor and owned several downtown Chicago buildings. His parents paid for his college education. He never played a down of football for Illinois. He never played anything. In fact, his college roommate was Art Petacque, who would grow up to be a Pulitzer Prize-winning reporter for the *Chicago Sun-Times*. Note to self: If you're going to tell lies, downright whoppers, you probably shouldn't bunk up with a journalist, who is also Jewish, and who belongs to Sigma Alpha Mu, the same Jewish fraternity as you do—but that's precisely what Irsay did.

Irsay left Illinois after only four semesters, and without a degree. He enlisted in the Marines on October 23, 1942, and lasted less than six months; no Navy, no Army, no fighting, no live grenades, no overseas, and certainly no Seabees. He bounced around and failed at several jobs before his "dead" father hired him into Accord Ventilating Company, the family business. He thrived as a secretary and salesman. His parents paid $5,000 for his Jewish wedding to Harriet Pogorzelski on July 12, 1947, at Temple Sholom, and his luxurious reception at the Belmont Hotel.

The more I learned about Irsay, the more common our upbringings had been. My father, Harry, had taught me the value of money, and Irsay's had done the same. The younger Irsay was charismatic, had a gift for gab, and had no problem selling his way to the top. But that's where our similarities ended. He had issues when it came to telling the truth, and spent his money on women, booze, and gambling faster than he made it, which created enormous rifts in his family. In 1951, after the family accused him of stealing from its company, he set out on his own, taking with him five of his father's employees, several major accounts, little overhead, and a determination to humiliate his own relatives. He succeeded. Two years later, his father suffered a massive heart attack, and shortly thereafter, Accord went out of business.

The Robert Irsay Company, however, was thriving, and Irsay himself was basking in the power that money brought him. In no time, his biggest projects were the 100-story John Hancock Center and 103-story Sears Tower, Chicago's two largest buildings and two of the world's tallest skyscrapers. He took up space in a penthouse office of the Hancock Center, then promptly denounced his parents, family, and Jewish heritage.

Rumor had it that he spent his mornings in profanity-laced tirades with frightened employees, and spent his afternoons at a local bistro, where he drank long into the night. He purchased a men's clothing store in Wilmette on Chicago's North Shore, and at night used it for illegal poker games. He made headlines for driving his own trucks through Teamster picket lines to get supplies to his job sites. For thirteen years, Irsay was involved in a major Chicago association that engaged in illegal bid-rigging. He escaped prosecution by accepting government immunity for his testimony against his own confidants.

By 1970 the Robert Irsay Company was the largest sheet-metal business in Chicago, grossing nearly $13 million in sales and posting after-tax profits of about $650,000. In 1971 Irsay sold the company to Zurn Industries in exchange for some $8.5 million in common stock, although he claimed to the press he had sold to Zurn for "$50 million." He stayed on board with Zurn until 1978, when he was told that his purchase of the Baltimore Colts "was a distraction."

When Irsay turned his full attention to the Colts, it pulled the trapdoor on whatever decency remained in the Baltimore organization, and the bottom fell out.

Irsay's purchase of the Colts was the ultimate practical joke played on the National Football League, engineered by none other than former Baltimore owner Carroll Rosenbloom, a savvy, conservative, and sophisticated businessman who owned the team from 1953 to 1972. For years leading to the sale, he desperately wanted out of Baltimore because of the limited potential of Memorial Stadium on 33rd Street in a residential neighborhood, two miles north of downtown.

The park was shaped in a horseshoe and designed for both football and baseball. It was poorly designed, like a chunk of steel and concrete that had been dropped into a large vacant lot in the middle of a suburb. There was no parking. The pillars supporting the upper deck blocked the views of the pricier seats that sat below it. There were no box seats. Rosenbloom battled back, raging about new luxury stadiums in other markets and soon-to-be NFL markets like Tampa, which created an unfair competitive advantage.

The Baltimore press, specifically John Steadman of the *Record-American*, fired salvos almost daily, and won the war of attrition and public opinion. Remember, it is difficult to win a fight against someone who buys his ink in barrels, and Rosenbloom didn't stand a chance. He sought relief from NFL Commissioner Pete Rozelle, as well as other owners, but none came. In fact, some owners—whose teams had been soundly whipped by the mighty Colts in years past—reveled in Rosenbloom's frustration.

But when the owner of the Rams grew ill and the Los Angeles franchise and market became available for $7 million, Rosenbloom leapt at the opportunity. He concocted perhaps the most amazing scheme in professional football history, one in which he would put the Rams in his pocket for virtually zero money: He would swap the Colts for the Rams, even-up. All he needed was someone to buy the Colts and make such a deal.

Enter Robert Irsay, who had been introduced to Rosenbloom by Joe Thomas, a personnel guy who had been fired by the Miami Dolphins. Thomas and Irsay crossed paths after Irsay's boundless ego led him to actually inquire if George Halas, the founder of the Chicago Bears, would be interested in selling the NFL's most prestigious franchise. Rumor has it that Halas told Irsay to go to hell. Thomas, no fool himself, stayed in touch, and when Irsay sold his company and was flush with cash, Thomas put him in contact with Rosenbloom.

The sting was on.

Incredibly, Irsay wrote a $19 million check for the Rams—the highest price ever paid for an NFL team.* Then Irsay, acting on prearranged contracts with Rosenbloom,

---

* *Sports Illustrated*, Dec. 15, 1986

swapped franchises without a penny changing hands. As he was laughing all the way to the bank, Rosenbloom disclosed after the sale that during his entire tenure as Colts owner, he had never spent more than $1.2 million total. He had pulled the ultimate sleight-of-hand over some of the slickest businessmen in the world.

Baltimore wasn't so lucky. The Colts got the double-whammy: first, Irsay as an owner; second, Joe Thomas as a GM, who came along with his new boss for orchestrating this magnanimous deal. The NFL had not just allowed a rogue owner in its midst, but now had a bid-rigging, price-fixing, scotch-slugging poker player on its hands; one who had no loyalty to or respect for his own heritage and family, much less his new business partners, players, coaches, or NFL peers.

Irsay was now the proud owner of perhaps the NFL's most storied franchise. The famed Unitas, whom Irsay had claimed to "worship" as a kid, was benched by Thomas, and then shipped unceremoniously to San Diego within six months of meeting the famed heating-and-air-conditioning aficionado.

"When Irsay introduced himself to the team, he came in sloshed," said fullback Tom Matte. "He stared at his shoes. He was an hour late. He buried his hands in his pants pockets. He said, and I quote, 'I'm the new owner. I was in the Marines. And I'm married to a nice Polack. . . . ' I looked over at Unitas, and we both started laughing. I was thinking, 'How in the hell could this guy make $19 million if he can't even look me in the eyes?'"*

He never could. He and Thomas told Unitas—the greatest quarterback in history—that he had been traded over the phone.

The great Tom Matte fared even worse. On injured reserve with torn knee cartilage and bleeding ulcers, Matte was told to quit on his own, that he wouldn't be cut. Quitting meant Irsay wouldn't have to pay him. So they activated Matte—Super Bowl hero, pride of Baltimore, an eleven-year veteran—and made him cover kickoffs on special teams until he could play no more.

Injury-riddled, Matte was forced to walk away.

If these men could destroy the careers of living legends, publicly, callously, and financially dismantle an entire franchise, and thumb their nose at the league commissioner himself, what chance did introverted Curtis Dickey—all of twenty-two years old, fatherless, and docile as a kitten—have against them? None!

Except Curtis had an ace in the hole: me.

---

* *Sports Illustrated*, Dec. 15, 1986

22

I'M NOT DEAR ABBY

I AM NOT DEAR Abby. My opinions are not advice directed toward only less fortunate people and how they deal with misfortunes. My hope has always been that better policies—by the NCAA and the NFL—would reduce the misfortunes.

Curtis Dickey exemplified all that was wrong with the system, then and now. If it's true that childhood is the father to the man, it would explain why Dickey could endure all outward indications of disadvantage but still have the key inner ingredients to advance against ridiculous odds. It might also explain why he was so damn fast, because the kid had to outrun disaster from the moment he could walk.

While the environment in which Dickey was raised was deficient in many things measured by sociologists as "necessary" for advancement, it also provided some keys to his character. Curtis was born and raised in the tiny, predominantly white town of Bryan, Texas, where more than one-fourth of its 50,000 residents—especially the Dickeys— were below the poverty line. His mother worked to support the family, and his father was frequently ill . . . and often absent.

Curtis was introverted, shy, and suffered from a speech impediment. Ridicule from other kids made him all the more quiet. But wow, could he run. Merrill Green, his high school coach, remembers mistaking his shyness for indifference, until he was handed the football. "The first time he gained 300 yards in one game that went away. He stuttered, and that was misleading. Curtis didn't run, he flowed. He was grace and grit, and he could do everything, and I mean everything. And while he loved football, he hated the attention. He had no idea how great he really was. It took Curtis only two days to make varsity."

Two days? "First day was picture day," Green said.

College recruiters beat a path to his door. White men in pressed khaki pants, shiny shoes, and coaching shirts bearing the many colors of every glamorous university in America descended on little Bryan, Texas. They waited on his front porch. They visited his high school. They called his coaches. Dickey was told about wealthy alumni who couldn't wait to meet him; about bouncy and buxom coeds eager to show him campuses; and told that head coaches would "change their offense" to accommodate his unique and rare talent. Curtis didn't know who or what to believe, or what to make of the offers being waved in his face, so he chose not to believe any of them.

There might have been better college opportunities for him, but we'll never know. He so shunned the outside world that he just preferred to stay as close to home as possible. So, he turned down visits to places like USC, even Oklahoma, and went down the street—less than five miles from his mother's front door—and enrolled at Texas A&M, where 26,000 of the school's 31,000 students bought season tickets. Even still, roughly only about 100 of those kids were, like him, African American, and Curtis further immersed himself in his studies and sports to hide from public glare.

He joined the track team, but winning NCAA sprint titles—he ran 60 yards in 6.15 seconds—didn't help his anonymity. Hiding behind his offensive line, he rushed for 3,658 yards to become the second-best rusher in Southwest Conference history, behind Earl Campbell. Aggie head coach Tom Wilson actually ditched Texas A&M's wishbone attack in favor of the I-formation, and Dickey responded with explosive elusiveness, simply gliding and sliding through opposing defenses. "He just . . . moves," said Wilson. "Nobody gets a clean shot. Every time he runs, he's one missed tackle away from a touchdown."

Gil Brandt of the Dallas Cowboys had Dickey higher on the draft board than Billy Sims, and cautioned coaches that even though Curtis was quiet, he was anything but dumb. In fact, by the NFL draft his senior year, he lacked only three hours toward his degree in physical education. "I think he should be the first back taken, ahead of Sims," Brandt said. "It's hard to find a back as big and strong as Curtis. He's 6-1, 213 pounds. He's a sprinter packed into a football player's body."

No kidding. In the NCAA outdoor track finals, Curtis ran the 100 meters in onetenth of a second off gold-medal time. He never ran a full track season, instead reporting for spring football. One spring weekend, he rushed for more than 100 yards in a full scrimmage on a Friday, then went out on Saturday and promptly won the 100-meter dash in the Texas Relays.

Curtis found shelter in the college football system, namely in the form of towering 6-3, 255-pound defensive end and team captain Jacob Green, his roommate at Texas A&M. Both men were put on my radar screen by Gene, who explained that Curtis—in

addition to being shy—had signed with Mike Trope. Green, while leaning that direction, had yet to pick an agent, but after setting the Aggie single-season record his senior
year with twenty sacks, was being chased furiously by every guy with a business card.

Fortunately, College Station was a quick jaunt from Houston, and Gene made
many trips. As was my stance, I never talked to the players while they still had eligibility,
but Gene kept me current. "They won't open the door to talk to me. I have to catch
them after practice, or wait until they come out. Curtis is very, very shy, but Jacob is willing to listen. If we get Jacob, we'll get Curtis, too."

Jacob, like Curtis, was very smart, but his personality was the opposite—gregarious,
outgoing, effervescent. After the season, they both came together to see me in Houston.
Jacob was from Pasadena, Texas, just fourteen miles outside of Houston, which was important to his mom and dad. Jacob and his family had great common sense, and he really
liked me, Gene, and our way of conducting business. Curtis watched his every move, and
they both signed with us on the same day.

I took Curtis to the bank and co-signed a note for him, and he repaid his debts. We
then set up a budget for Curtis and taught him how to write a check and balance a
checkbook.

Green was the tenth player drafted, taken by Seattle, and we did quick business
with the savvy Seahawks, who made him one of the highest-paid defensive ends in football. Curtis, however, had been dropped into the teeth of the Colts and Irsay.

I couldn't wait.

By the time Dickey was drafted, Irsay had been at the helm of the Colts for eight
years, hiring and firing so often that players, coaches, and administration never knew
from one day to the next if they were employed. His young son, Jimmy—today the
owner of the Indianapolis Colts—would repeatedly go behind him and apologize for
his father's actions. Things were so bad that it was public knowledge that if you didn't
speak to Irsay before he started having his noon cocktails, he wouldn't even remember
talking to you. Irsay had publicly humiliated and fired crony Thomas, replacing him
with Dick Szymanski. Dick had enjoyed a gritty thirteen-year career as first a linebacker,
then a center for Johnny Unitas and the Colts. He was a three-time All-Pro, and played
on three championship teams and ended his career after the 1969 Super Bowl.

Szymanski was a Polish American who had played four years at Notre Dame.
Though he never earned a degree, he had served the Colts as a scout and personnel director before becoming general manager. Irsay had then promoted long-time public relations director Ernie Accorsi to assistant GM. Szymanski was a great guy, no doubt
about it. Unlike his boss, he really had served in the Army, where he battled with the
Special Services in Germany. But Irsay treated him like he did everyone else: as a mind-
less, spineless puppet. During this era, Peter Hadhazy, who would later work with me in

the United States Football League, was the Browns general manager in Cleveland. He told me about one particular postgame conversation with Irsay, which they had in their native Hungarian.

"We had just beaten the Colts," recalled Hadhazy, "and Irsay, Dick, Ernie, and I were having some drinks after the game. With Ernie and Dick sitting in front of us talking, Irsay told me in Hungarian, 'Dick Syzmanski is a piece of shit. Ernie Accorsi is a good guy. I've got one idiot working for me, and one good guy.'"

The team counsel was Mike Chernoff, Irsay's Chicago attorney, and the only guy representing the franchise who actually finished school. "When Thomas left, there was no buffer between the team and Irsay," said safety Bruce Laird, who would later flee the Colts for the USFL. "Everybody liked Dick, but nobody respected him. He had no authority. Suddenly everything had to go through Irsay and Chernoff. Money became nonexistent, and everything they touched turned to manure. I came into lift weights once and the Jacuzzi was turned off. I told the trainer to turn it on. He said, 'I can't. The boss says we're spending too much money on electricity.'"

Tom Matte recalls when linebacker Ted Hendricks had literally picked up the diminutive Thomas and physically carried him out of the locker room. "You don't belong here," Hendricks told him, then stepped back inside and locked the door. "Chernoff knew better than to go in the locker room," said Laird, "because he would've been treated worse."

The new head coach was Mike McCormack, who must have been praying Curtis Dickey would provide the theater necessary to draw fans, calm nerves, and win enough games to pacify Irsay.

No chance.

23

IF YOU CAN'T BEAT 'EM, BRIBE 'EM

AS EVERYONE HAD predicted, talks with Szymanski went nowhere. They weren't hostile or confrontational (like Russ Thomas), they just went nowhere. We had a number, they had a number, and nobody was budging. Like the Lions, they offered a bare-bones contract, and we simply said "no thanks." This went on for months, and it became obvious Dick was powerless. After the Colts had played two preseason games, I made a statement to the press; admittedly, I was too tough on Dick. "Syzmanski has an IQ of nine," I said, "and if the owner would just get involved, we could have Curtis Dickey's contract worked out the next day."

Sure enough, they took the bait. The very next day, I got a phone call from none other than Irsay himself. "Argovitz," he rasped, "this is Bob Irsay, owner of the Baltimore Colts. You wanted to talk to the owner and said we could get this thing worked out in a single day, so here I am. How much are you getting paid to negotiate this kid's deal?" This question made me suspicious, and I flipped a switch to record the conversation.

"Six percent—my standard rate for every contract," I answered.

He paused, lowering his voice. "I will give you 6 percent," he said.

"I don't understand," I said. "What do you mean?"

Irritated, he retorted, "I will pay you 6 percent. And the player will pay you 6 percent. That's 12 percent."

"I can add, sir, but why are you paying me 6 percent?" I asked, incredulous.

"For signing the contract," Irsay replied.

126

"Are we referring to the contract I've proposed for Curtis Dickey?" I said. "You don't have to pay me 6 percent for that."

"Hell no," he roared. "I'm referring to the contract I originally offered."

"So, let me get this straight," I said, "if I sign Curtis, my client, to the contract presented to us by your GM, which we have turned down, you'll pay me an additional 6 percent, on top of what the player is paying me?"

"You got it, Argovitz," Irsay said. "And that's between you and me."

"You sonuvabitch!" I yelled. "You call me, and you try to bribe me because you won't pay a player his fair salary? Who in the hell do you think you're talking to?"

Irsay retreated, and laughed out loud. "No, no, no," he backpedaled, "I was just trying to see what you would do."

"Mr. Irsay, you just offered me a bribe," I said. "I'm going to call Pete Rozelle and tell him what just occurred. You need to make Curtis Dickey an unrestricted free agent immediately."

Irsay slammed down the phone. I called the NFL and asked for Rozelle. Anybody can say what they want, but Rozelle was a slick businessman. Regardless of the situation, he could handle it with such ease and confidence that it made you feel important. If you weren't careful when dealing with him you wound up under his ether, which was part of the sneaky charm that made him great.

True to form, Pete immediately took my call.

"Pete, we have a situation here that needs to be addressed," I said. "Bob Irsay just offered me a bribe of 6 percent—under the table—to hand-deliver Curtis Dickey to the Colts. You need to do something about this, and I believe the only remedy is to make Curtis an unrestricted free agent, or we will have to bring this to the attention of the media."

"Jerry," Pete said, "don't do anything. I'll call you right back. Give me twenty minutes."

Twenty minutes later, my secretary buzzed me. "There's a Jay Moyer from the NFL on the line for you."

Jay Moyer? I picked up the line. "Jerry, this is Jay Moyer, special counsel to the National Football League. I just spoke to Mr. Rozelle, and he tells me there's a problem. Tell me what happened with Mr. Irsay."

I reiterated the entire discussion. "Mr. Moyer, I can prove this, verbatim. I have irrefutable proof. Now the only way to get this done is to make Curtis Dickey a free agent."

"Calm down, Jerry," he said. "Did you tape the conversation?"

I laughed. "Are you listening? I have irrefutable proof. You decide whether I taped it or not. But what else would be irrefutable proof? I can't deal with Baltimore after the owner offered me a bribe to screw my own client."

He hesitated, and I upped the ante. "If the league doesn't do something, I'll just hold a press conference in Baltimore and handle this myself."

"Jerry, don't do that," he replied. "I'll call you right back."

In no time, he was back on the line. "Jerry, Mike Chernoff, the attorney for the Colts, wants to meet you, wants you to bring Curtis with you, and they want to get this deal finished. Get your client and get up there, meet with Mike, and let's see if you can resolve this."

Curtis and I arrived in Baltimore, and I was dressed in all black, from my boots right up to my black cowboy hat. Whenever I was in tense negotiations, I wore my black cowboy hats. Whenever my guys were there to sign their deals, I wore a white hat. You could measure the current state of the negotiations by the color of the cowboy hat I was wearing. As we drove to the Colts' offices, I could almost hear Clint Eastwood whistling in the background for this showdown.

The team was practicing at its Owings Mills, Maryland, facility, and Curtis and I made our way down to the sidelines. McCormack and his staff seemed surprised, and relieved, to see us. Roughly twenty television, radio, and newspaper reporters were there, and they gathered around us. Curtis, of course, was in street clothes, so it was obvious to them the contract wasn't done.

The press began pounding him with questions, and Curtis shyly lowered his eyes and managed to stammer out a few words. "I . . . I . . . I look forward to, to playing for the, for the Colts," he said. Nervously, he glanced at me, and I stepped forward. "Listen, guys, we came here for one reason, and that's to get this contract resolved," I said. "Hopefully, we can. Curtis brought his bags here, and he's prepared to stay, but if the Colts don't budge, airplanes fly in both directions. We don't want to leave, but we're prepared to."

A team assistant whisked Curtis away to introduce him to staff and allow him to watch the rest of practice in privacy. I made my way up to the offices, and into a boardroom where Dick and Mike Chernoff were waiting. In Chernoff, I'd half expected a slick car salesman with a bad suit, but I was pleasantly surprised. He was dignified, well-groomed, and very much at ease. After informal introductions, we got down to brass tacks.

"Just curious," Chernoff said, "but what time did this alleged phone call take place?"

"Around two in the afternoon," I said. Chernoff smirked; it had clearly been after the unspoken "before noon" Irsay rule. In other words, the owner had probably been drunk when he called me.

"Can you tell me specifically about the conversation you had with Mr. Irsay?" Chernoff asked, scratching away on a legal pad. "Mr. Irsay says he never offered you a bribe, period."

"Not only can I tell you specifics," I said, reaching into my briefcase, "but I can prove it." I set the cassette tape on the table next to my notebook. "This is my property, and it's all right here on the tape."

"Can I borrow it?" Chernoff asked.

"Well, it's my property, but you can borrow it as long as you give it back," I answered. "But keep in mind, that's a duplicate. I have the original."

Chernoff grabbed the tape, and the men excused themselves. I sat alone in the room reading the paper until the door burst open and Chernoff reentered, alone.

"So, Jerry, let's cut the crap," he said. "What are your plans?"

"I'm here to finalize a deal for my client Curtis Dickey," I said. "That's why the commissioner told me to come here."

"Well, what if we don't? Then what?" he asked.

"Well, I intend to spend the rest of the day and night trying, but if we don't, then I'm calling a press conference right on the practice field," I said.

"What will you say?" Chernoff asked.

"I will tell them I was offered a bribe by your owner, and that the league office told me to come here, and that the Colts refused to negotiate in good faith."

"Let me make sure I understand," Chernoff said. "If the Colts don't meet your contractual demands now, you will play the tape at a press conference in the morning?"

"That's correct," I said.

"Let's break for lunch," Chernoff said, "and meet back here in about an hour."

An hour later, I returned. Chernoff walked in, handed me a brown envelope, promptly wheeled, and walked out. I was excited—I thought maybe they had come to their senses—and that we had a legitimate offer on our hands. I dumped the contents on the table, and instantly, my heart sank.

First, there was a cover letter from Chernoff on Colts' letterhead, stating that my actions and activities constituted an attempt to blackmail the team and its owner for refusing to meet my demands. This was followed by a stack of case law and other supporting documents in the State of Maryland regarding bribery, blackmail, and using illegal recordings for the purpose of illicit gains. None of it would hold up in court. But the veiled threat was clear, and Irsay was used to getting his way through intimidation tactics and brute force.

That night, Curtis and I had dinner together. Sitting in front of me, he looked like an absolute stallion, and my heart broke for him. As usual, he was polite, quiet, and reserved. Behind his soft eyes was a fatherless kid who had spent his entire young life fighting to hold his head above water, never knowing who or what to believe. He had supported his mother and lived up to her expectations. But now neither she nor Jacob Green was here to protect him and tell him it would be OK. Other than Aggie away games, Curtis had never been outside the state of Texas. Earlier in the day, I had seen the look in those same eyes at the Colts practice. They absolutely twinkled each time quarterback Bert Jones took a snap and handed the ball to another running back. He didn't understand why he couldn't play, right now. He squirmed, like Secretariat bucking in the starting gate.

"Doc, you're my m-m-m-man," he said softly. "But this is building in the p-p-papers. I just want, I want to g-g-get this over with. I want to, I want to play, Doc."

"Curtis," I said, "I understand. But we're at what's called a stalemate. Just get packed tonight and be ready to go home in the morning." Curtis took a deep breath, exhaled, and toyed with his food. His lifeblood was football, and at the moment, I felt like the Grinch who stole Christmas.

I put my hand on Curtis's shoulder. "We've got these cheap bastards between a rock and a hard place," I said, "and the price of poker is going up. I'm going to make them pay for putting you through all of this, I promise."

It was impossible to explain "your best interests" to a kid who only feels normal when he explodes past the line of scrimmage, through the secondary, and—wind in his face—into daylight, while 70,000 people stand and roar in unison. That is the only place where Curtis Dickey found freedom, and anything less left him empty, scared, and alone.

Sensing that his spirit was about to break, that night I left an urgent message for Chernoff: Meet me at nine the next morning. I needed four aces, and I was ready to deal. There was no way in hell the Colts wanted a long, protracted lawsuit, or to have the tapes released. Curtis might have to wait a few more days, but he'd be the benefactor of what I had up my sleeve.

Chernoff seemed surprised when I walked into his office the next day with Curtis at my side. "Morning, Jerry," he said, smirking. "Last time we spoke, you were going to have a press conference on the practice field this morning."

"What?" I asked. "I don't know what you're talking about. But Curtis and I are just here to say goodbye. We're going back to Texas."

"Do you want to continue talking?" he asked. I bit my lip, and shook my head. "Listen, Mike, Curtis has now missed three preseason games. The last contract I submitted is off the table. If you want to sign him, it's going to cost a little more for what we've been through."

"What about the tapes?" he asked.

I called his bluff. "When I get back to Texas, I'm taking the tapes and your package and turning it over to my attorneys," I said, "and we're going public with everything. You do what you have to do, and we're going to demand that Curtis become an unrestricted free agent."

"Give me a chance to get something to you," Chernoff said. "I don't think that's necessary."

I returned to Texas with a very sullen client. However, within a matter of days, the Colts tendered him an offer that would make him the second-highest paid player in the draft, behind a guy named Billy Sims. We had increased our demands by several hundred thousand dollars for our trouble. Irsay removed both Chernoff and Szymanski from the final negotiations, and placed Accorsi in charge to close out the deal.

Knowing the fragility of Curtis's psyche, I asked that Gene remain in Baltimore with him until he was settled, comfortable, and acclimated to his new teammates. Gene helped him find an apartment, buy furniture, and get an automobile. We set him up at the bank, vowed to take care of his mother, and then told Curtis to do what he does best: run like the wind, and never look back.

For the record, the NFL contract of Dickey was the first and last that required the team receive both audiotapes of unknown origin and content from the player's representative.

The Colts got the damn tapes, but let the record show: Curtis Dickey got paid fair-market value for his unique skills and abilities, in spite of all of the king's horses and all the king's men. There is no fairness in greed. You defeat a greedy person by having something he really wants and not giving it to him. If you're a partner with a greedy person, you usually end up in a lawsuit, or in football, another holdout. If one person consistently and constantly wants more, but offers less and less, you're in perpetual trouble.

For once, I wasn't the Jew bastard—that honor had to go to Mr. Israel. I was a long, long way from being finished with Bob Irsay, or his ilk, and before it was over, it might have cost him a Super Bowl.

24

"DOES ANYBODY IN THIS LEAGUE TELL THE TRUTH?"

JOE STEINER CRIBBS grew up in Sulligent, Alabama, home to 2,151 people and Mr. Gene's All-American barbecue on Highway 278, where you can find ribs stickier than the Deep South humidity. Just around the corner on Elm Street, "Little Joe" was a legend at Sulligent High, where he was a two-time Parade All-American and the reason long lines of car headlights snaked for miles to get a bleacher seat at the football field on Friday nights.

Historically, Sulligent's primary export was cotton, and mostly black folks did the picking, while mostly white folks employed them. On Friday nights, however, color and creed took a backseat to the ritual of high school football and the thrill of watching Little Joe outrace the opposition to the collective gasps of the crowd. Even as a prep star, Cribbs' signature stutter-steps, limp-legs, and stiff-arms worked as equalizers against aggressive defenders and made him a fan favorite.

He was the kind of hero that only a small town with a single stoplight can produce, the local boy who plays his ass off on Friday, works all day on Saturday, and then shows up with his mom and grandma, a couple of aunts and two older brothers at the Baptist church on Sunday, where he sang with the same passion with which he played. His brothers played the role of his missing father, but Joe didn't need discipline. Something deep inside him burned to be the best, and he had no time for the foolishness of youth. In all the years I've known him, I've never heard him cuss.

"God has given me a gift, and my faith enables me to do some great things," he told the locals, which made them beam with pride. "I will never allow myself to be in a situation that reflects negatively on God, my family, or my teammates." Little Joe, at 5 feet 9 inches and 190 pounds, represented the people, their integrity, and their work ethic, three things that—along with his staggering statistics—caught the eye of the football coaches at Auburn University, who frankly didn't care if he was Christian, Jewish, or Muslim. All they knew was every time they looked at film, Joe ran over, around, or through a different color jersey.

"He plays like it's a sin to lose," exclaimed Tiger head coach Pat Dye, "and that's fine with us."

From 1976 to 1979, Little Joe gained 3,368 rushing yards and 4,561 all-purpose yards and scored 34 touchdowns. He set numerous Auburn records, including his seven 100-yard games in 1978, which shot him up the draft charts. Combined with James Brooks, the two backs became the only tandem in Southeastern Conference history to both rush for 1,000 yards in a season.

On weekends, he'd return to steamy Sulligent, where he'd help his mother and grandmother, attend church, and visit family friends. When he was spotted in town, the local coffee shops and gas stations buzzed to life with energy, and the Little Joe stories just got bigger and better. There was the time when he was a sixth-grader and almost never became a running back because he exceeded the weight limit, and they moved him to offensive line. And then the time he broke his nose during his first practice with the Sulligent varsity, but refused to quit. Or the time opposing teams would send in reserve players to beat him up, but Little Joe would prevail like a comic-book hero.

Gene adored Joe; the two shared great rapport. As soon as Cribbs was eligible for the 1980 draft, we flew him to Houston. To be from a town as small as Sulligent, it was surprising to see how mentally, physically, and emotionally ready Joe was for the NFL. Like all our other prospects, he was wide-eyed to see our cathedral offices and glass walls. But he didn't say a word. He just observed, like a gunfighter counting paces.

Joe scrutinized every document we showed him, and he listened intently. He made it clear that he was already thinking about life after pro football, before pro football. We talked at length before he finally mustered the nerve to tell me what he was really thinking. "Doc, you've got a lot of stuff, and you wear a lot of jewelry, but none of that impresses me," he said. I loved the kid's moxie.

"What I'm impressed with is that I believe you are the right man to help me long-term, but short-term, to help my mom, and to help me build her a house. That's all I really care about. All this other stuff . . . " he pointed around my office at real-estate blueprints and architectural plans " . . . just convinces me you're on top of everything. I trust you. But the most important thing to me is I made a promise to myself that football would change my mom's life, and I mean it."

Joe realized he couldn't play football forever. "Doc," he said, "I appreciate that it's your goal to make me a businessman, too. I've never had anyone in my life that had the knowledge or success to help me."

"Well, let's get to the bank, and you can borrow some money to make some money," I said.

Over dinner, he told me he'd never owned a watch. The next day, we took him to a friend who owned a jewelry store, and Joe bought himself a watch at a discounted price that I—of course—negotiated. We didn't play favorites. He got the same treatment as the rest of the Argovitz family: first class.

The Washington Redskins had spent almost as much time on the Auburn campus as Joe, and had us all convinced they would take him with the eighteenth pick of the first round. When they chose future Hall-of-Famer Art Monk, Joe was devastated; little by little, the first round slipped away. Five other backs went ahead of him, and two of them were ours; after Sims and Dickey, Earl Cooper, Vegas Ferguson, and Charles White were taken.

"Doc, I've lost faith in these guys," he said. "Does anybody in this league tell the truth?"

Obviously, I was the wrong guy to ask.

The good news came with the first pick of the second round, when Joe was taken by the Bills with the twenty-ninth pick. The blue-collar fans of Buffalo were thrilled to get their blue-collar, every-down running back from Auburn. When we arrived in upstate New York, the airport was packed with cheering fans. Joe was surprised—and thrilled—at the sincerity and overwhelming warmth of the Bills rabid supporters. "I feel like I'm back at Auburn, Doc!" he grinned.

Negotiations with GM Stew Barber went briskly, though after Russ Thomas, anything was a relief. "We are enthusiastic to get Joe!" Barber exclaimed when he met us. "In fact we had him rated much higher, and we couldn't believe he was still available in the second round!"

Barber had been a five-time NFL all-star as an offensive tackle for the Bills; odd, because it seemed every team—the Lions, Colts, and now the Bills—incorporated former linemen as general managers. I could only assume because they're used to blocking and protecting, which is how owners wanted their affairs handled.

In this case, Barber was still stinging over the loss of Tom Cousineau to Canada the year before, so he was treading lightly with Joe. "Jerry, we've been following your negotiations with Russ Thomas and Bob Irsay in the media, and if possible, we'd like to keep our negotiations out of the press," he said.

I agreed. "Stew, treat us fairly, don't attack my player, and we'll get this done in a hiccup." Joe signed for more money than any second-round pick in NFL history, and more than most of that year's first-round picks. Barber, like Thomas, agreed that if Joe out-performed his contract, the team would be willing to sit down and discuss new terms, as well as an extension during his option, or fourth, season.

As with our other clients, Joe got career-ending-injury insurance, and an array of performance bonuses. "Doc, give me a year, and I'll be the best running back in the league," Joe said. "My goal is to prove that I should've been a first-round draft pick. I will make every team that passed on me regret the day they did."

We believed him. Still, Gene and I had some unfinished business to do, back in Sulligent, Alabama: Build his mom a house. "Little Joe," I chuckled, "you know we've got a little experience with real estate. I think we can handle this."

Joe was surprised to see Gene show up in Alabama. I worked the phones from my Houston office to find and buy the right property as well as direct the right contractors to build a home for Joe's mom. Gene quarterbacked the show, and he and Little Joe drove all over Sulligent until they found the right plot of land and broke ground. "Doc, you have no idea how happy my mother is!" Joe said. "She will never forget this. To know that your big sports agency in downtown Houston cares this much about me and my mother down here in Sulligent . . . this is unbelievable."

Joe's faith was unshakable, and you couldn't help but admire him as a son, a man, and everything he stood for. "Heaven ain't a place to learn, Doc," he said. "It's a place to become. Character produces destiny, and the purpose of life is growth of character. I see God in my world every day, and I trust Him to deliver."

The feeling was mutual. We trusted Little Joe to deliver, and he wasted no time. Almost overnight, he unseated Terry Miller and Curtis Brown, the Bills' starting featured running backs. In the season's first game against the Dolphins, he rushed for 60 yards, caught passes for another 71, and dove in from two yards out on a gutsy fourth-down call to seal the game 17-7.

The win snapped a twenty-game, ten-year losing streak to Miami. Joe led Buffalo to a 5-0 start, scoring in each game, and he would finish with 1,182 yards, and eleven touchdowns on the ground. His fifty-two receptions netted another 415 yards, and—true to his word—he was named AFC Rookie of the Year and was the only rookie to start the Pro Bowl.

Of course, I called Stew Barber. "Maybe we should talk about that new contract now," I suggested. "Joe did exactly as he promised."

"Jerry, I'm not sure what you're talking about, but let's discuss this after next season," he said.

That was ominous. I hung up, scratching my head.

Joe had said it best on draft day. "Does anybody in this league tell the truth?"

25

OPEN WOUNDS

AFTER OUR FIRST full "season" in the National Football League, Gene and I had made quite a splash. All seven of our players had been drafted; four in the first round, and three in the second. In addition to Billy, Jacob, Curtis, and Joe, things had gone smoothly with George Cumby in Green Bay, Cleveland Crosby in Cleveland, and Perry Harrington in Philadelphia. Every single one of our clients had received substantial compensation that exceeded the previous slotting system the NFL had used effectively to artificially control the money paid to their draft picks. I created a special bond with these players that will last a lifetime.

Sims was the NFL and NFC Most Valuable Player. Little Joe took the AFC honors. Dickey led the Colts in rushing. Green started thirteen games in Seattle and had six and a half sacks. Cumby became a starter for the Packers. Harrington, expected to start in Philadelphia, suffered serious injuries and missed most of the year, and Crosby had nagging injuries throughout the year.

Of our players, all but one had been raised at poverty level. It felt good to be in a position to right so many wrongs, and to help heal and assist so many families, whether via housing, financial planning, or life coaching. Laugh if you must, but each of our guys walked away with a copy of *Think and Grow Rich*, and some of them actually read it and applied it.

We had gained national notoriety among college prospects, in spite of how negatively I'd been portrayed as the "Houston dentist moonlighting as an agent." For the record, I was effective, and all my players were happy and satisfied with their contracts

136

and our continued presence in their everyday lives. I spoke to each player at least once a week. I would travel to see each player in a game. I didn't do it for the money—I did it for these young men who had placed their trust and confidence in me.

Still, we had walked into a maelstrom. For one, we were no longer under the radar, and we'd infuriated other agents who vowed revenge. Also, Gene and I were being told directly from our league sources that a work stoppage and player's strike was brewing when the collective bargaining agreement was to expire in 1982. The owners and general managers were really vocal and upset by having allowed a dentist to come in and totally annihilate their salary structures. My friends Peter Hadhazy and Carl Peterson, a former assistant to the Eagles, both told me I had brought a new level of sophistication to the negotiating table, because a lot of the general managers and agents never based negotiations on present-day value.

I was also told to watch out for Irsay, Thomas, and Barber—they each had a vendetta against me, and we had open wounds in Baltimore, Detroit, and incredibly, now Buffalo.

While my professional life had its share of "challenges," my twenty-two-year marriage had collapsed. Clearly, things were about to get a little sporty, and we would be at the vortex of the storm. Meanwhile, I'd received an odd phone call from a New Orleans entrepreneur named David Dixon. He had left a message about discussing an idea for the development of a professional spring football league.

Could be interesting, I thought.

I made it a point to call him back.

ACT FOUR

In war, truth is the first casualty.

—Aeschylus

26

DECLARING WAR ON
THE NFL CARTEL

YOU DON'T JUST wake up in the morning and poke a stick in the eye of the NFL. But what was occurring in 1980—still as relevant today as it was then—didn't require a Rhodes Scholar to realize the NFL was not only violating the Sherman Antitrust Act and its own exemptions, it was dancing all over case law with a top hat and a cane. The whole purpose of the Sherman Antitrust Act was to limit cartels and monopolies and to prevent restraint of trade. Everywhere you looked in the NFL, it was an immoral Never Never Land.

A cartel is defined as "a collusive association of independent enterprises formed to monopolize production and distribution of a product or service, control prices, and eliminate competition." It took me less than a single NFL season of work to realize the suffocating power of Pete Rozelle's cartel. The NFL boldly marched forth like a superhero behind its obnoxious and intimidating big red, white, and blue shield and simply controlled production of football. That control included its distribution via television and radio, the sale of all merchandise, fixed labor prices, and prohibited player movement. Collectively, it held down costs and would stop at nothing to not only eliminate competition, but also kill it.

Section One of the Sherman Antitrust Act states that "every contract, combination in the form of trust or otherwise, or conspiracy, in restraint of trade or commerce . . . is hereby declared to be illegal." Notwithstanding that the antitrust laws have been used to favor particular competitors rather than the competitive process, the act implies that the federal government stands for open markets.

Without a doubt, the NFL was specifically price fixing, defined as an agreement between competitors (teams) selling the same product such as tickets and merchandise. Arguably, bid-rigging, too; NFL teams through the illegal draft were not only winning bids, but also slotting and fixing salaries to restrain trade and control spending. Furthermore, each team had a prearranged agreement not to sign other teams' free agents. The league in turn negotiated blanket television agreements and divided the wealth evenly among its members.

Through 1980 only three leagues had challenged the NFL. Three teams from the All-America Conference—the Browns, the Colts, and the 49ers—were absorbed by the NFL in 1950; twenty years later, ten teams from the American Football League merged with the NFL. The poorly formed and woefully underfunded World Football League took a shot in 1974, but drunkenly staggered through almost two seasons before falling face down and flat broke.

Obviously, many NFL teams could make more money if it broke rank and sold its product(s) at lower prices or even competing prices. But Rozelle's sorcery over the television networks' pot of gold made it crystal clear: Mess with the wizard, and you don't get the pixie dust. Many of the team owners had been hustlers since they had baby teeth, but they were smart enough to hedge their bets; acting in collusion rather than acting alone, they eliminated risk. By 1980 Rozelle had turned the National Football League into a public entertainment "drug" that allowed owners to profit without a single ticket being sold.

This wasn't about free enterprise, fair market value, or sport at all.

Plain and simple, this was about greed.

As with any good cartel, once you control the product, the prices, the markets—supply and demand—then you have to control the labor. This had been a hot topic dating back to June 18, 1921, when the NFL ratified its first constitution. The reserve clause in the constitution was similar to that of Major League Baseball at the time, which stipulated that a team had the first opportunity to sign a player after the length of the contract had expired. If the team chose not to offer a contract, then the player could try to sign with a team of his choosing.

Former NFL commissioner Bert Bell had instituted the NFL draft in 1935 as a means to restrain payrolls and reduce the dominance of the league's perennial contenders. Without consent of the players, the draft was illegal under antitrust law, because it restricted—then and now—free enterprise and competition, while encouraging collusion among owners to hold down costs.

Worse, theoretically, once a player was drafted, it bound the player " . . . to his employer in perpetuity." The "option clause" replaced the reserve clause when it was abolished in the NFL constitution in 1948. The option clause stated that a team may choose to automatically keep a player on its team for another year, at the same pay, after his contract had expired. The term "option clause" was not used by the print media, and was instead referred to as the reserve clause. Nevertheless, in the NFL's attempt to gain antitrust exemption from Congress in 1957, then-commissioner Bell still referred to the clause as the option clause.

This is where it gets particularly messy and confusing. When Rozelle came to power in January 1960, he left no stone unturned. He created the "Rozelle Rule," though he preferred to call it the "player compensation rule." This allowed the commissioner—at his own discretion—to "compensate" any team who lost a free agent to another team by taking something of equivalent value, usually draft picks, from the team that had signed the free agent and giving it to the team the player had left. This eradicated free agency, because teams feared the loss of several future high draft picks—at Rozelle's whim; nobody wanted to sign a veteran player only to learn that it would lose, for example, its next two first-round picks.

The owners had a gentleman's agreement that they would not sign another team's free agents, because "if you sign mine, I'm signing yours."

Absolute power corrupts absolutely, and Rozelle absolutely had it all, but he had to convince the player's association, or NFLPA, which didn't want Rozelle himself to be the arbitrator of his own rule. Go figure. Owners had either battled, or patronized, the NFLPA since its founding in 1956, and the union had struggled to unite and defend its rights. Rozelle himself hated public controversy, but masterfully controlled the strings behind Joe Browne, his executive vice president. Players were like puppies; they would test the fence, owners would reprimand them, then concede on smaller, nonimportant issues. The confrontation would dissolve, and the players would go home with their collective tails between their legs and lick their wounds while gaining no real traction and wondering what in the hell just happened.

Nice guy or not, Rozelle was the Pablo Escobar of football. If he figuratively ordered you dead, you were dead the same day, regardless which member of his staff—including a brilliant young attorney named Paul Tagliabue—would carry out the execution.

"It's my job," said Rozelle, "to keep league issues from becoming public issues, for anything that distracts us from the purely athletic aspects of our sport is bad for us."

No kidding. That clearly veiled threat from the glib commissioner demonstrated his brilliance at protecting his cartel. Anything bad for him was good for the players, and vice-versa. He was a mastermind at keeping salaries low, preventing free agency, and maintaining league parity. Furthermore, there was no way the league or the owners would ever reveal their books and share the real wealth with the players creating it. Sound familiar?

This tennis match went on until Ed Garvey entered the fray. Garvey had graduated from the University of Wisconsin, spent a couple of years in the Army, and then earned his law degree. He joined a Minneapolis law firm that worked for the NFL's player union, and was assigned to work with union president and former Colts tight end John Mackey regarding negotiations over a new four-year contract with the league's owners. As months went by, Garvey slid into the driver's seat of the union as its executive director.

In 1974 the NFL was on the ropes. It was clearly in violation of antitrust. Without a collective bargaining agreement, the draft and Rozelle's compensation rules were illegal. With the Mackey suit pending, players—declaring "no freedom, no football"—held out of training camp over the outstanding issues. Meanwhile, the young, militant Garvey used heated rhetoric to explain his unreasonable list of nearly 100 player demands, including total free agency, elimination of the Rozelle Rule, and the right for veteran players to veto any trade.

With teeth bared, the NFL viciously responded. First, its teams stopped collecting dues for the NFLPA. To that point, players could merely "check-off" on their payroll slips that they wanted their union fees deducted automatically. Without the deductions, union dues plummeted. Then the NFL teams offered players raises if they crossed picket lines and went to camp, and players returned in droves. Weakened, Garvey sent his union back to work with no contract and turned his focus to the Mackey trial. The question was if the union is supposed to be protecting the players from management, who was protecting the players from their own union?

Garvey, overmatched and incapable of sparring with a veteran like Rozelle, directed the NFLPA back to court and into battles that led, in 1975, to the ruling in *Mackey vs. NFL* that antitrust laws applied to the NFL's restrictions on player movement. In other words, he had a chance to win free agency for the players. In 1976, now armed with leverage regarding player movement from team to team, Garvey and the union claimed to win major concessions from the owners.

In my book, that's not what happened. The real ramifications would last another thirty years.

In my opinion, Garvey had pulled a naked bootleg, a reverse-psychology smokescreen to protect his own interests and his position with the union. Garvey claimed that his negotiations had "successfully" exchanged the players' threat of pursuing a system of unfettered free agency for an improved package of player benefits. Are you kidding me? Garvey gave back the draft, gave back the Rozelle Rule in exchange for the check-off system. He gave back free agency, the lynchpin of the NFLPA's case! Hiding behind fancy-sounding line items like minimum-base salaries and a so-called viable pension plan and medical benefits.

I had been incredulous as an observer and a fan, but now, as an agent battling on behalf of a half-dozen marquee players already in the league and facing another draft of my players in 1981, I was incensed. The union's own leadership had agreed to allow the NFL to continue its cartel as business practices in a closed system that grossly favored the owners and stripped the players of all their rights. In my opinion, Garvey couldn't have done worse had he sold the players into outright slavery.

What became of Garvey's list? The owners rejected nearly every single one. He harped about "victories" like the NFLPA becoming recognized by the owners as a full-fledged National Labor Relations Board union and damages totaling $13.65 million that were awarded to past and present players for antitrust violations against them. Big deal. That was a fraction of the league's annual income, and that small judgment would cost hundreds, if not thousands, of players much of their livelihoods over the next fifteen years.

The Rozelle Rule was struck down in 1976, but with no help from Garvey. Wide receiver Ron Jessie had played out his contract with Detroit, and Carroll Rosenbloom of the Rams immediately signed him. Rozelle awarded the Lions a first-round draft pick, plus Cullen Bryant, a valuable Rams running back. The Rams filed a temporary restraining order, and a judge in Minneapolis killed the deal. Free agency reverted back to collective bargaining and wouldn't be tested again for many more years.

Of course, Rozelle took the high road. "Rather than just saying I'm hired by the owners and I'm subservient to them," he said, "you have to look at whether the players are getting a fair shake." Really? Was Rozelle seriously trying to run that flag up the pole? During the Mackey trial, Cleveland owner Art Modell had testified the opposite. "We pay Mr. Rozelle to be neutral," he stated, under oath and directly from the witness stand.

Right. And John Gotti was an honest plumber, a philanthropist, and just a regular Joe.

The bottom line is that if your path crossed the NFL, all roads—college and pro—led through Pete Rozelle. This explains the sweetheart deal between the NFL and the NCAA, which further infuriated me. Who made the rule that underclassmen couldn't be drafted, and why? Who decides that a grown man can't get a job at his chosen profession whenever he chooses if his talent merits the opportunity? When I looked at the NCAA, I saw a tax-exempt organization also operating as a monopoly, with a rulebook denser than the New Testament. Meanwhile, the NFL enjoys fruits of a minor league feeder system without having to pay for one, like baseball or hockey.

The support of college football coaches for the NFL policy was not shocking. College coaches depend on these athletes for their own success, in spite of the fact that some of them may be good enough to play professionally before their graduation or the end of their collegiate eligibility. League restrictions on young players punished the kids but greatly benefitted both the NFL and NCAA. Let's face it: These restrictions provide colleges with exclusive control of pre-professional talent for a four-year period and insulate the college programs from competition for cheap labor.

My friend and famed antitrust attorney Jerry Tockman in St. Louis spent hours guiding me through the labyrinth of case studies and loop holes that made the NFL a slicker operation than the New York mafia. Trying to navigate one's way through Pete Rozelle's house of mirrors was like following Alice in Wonderland down the rabbit hole. I wondered aloud how the NFL was still operating.

"The NFL's practices," Tockman readily agreed, "totally violate the Sherman Act's proscription against restraints of trade. And the policy against drafting underclassmen imposes unjustifiable hardships on college athletes and is also legally insupportable. It constitutes a conspiracy by all employers in this industry to bar from gainful employment a group that is ready, willing and able to work."

To me, it was unconstitutional. Who takes care of the kids that have career-ending injuries?

"Well, we need to fight," I told him in 1981. "I've got another class of kids about to be drafted. I've got at least three—Billy Sims, Curtis Dickey and Joe Cribbs—who I believe are about to be screwed by the people who signed them. NFL management is already manipulating the draft and system in Canada to stop the flow of players going north. Somebody has to do something, Jerry, and I think that somebody is me."

Tockman looked at me like I was Evel Knievel and I had just announced my plans to jump the fountains at Caesar's Palace. "Doc," he said, "you're not a big agency, and you're not a conglomerate. You're just one man. You are also asking questions that can get you silenced. *If* you fight, it will be the fight of your life, and the NFL will seek to first blackball you, then destroy you."

"I could not care less how 'little' we may seem to the big, bad NFL," I said. "I simply refuse to back down and turn my back on my own players, and the rest of the players as well. What they are doing is patently illegal, and needs to be exposed. Damn the union; damn political correctness; damn the torpedoes. This is about the difference between right and wrong. If nobody calls them out, the next thing you know they'll monopolize all of the networks, and probably start their own and compete with themselves to gorge more money out of the public and rape the players even more."

Tockman laughed. "You're probably right," he said. "One thing's certain. The players eventually are going to strike. If you're going after them, the next few years are the time to do it. The NFL without a collective bargaining agreement is going to be vulnerable, and Rozelle knows it."

"Without a CBA," I concurred, "Pete is just polishing the brass on the *Titanic*."

"I can't tell if you're just a glutton for punishment or the reincarnation of Abraham Lincoln," Tockman chuckled. "But I will say your idea of decertifying the union is a brilliant strategy. This will definitely level the playing field."

"Jerry, it's not just about the money," I said. "I was raised on principle. That's how I sleep at night. I'm going to challenge the Rozelle Rule, or whatever they call it now. I'll find other leverage somehow. I'm going after underclassmen and test the limits of the law. I'm going to war with these bastards! Are you in?"

"Of course," Tockman growled. "If you go, I go. But," he paused, "don't say I didn't warn you."

27

A CONTRAST IN HUGHS

FOR MY MONEY, Pete Rozelle had unwittingly shifted the balance of power in the National Football League when he made television the league's profit center. This meant that owners could no longer argue that, without them, there would be no league or players. The players could now argue that without them, there would be no television contracts; they quickly became as important as actors are to a movie studio or network, or as musicians are to the recording industry.

Players to that point had been treated like little more than slave labor, but now the paradigm was shifting, beginning with Billy Sims landing the NFL's first million-dollar contract.

Convincing the egomaniacal owners, however, would take time. This made for interesting theater when the Tampa Bay Buccaneers drafted the University of Pittsburgh's Hugh Green in 1981. The Bucs were owned by Hugh Culverhouse, a former accountant and attorney who purchased the team for $16 million in 1976 and chaired the NFL's Finance Committee and the Executive Committee of the Management Council.

That wasn't the best part. At the University of Alabama, Culverhouse had competed on the boxing team, where he fought the likes of former Alabama governor George Wallace. He served in the Army Air Corps, had been the assistant state attorney general, and became legal counsel for the Internal Revenue Service. Much of his nearly $400 million net worth had come from—get this—real-estate syndication, and he once served as a personal representative of President Gerald Ford. We had a lot in common—right!—give or take $375 million, a president, and a governor.

I was about to spar with a man who steered the two most powerful groups in the entire league. Culverhouse could care less that my client Hugh Green was leaving college as arguably the best player in the game; he had already vowed publicly he would never pay a player a million dollars, much less a defensive one.

By contrast, these two Hughs were about as far apart as the antebellum plantation houses and the shotgun shacks that split Natchez, Mississippi, once a hotbed of Southern slavery and a key city during the civil rights movement. Natchez was also the boyhood home of one Hugh Green, where he had been raised in tragedy and barely a step ahead of poverty.

I met Green in 1980, at the Senior Bowl in Mobile, Alabama, when he was a junior linebacker at Pitt. Gene and I had been in Mobile to watch Little Joe Cribbs play in the annual college all-star game, and Green was seated behind us in the stands.

"Do you know who's sitting behind you?" Gene asked.

I turned around rather conspicuously, and I made eye contact with Hugh.

"Who is he?" I said.

"That's Hugh Green," Gene replied. "He's the best defensive player in football, and he'll be one of the top picks next year."

Hugh and I hit it off immediately. I told him to keep working hard, stay the course, and to come see me after his senior year. And what a senior year it was. Hugh appeared on the cover of *Sports Ilustrated*, then went on to win the Walter Camp Award, the Maxwell Award, the Lombardi Award, the Sporting News Player of the Year, and finished second in the Heisman Trophy balloting, the best a defensive player had ever attained to that point. In 1997 Michigan defensive specialist Charles Woodson beat out Tennessee's Peyton Manning for the Heisman.

In the same draft that produced North Carolina's Lawrence Taylor, Green was the dominant defensive player in the nation. In his four years with the Panthers, he appeared on a total of twelve different All-America teams, and the University of Pittsburgh retired his jersey—#99—at halftime of his final home game. In his college career, Hugh racked up 460 tackles and 53 sacks.

We believed Hugh should command the same money or more than Billy Sims—$1 million to sign, plus three years at $600,000, and up to $500,000 in bonuses. "Doc," he said, "get me as much as you can. Let's face it. Football is all I know how to do."

During Green's four-year span, Pitt was nationally televised thirty-one times, sold out 69,400 seats at home twenty-four times, reaped millions of dollars in football merchandising revenue, and was paid to play in four major post-season bowls, three of which the Panthers won.

Other than the value of his scholarship, Hugh lived in a dorm at Pittsburgh on a monthly $130 Social Security check as a result of his mother's death. His car payment was $129.10, leaving him with ninety cents a month for gas, clothes, and food.

Martin Luther King Jr., once said that "faith is the first step . . . especially when you can't see the stairs."

Nobody had a harder climb to the NFL than Hugh Green.

Born in 1959, Hugh grew up on the banks of the Mississippi in the segregated and racially charged city of Natchez. At that time, less than 12,000 people lived there, and the city had been rife with hate and betrayal since the Civil War. White families lived on one side of the street, and blacks on the other. The city's showcased mansions were a far cry from the poverty of its black population, most of whom were direct descendants of the horrors of slavery.

Hugh never met his father. His world contracted painfully after his mother died suddenly when he was six years old, and he was taken in by his aunt, Lucy Berry, and her husband, Eltee, a bricklayer. They lived in a one-story house, one of fourteen in an un-paved cul-de-sac at the top of a hill. Every family who lived there was somehow related, and the kids grew up playing in the streets or in the bayous. Hugh would cut vines and swing off the hills into the river.

The only book he remembers seeing in his house was the Bible. Aunt Lucy was always in the kitchen, cooking collard greens, macaroni, chicken necks, and potato pies. From the time he was a boy, Hugh was always soft-spoken and tended to avoid confronting situations where he felt awkward and out of place. As soon as he was old enough to help Eltee, his uncle made him work. The older men worked up on scaffolds and forced Hugh to mix the concrete and tow it by rope up to the other workers. Eltee refused to ever watch Hugh play ball in junior high, high school, or later at Pitt.

Back then, a big time for Green consisted of rolling a tire down the street with a stick during the day and sitting on the bluffs overlooking the Mississippi at night. The empty afternoons were lonely, and they tortured him. He would sneak away by himself to the bridge that leads to Vidalia, fishing for perch and catfish, where he mainly stared at the water and longed for his mom. "I never caught much," he said. "I'd just beat at the water with my pole."

He was thirteen years old the first time he ran away from home, and not knowing where to run, he spent the night asleep in the back of a parked bus. A white policeman found him and threw him in jail. The judge took a look at Hugh's unnatural size and suggested football, and Hugh took the advice to heart.

Pitt head coach Jackie Sherrill discovered Green by accident while recruiting a running back from nearby Pascagoula named Rooster Jones. While studying one particular film of Jones, the Pitt staff couldn't help but notice one lineman—Green—from

North Natchez High, who was single-handedly disrupting every play. Sherrill sent his assistants to get Rooster and Green and bring them to Pitt, and both eventually signed with the Panthers.

"I hated it there at first," Hugh told me. "The only reason I stayed was because Tony Dorsett called me and told me they really wanted me, and because Coach Sherrill told me that I'd get more publicity there than any school in the South. Besides, if I had stayed in the South and a coach called me 'boy,' there was going to be a problem. So I stayed."

He recounted how he would be the first to show up for team meetings, sit up front, ask questions, and be the last to leave. He was so good that Pitt coaches wouldn't let him practice against the first team. "Coach said there was no need to embarrass our own players," he recalled with laughter. "Because of how I grew up, I always felt a great obligation to do my very best. I take nothing for granted, Doc, not even you."

Green blossomed into one of God's most impressive engines; watching him play football at the University of Pittsburgh was irresistible. Normal football players were laden with handicaps, but not Hugh. By virtue of his awesome physical gifts, Hugh played more like a god than a mortal. With balance, coordination, and cat-quick reflexes, he flew all over the field, his body a paradox of mass and lightness.

"I can't imagine carrying the football against him," said former Pitt assistant Jimmy Johnson, who went on to a very successful career that included NCAA and Super Bowl championships. "He never leaves the balls of his feet. When he arrives at the point of attack, he's always coiled. In the back of your mind, you know he's coming for you, with very bad intentions." Facing Green, Johnson said, "is like running through a tiger compound wearing a meat suit."

Hugh was a mix of superlative courage, capable of pushing beyond defeat, beyond exhaustion, certainly far beyond the limits of those who would attempt to stop him. He could cover the entire field with dazzling speed—there were moments when what you were seeing and what he was doing simply didn't add up. A football field is 53-and-a-third yards wide by 100 yards long, and he could defend every inch with freakish talent. No human being should be capable of starting on one side of the field and ending up on the other before an opposing ball-carrier—considered to be a great athlete in his own right—can even reach the corner on a sweep.

Not only did Hugh perform this feat time and again, he came with such force and destruction that opponents gave up blocking and found themselves watching him, with a mix of awe, sadness, and respect—the way you watch an F5 tornado rip your dream house from the foundation and twist it into scrap. He smelled the fear of others and exploited it mercilessly. "If you show even the slightest cowardice against Green," said former Notre Dame coach Lou Holtz, "it can get even worse for you out there. Usually, we ran against a team's best player as a strategy. Against Hugh, we ran at him because he ended the play so fast it saved us money on game film."

Hugh played in a vortex of supreme power and unparalleled exhilaration. "You don't take Hugh Green," said Pitt quarterback Dan Marino at the time. "He takes you."

In full stride, Green would completely forget the crowds. He and football became one. While the rest of the field moved in slow motion, as if swimming in molasses, Hugh exploded with dynamic balance and ballistic opportunity, and he reveled in the crucible of strength, power, and reckless adolescence.

He lined up at defensive end. He lined up at linebacker. In fact, he lined up anywhere he chose, just before the snap. Opponents could not key on him, or game-plan against him, because there was no way to tell from one snap to the next where he might even be.

"Marino was obviously great, but he didn't run or catch," says former Dallas Cowboys guru Gil Brandt. "But Hugh Green, by himself, could change the whole game. Hugh was ready for professional football long before his senior year."

My first negotiation for Hugh occurred at the Hula Bowl, after his senior year. Hugh came to my hotel room to inform me that Coach Sherrill was in another suite, and had ideas for how Hugh should pursue his professional career. Remember, agents still were not commonplace, and Sherrill had me lumped in with all the other fly-by-night operators.

My chance meeting with Hugh when he was a junior had worked in my favor, because it had given Hugh the opportunity to witness the impact I had on my other players. But he was also torn in his loyalty to Sherrill, and rightfully so. Sherrill had smothered him for four years; as his head coach, Jackie had been his sounding board for everything from social issues to personal problems. I understood. However, I also realized that without proper representation and a skilled negotiator, Hugh would be ambushed like everyone else.

Along with Gene, we visited Sherrill in his suite, and once we got the informalities out of the way, Sherrill wasted no time. "Argovitz," he said, right to my face, "you're nothing but a fucking pimp. I've got other plans for who will represent Hugh, and he's going to make a sizable donation to the University of Pittsburgh." Hugh was caught in the middle, because of the respect he had for his head coach. I told Hugh, "You don't owe Pitt another second. You've served your time and paid your dues."

Turning to Sherrill, I said, "Coach, I'm sorry you feel that way about me, but this is not your decision. His college days are over and now it's up to me to be his financial coach and business manager."

My instincts were to beat the hell out of Jackie, but in retrospect, I could understand his position. Agents at that time were considered bottom-feeders; most of them were, and many today still are. Jackie had based his opinion of me on what he was hearing and reading, which admittedly, wasn't very good. On the way back to my room, Hugh thanked me for restraining myself and being professional. "If we had fought, who do you think would've won?" I laughed.

"Doc, I'm not betting against you," Hugh said. But with that meeting, the baton had been passed from Jackie to me as the caretaker of Green, and I took my job seriously. In dealing with my players, I had learned to ascertain their hopes, dreams, and goals for the future, and help them transform from a collegiate football player to a businessman. This was part of the constant process of teaching them they were the employer; I was their employee.

"With the fifth pick of the 1981 draft . . . the Tampa Bay Buccaneers select Hugh Green, from the University of Pittsburgh." With those words, Pete Rozelle welcomed Green into the league—and into the waiting arms of professional football.

The Buccaneers, under Hugh Culverhouse and general manager Phil Krueger, were notoriously cheap. The franchise had only been in existence since 1976, but under quarterback Doug Williams and head coach John McKay, had fought its way to the 1979 NFC Championship with one of the league's smallest payrolls. The Bucs were building a ferocious defense behind the likes of Leroy and Dewey Selmon, and adding Green to that group would be downright frightening.

As we opened negotiations with the Bucs, I invited Hugh to come stay with me in Houston until he signed, and he moved into my twenty-third-floor high-rise condo across from the Houston Summit. He immediately took to the thriving city of Houston, and was like a man possessed when it came to his routine. He woke up before dawn and ran for hours. He hit the weight room at nearby Texas Southern. During the day, he was always moving.

At night, Hugh was just a big kid. He stared quietly out of the plate-glass windows at the sunset, and marveled as the twinkling lights of the Houston skyline began to wink back. "Only in the darkness, Jerry, can you see the stars," he'd say.

We would talk for hours. He wondered aloud why his dad abandoned him. He shared that—for a while—he had harbored anger toward God for taking his mother. He asked a million questions about my strong relationships with my own mom and dad. Some of these conversations, frankly, were heartbreaking. It helped me grasp the gravity and responsibility of my obligation to young men just like him.

Hugh loved my office. He looked at every signed picture on my walls, and commented on each one. Singer Kenny Rogers. Muhammad Ali. Angelo Dundee. Moses Malone. Sylvester Stallone. "Jerry," he said, "you need to clear some room on this wall.

When I get to the NFL, I promise I'll be so good you're going to have to put up more than one picture of me."

He'd engage me in daily conversations regarding business, investments, finance, and friendship. My friends from all walks of life embraced him. He met everyone from dentists to developers, brokers, bankers, car dealers, celebrities, restaurant and nightclub owners—anyone and everyone with whom I was friends or did business. Hugh loved to eat and hang out at Angelo's, a local Italian bistro. Through our network of friends, he met some of his heroes—Earl Campbell, Gene's brother, Kenny Burrough, and Astros pitcher J.R. Richard. Honestly, we enjoyed each other's company and had a lot of pure fun. This is exactly why I brought new clients to Houston. On the road, anybody can lie to you and be what I call the "out-of-town" expert. But when you bring them to your backyard, where you live, work, and play, you can't fake a charade and pass it off for real life.

The thing I loved about him was that he wanted to actively participate in his own negotiations, and together we created a textbook dichotomy of how NFL talks—even today—can be handled between a player and his agent.

The best part about Hugh was that he was already frugal. His senior year at Pitt, he counted among his possessions a stereo that he paid $90 for in junior high; a bike he bought in high school for $40; and a used black-and-white TV, for which he paid $100.

Hand-in-hand with Green's frugality was a down-home self-sufficiency and directness. He cooked, ironed—even sewed. One of his favorite outfits was a long-sleeved blue-and-white shirt that he had made himself. "It's a good idea, Doc," he'd grin, "if you're capable of taking care of yourself."

The negotiations with Phil Krueger were basically little more than phone conversations that bordered on ridiculous. It was obvious that just like Dick Syzmanski in Baltimore, Phil was merely doing his boss's bidding. The difference here, however, was that Culverhouse was no drunken, slovenly fool, but a wickedly intelligent financier with enough league firepower behind him to blow you to kingdom come. Dealing with Culverhouse was two-fold, because any decisions he made would be held up again in front of his committee cronies, whom he was supposed to be leading.

I saw this as a double-edged sword. I had the opportunity to kill two birds with one stone; Culverhouse, and the league's salary structure for defensive players.

I'd talk to Krueger on the phone and allow Hugh to discreetly listen in from a phone in another room. He heard first-hand as Krueger totally devalued him, called his integrity into question, and categorized him as less important than aging veteran linebackers. Occasionally, this would enrage Hugh. "He's talking about me like a piece of meat, like this is slavery," Hugh said. "They picked me, I didn't pick them."

I'd soothe his feathers and remind him it wasn't personal. "Let me work," I said. "Trust me. We'll get there." Hugh would listen intently to my conversations with other general managers regarding my other clients, and afterward, he would involve me in intense question-and-answer sessions. He loved to learn, and made it clear that once it came time to sign, he'd make his own decision based on what I concluded. "But I'm always gonna be my own man," he said.

Hugh and I flew down to One Buc Place in Tampa. The local newspapers were blaring Hugh's arrival, and judging from the press, the coaches couldn't wait to get him on the field. According to Bucs head coach John McKay, Hugh was already penciled in as a starter, and rightfully so.

We met with Coach McKay and talked to him for more than an hour. An intriguing man, McKay had won a national championship at USC; he clearly understood the psychological makeup of great athletes and wasted no time pushing Hugh's buttons. "I want you to be a leader on this team," he said. "There are a lot of football players out there, and I picked you."

Unbeknownst to them, I was already making my negotiations just by listening to Coach McKay, and would use his exact words when dealing with Krueger and Culverhouse.

When we walked into Krueger's office, the first words out of my mouth were Coach McKay's. "Phil, you drafted Hugh for a reason," I said. "Obviously, you expect him to be a leader. My job is to get him in here so he can provide all of his services for you."

Smiling at my tactic, Hugh excused himself and left us alone. In negotiations, I never like to be the first one to throw out a number, because usually the first one to shoot is the first to lose. It only took a few more minutes of verbal sparring to realize that I was wearing a bulls-eye. I had ruptured the NFL salary structure in 1980, and it was clear the general managers had discussed it and were not about to let it happen again.

Finally Krueger threw out the first number. "You're not even on the same planet," I said. "That's less money than I got for Curtis Dickey with the fifth pick last year, and less money than I got for Jacob Green with the tenth pick. I signed George Cumby to the Packers last year for more money than veteran All-Pro Robert Brazile, and you're offering me less than both of them, Phil. You're not even in reality."

He leaned over his desk. "Last year was, let's just say, unusual," he said. "Jerry, this is how it works within our structure. We don't care what other stupid teams do. What I'm offering is Hugh Green's value to our team." He did his best to intimidate me, but he was child's play compared to what I'd been through. His methods of negotiating weren't based on logic—merely the team's posture that it would only pay Hugh what it wanted to pay him, regardless of where he was picked. "If this is what you think he's worth," I shot, "then you should have waited until the third or fourth round, because that's the type of money you're offering."

I laughed at him. Krueger couldn't open a hole in a donut factory. Frustrated, I asked him who had the authority to make a different decision. "I have full authority from Mr. Culverhouse," Krueger said smugly.

"Well, I have full authority from my client to get up and leave," I said.

When Hugh and I flew home, he was highly irritated. I told him a story about when I was in dental school, where I had been an outcast for being Jewish, and I was discredited and sent packing. "The bottom line, Hugh, is that we persevere, and triumph in the end," I told him. "Patience is power. Keep working out, keep training, and just have fun before you start your job."

Bottom line: I got a number out of Krueger, but he never got a number out of me.

I hammered the Buccaneers in the media, and thanks to Culverhouse's brief miserly history in Tampa, the press was sympathetic to us. The owner was hardly popular: In spite of its recent success, the team had lost its first twenty-six games after becoming a franchise in 1976. Off the field, Culverhouse had been heavily criticized for—among other things—trying to force an extension of Interstate 75 directly through land owned by him, of course, and the Florida governor.

When my talks with the team finally culminated with a face-to-face with Culverhouse himself, it was quickly evident why past employees described working for the man as "living in an atmosphere of fear." He was arrogant, brash, and rude. This was the same man who had fired his marketing director due to public backlash over ticket prices, when it was Culverhouse himself who had set the prices. With a strike looming for 1982 and Culverhouse on the NFL's Executive Committee, I could tell immediately he was going to cause the players lots of grief before he was done.

"Argovitz?" he asked. "Is that Jewish?

"Yes sir," I said. Sitting behind a broad wooden desk, he smiled like a fat, white-haired Cheshire cat. "I've got some good friends who are Jewish." Smiling on the outside, seething on the inside, I went to work. I was willing to defer some of Hugh's money for two reasons: One, I knew that Culverhouse wouldn't want to admit publicly to any contract worth a million bucks; and two, I wanted Hugh's money to last him long into the future.

However, I stuck to my guns on present-day value, and we were able to compromise over a deal that would pay Green handsomely for years to come, including far more than a million dollars in present-day value. The Bucs could report it to the media however they chose. Culverhouse was only concerned about his money and his reputation. I had played to his enormous ego and gave him a way to save face. It worked.

When Green came in to sign his contract, Culverhouse made a feeble attempt at humor.

"The only reason I like you is that we share the same name," he said, shaking Hugh's hand.

For once, he probably told the truth.

As expected, Green instantly became a team captain and earned Rookie of the Year honors for the Bucs and made the Pro Bowl. He became an outspoken team leader and was considered one of the best linebackers to ever play the game. The rest of the team played incredibly, too. Attendance records were set, Buc jerseys were sold by the thousands, and Tampa Bay appeared on national television throughout the season. And when it was all said and done, the season culminated with Green's Buccaneers facing the Lions—and Billy Sims—in the Silverdome for the division title and a shot at the playoffs.

The Bucs defense shut down Billy, and handed the Lions a stunning 20-17 loss.

After the season, it was revealed that the Buccaneers had earned the third-highest profit in all of football, though Culverhouse had told me face-to-face they were dead last in the league and had "nothing to work with."

All I knew was that whether or not people considered me a pimp, Hugh Green had earned enough of Hugh Culverhouse's precious, almighty money to buy himself a whole block of antebellum houses in Natchez, Mississippi, if he so wished.

Green was no longer sleeping in the back of the bus.

He was driving it.

28

DISCOVERING MY "OLLIE BROWN"

IT WAS JUST after the 1981 draft, and my mind was a blur as I whipped my Mercedes through side streets in downtown Houston en route to meet my father, Harry, for lunch. Dining with dad was cathartic for both of us, especially me, in spite of the fact I was forty-two years old. My dad had an innate ability to instantly bring focus to any abstract situation. Whenever I got in over my head, the sage advice of my father was always a lifeline. He was always armed and ready to listen—with the same gusto and passion of my boyhood.

Right now, I felt like I was drowning, and my mind was all over the place. I was battling the Miami Dolphins and Pittsburgh Steelers over two of my other first-round draft picks—running back David Overstreet and defensive end Keith Gary, both from the University of Oklahoma. I had been vilified in the national press for my adversarial positions against the NFL, the NCAA, the NFLPA, individual teams, general managers, and other agents. In a few words, I had pissed off most of the football establishment, and it had taken me less than a year to do it.

My dad and I spoke every day on the phone, but when things got particularly slippery, we did everything face-to-face. This was one of those "serious" days; a day when only Dad could calm me. These were special afternoons when I threw out my entire schedule and time stood still. We liked to meet at Luling City Market, which was as close as you could get to a Borger barn inside of metropolitan Houston.

Tucked away in a Richmond Avenue strip mall only minutes from the hustle and bustle of my offices in the Galleria, Luling was a place where I could go in my blue jeans, boots, open-collared shirts, and cowboy hats and feel right at home. TVs chatter at each end of the polished bar. No hostess, no wait, no table service. Get your food, sit down, prop your boots up, and eat. The interior resembled any Texas roadhouse, with wooden walls, hard wooden floors littered with peanut shells, and bench seating. The smell of smoked chicken, turkey, and ribs was so thick you could taste it.

I hugged my dad, kissed him, and relaxed in his iron grip. We grabbed some grub, and for a few minutes we sat lunching and munching. There's nothing like real Central Texas barbecue cooked over Post Oak wood pits.

On a warm spring Houston day, there's nothing better than a large sweet tea and a plate of ribs and smoked brisket on a paper plate, with slaw, potato salad, pinto beans, and a Texas-sized brownie.

And my Dad.

"How's the divorce coming along?" he asked. "OK," I answered. Truthfully, like any divorce, it had been excruciatingly painful, emotional, and expensive, but I didn't want to talk about it today. Elaine and I had a lot of respect for each other, and we both deeply loved the kids; I knew that, in time, we would remain friends. Sometimes people just grow apart. Elaine was my wife of twenty-two years and the mother of my children, and I had ensured she would be fine financially. Dad and I had spent enough time on that topic, however, and on this day, I was here for other reasons.

"I'm just a little overwhelmed with everything, Dad," I said. On the outside, I explained, I had run through the NFL like a crazed revolutionary, raging against the machine. Inside, though, I was scared to death. I was still earning a small fortune in real estate and land development, but I was now totally consumed and driven by football and the challenges it had placed on my doorstep.

Dad's sheer presence alone was comforting. In general, I could talk to him about anything—philosophy, religion, psychology, sports, women, business—you name it. But when I was stressed or compressed, like today, he would challenge my theories, re-center my perspective, identify my purpose, and "clear the mechanism" in my wheel-house. Most importantly I was just grateful that I had a dad to talk to, when so many of my friends and clients—like Hugh Green—did not. The best thing about a true father-son relationship is that, regardless of age, he's still the father, and you're still the son.

"Don't tell anybody, Dad," I admitted, taking a long pull of iced tea through my straw, "but I may have bitten off more than I can chew. I really think the NFL is conspiring against me, and it's going to have a negative impact on my players."

My dad was still a muscular man, with thinning salt-and-pepper hair and brown eyes, and tufts of graying eyebrows. His personality simmered with energy, and he still possessed a personal magnetism of astonishing power. When he smiled, he made you smile with him, as if you'd just heard the funniest joke in the world.

"Jerry, you've done more than that!" he roared. "You've picked a fight with somebody a lot bigger than you. You've made so much noise in the press and the media that the NFL is going to cut your nuts off if you're not very, very careful. They don't need Jerry Argovitz. They can blackball you. Every time I open the paper, you're in it. Every time I turn on the radio or television, you're on it. Just do me a favor"—he smiled broadly—"don't show up on the wall at the post office."

I tried not to laugh. I was there to vent. "Dad," I ranted, "the players have been sold out from the time they're kids. First, the NCAA exploits them. Then the NFL exploits them. Most of these kids don't have a father. What's being done to them is illegal. Talking to the Steelers and the Dolphins is like talking to the same team. They are price fixing. Every time one of the teams talks to me they call the other teams and relay my negotiation points and strategies. I can't just stand around and allow this to happen in America, and no one gives a damn. These two teams are stonewalling me and refusing to negotiate in good faith. I feel like they are colluding against me and my players.

"The NFL takes away all the leverage," I continued. "If they can get you for less than you're worth, they will. If they have you for $1, and you turn out to be the best player in football, they will still pay you $1. But if they sign you for $2 million and they decide to waive you or terminate your contract, they will—they'll just cut you. If they find out the next day you can't chew gum and walk, you're gone."

"What do you mean by cut?" he asked.

"When a player signs an NFL contract," I said, "it is nothing but a series of one-year contracts. Each year, the player has to make the team and pass his physical. The only guarantee to the player is the signing bonus."

"So the teams have the options to keep or cut a player, but a player is obligated for the entire three or four years?"

"You got it!" I said. "That's why these guys need free agency, like the rest of the working world. I'm willing to stake my career—my life, if necessary—to do something about it. But it's gotten so big so fast, I just don't know where to begin."

"Seriously, I'm proud of you, son," he said. "But you have to be methodical in your behavior. One man can't fight everybody all at once. We've talked about this your whole life—pick your fights. Keep your chin tucked in and your eyes open. Don't get diverted by all the variables outside your control. Don't let all the crap eat away at your vision and self-confidence. Detours will doom you; lose faith in yourself, Jerry, and you'll fulfill your own worst prophecy. There are no safe harbors. If you don't have leverage, then create it. If you don't like the environment, then change it."

His eyes grew narrow, and his voice deepened.

"Remember when you started out as a dentist?" he asked. "You hung your shingle out in front of the door in Houston and you started with no patients. One by one, they came to you. They'd walk in with horrible pain. Then you, with your magic needle and your drill, would send them home pain-free. You built on trust. Then, when you decided to get into real estate, there was that grocery store down the street. You worked out a deal for a little money down, and paid it off in increments. You built on knowledge and trust. Then you enlisted that endodontist pal of yours to go in halves. Again, you built on trust. He made money, you made money, and then more and more people wanted in on your deals. You made some people really wealthy, one deal at a time.

"You're doing the same thing now in this agent business," he said. "All your success is predicated on trust—one good deal at a time. Except now you've got this 4,000-pound elephant called the National Football League sitting on your shoulders. If I hear you right, the NFL wants to dictate unacceptable terms, destroy you and the trust you've earned from the players. The way you eat an elephant is one bite at a time, remember? Sometimes the answers are staring you right in the face, son, but you need to take a step back to see them.

"So let's keep this in perspective. Do you remember a few years ago, when you bought that commercial property for $40,000, because you knew that 7-11 wanted to put a store there? If you recall, the city of Bellaire wouldn't change the zoning to allow them to sell alcohol, and you were stuck."

Where was he going with this? I wondered. What did this have to do with football?

"So you went out and talked to some minister . . . " he continued. "What was his name?"

"Ollie Brown?" I asked quizzically. "He is the pastor of what will be the first Negro Baptist Church in Bellaire."

"Yes, Reverend Brown," my dad continued, and we both remembered my "negotiations" with the city of Bellaire. When my request for liquors sales was denied, I told the city that since it refused to change the zoning, I would simply listen to my accountants and donate the property to the good reverend and take a tax write-off. I also made sure to inform him that Reverend Ollie Brown would very soon be pitching his big tent and conducting revivals on the property every night. The city manager went nuts, and the city of Bellaire's lawyers were furious. And while they called me some pretty choice names, about thirty days later the zoning was indeed changed, and I sold the property to a developer for $2 a square foot. Ultimately, I made $170,000 on that initial $40,000 investment.

Are you kidding me? Instantly, I got it. My dad's wisdom pierced me like rays of sunshine poking through the curtains of a darkened room. When he pulled those shades wide open, the truth was blinding.

"You want to beat the NFL, son?" he asked, leaning forward and grabbing my arm. "You've got to find another Ollie Brown, kid. Patience is power, but leverage is everything. Beat these NFL owners in Pittsburgh and Miami at their own game. You find the equivalent of an Ollie Brown, pitch your revival tent, and it will change everything."

"Dad, I think I have my Ollie Brown," I said. "His name is Nelson Skalbania. He owns the Montreal Alouettes of the Canadian Football League. He's willing to spend money for American stars. He's a little goofy, but he's just smart enough to be dangerous."

"Sounds like someone else I know," my dad smirked, eyes twinkling.

"If you want my advice, son, I'd call Mr. Skalbania and start pitching my tent."

29

PENGUINS AND MIDGETS

RUNNING BACK DAVID Overstreet and defensive end Keith Gary were still in at Oklahoma and had never even heard of Bill Gates in the late 1970s, when IBM and DEC were both considered insurmountable computer behemoths.

Of course IBM, as a creative leader, came under attack. Under the burden of a thirteen-year antitrust case spanning most of the 1970s and early 1980s, IBM lost its edge—and much of its creative talent—to competition. In 1981 computers were the stuff of NASA and the military. Microsoft and Apple jumped through those antitrust loopholes, however, and put computers in your pocket at a price everyone could afford.

Commissioner Rozelle, on the other hand, was watching the troubled antitrust landscape with the cunning of a jackal. He was no idiot. He understood business far better than he understood the actual game of football. His game wasn't the game—that was just the drug that he peddled to a never-ceasing supply of end-users. His game was money. To grow more money, he had to eliminate competition, and this would be as critical to his legacy as his creation of Monday Night Football. Like a heat-seeking missile, once Rozelle took your television set at prime-time on Monday night, he realized that without opposition, he could one day command the football world.

By 1981, when David and Keith were drafted by the Dolphins and Steelers, respectively, I knew from my own dealings in real-estate syndication and dentistry that competition in a free, unrestricted system is the only way to determine fair-market value. If there is only one buyer, such as the NFL's restricted system—an illegal draft and no free agency—the seller, the players, have zero negotiating power.

Rozelle, however, saw pro football as a fixed hunk of meat, one he refused to allow rivals to tear from his jaws. Forget those age-old American birthrights of effort and ingenuity to improve and achieve higher standards and to attract more dollars. Competition under capitalism should lead not to the restriction of output at ever-higher, wallet-gouging prices, but rather to an abundance of output at ever-lower prices.

The image of competition as leading to monopolies, in which stingy, NFL Scrooge-types hoard their wealth and parcel it out in mean-spirited ways, is the image held by those who've never grasped the creative essence of capitalism.

The Commissioner and his cartel cohorts in the NFL were backpedaling furiously to close the market entirely. Rozelle and his minions sought to create an environment where each team owner would capture and protect his respective territorial slice from a fixed pie. To ensure his success, Rozelle had run crying to Washington to save his ass from antitrust. Operating under the safety of what should have been an illegal umbrella, Rozelle could then carry on like any good godfather, eradicating any who dare challenge him with such brutal force that no one dare try a stunt like that again.

The result? The same as any other monopoly: The NFL began an unfettered feast that continues today. The league price-gouged the networks, added additional games, increased ticket prices, inflated the price of everything from parking to hot dogs to beer, and prohibited any transactions that might threaten the greater good of the cartel.

Better yet, America bought it . . . hook, line, and sinker. The national media was seduced by the NFL's rank cologne and followed along like school marms at the prom and became willing accomplices.

Some people steal to enrich their lives, while some steal to define their lives. Publicly, Rozelle preached the integrity of "the game, the game, the game," then—like Tony Soprano at the Bada Bing Club—gathered his fat-cat owners in smoky backrooms at private NFL meetings and mocked the general public as they divided untold wealth. The owners drafted players like they were picking slaves from the trading block—the best, biggest, brightest, fastest, and strongest went first. The rest were left to die.

The owners rode the backs of these great athletes to exponential fortunes, while telling them how lucky they were to just be cogs in their giant money-making machine. Challenge them, and you were quashed, black-balled, outcast, excommunicated, and publicly harassed.

The public's insatiable demand for football was matched only by the owners' demand for more money. Beating up the players wasn't enough. In a clear abuse of power, NFL tanks rolled into city democracies and pointed their guns at the heads of civic leaders, ordering them to either pay them by subsidizing stadium renovations, building new stadiums with private boxes, tax-free loans, and fixing rent prices—or they would move their business elsewhere.

Leading these threats was none other than Bob Irsay of the Baltimore Colts. Overnight, money that should have gone toward education, street lighting, lighthouses, police and emergency services, air defense systems, roads, flood and disaster protection, public parks, and beaches was redirected to pacify the NFL. And don't forget my old pal Bud Adams for taking our beloved Oilers to Tennessee because the mayor wouldn't support funding a new stadium. One can't blame him for moving his team; every owner has the right and freedom to move his team to make more money; everybody has the right to move except the players. The NFL owners are powerful and smart businessmen. It's all about the money.

The NFL in those days would have eaten today's agents for lunch. If you think being one of the early agents in the NFL was easy, try telling a couple of sizzling twenty-one- or twenty-two-year-old rookies from Oklahoma that the league in which they dreamed of playing had become nothing but a lawless and legalized thug. In my opinion, every practice in the NFL involved either coercion, force, or fraud. It could not have been worse if owners and GMs wore ski masks and gloves, and the first words in each contract said, "Get on your knees and clasp your hands behind your head."

In Texas, however, we have special laws for thugs. We practice the right to bear arms, and deadly force is justified when and to the degree one reasonably believes the force is immediately necessary to protect oneself.

Just as the Dolphins and Steelers were about to hustle out the back door carrying my two clients like stolen TV sets, I raised my weapon and said, "Stop, or I'll shoot!"

Keith Gary grew up in Bethesda, Maryland, where he dreamed of one day being a part of the immortal Steel Curtain defense of the Pittsburgh Steelers. "Mean" Joe Greene and Jack Lambert were his idols, and he emulated them on and off the field. Meanwhile, 1,262 miles away in Big Sandy, Texas, population 912, David Overstreet was a blue-chip running back. He had power, speed, and balance. In Texas, David was a legend in high school football. He was recruited by most of the top colleges in the country. He had been a boyhood fan of the Miami Dolphins, and likened himself to Eugene "Mercury" Morris, a fearless scatback who had terrorized defenses with blinding speed en route to the Dolphins' 17-0 season in 1972.

Overstreet was a legend on the football field long before he went to Oklahoma. His high school team, Big Sandy, dominated their opponents, outscoring them by 824-15 his senior year. One of his teammates was Lovie Smith, now head coach of the Chicago Bears. They won three consecutive Class B State titles. His senior year, David had just thirty-four students in his graduating class.

Both David and Keith would later tell me that, as boys, they prayed at night to one day wear the jerseys of the Miami Dolphins and Pittsburgh Steelers. Both did their part in college to earn the chance. David, in spite of playing in the same backfield at Oklahoma for years with Billy Sims, Kenny King, and Elvis Peacock, still rushed for 1,702 yards and averaged nearly six yards a carry. Keith terrorized offenses and was a combination of height, speed, and strength. Imagine their elation on draft day when, as only fate would have it, Miami, with the thirteenth pick, grabbed Overstreet, and Pittsburgh, with the seventeenth pick, took Gary.

A predicament is at best an unpleasant situation, so try to imagine mine. I had two players desperate to play for these two particular teams. The Dolphins had won two Super Bowls in the past decade, and were the only NFL team to have an undefeated season. The Steelers had become a virtual dynasty in the 1970s with four Super Bowl wins. David was gushing at the thought of playing for legendary coach Don Shula; Keith couldn't wait to get on the field with equally renowned coach Chuck Noll. I was up against two of the most feared franchises in the league, and dealing with Miami's Shula and Steelers owner Art Rooney and Dan, his son and general manager, was going to be tougher than doing a root canal on a pair of silverback gorillas.

I was instantly stonewalled by both clubs. Talking to owner Joe Robbie, Shula, or Dan Rooney was like talking to exactly the same person. It was so blatant it seemed contrived. Obviously, there had been a clear exchange of information between the two teams, and I was getting nowhere fast. Both teams talked about "the family business" and that they "couldn't afford" to pay any more than they had the year before for the same pick.

I asked Shula point-blank if David was important to the Dolphins. He was belligerent. "If I didn't believe in Overstreet, I wouldn't have drafted him number one," he said. The Rooneys were at least polite, but it was the same wolf in sheep's clothing. I wasn't holding my breath; the last time the Steelers had paid out the league's biggest contract was in 1938 when they signed Byron White, a future justice on the U.S. Supreme Court.

"Jerry, we've got nothing but time," Dan Rooney told me on the phone. "Make it fit within our salary structure, and we'll do it. But if it doesn't . . . we're not willing to pay the preposterous money you've been demanding for your other guys." I didn't have time. I took the advice of the immortal Vince Lombardi—winning isn't everything, but finding a way to win is. I grabbed the phone and called Nelson Skalbania in Montreal, Quebec. A perky female voice picked up.

"Merci d'avoir appelé les Alouettes de Montréal!"

The only French I knew was a Burger King croissant and French fries.

I said, "Hi—this is Jerry Argovitz in Houston, Texas," I drawled, throwing my boots up on my desk. "Can I speak to Nelson? We've spoken several times regarding my two players. He knows me. Tell him we're ready."

Within seconds, the line buzzed. "Jerry!" Skalbania blurted. "When can you be here?"

There was a time when the Canadian Football League paid as much or more money than the NFL. The CFL in 1952 signed Heisman Trophy winner Billy Vessels, along with Eddie LeBaron and Gene Brito. Other big-name players like Kenny Carpenter, Mac Speedie, Neill Armstrong, Bud Grant, Frankie Albert, and John Henry Johnson also made the leap. In 1955 LeBaron, Brito, Norb Heckler, Alex Webster, and Tom Dublinski left the CFL for NFL teams after representatives from the two competing leagues failed to work out a no-raiding treaty.

At that point, for the most part, Canadian teams and owners did their best to pay homage to the NFL. But names that are saluted now—Halas, Rooney, Tim Mara, and Bert Bell—were second-rate thinkers compared to Rozelle and his vision for a global NFL product. It seems absurd to think that Montreal could outbid an NFL team for talent, but given the right maverick owner, it was true.

Enter real estate and sports mogul Nelson Skalbania, a short, flamboyant, fiery, cigar-smoking, low-buying, high-selling short-seller who had purchased the storied Montreal Alouettes of the Canadian Football League. To listen to him talk, you'd think the sun came up just to hear him crow. As owner of the Indianapolis Racers in the World Hockey Association, he had sold a young hockey star named Wayne Gretzky to the Edmonton Oilers. He was an entrepreneur, and always making a quick play for a fast buck. He made no bones about his desire to rebuild the Montreal franchise to glory—and to sell it just as fast.

That was fine with me. I only cared about ensuring that David and Keith had alternative options besides the Dolphins and the Steelers and earn as much money in as short a time as possible, and get them back to the NFL—with leverage. "Watch that guy," Gene warned about Skalbania. "Some people say he's big hat, no cattle." I checked deeper into his background, and I found enough financial evidence to proceed, albeit with caution. Personally, Skalbania didn't mean a fart in a skillet to me, but I liked him. He was bright—he graduated with a degree in civil engineering—and he had made millions in real estate. As long as he could personally guarantee my players their money, I was interested.

I called David Overstreet. "Hey, Doc!" he said. "I just bought myself a new Miami Dolphins hat today. Looks great. When are we going to Miami?"

"You might want to trade that hat for a jacket," I said. "Get your wife Johnnie May. We're all going to Quebec."

My biggest fan, my mom, at homecoming, junior year. Berger Bulldogs.

Me in elementary school.

This is me: No more Jew bastard! I was the light heavyweight regional champion.

Sports Illustrated

SEPTEMBER 22, 1980 $1.50

PRIDE OF THE LIONS

Detroit's
Super Rookie
Billy Sims

"Doc. J."
Best friend a
person can have
Billy Sims
#20

Herschel Walker, Marcus Allen, Doc, and Billy Sims at the Walter Camp awards.

Billy and I participating in a children's charity event, 1980.

Jim McMahon, my friend and a fearless competitor. He is also the best shoeless golfer I know.

Commissioner Chet Simmons and me in happier times, before Donald J. Trump.

Gene Burrough and me at a Gambler's game. "A great partner."

Here I am with a couple of my clients. On the left is Joe Cribbs, Rookie of the Year in 1980 and All-Pro running back with the Buffalo Bills. On the right is Hugh Green, Rookie of the Year in 1981 and All-Pro for the Tampa Bay Buccaneers. "Men of Character."

Herschel Walker

Signing Bonus: $2,000,000

10 years = $200,000 per year.
(Pledged as collateral for loan.)

LOAN:
$1,000,000 (Interest Free)

Contract fully Guaranteed by Team + Owners personally.

Injury Guarantees: Player will purchase insurance from Lloyds of London.

Educational benefits: Team guarantees payment, for the life time of Mr. Walker, of tuition for undergraduate and/or postgraduate education

Graduation Bonus: $25,000 cash Bonus payable upon completion of Bachelor's Degree.

Herschel's signature changed the course for all collegiate football players.

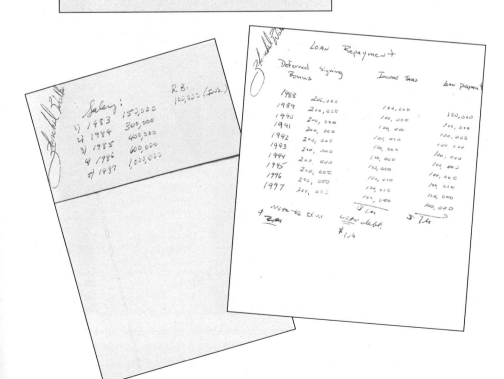

Salary:
1) 1983   150,000
2) 1984   300,000
3) 1985   450,000
4) 1986   600,000
5) 1987   1,000,000

R.B. 100,000 (Ins.)

LOAN Repayment

Deferred Signing Bonus		Income Taxes	Loan Payment
1988	200,000		
1989	200,000	100,000	100,000
1990	200,000	100,000	100,000
1991	200,000	100,000	100,000
1992	200,000	100,000	100,000
1993	200,000	100,000	100,000
1994	200,000	100,000	100,000
1995	200,000	100,000	100,000
1996	200,000	100,000	100,000
1997	200,000	100,000	100,000
		$1M	$1M

Note to H.W.
$2M

Loan debt:
$1M

Don't Mess with Texas: The author (left), Gov. Rick Perry, Loni Argovitz, Rep. Harold Dutton, and a Gov. Perry aide, at the signing of House bill 1123.

Dinner with my good friends Marla, Congressman Tom McMillen and date, "TF" (Jim Kelly) and friend.

My father Harry, wife Loni, and me, celebrating life on Dad's ninetieth birthday.

Skalbania and Joe Scanella, his head coach, were wonderful. Team executives rolled out the red carpet. In a single weekend, we crammed in enough French Canadian history to pass a high-school exam. We gazed at the city's beautiful, sweeping architecture, walked the banks of the St. Lawrence River, browsed Quebec's Old City, toured the Parliament, and saw the Plains of Abraham, where the famous battle between the French and English armies took place in 1759.

"My job is to present options," I said, as we toured the town.

Montreal's gorgeous Olympic Stadium sat right in the middle of quaint, single-story brick houses and small shops. It was as if somebody had dropped a football stadium right into the middle of an Aesop fable. Once inside, David and Keith were a bit shocked at the size of a Canadian football field, which is 110 yards long and 65 yards wide. Coach Scanella showed them a little film and covered the rules—twelve men, three downs for a first, and emphasized how their speed could make them instant CFL stars.

Because of our prior discussions, it took me little time to negotiate with Skalbania. I was able to get David and Keith more money from Canada—for two years—than the Dolphins and Steelers were willing to pay them for four years. I insisted that any taxes—Canadian—be paid by the Alouettes. Then I asked Nelson to personally guarantee them both. He agreed, and just like that, we were done. The money was on the table.

On the flight back to the states, I did my best to reassure both guys this was a prudent decision. "It's only two years," I said. "You'll be set financially and still realize your dream to play in the NFL. Don't worry about the mule, just load the wagon. Go to Canada, play your asses off, and by the time you get back to the NFL, you'll be leading the herd as a total free agent."

This made sense to David, but Keith just stared out the window. I hurt for him, but dreams don't pay bills. They were about to make more money individually than their heroes—Mercury Morris and Jack Lambert—had earned in their careers combined. And when they returned to play in the NFL, much to the chagrin of Rozelle, they would be total and unrestricted free agents.

The NFL was about to get a root canal.

In their wildest dreams, the Dolphins and Steelers never imagined—despite my insistence—that I would take both players to Canada. You don't judge a cowboy until you see him ride, and they could only watch as two of the league's best draft picks, for the first time in NFL history, thundered off into the sunset.

The reaction was about what I expected: All hell broke loose. In Miami on other business, I saw Shula in a restaurant, and he gave me the single-finger salute. "You took my first-round pick to Canada. You destroyed our draft! Why didn't you call me and give us the last shot?"

"Coach, I told [owner] Joe Robbie that if he didn't get serious about signing David, we had other options. You said yourself that you had other options, too, and that if David wanted to play in the NFL, it would only be for the Dolphins."

I remember Shula, red-faced, cursing at me as I walked away.

And if I had walked off an airplane in Pittsburgh, I would have been lynched by fans, but honestly, Dan Rooney had too much class to speak to me in that manner.

Rozelle's media buddies criticized my behavior as "self-serving and asinine," and claimed I'd ruined two of my players for taking them to Canada. Other owners screamed about how much money, time, and preparation went into the "welfare" of a first-round pick. "If the owners had their way," I shot back, "that's what these kids would be living on—welfare."

Other agents called my move "career suicide." Regardless, it was startling how fast their negotiations picked up, as NFL teams suddenly raced to sign their draft picks.

In my book, they were all mad at the wrong guy. "If my guys had turned into penguins and midgets the next day," I told the press, "they were getting paid. Those contracts were guaranteed."

Two years later, both David and Keith returned to the NFL and the Dolphins and Steelers. Nelson Skalbania eventually went bankrupt, and the Alouettes were sold. Tragically, David Overstreet died in a car accident after his first season with the Dolphins, and left behind a great wife and a talented son.

Rozelle, meanwhile, added the CFL to his hit list. Television was now the lifeblood of football; without it, any attempt to compete with the NFL would fail. Rozelle didn't want to do away with the CFL—he just wanted to control it, too, and eventually, over time TV would be the way to control everything.

The National Football League was fast becoming a dungeon of hellish injustice, where liberties went to die.

30

THIS BUD'S FOR YOU

IN 1974 THE National Football League—among other rules changes—narrowed its hash marks to the center of the field, creating vast outside alleys that put an emphasis on space and speed. Defenses answered by creating a hybrid linebacker: One who could rush off the corner and harass quarterbacks, blow up offensive linemen at the point of attack, chase down ball carriers from behind, or drop into coverage.

The Oilers found such a beast at Jackson State, where 6-3, 215-pound Robert Brazile—a college teammate of Walter Payton's—had been converted from tight end to linebacker, and had been nicknamed "Mr. Versatile" because he could play everywhere.

Houston acquired Robert when it sent John Matuszak to the Kansas City Chiefs for veteran Curley Culp and the sixth pick of the 1975 draft. New Houston head coach Bum Phillips quickly made Brazile the first prototype 'tweener: A ferocious mix "between" a defensive end and outside linebacker. Bum credited Brazile as the biggest reason why he switched defenses from the 4-3 to the 3-4, because Brazile could play anywhere. Robert stepped up to the challenge.

Fans nicknamed him "Dr. Doom" for his savage hits on Redskins quarterback Billy Kilmer and Dallas running back Tony Dorsett. He was strong enough to destroy fullbacks, fast enough to chase down tight ends, and roamed those wide sidelines like a cheetah chasing a white-tailed antelope.

So, after being named Rookie of the Year in 1975, leading the Oilers to back-to-back AFC Championship games in 1978 and 1979, and playing in five consecutive Pro Bowls, Brazile was flat broke by the early 1980s. His teammate and wide receiver Kenny

Burrough—Gene's brother—had introduced us, and called to ask me to look over his contract with the Oilers. I knew Robert and his wife Cookie socially. Robert was movie-star handsome, and had the world's greatest smile.

"Doc, Robert really needs your help!" Kenny told me. "He's our best player, and he has a terrible contract and the Oilers are really screwing him over."

Up to this time, all of my clients had been rookies. Robert was my first veteran player.

But when I sat down and assessed the situation, I was dumbfounded. Robert was the best linebacker in the NFL. I had just signed a rookie linebacker in Green Bay—George Cumby—for nearly double what Robert was making for five years. This was more proof of how ridiculous the NFL system really was, and how unfair to the veteran players on each team.

I thought to myself: How is it possible for a rookie, before he plays a down of professional football, to make more money than Robert Brazile? This discovery became the Achilles heel of the NFL—and eventually led to the rookie salary cap instituted in the CBA in 2011.

I told Robert I'd be happy to represent him.

"Robert, I'll call [Oilers' GM] Ladd Herzeg in the morning," I said. "When you find yourself in a hole, the first thing to do is stop digging. Ladd's an astute numbers guy, unlike some of the GMs I've had to deal with. He understands present-day value. We'll find a way to get this done."

When I spoke with Ladd, he agreed that Robert was the cornerstone of the defense, and he understood that most of Robert's contract had been deferred: good for the team, bad for the player. But while he was sympathetic, he made it crystal clear that—under order from owner Bud Adams—there would be no renegotiation.

"Jerry, he had an agent when we did his deal," Herzeg said. "He signed a contract. We are paying him. And we are paying him to the contractual terms, no exceptions."

"I want to meet with Bud," I said.

"Good luck," Ladd replied. "He won't even talk to you."

Immediately, I put in a call for Bud Adams.

For as long as one can remember, Adams has been riding a gravy train with biscuits for wheels. He won the lottery twice the day he was born in 1923 as the son of Boots and Blanch in Bartlesville, Oklahoma. First, he became an enrolled member of the Cherokee nation simply by virtue of his great-grandmothers, whose husbands had drilled the first commercial oil wells in Oklahoma. Second, his father worked for Phillips Petroleum, and would eventually become president. Adams' uncle became CEO of Phillips and was appointed chief of the Cherokee Nation by President Harry S Truman himself.

After graduating from college and a stint in the Navy, Adams was aboard a plane that was forced to land in Houston due to heavy fog. "I liked the area," he would later say, "so I stayed."

Houstonians, at first, were grateful. Adams launched a successful wildcat oil firm, and after several failed attempts to purchase an NFL team, he became a pioneer member of the "Foolish Club"—the original owners in the American Football League. The Oilers won three championships, and Adams was paramount in forcing a merger with the NFL. In those days, Bud was a maverick: As a new AFL owner in 1960, he signed Louisiana State's Heisman Trophy winner Billy Cannon out from under the nose of the NFL's Pete Rozelle, who then was with the Los Angeles Rams.

Adams signed Cannon in the end zone following LSU's Sugar Bowl victory. The Rams took him to court, and the AFL won a landmark victory against the NFL, which put the fledgling league on the map. Cannon was a man after my own heart—he became an orthodontist after his football career.

No one can seem to pinpoint when Adams became so cold, but all the people I know agree that it happened after the merger that he did not support. By the time I met him, he had burned through eight coaches in fifteen years. But that was hardly his legacy. For a professional football owner, his behavior was bizarre. He micro-managed the team and demanded that he personally approve all expenditures over $200. This created an unbearable log-jam in a business where a couple boxes of chinstraps or facemasks could be $300—and Adams might be gone on a week-long business trip.

Although Adams was initially a hero in Houston for bringing the city a major-league team playing in the AFL, with much success, his popularity tailed off during the Oilers early NFL years. In the late '70s the Oilers regained prominence under their popular coach Bum Phillips and the Luv Ya Blue era. Adams fired Phillips, and the team was terrible and would not be a serious contender until the late 1980s. Most of the Houston sporting public blamed Adams.

During the 1970s alone, the Oilers traded or waived George Blanda, Ken Houston, Charlie Joiner, Steve Largent, and Willie Brown, all of whom would one day make the Pro Football Hall of Fame.

When I first took a look at Brazile's existing contract, which I didn't negotiate, it was sad, and was full of more holes than a screen door. The Oilers knew it, too: They had purposely signed him to another long-term contract, and Robert had outperformed it, too. I tried to renegotiate with Ladd Herzeg, but that was like pissing up a rope.

Robert would have made more money parking cars, which at one point Herzeg suggested he do if he didn't like playing professional football. Adams flatly refused to renegotiate any deal, including Robert's, going as far to say he didn't care who represented him. I loved the challenge, and saw no recourse but to withhold Brazile's services.

I had earned the friendship and confidence of head coach Bum Phillips. So, when I held Robert out of camp, missing several preseason games, he called me—and wasted no words. "Robert Brazile is the best damn linebacker in football," he said. "He's one of only three guys we have who can play. Can you please get him back in here? We can't even line up on defense without Robert, and we're getting killed."

I asked Bum to set the table with Adams for a face-to-face meeting at the Oilers' training camp at San Angelo State University, 318 miles away from Houston. I was shocked when Adams agreed; but he insisted I bring Robert with me. I scooped up Robert, and we hit the road.

En route, Robert told me Bud Adams stories until I laughed so hard I nearly wrecked the car. During holidays, Adams would substitute $5 frozen hams for cash bonuses to Oilers staff. During the playoffs, he paid coaches $3,000 for winning the first round. The next week, when the Oilers won again, he paid them only $2,000. The following week, the Oilers lost in the AFC Championship, and the money stopped.

"Thank God we didn't win the Super Bowl that year," Brazile laughed, "the coaches would've owed Bud money."

I had told the Houston media "that a dollar bill says 'In God We Trust,' but in Bud, we don't."

When we arrived at San Angelo State and sat down in a near-barren room that consisted of a long cafeteria table and a few folding chairs, Bud saw little humor in my remark. Robert sat on one side of me, and Phillips was sitting on the other side of Adams.

"He's got a contract Argovitz," Adams said, skipping all the small talk. "He needs to honor it."

Now, I found humor in that. I love it when teams insist players should honor their contracts, when the owners can cut a player at any time. Basically, the NFL players are the only ones with a contract. The teams are the only ones with real options, and they can fire you. There is no loyalty from the majority of the owners to the players—football is a business, although the NFL is a monopoly.

"Bud, here's the deal," I said. "I've done my best to work with Ladd, your general manager, and we've reached a stalemate. Based on current contracts with players half as good as Robert statistically, he's making half what he's worth. So here are my options: Hold him out of camp, demand a trade, or I can send him back out on the practice field and I'll advise him to give you what you're paying for—half of his effort."

Bud looked right at Robert, and waved his hand like a magician toward me and Bum Phillips—as if to make us disappear.

"Robert, I know you are having some financial problems and need some money. I won't renegotiate your contract, but I will help you out."

Bud's offer shocked me. This was the first time I ever heard an NFL owner allude to "cash under the table." I asked Robert if he wanted to go to jail. He said, "no." I said I didn't either.

With that, we stood up and walked out the door. We barely made it down the hall before Adams sent Bum Phillips hustling after us. "He's reconsidered," Bum said.

Within a matter of hours, Robert had a new contract and a cash bonus to boot. "Doc," he said afterward, "I don't know how to thank you."

This was the most rewarding part of my job.

"Robert," I said—stealing a line from a recent popular TV commercial jingle— "This Bud's *for you.*"

Robert deserves to be in the Pro Football Hall of Fame.

31

DON'T SQUAT WITH YOUR SPURS ON

SOMETIMES IT PAYS to be a firebrand. All the publicity—good and bad—I'd received had caught the attention of David Dixon, a New Orleans entrepreneur, fine-antiques dealer, and football aficionado who had come to me with an intriguing idea: a spring football league. Better yet, it was only fitting that David had experienced quite a history with Pete Rozelle and the NFL's tangled web of antitrust deceit, dating back to the early 1960s.

With my boots squishing ever deeper into the home-grown fertilizer dropped by NFL owners, its management, and Rozelle, I struck up phone conversations with David that were downright mesmerizing. At this point, I was seeking any leverage I could get; I doubted the NFL would tolerate another firestorm like the one I'd created in 1981 with Gary and Overstreet and their foray into the Canadian Football League, which had left me scrambling for new options for the players.

Dixon's idea for a new spring football league represented more than just options. For me, he also represented a measure of justice against my antagonists. I invited him to Houston, not realizing the long-term ramifications our meeting would have on the future of professional football.

The first time Dixon appeared on the NFL radar screen was in the early 1960s, when Rozelle had come into power. After promoting NFL exhibitions at Tulane Stadium, he used his flair—along with powerful political and social connections—to seek a franchise for New Orleans. Ironically, in 1966, when Rozelle sought antitrust immunity from Congress, he turned to Dixon for help.

Representative Emanuel Celler of Brooklyn was the chairman of the House Judiciary Committee, and had vehemently opposed Rozelle. The commissioner called Dixon in New Orleans. Dixon was a friend of Hale Boggs of Louisiana, the House Majority whip, so Rozelle asked for a meeting, then sent a public-relations advisor to meet with them. In what could only be called a thinly veiled quid pro quo—an NFL franchise in exchange for the antitrust exemption—Boggs went into action, and circumvented Celler by attaching the immunity to a budget bill.

The exemption was approved in October 1966, and New Orleans was awarded its NFL team on All-Saints Day, November 1. The Saints were purchased by John Mecom Jr., a friend of mine who had Houston real estate holdings along with his father, John Mecom Sr. The Saints opened play at Tulane Stadium in 1967. In the meantime, Dixon had the support of Governor John McKeithen for construction of a domed stadium in downtown New Orleans, and relinquished his minority interest in the Saints to become executive director of the soon-to-be Superdome, where he remained until it opened in 1975.

Now Dixon, partly responsible himself for the NFL cartel, sought to compete against it, and he was seeking me for advice? Are you kidding me? Hollywood scriptwriters couldn't have written a better subplot, and of course, I was happy to help. If Dixon could pull this off, it would mean new teams, new markets, and new money, which meant higher value for my clients with their respective NFL teams.

"Come see me, David," I said. "Show me everything you've got."

Dixon bounded into my Houston office in the late summer of 1981 with an outward confidence that belied his sixty-one years. Before he opened his mouth, I could tell this guy could sell snow to an Eskimo. Dixon resembled a spry, bespectacled George Bush Sr., and had the manners of a genteel Southerner. Dixon shook my hand with a firm grip and looked me directly in the eyes as he sat down, grabbed a hanky from his sport coat, and dabbed a few beads of sweat from his brow.

"Jerry, I do believe with your help and a few men like you we can make history," he said. "I've been working on this idea for a long, long time." He flipped open his worn brown leather briefcase and started whipping out notebooks, colored pie charts, and a thick, spiral-bound document, all of which landed on my cherrywood desk one thud at a time.

"Spring football isn't far-fetched," he said. "Timing is everything, right? College and pro football is more popular than ever. Fans can't get enough. Here's the deal: The NFL's television contracts are winding down. The NFL's collective bargaining agreement is going to expire, and the players are bound to strike next year. This makes for a huge opportunity in spring of '83. "

No kidding, I thought. "Who do you have as owners?" I asked.

Like any good entrepreneur, David could knit great ideas with capital. He rattled off an impressive list of a dozen or more very deep pockets; many of them I either already knew, or certainly knew of. In Tampa, he had John Bassett, a Canadian film developer and businessman. In Birmingham, he had banking mogul Marvin L. Warner. In Michigan, A. Alfred Taubman, one of the richest men in the nation, a real estate developer and pioneer of the modern shopping mall. And in New York, he had Oklahoma oilman J. Walter Duncan. And this was just for starters. As the league grew and as territories merged, the list would include a young New York businessman by the name of Donald J. Trump.

"I'm already talking to two TV networks, and I've got serious interest," he added.

David now had my undivided attention. Half the owners he'd named were NFL-worthy, and if you threw in TV money, this could really work. He picked up his spiral-bound notebook and waved it like an evangelist holding a Bible. "This is a study I commissioned from Frank Magid Associates," he said. "Essentially, it conclusively suggests that a spring league would be fondly received by the public and that teams could turn profits. It further suggests that television networks could use spring sports programming, and that owners can make money."

"Where do I fit in?" I wondered.

Methodically, David painstakingly went through his presentation, which consisted of the Magid study and an array of supporting documents. Watching his breathless histrionics, I smiled—he got me excited sitting still. He was going to need players, and lots of them; he was going to need help negotiating contracts and advice on additional owners. He envisioned playing in the spring of 1983.

"David, you've got a chance to right a lot of wrongs in the NFL, and to give the public something to think about," I said. A page at a time, we went through his paperwork, and I made my suggestions while he took meticulous notes and asked great questions; he might have been a character, but he was incredibly gifted, and bright. He had the annual team budgets set at $1.8 million, which was reasonable, but he would need good negotiators. "You need at least two marquee players per team, like a quarterback or running back," I suggested. "That will tell the media and the fans how serious you and these owners really are."

I explained that the NFL demanded a prototype player, which left thousands of others—who were just as good—without the opportunity to play professional football. "There are countless players out there who will never have a chance because they're an inch too short, thirty pounds too light and a half second too slow," I said. "All the NFL's statistics and measurements leave one thing out: Nobody pays any attention to the size of their hearts, or their desire to play the game. Trust me, there are great players available."

The key, I noted, was a territorial draft. "You wouldn't believe how many all-conference, All-America players from major conferences—some of the most popular players—who never play professional football," I said. "A territorial draft immediately creates a rapport with the fans. They've known these kids since they were freshmen."

Finally, he asked me about rules.

"On the field, open up the game," I said. "Push for innovative coaches. Deepen the end zones if you have to. Bring back the two-point conversion. Stop the clock after first downs. Make receivers only get one foot down to rule it a catch. No fair catching on punts. Use instant replay if you can to overturn calls. Let the kids dance in the end zone. Make the game fun!"

Just to be sure I had his attention, I dropped a bombshell.

"And don't be afraid to sign underclassmen," I said.

David grabbed his water glass and took a gulp.

"Excuse me, Jerry?"

"I said, Don't be afraid to sign underclassmen! Listen, Billy Sims, Curtis Dickey, Hugh Green—half my players—were ready to come out during their junior years if the NFL and NCAA would have allowed them. They had nothing to gain by playing their senior years except risking a career-ending injury."

David almost choked. "We can't do that," he stammered. "I'm in discussions with a number of former NFL coaches and executives. They tell me not to mess with juniors—we'll enrage every college coach and the entire NCAA."

"To hell with the NCAA," I said. "You do realize they are just as illegal as the NFL, right?"

An ex-Marine, Dixon didn't retreat. To the contrary, he was fascinated, and wrote down every word.

"Answer this question, David—who makes the NCAA rules? The NCAA. And who is the NCAA? You fought for your country when you were eighteen, right? Tell me anywhere else in the United States where a man who is physically and mentally able is told he can't even try out? Why does a kid have to attend college to be a professional football player? What if every person in America lost his job right now if he didn't go to school? This is hypocrisy!

"The NCAA is just an unsubsidized farm system for the NFL," I told him. He was nodding his head. "The draft is illegal, too. Before I die, I promise you, the NCAA will implode under its own corn-fed wind; and the draft, without collective bargaining, will be dead, too."

I burst out laughing. "You're right about one thing, David," I said. "You've got a chance to make history all right—but maybe just not the kind you were thinking."

He dabbed his forehead a few more times, and spit out a question.

"This is totally hypothetical," he said. "But if we did look at an underclassman . . . "

I cut him off. "Herschel Walker," I said, without hesitation. "Best running back in football."

"He's a freshman!" Dixon retorted.

"Well, you said spring 1983, right? That's before his senior year."

"Jerry, you're nuts!"

I grinned. "But you know I'm right, don't you?"

Without a doubt, I wanted Dixon's plan to succeed. No question, his business model was spot on, and had every element necessary for a new league to make it. Competition means free enterprise—I had a chance to bust free agency wide open. A new league would severely hamstring the NFL, and—if David bought my argument—emancipate NCAA players. And the best part was that this would come from a guy, Dixon, whom Rozelle and the NFL had treated like a pawn to secure their existing monopoly.

I believed David was a straight shooter, and an honest man. He understood that my fiduciary duty was to my players, and not to any league, be it the NFL, CFL, or now, the USFL. It was to our advantage to get as many teams and leagues as possible to provide jobs and opportunities for the players. Houston and New Orleans were just three hours apart, and we agreed to meet often—with a promise that neither one of us would reveal we were doing so.

The NFL had done its best to throttle me, muffle me, and sit on me; it was about to discover why in Texas we don't squat with our spurs on.

When David left, I grabbed Gene and we headed out for some fine Houston cuisine—a couple of original Texas chili dogs at James' Coney Island. Gene couldn't believe his ears as I rattled off Dixon's strategy, and nearly choked.

"Do me a favor, Gene," I said between bites. "Gather every bit of information you can on the Herschel Walker kid at Georgia. I want to know what makes him tick. I want to know what he eats for breakfast."

"I can't," Gene said, smiling. "He doesn't eat breakfast. He eats once a day. He eats salad, soup, and bread. I'm already on it, coach. All over it."

32

SOCIALISM, COMMUNISM, AND THE UNITED STATES FOOTBALL LEAGUE

IN 1982 NFL union head Ed Garvey had drawn the line in the sand—a strike in the fall seemed unavoidable. The collective bargaining agreement between the players and the Management Council, which represented the owners, would expire on July 15. Deep distrust emanated from both sides, and Garvey, whom I considered to be little more than a liberal, flaming idiot, only added fuel to the fire.

The NFL had just signed another record-breaking TV deal, which further empowered Garvey. ABC paid $681 million for Monday Night Football; CBS paid $713 million for NFC games and two Super Bowls. NBC paid $638 million for AFC games and two Super Bowls. The total was $2.325 billion. Dividing this pie was hardly child's play. Garvey thinking he was a union boss was about as funny as me flipping burgers in McDonald's and calling myself a chef. Remember that Garvey had convinced players to hold out of camp for six weeks in 1974, only to have them concede and return. In 1977 he had signed away free agency. Now in 1982, I felt like he had a personal vendetta that could only hurt the players.

Since the day I became a player agent, I had argued for unfettered free agency. My ideas were simple. Over time (eventually culminating in the resolution of the 2011 NFL lockout) they would prove to be gospel: I was demanding three- or four-year contracts without penalties or restrictions to a player's original team, and no version of the Rozelle Rule should a player elect to play for another team.

While I was building a case for free agency, it seemed as if Garvey worked equally hard to destroy it and any leverage that came with it. He told reporters that "you can never have free agency in the NFL's closed monopoly," which was ludicrous. He told linemen that if they went on strike for free agency, they would be striking only so "quarterbacks and running backs can make more money." He wanted all NFL players to be represented by the union itself, not by individual representatives. He proposed wage scales: Regardless of position, every player would receive the same base salary, depending on the number of years they had been in the league, plus bonuses and incentives.

Garvey called the NFL a socialist society; he then countered with his own theoretical economic system characterized by the collective ownership of property and the organization of the NFLPA for the common advantage of all its members. I looked that up, by the way, and that was the pure definition of communism. Furthermore, for Garvey to even consider using only representatives of the NFLPA to represent each NFL player with their team was an outrageous conflict of interest, rivaled only by the collusion and monopoly of the owners.

All my players agreed with me: Just because a chicken has wings doesn't mean it can fly, and none of them trusted the union. They trusted me. Garvey would have had better luck telling a stranger's dog to sit, heel, or roll over.

About the only thing Garvey and I agreed upon was that players deserved a fair and equitable percentage of a team's gross revenue, something I believed then and now. In 1967, when the NFL had competed with the AFL for players, 68 percent of gross revenue had gone for player salaries. Without competition, except for players like mine who went to Canada, the percentage had dropped off to 25 percent.

The owners behaved like ranchers, and considered their players cattle—a belief so entrenched that Tex Schramm of the Dallas Cowboys would later admit to such in his own book, *Never Just a Game*. The Management Council included three owners—Tampa Bay's Hugh Culverhouse, Pittsburgh's Dan Rooney, and Philadelphia's Leonard Tose— all who had drafted at least one of my players. In my own conversations with Culverhouse, he had told me point-blank that owners would never allow "the inmates to run the prison, period."

Over just a few years, I had rattled cages around the NFL with record-breaking contracts, holdouts, renegotiations of veterans' contracts, and visible and vocal dissatisfaction—exposing the NFL's monopolistic system. Teams were now exchanging information and acting in collusion to keep salaries as low as possible; with fixed television revenues and equal profit-sharing, last-place teams had no incentive to win—earning just as much as those that won the Super Bowl. Garvey's plan not only would hurt superstars, but also put them on par, or worse, with their backups who never saw the field.

Despite the palpable unrest between the NFLPA and the Management Council, Gene and I had a banner draft on April 27, 1982. In the first round alone, Jim McMahon went to the Chicago Bears with the fifth pick; the Steelers took running back Walter Abercrombie with the twelfth selection; St. Louis picked offensive tackle Luis Sharpe sixteenth; and the Giants grabbed Butch Woolfolk with the eighteenth pick. With the second pick of the second round, the 49ers chose left tackle Bubba Paris.

Neither the owners nor players would budge on their positions of power or money. In the face of an imminent NFL players strike, I would have to do the unthinkable—negotiate with some of the toughest, most ruthless owners and general managers football had ever known. Chicago's George Halas and Jim Finks, New York's Wellington Mara and George Young, Pittsburgh's Dan Rooney and St. Louis's Bill Bidwill were tighter than bark on a tree, and I would be about as welcome as a skunk at a garden party.

I called Garvey and cussed his ass out regarding his artificial deadline to make a player sign.

"Are you crazy?" I asked. "You're taking away our leverage, what little we have."

"July 15 means July 15," he answered. "Our players will strike. This isn't fun, Jerry. Nobody gives up money or power for the fun of it. There is no economic incentive for free agency. It doesn't increase attendance. It doesn't increase TV money. It doesn't increase anything. Fighting for free agency is a dog chasing its tail."

Not so. A year earlier, Major League Baseball had gone to war with its union over the issue, and union head Marvin Miller stole a landmark victory that reshaped the sport forever. Garvey, meanwhile, was under the ether, and was ignoring and giving away free agency, incredibly, again.

Expecting the worst, I continued to work furiously behind the scenes on the little surprise Dixon had for Rozelle, the owners, the general managers, and Garvey, too.

The fledgling United States Football League.

The United States is the only country founded on a good idea, and how fitting that the USFL was about to demonstrate why: Unfettered free agency in the form of good ol' American competition, open markets, and democracy.

From every mountainside, I thought, let freedom ring.

Just days after the 1982 NFL draft, an excited Dixon popped into my Houston office. Our clandestine meetings had escalated to the point that we were meeting or talking so often that we had become good friends. I had already spoken with half the owners, coaches or GMs of the soon-to-be-announced USFL, and I was very impressed with David's work. From a personal standpoint, it was refreshing to see a guy actually implement many of the ideas we had discussed.

For his commissioner, David and the owners had convinced Chet Simmons, president and CEO of a new innovative cable network called ESPN, to come aboard. Simmons was also a former protégé of ABC's Roone Arledge and Monday Night Football, and it had been his idea to broadcast the NFL draft on ESPN. He was perfect for the job. Better yet, he had been instrumental in landing a pair of TV contracts for the new league with, of course, ABC and ESPN.

"Peter Hadhazy is on board and has agreed to join us as director of operations," David said. Hadhazy I knew well. He had been an assistant GM with the New England Patriots, GM of the Cleveland Browns, and at the time of his USFL hiring, he was working in the NFL front office. He was another excellent decision.

"Jerry, it's time," David gushed. "We're holding a press conference on May 11. Can you speak to the owners soon afterward? We're scheduling our draft for January 4, 1983. These owners have to assemble staffs, scout players, and prepare to sign players. We've got a lot of NFL guys coming on board, but your advice is going to be extremely helpful, especially when it comes to drafting and signing players."

I agreed. "You know I'm going to talk about the NCAA and underclassmen, too," I smiled.

He nodded, albeit nervously.

"David, Herschel Walker is already telling people close to me that he'd consider going to Canada right now, after his sophomore year," I said. "Can you blame a guy for wanting to get paid and feed his family, and avoid a major injury that would prevent him from playing professional football and making money? Why should any player have to wait four years to play in the NFL? What a stupid, unconstitutional rule. This is flat-ass wrong. Herschel could start for any team in the NFL right now, and make a lot of money.

"David, David, David—who's going to take care of Herschel if he gets a career-ending injury in his junior or senior year in college?"

"Can we deal with that after the press conference, Jerry," he replied, "one crisis at a time?"

No crisis to me. Frankly, I couldn't wait.

On May 11, 1982, just a short stroll from the Broadway theater district in midtown Manhattan, the United States Football League held a press conference at the "21" Club and announced it was open for business.

The league announced its first draft would be held in January 1983, and that games would commence in March that same year.

33

DA BEARS

JIM MCMAHON CURLED his body into the limousine at Chicago's O'Hare International Airport. Fresh off his final year at Brigham Young University, where he had claimed the Davey O'Brien award, the Sammy Baugh Trophy, seventy-five NCAA records, and two All-America seasons, McMahon's body was creaking.

He had rolled up 10,000 passing yards and 84 touchdowns on his college football odometer, and—having yet to play a single professional game—was already hurting, grimacing from a back injury suffered late in the season in which he played with padding taped to his spine. Twice he had missed games with a knee injury, and still managed to become the nation's best quarterback.

"Do they have beer in here?" he asked, lowering his sunglasses and glancing around the limo's interior. McMahon had been born in Jersey City, reared as a Catholic by his parents, Jim Sr. and Roberta. The family moved to San Jose, California, when he was three. At six, McMahon severed the retina in his right eye by accidentally poking a fork into it. The injury made him sensitive to light—the real reason, he said, for the sunglasses, even in a darkened limo.

I pointed to the mini-fridge. He grabbed a beverage and popped it open, settled back in his seat, and let out a long sigh. Chicago had taken him in the first round and insisted Jim come meet George "Papa Bear" Halas, the revered, iconic leader of the Bears and the founder of professional football.

Old Halas Hall was on the campus of Lake Forest College, about 30 miles north of the city, which gave me and Jim a chance to talk. As the airport disappeared behind us and we traveled up the interstate by Lake Michigan, I just smiled. The best part about Jim is his obnoxious personality and unapologetic attitude. He could care less if you like him, and chances are, he probably doesn't like you, either. He mocked my cowboy hat, boots, and open shirts.

"That's a lot of hair flowing out of your shirt," he smirked, dripping with sarcasm. "You have great style, Jerry. That's why I like you. The Bears are really gonna love you."

My style? This was college football's bad boy, who blew up at coaches, yelled at teammates in the huddle, and "changed the play at least 60 percent of the time," said Lavell Edwards, his BYU coach.

"Why wouldn't I change the play?" he asked. "If the coaches are wrong, I'm just doing them a favor before the whole world finds out."

I changed the subject. "Excited?" I asked.

"About what?" he said. "Are you hiding girls somewhere?" He laughed. "How far is the drive?"

"About twenty more minutes."

"How long will it take when we get there?"

"That's up to them," I said. "Mr. Halas wants to talk to you."

"Good," he said, guzzling his beer and wiping his mouth on the back of his hand. "Well, let's get it done and get out. Let's not sit around smelling his old farts."

There is only one Jim McMahon.

It was none other than Colts' owner Bob Irsay who dropped McMahon into the lap of the Chicago Bears. Baltimore had closed out 1981 with a 2-14 record, and had the fourth pick in the draft. The Colts made it known publicly they would draft Jim McMahon. Irsay had ended the season by bursting into the coaches' booth and sending down plays to his head coach, Mike McCormack. Irsay didn't just hate me; he hated everybody, which didn't make me feel any better. After the season, Irsay fired McCormack and—just after the draft—he would fire Dick Szymanski, his general manager and my old rival, which unwittingly played into my hands and may have cost him a Super Bowl.

The best quarterback in the 1982 draft was McMahon, whom I had met at the Walter Camp Awards. Jim had introduced himself to me, which is rare. "Jerry Argovitz," he said, "every GM in the NFL hates you, so you must be doing something right. I know you've got Curtis Dickey in Baltimore, and I heard about your issues there. I don't want to play for Irsay. If you can keep me out of Baltimore, you're hired."

"I promise you that if I represent you, Baltimore won't draft you," I told him.

I went to Utah, met with Jim, and he and I swiftly saw eye-to-eye. Jim and I shared the exact same philosophy. He laughed when I told him that all my clients had an escape clause in their agreements. "Send me a letter if you don't like me, and you can fire me on the spot," I said.

"But remember . . . I get to do the same."

He agreed. Jim liked the fact that my product was my players, and my product—and record—was perfect. The NFL was a world of sheep, and leaders like Jim McMahon immediately stood out like goats and commanded the highest respect, as well as the entertainment dollar. But with Jim, it wasn't all about money. He was a game-changer, in every sense of the word. He had a way of not conforming that made the establishment resent and love him at the same time. The kid was one of the most competitive people I've ever known. He would go after his grandmother to beat her at tiddlywinks.

Unlike Bob Irsay, who blasted away like a band of pirates firing on a passenger ship. "If Jerry Argovitz is McMahon's agent," he told my friend Peter Hadhazy, "then I'll draft Ohio State's Art Schlichter."

Trust me, it was mutual. Without me lifting a finger, Irsay's public hatred for me cemented my new client's number-one goal. Call it "seren-fucking-dipity." But as soon as I called the Colts and Szymanski to tell him I was representing McMahon—and reminded him of the Curtis Dickey bribe—all of a sudden, Schlichter's spirals got tighter and he became the superior quarterback.

This left Jim available to the Bears and the grand stage of Chicago. I couldn't have drawn this up any better, because from the very moment I met him, I knew Jim was destined for greatness.

"Outrageousness," he said, "is my way of waking people up."

The greatest fear most people have is not being who they are, and instead, resigning themselves to simply follow the crowd. Jim never shied away from being the one thing that made him uniquely different—himself. If I was ever in a war, and I could be in a foxhole with one soldier, it would be Jimmy Mac.

Mac stunned the nation in the 1980 Holiday Bowl after the Cougars trailed SMU 38-19 midway through the fourth quarter. McMahon started a rally for the ages, at one point refusing to leave the field on fourth down. Behind 45-25 with 4:09 to play, Jim marched BYU to consecutive scores; the Cougars blocked a punt, and then he threw a forty-one-yard Hail Mary to Clay Brown with no time left to beat the Mustangs 46-45 in breathless fashion.

BYU head coach Lavell Edwards would later call McMahon clearly one of the best he'd ever coached. The evidence was evident by his junior year, when McMahon—exuding uncanny presence in the pocket—had a whopping passing efficiency of 176.9. While nobody would ever accused Jim of being Steve Young, he was mobile, could throw on the run and, when necessary, run over anyone to get a yard. The truth about football is that, while the casual fan considers it a game of incredible precision, in reality it is a game of breakdowns. If all plays happened the way they are drawn on the chalkboard, the game would be easy. However, because of mental errors and missteps, the pressure breaks the weak, but creates an opening for pure genius for the impresarios.

Scouts call that leadership, which really is a combination of fearlessness and pure will. McMahon was a rebellious and fierce competitor, a great leader who could read defenses. He marched to his own drummer and wasn't afraid to change plays, run recklessly for first downs, confront linebackers or linemen, scream back at fans, or argue with coaches. He was more brave than tough, because for him not to be meant a potential loss of manhood, and for McMahon, that was too great to face. He turned obstacles into opportunity, and used his rock-star energy to corral morale. Jim was a tough act to follow, because few could pull it off. He made everyone around him better. He provided the extra confidence necessary to win.

He was a sixteen-year-old junior when his family moved to Roy, Utah, a blue-collar town with year-around rain and heavy winter snow, a perfect proving ground for a future Bear. His father, Jim, was a Catholic, his mother, Roberta, was a Mormon. His parents routinely told him to believe he was the best, so he did.

Jim cared for neither parents' religion, but hoped that his three-sport excellence at Andrew Hills High might get him a shot at Notre Dame. It didn't. BYU, Utah, and Utah State, however, did, and he chose BYU, where his ornery aggression immediately clashed with the school's long-held Mormon traditions.

He drank beer and played golf on Sunday. He said he was harassed daily to convert to Mormonism, but refused to hide behind the prison walls of BYU's "hypocritical" honor code and fought to get out of its circle. His staunch refusal to "conform" was met with enthusiasm by the public and disdain by his college deans. They asked him to pull in the same direction, yet McMahon insisted that if everybody pulled in the same direction, the whole world would keel over.

On and off the field, his presence was commanding. His own frustrations, aspirations, resentments, and jubilation sizzled through college crowds—and nightclubs—like electricity, and fans lived vicariously through his eccentricities, wild temper, and ego. BYU, meanwhile, handled McMahon like they were bathing with a leper.

"What was the best part about BYU?" I asked him then.

"Seeing it in my rear-view mirror," he replied.

"Did you feel used as a college player?" I asked.

"Anybody who ever plays college football," he said, "gets used."

Shortly after the NFL draft, the USFL was holding tryouts and preparing for its inaugural draft and season. Longtime NFL veteran coach George Allen had jumped to the new league to become head coach of the Chicago Blitz, and was already leading the USFL in free-agent signings. George's son Bruce was serving the Blitz as general manager, and it hadn't taken them long to contact me and inquire about the availability of McMahon. I told them I was already having discussions with Dr. Ted Dietrich, owner of the Blitz and a long-time personal friend of mine. He had performed heart surgery on my mother back in Houston as a top resident, and he had been an investor in some of my land syndication deals.

Once again, history came within an inch of being completely rewritten, and with fascinating subplots.

Allen had strong ties to the Bears, having been hired by Halas in 1958 as a scout. Papa Bear was so impressed with Allen's attention to detail that he eventually earned a position on the Bears' coaching staff, and worked his way up to defensive coordinator. His strategies and motivational skills helped lead the Bears to the 1963 NFL Championship. Allen quickly proved his mental agility at the NFL draft, choosing legends like Mike Ditka, Gale Sayers, and Dick Butkus.

It was widely reported that Halas had told Allen for several years he would become the next Bears head coach, but Halas kept winning, and kept extending his coaching career. Finally, in a heated contract dispute with Halas, Allen finally left to become a head coach with the Los Angeles Rams and the Washington Redskins, where he took the latter to a Super Bowl.

Now Allen had the opportunity to one-up Halas in his own backyard—if he could convince Dr. Dietrich to sign McMahon with the Blitz, a team that had yet to play a game. After going nowhere with the Bears, I proposed to Dr. Dietrich a deal with the Blitz: $600,000 a year for four years, guaranteed, and 5 percent ownership in the team, which would be the first contract of its kind.

I asked for the offer in writing, and then let it be made known to the Bears. Halas, certainly no stranger to the recruiting wars between the old AFL and NFL, immediately called for the meeting in Chicago. The new head coach of the Bears was Mike Ditka himself, who certainly didn't want to be upstaged in his own town by Allen, his old coach.

The written offer from the Blitz never materialized, but the Bears never knew how close they came to disaster. Had the Blitz, Dr. Dietrich, and Allen moved quicker, McMahon had given me the go-ahead to draft a special-services contract with the Blitz and the USFL. Such a move would have sent shockwaves through Chicago, crippled the Bears, and given the new league overnight credibility before it pumped up its first football.

If the USFL is going to compete against the NFL for its top players, I thought, it's going to have to learn to get offers on the table, and quick. The Blitz brass had drug its feet, and it cost them one of the best players in football.

Owners of most NFL teams were scrambling to sign players before the strike and to avoid USFL competition. After losing Keith Gary the year before to Canada, Steelers' GM Dan Rooney took no chances: He flew into Houston and drove to my house to resolve Walter Abercrombie's contract, and it went smoothly. George Young of the Giants came to my Houston office to hammer out Butch Woolfolk's deal. George was one of the nicest "tough guys" to ever grace the NFL, but nobody ever accused him of being thin. The day he came to Houston, it had to be 110 degrees. I turned the heat up in my office, and we had Butch's contract done in record time.

Bubba Paris, who was drafted by the 49ers in the second round, benefited greatly from a single published quote from his head coach—the legendary Bill Walsh. "We were shocked Bubba was still available in the second round," he told the San Francisco fans and media. "We had Bubba projected first-round all the way." That worked well when I asked for first-round money, and surprisingly, the 49ers quickly paid it.

When it came to Luis Sharpe and the Cardinals, Bill Bidwill, the St. Louis owner, brought in an outside attorney to negotiate with me. Bidwill was absolutely notorious for being cheap, but when dealing with me he clearly decided that there were more ways to skin a cat than sticking his head in a boot jack and jerking on his tail.

"Can we keep this out of the press?" Mr. Bidwill asked me.

"That's up to you," I said.

His designated hired gun—in our first meeting—said, "I've done my homework. I intend to accomplish this in record time."

"What's your proposal?" I asked.

God is my witness: His first offer was more than my number. So I added another 35 percent to that, and they agreed.

Luis was ecstatic, to say the least.

This is how Jim and I wound up driving to Old Halas Hall at Lake Forest College hoping to sign a deal with the Bears before the expiration of the NFLPA's collective bargaining agreement on the evening of July 15. After that date, Jim—under Garvey's rule—wouldn't be allowed to have representation. The drive to Old Halas Hall was picturesque, and I couldn't help but think of the generations of legendary Bears who had made this same trek in bygone eras—Johnny Lujack, Bobby Layne, Red Grange, Dick Butkus. Dusk was settling, and now we were passing through a series of neighborhoods. Jim began to wonder aloud where we were going.

"This is the NFL?" Jim said. "I feel like I'm headed to a Pop Warner practice. Are you sure we're not headed back to Utah?"

As it came into view adjacent from two practice fields, Old Halas Hall—a one-story, red brick ranch house with a chimney stuck right in the middle—looked more like a Moose Lodge than the home of the Monsters of the Midway.

Scrambling media swarmed outside the building, and one reporter noted I was wearing my black hat. "He's wearing the black hat! There's going to be hell to pay!" he shouted into the camera. Bears' personnel hustled us into the building.

The tensions inside the building had been escalating long before our arrival.

The Halas family had hired Jim Finks, a football executive, to run the team in 1974. I actually had a liking for Finks; at one time, he had been a maverick and a front-office innovator. He understood fair-market value and the importance of competition, including the value of other leagues. He had been a backup quarterback at Notre Dame, jumped to Calgary of the Canadian Football League, became the team's general manager, and eventually won a championship. He switched to the NFL as GM of the Minnesota Vikings, where he hired Bud Grant, another CFL legend, as head coach. The Vikings played in four Super Bowls, and Finks became NFL Executive of the Year.

After Finks became the Bears' executive vice president and GM, he surprised everyone with his hiring of Jack Pardee, a former NFL linebacker whose only coaching experience had been in the defunct World Football League. Not surprisingly, this thinking clashed with the old-school Halas, who staunchly believed in clean NFL bloodlines and the pedigree of his own stall. Just prior to drafting McMahon, Halas had hired former Bear Mike Ditka without consulting Finks, and it created enough friction to start another Chicago fire. Now Halas was applying enormous pressure on Finks, and had reclaimed much of the power he once had entrusted to him.

Finks and I already had butted heads the previous year. I represented wide receiver Ken Margerum, who had played at Stanford University, where Bill Walsh had briefly been his head coach prior to joining the San Francisco 49ers. Finks called Walsh, and had him call Kenny.

"You are a third-round pick," Walsh had told him. "You need to fire your agent and sign a contract now if you want to make the team."

When Ken called me and informed me of what Walsh had said, I was furious. First, it demonstrated the collusion among teams. Second, it proved that if you shoot holes in the NFL's closed system, they will stop at nothing to plug them. Kenny was distraught.

"Ken, you hired me for a reason," I said. "This is proof—otherwise, why would competing NFL teams work together to torturously interfere with my ability to do my job?" He agreed, and I called Bill Walsh. My first question: "Do you even know what the Bears are offering him?"

Walsh said no. I said, "Is Kenny a good player?"

"Of course," Walsh answered.

"Then why should he make 35 or 40 percent less than what he's worth?" I asked. "If you really care about him, tell Jim Finks to sharpen his pencil and get the job done."

Finks and I battled all the way to the finish line of Ken's short-term contract, which included a signing bonus and was laden with incentives.

I knew Finks wouldn't be too happy to see me again. Not with a pending strike and a wildcat draft pick like McMahon; you can only imagine the maelstrom that Jim and I walked into that night with the hopes of negotiating a fair and equitable contract. Before I arrived, Finks and I had discussed numbers over the phone; it would be interesting to see if he lived up to them.

"Hold on tight, Mac," I said, as we walked toward the front door. "This is going to be a hairy ride."

Jim squinted, and gave me a quick nod. He didn't seem overly concerned as he blew his nose—by holding each nostril shut, one at a time—on the ground.

Finks was wearing a starched white shirt, a red tie, and a pair of wide silver-rimmed glasses that matched the color of his hair. He looked exhausted, with dark circles under both eyes. The stress he was under was evident by the cigarette-induced wrinkles around his mouth. In Minnesota, he had been able to carve out his fiefdom. In Chicago, Finks was clearly the doorman of the Halas Empire, and it had become his prison.

Out of respect, I took off my cowboy hat. We all shook hands and headed back to a dark, paneled, musty office, shelved with books. Rows of old gray filing cabinets were against the wall to the left. It smelled like old cigars. We took our seats in thick, padded leather Victorian chairs facing a gigantic wooden desk big enough—and old enough—that I swear George Washington could have used it to cross the Delaware. We talked with Finks for about a half hour.

Like a Broadway play, George Halas shuffled in stage right from a side door, wearing what appeared to be silk pajamas. His body was bowed, but even after eighty-seven years, the slight forward hunch still gave him an aura of barely restrained power. The aging patriarch still looked ready for something. What, exactly, I wasn't sure. His chiseled face looked like a pencil sketching, etched by countless games in the teeth of bitter Chicago winters.

It's one thing to think how you might respond when you meet history face-to-face, but actually witnessing it is quite intimidating, especially when you're not there for an autograph. Standing in front of me was the man who had helped start the NFL. This was the man who brought the Decatur Staleys to Chicago, renamed them the Bears, and in the new league's early years, played offense, defense, and special teams. He also sold tickets to Wrigley Field and ran the business. In a 1923 game, he had stripped the ball from Jim Thorpe—Jim Thorpe—and returned the fumble ninety-eight yards for a touchdown, a league record.

He signed the great Red Grange right off the Illinois campus before the Galloping Ghost graduated—at that time a move considered totally taboo. He was a cut-throat coach who implemented a revolutionary offense in the T-formation, piled up statistics, and ran up scores, once beating the Washington Redskins 73-0. He won 321 games in the National Football League.

Then I looked down. The great feet that had carried George Halas like wings down the immortal sidelines of time were now gnarled and stuffed inside soft, puffy slippers. It was a freeze-frame moment I will never forget.

Thinking the same thing, Jim and I exchanged glances.

Did we wake him up? And where was he sleeping?

Mr. Halas sat down behind the giant desk; Finks rode side-saddle in a chair to his left.

"Son," he rasped, his eyes boring into mine, "we've been doing this a long time, longer than you've been alive, and way before your boy's folks"—he pointed a scraggly finger at Jim—"were even born."

Both Finks and Jim sat smugly across from each other, with arms crossed. Jim clearly didn't appreciate being called "boy," and with McMahon likely to say anything at any time, I hurriedly kept the dialogue moving along.

"Mr. Halas," I said, "I'm a huge fan. I have tremendous respect for you and what you mean to professional football ... "

"Mr. Staley gave me $5,000 to move this team to Chicago," Halas said, interrupting as if I'd never said a word. He coughed wetly. "We worked our asses off building this franchise. Hard work. Disciplined work. We've had some great quarterbacks here: Billy Wade. George Blanda. Sid Luckman was amazing. Your boy there is coming into a great tradition."

At the moment, I was praying to God "my boy" didn't blurt out something we were all going to regret. I spotted Halas's autobiography on a shelf behind him, and asked about it. To my amazement, he grabbed it and opened it. A pen appeared from nowhere, and he began to sign it.

"Sid Luckman was the best quarterback ever," he growled. "He was the best of his era, and all eras to come. I played him at halfback before I moved him to quarterback. He understood the machinations of how the game was supposed to be played. He earned every nickel." Halas chuckled to himself. "I told Sid to keep his money in his sock, and at night, to put it in his pillowcase. That way he'd never lose it."

Looks like "my boy" is going to need some bigger shoes, I thought.

Halas looked up, slid the book across the desk at me, and didn't crack a smile.

Finks handed me Jim's contract. I immediately noticed some zeroes were missing.

"Son, this is a family business," Halas continued. "We lose money every year. Mr. Finks here will tell you that we can't afford the money you guys are talking about. This annuity stuff and insurance you're asking for—we've never done that. It's a miracle we're still in business. The only way I'll ever make money here is to sell the team."

On the spot, I offered George Halas $50 million to buy the Bears.

"I'll buy the team right now, Mr. Halas," I deadpanned. "I'd be happy to take on the awesome responsibility of owning the Bears. No one should own a business that isn't profitable."

He cupped his hand behind his ear and leaned across the desk.

"How much?" he asked.

"Fifty million," I repeated.

That forced a smile from the old man. He changed subjects like he used to break open-field tackles, and immediately turned on Jim.

"Your boy there could probably go play in Canada," he said. Finks grinned at the obvious cheap-shot, which could've been directed at either one of us. "I've seen the tapes. He's got a weak arm. He's damn near blind in one eye. He's missed several games because of injuries. He's got a bad back and a bad knee. And his mechanics look nothing like Sid's."

By this time, McMahon was simmering. He was tired of Halas's stroll down memory lane and was clearly fed up with being called my "boy." He was at his breaking point.

"If I'm all those things," McMahon said, "why in the hell did you draft me?"

Halas ignored him and pointed to the contract, which I was quickly scrolling—$300,000 to sign, three years with an option, worth over a million dollars total—far below what I'd discussed with Finks. Clearly, they were using the strike deadline against us: It was July 15, and midnight was three hours away. If Jim didn't sign his contract, I could no longer represent him, and he might lose his rookie season.

Time was slipping. I had to think fast.

"That's more money than we've ever paid any rookie who ever played here," Halas said. "That's a bigger signing bonus than Ditka, or Payton, or Butkus ever received."

It was actually more than all three of them combined.

"Mr. Halas, the NFL just signed a multi-billion-dollar television contract, and it has to be reflected in these negotiations," I said.

Jim and I excused ourselves and went into another room. I flipped open my legal pad, and quickly began penciling out numbers.

"Can you believe these cheap bastards?" Jim said.

"Welcome to the NFL, Jim," I said. "Don't take this personal. Finks knows talent and Mr. Halas really wants you."

"Doesn't sound like it to me," Jim said. "They're talking to me like I'm a piece of shit."

"We can call Dr. Dietrich with the Blitz, and up our ante with the USFL," I said. "But where's your heart? Do you want to play for the Blitz, or the Bears? Where's your heart?"

"Doc, I've always dreamed of playing in the NFL," Jim said. "I want to compete against the best."

His answer didn't surprise me.

"Here's the deal," I answered. "I'm going to escalate the guaranteed money and increase the incentive money. We can live with the salary. Ed Garvey and his madness have left us in a terrible situation. We're in never-never land. I've got forty minutes to do a deal, and I'm not going to leave you exposed and unprotected. It's forty minutes to midnight. You might be the last player out there who's unsigned."

I ripped a clean sheet from my legal pad and scrawled a sentence.

"Jim, read this, and sign it," I said. "Hand it to Finks the second you sign your contract."

McMahon read it, smiled, and folded it.

"Have you ever seen a Bear with a little tonic on its ass?" I said.

Jim laughed "No, I can't say I have," he said.

"Well, you're about to," I chuckled. "Watch this."

We went back in the room with Finks and Halas. The clock over the desk was now poised at five to midnight. Jim did exactly as I instructed: He took the contract I'd amended and signed it. Then he signed the yellow piece of legal paper that I'd handwritten. Simultaneously, he handed Finks both documents.

Finks looked at the contract and the changes, and smiled. Then he unfolded my note on the yellow legal piece of paper, and turned redder than his tie.

"WHAT IS THIS CRAP, ARGOVITZ?" Finks roared. He was enraged. He made a guttural noise and viciously wadded the paper and spiked it into the floor like a basketball. Jim and I were trying not to burst out laughing. Halas bolted up out of his chair, if you can believe that.

"What's going on here?" Halas cried.

I jumped up, grabbed the crumpled yellow paper off the floor and unfolded it for Mr. Halas to see. On it, I had written the following:

"I signed this agreement under duress and distress, and reserve all of my legal rights. Signed, Jim McMahon."

"This isn't over, Argovitz!" Finks screamed.

McMahon could no longer contain himself, and laughed out loud.

Weeks later, McMahon called me from training camp. He was struggling under Mike Ditka, who favored the predictability of veteran Bob Avellini over McMahon's petulant personality. "We're fighting a lot," Jim said. "Not a little. Every damn day. All I get is criticism. Playing for Ditka is a nightmare. All he does is yell." I had always told my players if they had a problem, just call me and I would handle the problem. They could go back to bed assured that it would be addressed, and Jim did exactly that.

The following day, I called Coach Ditka and asked if we could meet without Jim's knowledge. I flew in and met privately with Ditka, who is no poster boy for patience himself. We met in his office, and even though his t-shirt and coaching shorts were XXXL, Ditka made them look small.

"Jerry, tell Jim I'm not going to cuddle him," Ditka said. "College ball is over. He's getting paid a lot of money, and my ass is on the line."

"That's not what he wants, Coach," I told him. "I know this is your first head coaching job. I want to do everything I can to help you succeed. Coach, I've spent a lot of time around Jim. Nobody puts more pressure on Jim McMahon to win than Jim McMahon. I've been getting phone calls from him every other night, especially after the preseason games.

"Nobody wants to win more than Jim does. He is afraid to make a mistake or make a decision because of your constant criticism. He's afraid to call an audible because if he screws up, you'll pull him out of the game."

"I'm just trying to make him better," Ditka said, slamming his fist on the desk.

"Coach, I'm not trying to over-step my boundaries," I said. "But I'd like to make a suggestion that might make things a thousand times better for you and Jim both."

"Fire away," Ditka said.

"First, Jim will never know we had this private meeting," I said. "But if you have a one-on-one talk with Jim and tell him, 'Jim, we've got one more preseason game, and you are my man. I'm prepared to win or lose with you. The quarterback job is yours.'

"Coach, please sleep on it, just put the ball in his hand and he'll give you everything he's got. Just show him a little love.'"

The next night my phone rang.

"Doc, Mike said he's gonna give me the chance to earn the starting job," Jim said.

How fitting that Bob Avellini would start the season opener against my old friend Russ Thomas and the Detroit Lions? Avellini suffered a broken nose, and was forced to come out of the game. Jim McMahon replaced him, and soon would become a Chicago icon.

Over the next several years, the fighting didn't stop between Ditka and Jim, but they begrudgingly learned to respect and appreciate each other. Jim finished 1982 as the NFL Rookie of the Year in a strike-shortened season, and eventually led the Bears to their only Super Bowl victory in 1986, securing his place in Chicago lore alongside George Blanda, Billy Wade and of course, Halas's favorite quarterback, Sid Luckman. By the end of his career, Jim would play sixteen NFL seasons for seven teams, and—bad eye, bad leg, bad back and all—throw 100 touchdowns.

The 1982 players' strike lasted fifty-seven days. It cost $240 million. Garvey never got his wage scale, free agency was struck down, and the union gained nothing in terms of power. The players had been unprepared emotionally and financially for a strike. The players and the public were misinformed by both sides during the strike. The rivers of hatred and mistrust between the players, its own union, and the owners ran even deeper still. Many players returned from the strike flat broke.

Then there was the sad case of Art Schlichter, the quarterback Irsay had hand-picked ahead of Jim McMahon. It was well known that Schlichter sadly had a gambling addiction. During the strike, he lost nearly $100,000 on college football games. Within three years, he was out of football. In and out of prison for decades, today Schlichter sits in a cell awaiting trial on federal fraud charges that may put him away for life.

I'll take my guy. Jim McMahon: Bad eye, bad leg, bad back, and a heart so big that even in the face of the toughest critics, it's immeasurable.

If you had to line up today, pick Mac. It's impossible to go wrong.

34

OH YOU, HERSCHEL WALKER

AFTER IT RAINS in the heart of Georgia on a hot summer afternoon, everything seems brilliantly clean. The towering pine trees that line the roads seem taller, the fresh-cut blades of grass on the medians seem greener, and you swear you can smell pine cones. The year was 1982, and Gene was driving a rented sedan—with me in the front seat and attorney B.K. Watson in the back seat—as we raced toward Wrightsville, Georgia. The undulating landscape flickered past outside the windows as we barreled down the simmering two-lane asphalt highway that separated tiny farming communities. There seemed to be one about every ten miles.

We were headed to the boyhood home of Herschel Junior Walker, arguably the greatest college athlete ever known to man. Walker was a football phenom, a phoenix who had mythically risen from a place where the deep, dark soil matches the skin of his ancestors who had toiled there in stifling cotton fields. The last beads of rain chased each other off the windshield, and Gene rolled down his window to get a better look. We felt the humidity instantly, and it was suffocating. Gene rolled the window up faster than it took to roll it down.

"Hotter'n a goat's butt in a pepper patch," I muttered. "Hard to believe Herschel ran up and down this road every day in this humidity." I tried to imagine, and couldn't.

"That's Herschel for you," Gene said. "The kid is a beast. He's built like a tank and weighs 222 pounds, every day.

"And he doesn't lift weights, only pushups and sit-ups. He can run in this heat all day long; in fact, this car would break down before he would. It's hard to believe he was short and fat as a kid, but that's what they say."

"He's just a freak of nature," I replied. "Herschel is like Superman."

I stared at the map. We were just a few miles out. I smiled at the thought of how college coaches from Clemson, Southern Cal, Georgia Tech, and UCLA had all zoomed up and down this same little road, headed toward Johnson County High School in an effort to snare the services of Herschel, whose high-school heroics quickly made him a once-in-a-lifetime trophy. When you rush for 3,167 yards and 45 touchdowns in a single season, the world of college football beats a path to your door, no matter how small your door might be.

Now we had joined the safari, but for far different reasons. If you're going to upset the apple cart of the sanctimonious, hypocritical, self-serving, sacrilegious National Collegiate Athletic Association, you may as well start by poaching its best player.

Approaching fast was a cylindrical, silver water tower. Painted on its side was the image of two hands shaking and words declaring Wrightsville as "The Friendliest Town in Georgia."

We reached a four-stop intersection with a two-pump gas station on the corner, and whipped in to ask directions. A bell rang twice when we ran over the cord, and a rugged man in blue jeans and a sweat-soaked, cut-off flannel shirt ran out to meet us.

"Here to see Herschel?" he asked, before we could even speak.

I took off my cowboy hat, and wiped my brow. Grinning, I said, "What makes you say that?"

"Just a guess," he said. "Everybody who comes through here with a map is here to see Herschel."

He pointed in a general direction. "About six miles," he said, "thataway."

The University of Georgia ultimately won the Herschel Walker lottery, but like any lottery, it was pure chance. Some college football purists argue today that Herschel made National Signing Day what it is today. As a Parade All-American, the kid literally put Georgia on everyone's mind. On Easter Sunday in 1980, fans of universities from coast to coast held their collective breath while scrambling through AM radio stations searching for news, any news.

What started as more than a hundred schools around the nation had been whittled to roughly ten by Walker's senior year, and two or three by signing day. Hundreds of thousands of dollars were spent on the recruiting of Herschel Walker, and twice that many miles were logged. His high school games and track meets had been attended by so many coaches that they often arrived before the players in an effort to be the first to greet him. During his visit to USC, Herschel took his first ride on a plane. Upon their arrival, his mother was escorted by O.J. Simpson himself.

Herschel was a football messiah; a pigskin Elvis. Girls swooned in his presence, nearly as much as the grown men in coaching shirts who followed his every move. Landing Herschel could and would make a coach's entire career. He couldn't answer the phone or open the mail without hearing from a Coach Somebody from University of Somewhere. Whatever school he picked would feel the immediate impact. So much so, that to hopefully gain an edge, Georgia had created a woman's track team in order to award Herschel's older sister Veronica a scholarship two years prior.

On signing day, Herschel bunkered with his folks in their neat, one-story, white clapboard house six miles outside of Wrightsville, which then sat on a green hill just over a set of railroad tracks. Leading to the doorstep is a well-worn dirt road where Georgia assistants Mike Cavan and Steve Greer had spent many evenings in their cars waiting on the seventeen-year-old to make up his mind. There were no motels in Wrightsville; Cavan had been camped out in a nearby cabin owned by a wealthy Georgia alumnus for nearly six months.

Now it all came down to this. Legendary Bulldog head coach Vince Dooley, in his Athens office ninety-one miles away, waited anxiously by the phone. And waited. And waited. This was the moment over which grown men had fawned—mostly white men, by the way, from universities that had only begun awarding scholarships to African American athletes barely more than a decade before. An entire cottage industry of people had exhausted thousands of hours chasing Herschel through local restaurants, his own high-school cafeteria, highways and byways, airports and thoroughfares. Helicopters had hovered above his house. Imagine all of this occurring in Wrightsville, a town so small that Herschel would later say "as a little kid, my lifelong dream had been to just go to Atlanta."

When it finally came to make a decision, Herschel's formula would be very unscientific: He simply flipped a coin.

It was heads. Georgia had won the toss, and elected to receive.

Herschel was the last freshman to sign that year.

In Herschel's first collegiate appearance against Tennessee, the entire nation would learn what the hoopla was all about. With the Georgia faithful glued to transistor radios, the legendary Voice of the Bulldogs—Larry Munson—made his now-famous gravelly call that forever will resonate in the hearts of Bulldog fans:

"He hands it off to Herschel. There's a hole. 5-10-12. He's running over people! Oh you Herschel Walker! My God Almighty! He ran right through two men! Herschel ran right over two men! They had him dead away inside the nine! Herschel went 16 yards. He drove right over orange shirts driving and running with those big thighs! My God, a freshman!"

One of those would-be tacklers was future NFL Pro Bowl safety Bill Bates, the first of many casualties en route to Herschel's NCAA record-setting freshman season. He averaged nearly six yards a carry, rushed for 1,616 yards and fifteen touchdowns while leading the Bulldogs to an unlikely 12-0 record. In the Sugar Bowl for the national championship against vaunted Notre Dame, Walker carried Georgia on one shoulder, rushing 36 times for 150 yards with a separated left shoulder in a 17-10 win. Every time he slammed into a train-wreck of helmets and jerseys and disappeared, he would miraculously emerge on the other side, still running. He was the first freshman in the twentieth century to make the All-America team. He ran on the track team and recorded Olympic times as a sprinter.

The following year, Herschel tacked on another 1,891 yards and 18 touchdowns, and entrenched himself as a college sports icon. By the time Gene and I headed to Wrightsville, Herschel had graced the cover of *Sports Illustrated* three times. Sportswriters across the country had run out of ways to describe him; writing about Herschel had become harder than tackling him, because every single cliché, adjective, and expression already had been used.

"He's a masterpiece of physical construction who can run around you or through you . . ."

"Herschel is a combination of power, anxiety, nerves, diet, and skill . . ."

"Great balance . . . he holds a football like an egg, with the fingers of a pianist . . ."

"If he's even, he's leavin' . . ."

"He knows when to accelerate, when to hold back, shifting like a racehorse behind the thundering hooves of 2,600 pounds of moving flesh and muscle . . . before bursting into open field with the weight and power and speed of a runaway stallion . . ."

And every one of them was true.

We weren't just showing up at Herschel's home unannounced, mind you. This meeting occurred after my numerous conversations with David Dixon regarding the United States Football League, which was set to begin play the spring of the following year. David had gone from totally uninterested, to scared and interested, to now downright interested—if I could pull off the coup of the century.

David's drastic mood swing occurred shortly after I informed him that my Canadian friend Skalbania had the same idea. Nelson already had two of my first-round NFL picks on his roster, and he had made the trip to Wrightsville to meet with Herschel's family and discuss a possible CFL future with his Alouettes. I wasn't there when Herschel's mother took the contract to Athens to show Vince Dooley, but I can only imagine the revered college coach probably didn't know whether to scratch his watch or wind his butt. The message was clear: Herschel knew his value.

"David, the kid just wants to earn a living," I told Dixon. "Family is everything to Herschel. I talked with Gene, and helping Herschel is on our bucket list. We're not in this for money. If Herschel gets hurt, he has nothing."

This was a fact. Herschel could run roughshod over anything except his fear of a career-ending injury. No question that by now, he had everything to lose and nothing to gain by playing college football: The snap of a single bone could mean the difference in the number of zeroes at the end of a signing bonus.

Herschel was far too smart for this—he was as quick in the classroom as he was on the field. He could engage on subjects at all levels, quote Macbeth, recite authors, and discuss politics as easily as he absorbed a playbook. While Georgia fans were content to keep him between the hedges, canonize him as a life-time recruiting tool, and cherish his school-licensed bobble-heads, jerseys, and likeness, Herschel had other plans.

He had no beefs with the University of Georgia. In fact then, and now, he valued his education. He respected Coach Dooley. The real story was that Herschel Walker refused to be ground in the teeth of the most corrupt system in all of sports: the National Collegiate Athletic Association. He knew, like I did, that his recruiting was illegal, that his unique gifts and talents were exploited, and his civil-rights violated.

You had to love his spirit. He tried to open the Herschel Walker Insurance Agency, a business wherein he would work the NCAA-equivalent of "an off-season summer job" alongside a couple of businessmen and "friends of the family." The idea alone never made it past Coach Dooley's desk, but can you imagine the surprise of the NCAA when it learned that the best player in the world was testing its boundaries?

Clearly, Herschel was no "yes man." With subtle force, he was willing to shred the barriers placed in his path by the NCAA and weave his way like a battering ram through its hypocrisy. Before he was through, he would do something never before done by an athlete of his fame or stature: Use the NCAA system just as it used him, and escape its grasp while he could still earn a living at his chosen profession; a Frederick Douglass, of sorts, in helmet and shoulder pads, and coming at you like a freight train.

"I grew up in America and I don't think anybody should have to leave the country to make a living," he said publicly about his offer to play in the CFL. I knew the NFL would be a different story. While Walker had correctly figured out that a legally grown man could not be deprived of a job due to his age, to challenge the NFL's underclassman rule could threaten his pro future.

"Don't ever underestimate Herschel," I told Dixon. "I think I can sign him. I just hope your owners are smart enough to take advantage of this unique opportunity. The Herschel Walker signing will put your league on the map."

"If anyone can do it," Dixon said, "you're the man. Good luck."

By 1982 I was convinced Herschel was ready for just the right opportunity to blow the lid off college football. I was all too happy to oblige. This is how Gene, B.K. and I ended up in Wrightsville, burning down a dirt road in a rental car for a sit-down pow-wow with Mr. and Mrs. Walker.

We parked in the driveway and walked up to the very front porch where Herschel's family had listened to Munson's famous call his freshman year. That special night, his father, Willis, had parked the car in the front of the house and cranked up the volume, and the crackle, of the AM radio.

It's a wonder that all 812 households in Wrightsville—with a median income of $10,000 and where 50 percent of its inhabitants are below the poverty line—couldn't hear Herschel's family screaming, "Do it Bo! Do it Bo! Do it Bo!" while he slammed his way through eight separate guys en route to the end zone. The hopes of an entire family, maybe this entire town, were willing "Bo" through every tackle, and he had obliterated them all.

So this was the house where it all began. I looked around the yard, where, as the story goes, Herschel had kept his horse, Smoky. As a boy, he kept to himself, and had been content to play with his dogs, ride his horse, read, go to school, play football, and not much else. It wasn't until he was in junior high that he began to burst from his roly-poly M&M shell into a mind-numbing physique.

I tried to picture all of this in my mind. How could a Division I coach come to this house, in this town, and not realize that this kid can't fulfill four years of a so-called scholarship without money? Herschel's parents had taken out a second mortgage against their house so he could have a car to drive back and forth to Athens. Of course, the dealership where it was purchased was owned by a Georgia alumnus, and the car was purchased at wholesale, but hey, it was legal, right? The cabin where Georgia assistant coach Mike Cavan had stayed during Herschel's recruitment was owned by the same alum, but hey, who's counting?

And the University of Georgia, with its offices chock full of well-heeled attorneys, compliance officers, coaches, and recruiting war chests stuffed with cash pursued a seventeen-year-old boy and coerced him to sign a document without any legal representation or financial consultant of his own? But hey, you're getting a scholarship, right?

"Gene, the system is so wrong," I said, as we climbed the creaky but well-tended steps on Herschel's front porch. "These kids are pro athletes from the time they go to college. It's time they get paid."

"First things first, Jerry," Gene said. "Let's talk to momma."

Word was already out that Jerry Argovitz had shown up in town, and hey, there must be something illegal going on. God forbid, I thought, that we make Georgia compete for the rights of a grown man to earn a living in his chosen profession—football.

The mat on the front porch read WELCOME. I took off my hat, rapped on the wooden door, and waited.

Willis and Christine Walker ushered us into their simple, but beautiful home. I introduced Gene and B.K., and we all sat down. The den was full of trophies and awards earned by their seven children. Herschel was the fifth of the litter, behind Willis Junior, Renneth, Sharon, and Veronica. Following his giant footsteps were Lorenza and Carol. All were outstanding athletes, and Christine had a story for each one. The joy on her face as she spoke of each child was contagious and exuded pure pride; she showed no favoritism whatsoever.

When a woman is gushing over her kids, never miss a good chance to shut up. This was one of those times. Her husband, Willis, had obviously been to the rodeo a few times, and he didn't interrupt, either. I listened and played with their toy Chihuahua while a pit bull stared us down from the kitchen. The thing I remember most was how gentle and courteous she was. Christine and Willis were factory workers now, still earning a pittance but supporting all these kids while managing to spend quality time with each and every one. The house was warm and perfectly kept, and there were books everywhere, including an open Bible someone recently had been reading. There were other good books, too—a few so thick that even I wouldn't have taken the time to read. These folks are self-taught, I thought, and true products of the Old South.

Herschel, I told her, is a Jewish name. "My dad's name is Harry; his Jewish name is Herschel," I said. "Herschel means deer." She smiled a megawatt smile. "Well, I don't know about all that," she said. "But we have many generations of Herschels. Big Herschel and little Herschel were brothers, and Big Herschel was my Herschel's grandfather."

Gene and I exchanged glances. There's a "bigger" Herschel out there somewhere?

The Herschel we were there to talk about briefly was home from college, but at the moment, was out running. Legally, I could only speak to them with an attorney present.

"Mr. and Mrs. Walker," I said, "I know Herschel has considered the CFL. I'm not here to represent Herschel. In fact, that's why we brought along B.K. Watson, a Houston attorney. Give him a $1 retainer to represent you, and I'll give you some information that you can take under his advice."

B.K. nodded, and pulled out a simple, one-paragraph retainer, limited to this conversation only.

I did my best to paint the picture. "Here's the deal," I said. "Obviously, Canada would be a drastic mistake. But I'm involved with the founder of this new league, the United States Football League. I can promise you guaranteed money. We're talking over a million dollars to sign, tax-free, plus millions more. Guaranteed, cash money.

"There will be a provision in his contract to pay for Herschel's tuition to finish college and an extra bonus when he graduates."

"Hallelujah!" his mother whispered, clasping her hands. "We've been praying for answers!"

"This new league will make Herschel its face," I said. "It will be a historical event. Herschel will be the first junior to ever come out and sign a professional football contract. We're not here to negotiate, or even make a deal. We're here to inform you and to make sure he knows about the USFL before he commits to play in Canada. Herschel can still play this fall at Georgia, win the Heisman, and we'll be back with a contract after his junior year."

By now, Willis was sitting up in his recliner. "My dad's name was Herschel Walker before his name was Herschel Walker," he smiled. "My Herschel needs to take advantage of this opportunity." Then, Mr. Walker asked, "What about the NFL?"

"Well, Mr. Walker," I replied, "as you are probably aware, the NFL's rules prohibit him from coming out as a junior."

The screen door opened suddenly, and there he was. Soaked with sweat, in a cut-off t-shirt, gym shorts, and tennis shoes was a 6-foot, 2-inch beast built like an ox, with a neck nearly the size of his tapered 31-inch waist. His thighs were the size of fire hydrants. He didn't appear to have an ounce of fat on his glistening, onyx body.

"Hi, Momma," said Herschel Junior Walker, softly.

Dear God, I thought. This is "little" Herschel?

For a split second, I actually felt sorry for Bill Bates.

"Herschel, these men want to talk to you," his mom said. I walked back through our plan, thoroughly explaining the potential of the United States Football League, the money that he would earn, and that he would get every penny, regardless of the fate of the league.

Herschel mostly nodded, didn't say much, and occasionally glanced at his mother.

At that point, there was little left to discuss.

"If everybody's on the same page," I said, "we'll let you folks get on with your business. I'll go back to the owners in this new league and tell them you're interested. We'll keep everything quiet." I looked at Herschel. "Best of luck to you, young man—just stay healthy, have a great year, and we'll get the details worked out. I'll be back after your junior year."

We all stood up, shook hands, and we turned to leave.

"You gentlemen have a safe trip," she said, then added with a twinkle in her soft eyes, "You are the answer to my prayers."

"Thank you, Ma'am," I said, tipping my cowboy hat to Mrs. Walker.

As soon as I was convinced our taillights had disappeared from the Walkers' driveway, I turned to Gene.

"Herschel Walker is the American dream," I gushed. "He debunks the myth that it can't be done. He's evidence that if you believe it, you can achieve it. It is possible to fight your way up from the lowest rung of the ladder. This is how America crowns its heroes."

"You sound like Don King," Gene said.

"Laugh if you must, but before this is over, I'm going to build a statue of Herschel Walker in full stride on the doorstep of the NCAA in Indianapolis," I said. "The inscription at the bottom is going to read, 'Free at last, free at last . . . no thanks to the NCAA, I'm free at last.'"

"You're crazy," B.K. said from the back seat, "but you're not wrong."

"Yeah," Gene said, "you're crazy like a fox."

"Whenever truth is denied, B.K.," I answered. "corruption follows. Well, truth for once just won. This kid has it all: He's handsome, intelligent, proud, and a world-class athlete. To hell with the NCAA and their self-serving rules. All Herschel wants to do is play professional football and help his family.

"The fact is, Herschel Walker could start for any team in the NFL right now."

As we zoomed into the night toward the airport, I couldn't wait to get David Dixon on the phone.

Herschel Walker was the USFL's for the taking, and all that remained now were the simple details of which team he would play for, and how much he'd get paid to work.

ACT FIVE

Let us trust God, and our better judgment, to set us right hereafter. United we stand, divided we fall. Let us not split into factions which must destroy that union upon which our existence hangs.

—Patrick Henry

35

NEVER ASK A BARBER IF YOU NEED A HAIRCUT

PROFESSIONAL FOOTBALL IS a rite of passage for millions of people, and but for a select few, most are content to simply count themselves among its fanatical observers. The rest are divided into participants and owners. Participants include the players themselves, where opportunity is strictly limited by talent and youth. Then there are the supporting casts of managers, coaches, trainers, and other administrators.

But ownership of a professional football team is something chased by only the richest and most powerful men, all of whom are unaccustomed to being told "no" in their outside professions. Since most teams are "family" businesses, as Mr. Halas had so deftly explained to me in Chicago, the opportunities to break into this rarefied air are somewhere between slim and none, and—as the saying goes—Slim just left town.

This is why the exclusive men's club of the National Football League is forever challenged by the idea of new leagues with rich, powerful men who have been excluded from their ranks attempting to get a piece of this exorbitant privilege, without the exorbitant price.

David Dixon amazingly had assembled twelve such extraordinarily wealthy, ridiculously powerful men, all of whom—had they been given the choice—would have purchased an NFL team. Yet by announcing the United States Football League as a spring league, Dixon had convinced these guys the USFL wasn't the "next best thing," but a ground-breaking, brilliant, first-best thing, an idea whose time had come.

These were shrewd businessmen with vast wealth who conceivably could move any mountain but one: The Gibraltar called the NFL. Simply having financial acumen to

206

buy your way into the tight-knit NFL fraternity wasn't the issue: More teams meant a smaller piece of the television pie, and NFL owners weren't keen on sharing. So, shut out by the NFL, they were left with only one option: Start their own league.

And why not?

The USFL would play a spring season—in a calendar free of competition from high school, college, or pro football. Stadiums that normally sat dormant would be thrilled to have tenants. Jobs would be created for thousands of administrators, stadium workers, coaches, and players. Owners would enjoy national television notoriety and a chance to make money against shoestring budgets.

Fans, for the first time, would have year-round football, as opposed to reruns of Wide World of Sports. By the time David asked me to address his owners in a private New Orleans meeting late in the fall of 1982, he had convinced them all he was right, and he had nearly two decades of research and reams of recent marketing studies to support his claims and projections.

For nearly two years I'd been sharing my ideals with David on how to make the USFL a solvent enterprise, and I jumped at the opportunity to share my plan first-hand with the owners.

New Orleans in 1982 was abuzz with hope. The World's Fair was just two years away, and the city was booming. Architects, builders, and developers were buying up empty warehouses and run-down factories and converting them into restaurants, hotels, and shops in preparation of the historic city's latest renaissance. Many of the city's building codes were ignored as people flocked to New Orleans and packed its soft soil to near capacity.

Aboard a Pan Am jet flying toward New Orleans International Airport, I could see the signs of optimism that accompany abundant progress. From the air, I could see the city straddling the mighty Mississippi River, which pumps like a steady heartbeat into the Gulf Coast. Transport ships appeared to be sea-bound worker ants, carrying cargo to and fro on the horizon. In a cab bound for downtown, I could hear the clatter of jackhammers and see yellow cranes spotting the shadows of the city skyline.

New Orleans is famous for its unique architectural styles, which reflect its multicultural roots. The shotgun houses on the city's outskirts give way to antebellum mansions. Large, European-style Catholic cemeteries dot the landscape. The Creole cottages of the French Quarter—with their large courtyards and intricate iron balconies—charm even the most reluctant visitor. The smell of fresh baguettes made me hungry as I made my way to the downtown hotel for my first face-to-face meeting with the owners who would decide the fate of the new league; I bought into the optimism of the city itself.

Fires, floods, and hurricanes had battered New Orleans through the years, only to create a quiet resilience beneath its cool, Southern façade. On his home turf, Dixon personified every one of these traits to a tee. He was flush with excitement, and I swear he shared the same mannerisms of an expectant mother with just a few weeks before delivery.

"Can you believe we're going to pull this off?" he asked me breathlessly when we met in the lobby of the hotel where his top-secret meeting would be held. "Jerry, they're all here . . . Alfred, Marvin, Walter . . . "

Alfred Taubman was from Detroit; he had built the most elegant, lavish malls in America and could stand toe-to-toe with any NFL owner. I relished the thought of him doing battle in the same market as Bill Ford and the Detroit Lions. Marvin Warner's Home State Savings Bank was a financial empire at the time, and he was a former U.S. ambassador to Switzerland who had owned 10 percent of the New York Yankees and 48 percent of the Tampa Bay Buccaneers. Warner would anchor the south in Birmingham.

Walter Duncan's oil-lined pockets were deeper than his Oklahoma wells. However, a young, ambitious developer named Donald J. Trump was watching the USFL proceedings with piqued interest—and would buy the franchise from Duncan in 1983. Trump, from day one, was more than thrilled to let others blaze the path before he determined his own route.

Trump's initial hesitation didn't discourage others. Jim Joseph and Tad Taube, both descendants of Jewish immigrants, would own the Phoenix and Oakland teams. Joseph made his name as a San Francisco developer; Taube had rolled his computer-silicone fortune into massive real estate holdings as well. Joseph would field a team in Phoenix; Taube would play in Oakland. Cable television moguls Alan Harmon and Bill Daniels had grabbed the Los Angeles market. In Washington, D.C., slick attorney Berl Bernhard had compiled "an amazing series of accomplishments" in the legal, political, academic, and athletic arenas. Denver would be under the charge of developer Ron Blanding.

Of course, my friend Dr. Ted Dietrich, an internationally renowned cardiovascular surgeon who founded, owned, and operated the Arizona Heart Institute in Phoenix, was solid in Chicago. Tampa Bay had tremendous promise behind the aggressive, creative marketing of savvy owner John Bassett, whose holdings included real estate, motion pictures, and computer software. "In all my other ventures," Bassett told me, "I was the richest guy in the room. With the USFL, I'm the poorest." Myles Tanenbaum was a powerful Philadelphia attorney. Boston was led by prominent local businessman George Matthews and former NFL player Randy Vataha.

The league office was shaping up, too. With Chet Simmons at the helm as commissioner and long-time NFL executives John Ralston and Peter Hadhazy aboard, the USFL was swiftly being taken seriously. Steve Ehrhardt, an attorney and former agent, became league counsel and Simmons' right-hand man.

Interestingly, Alex Spanos, owner of a massive construction-services enterprise in Southern California, had excused himself from the USFL to become part owner of the NFL's San Diego Chargers.

Equally impressive was the front-office talent being assembled by the USFL owners. To name a few, Warner had Jerry Sklar; Tanenbaum had Carl Peterson, the former GM of the Philadelphia Eagles. Chicago had George Allen and his son, Bruce.

The media had its own ideas, and I certainly had mine. Very few people had access like I did to both the NFL and USFL. I had been behind closed doors with NFL owners like Irsay and Adams, men who consistently proved that if common sense was dirt, they couldn't cover an acre. I'd battled with NFL executives like Thomas and Barber, a couple guys who couldn't pour piss out of their boots if you wrote the instructions on the heel.

Being around NFL offices was like hanging out in funeral parlors. The older league had forgotten about the most important ingredient in sports: the fan. The NFL had become predictable and boring—three yards and a cloud of dust, followed by a sixty-second television commercial. NFL coaching staffs and front offices were predominantly white, which was strange to me when more than half of its players were black.

On the other hand, the men who gathered to form the USFL were full of energy, ideas, and life; and at the very least, seemed downright stimulated by the daunting challenge facing them. Like the very season of spring itself, it was an intoxicating breath of fresh air. Not one of these men had built his reputation by running from a fight, and I fed off the excitement of each one. Now they had something the NFL didn't: A six-month spring season all to themselves. When I took my place at the front of the meeting room, I loved the sheer hunger in their eyes.

"Gentlemen," I began, "I know just a little about a lot of things, but I do know a lot about football." I pointed to my Gene and asked him to stand. "Gene and I represent some of the top talent in the NFL. Football is our business. I can promise you there are a lot of players and agents who will welcome the chance and opportunity to play in the USFL. I'm so sure of this fact that I believe the NFL will expand its rosters, or stash players to reserve rosters to keep them from your league."

I knew Carl Peterson from my former dealings with the Philadelphia Eagles. "Carl," I asked, "what do you think?"

He laughed. "Like I've always said," he remarked, "don't ever underestimate the NFL."

"Well, guys," I continued, "like it or not, the NFL is your enemy, and it will stop at nothing to put you out of business. I've heard a few of you comment that you're 'not competing' with the NFL. Think again. You are competing with the NFL for players; and if you don't act swiftly, you'll lose. You cannot fool football fans—they know the game. They want to watch professional football, and if you slap together an inferior product, the fans and media will tune you out."

I began handing out a printed summary of my ideas. "David has asked me to share information regarding players' salaries, structure of contracts, and my recommendations for the type of players that each team should sign," I said. "The USFL has a proposed budget for signing players of $1.8 million. I personally believe each team should be required to sign two impact players: Either a quarterback, running back, or wide receiver. These players should be a top draft pick or an NFL free agent. These players must be recognized names by the sports fans and media. Each team should have a wild card to spend necessary funds over and above $1.8 budget to sign these two players. Here is my five-year game plan for the league . . . "

My five-year plan was relatively simple:

- First year: Awareness
- Second year: Credibility
- Third Year: Acceptance
- Fourth year: Parity between NFL and USFL
- Fifth year: Profitability

I broke it down into five categories: (a) Team Equity; (b) TV Revenue and Pay TV; (c) Attendance; (d) Promotions; and (e) Expansion. My firm belief was that in five years, each franchise in the USFL could and should gross somewhere between $20-$24 million a year, and each team in the league should be worth a minimum of $40 million dollars.

"The league must generate an overall game plan to protect its investment and insure the profitability of the fifth year," I said. "The ultimate profits will be based solely on attendance and television ratings. There is nothing magic about building a successful league; it only requires a sound business practice on the part of each franchise to have an entertaining and exciting product designed for the benefit of the fans."

I stressed to each owner a significant fact: They were no longer individuals, but partners, and must all act and react to the sole best interests of the total partnership.

"There is no way this five-year game plan can work if you are divided in business philosophies," I said. "You must be willing to trade short–term losses for long–term growth and profitability."

Some owners still believed they could build a competitive team and TV ratings by not signing top-quality players; while other owners believed in signing top-quality players from the draft, along with some "name" players from the NFL.

"The things that make football ownership different than any other sports ownership are that all the owners are partners and share equally in the revenue," I said. "The draft controls player movement and salaries; and the sport itself is the most appealing of all sports to TV networks, cable television, and fans."

Pointing to Major League Baseball, I explained that an 8.0 television rating had equated to a $1.2 billion television contract. "What if, in our first year, the USFL can pull out a 6.2 overall? What happens next year if each team signs some top-name draft choices and highly regarded NFL talent? This will give you credibility with the media, football fans, and sporting public in your second year, which will certainly increase the value of the future television contracts."

At this point, everyone in the room was listening and attentively taking notes.

"The NFL is successful because of revenue-sharing and the draft," I continued. "You must do the same. The formula is simple: exciting football. It is incumbent on the USFL to adopt some rules that will differentiate your product from theirs."

Myles Tanenbaum interrupted. "What kind of rules?" he asked. "How can you change the rules of football?"

"It is simple, Mr. Tanenbaum—and I've already shared a lot of these ideas with David. These are subtle changes, but they will make the game a helluva lot more exciting. For instance, no game should end in sudden death or be decided by a coin flip. There should be no fair catches. In the passing game, you should only need one foot in bounds for a reception, instead of two.

"I've already suggested instant replay as an idea, to challenge bad calls. Use the two-point conversions. And let players celebrate after a touchdown, or a big play, to make the game personable.

"And when it comes to the draft, the best way to compete with the NFL is to hold your draft before they do," I added. "Utilize a territorial draft, where local boys play close to home."

I had saved the best for last, however.

"And if you want to be on the front page of every paper and newscast in America, sign Herschel Walker."

For a moment, you could've heard a pin drop.

"You're kidding, right?" gasped Peter Hadhazy.

Within seconds, bedlam ensued. Everyone was screaming "sacrilege." You would've thought I had just suggested raping a nun. The guys with NFL experience shared the same facial expression, like they'd been sucking green persimmons.

You're crazy! College coaches will blackball us!

The NFL will put us out of business!

The networks will sue us!

Herschel will never sign!

I grinned with the satisfaction of a man who had an answer to all of the above.

"First of all, the college coaches can't blackball you," I said. "The NFL and NCAA cannot prevent grown men from working, and they both know it. It's just been an unspoken rule, and it's only a matter of time before it goes the way of the Edsel. I predict that if you do this, the NFL will be forced to follow suit.

"Second, the networks can't, and won't, sue you. Curiosity alone will drive your early ratings through the roof. Third, I've met with Herschel Walker himself. I've been in his home with his parents. Herschel will sign! I promise you! Herschel will sign!"

Stark terror and concern slowly gave way to common sense. Looks of bewilderment slowly changed to smirks of beguile, as if they were about to commit the heist of the century. Gradually, it was glaringly obvious: Herschel Walker could put their new league on the map.

"Who gets him?" somebody asked.

For me, this was easy math: In total marketing dollars, what would the signing of Herschel Walker be worth? Now, divide that number by twelve teams, and amortize it over the gross marketing budget. In 1976 model and actress Farrah Fawcett—posed in a red bathing suit—had sold twelve million posters at six bucks a shot. Likewise, Herschel Walker had football cleavage, and the owners knew he was worth every penny in yards, ratings and sales. I suggested they put him where it would have the impact of a meteor slamming to earth.

New York.

Later that night, I boarded my Pan Am flight back to Houston. It took off from the same New Orleans runway where just a few months before, Flight 759 had ascended into the teeth of a thunderstorm, bound for the bright lights, energy, and thrills of Las Vegas. Optimism aboard that aircraft was rampant, as gamblers readied for the ultimate challenge of beating the odds and returning home with untold riches. Seconds after takeoff, the plane was slammed to the ground by gusty, swirling winds, hitting trees and houses before bursting into flames, killing all 145 souls aboard.

Ironically, the name of the clipper had been Defiance.

Exhausted, I ignored the obvious parallels. I put my head on my seat pillow and went to sleep.

The University of Georgia had stormed through the 1982 regular season, scoring 338 points behind Herschel Walker, who earned the coveted Heisman Trophy. As soon as the Bulldogs finished their regular season, I made arrangements to meet Herschel at the Athens airport, twelve miles from the Georgia campus. I hopped a private Learjet 25D for a quick, 531-mph direct flight from Houston. In less than ninety minutes, the plane dropped into a forest of green trees. Runway lights trickled through the fog, and the control tower suddenly appeared, adorned by the university's giant black, white, and red "G" logo.

History in the making, I thought.

The engines whined as we taxied off the main runway toward the terminal tarmac. I never got off the plane. Herschel hastily was escorted inside the plane, and we shook hands. Collapsing comfortably into the plush, cream leather seating, he filled up the cabin, literally and figuratively. Herschel could step into any situation, any space, and you immediately felt his presence, his greatness. He was Superman, and he knew it. Anyone who thought they could outsmart this kid was dreaming: He had a master plan, and he was sticking to it. The rest of us were bit players in a big dance; Herschel was pulling the strings and at the end of the day, the only guy who was going to carry the rock.

On my legal pad, I had sketched out a five-year deal, which I laid out across the dual-executive, burl wood cabinetry table.

"Herschel, here's what I'm thinking," I said, pointing to rows of numbers, written out year-by-year, over three pages. Outlined were signing bonuses, annual salary, and incentives. Patiently, I explained each one. Herschel reviewed every item carefully, and nodded as I spoke.

"Your entire deal will be worth over $4 million for five years, about $4,550,000, to be exact," I said. "Officially, this is not a contract, or an offer. All of it will be personally guaranteed by a USFL owner. This is more money than any player today is making. You can choose the market where you want to play. Technically, your USFL draft rights are owned by my friend Dr. Ted Dietrich in Chicago, but rules are made to be changed. I'm thinking you belong in New York. But I'd like you to meet Dr. Dietrich, who'll get the ball rolling with the USFL. Take your time, read through this again, and if this is amenable to you, I'd like you just to acknowledge it by signing the top of each page. Your signature isn't binding; it just means you read it, you understand it, and you have no disagreements.

"The USFL is going to present a contract to you," I added. "You need to have proper legal representation, and at that time, you can compare the contract with the information on these pages that have your signatures on them. This way you'll be able to identify the specific terms we've discussed against whatever they are offering."

One page at a time, Herschel read every word; then, oh-so-patiently, signed his name. Just like his open-field running, his handwriting was prestigious, swirling, and beautiful.

Herschel Walker. Herschel Walker. Herschel Walker.

The Bulldogs were the number-one team in the nation, and on New Year's Day, just a few months before the start of the USFL season, would play Penn State for the NCAA title in the Sugar Bowl.

"Herschel, I will see you at the Sugar Bowl," I said. "I will introduce you to an owner of a USFL team that is willing to sign you."

"Doc," he said, "My focus right now is on Penn State . . . " his voice trailed, and he never cracked a smile, "but if it makes you feel better for me to meet the owner, I'll be happy to."

Like a puff of smoke, Herschel disappeared from the cabin. In minutes, the plane screamed back into the clouds nose up toward Houston, as the twinkling lights of Athens disappeared behind us.

The next morning, I was on the phone. "May I speak to Dr. Dietrich?" I asked.

"He's prepping for surgery," the voice on the other end said. "Who's calling?"

"Dr. Jerry Argovitz. He knows me. It's important. Tell him it's about Herschel."

Within nano seconds, the phone picked up.

"Jerry, hey, this is Ted, what's up?"

"Ted, I've got Herschel to agree to meet with us. Can you meet me at the Sugar Bowl? I think Herschel is ready to sign with us. Regardless of what team he ends up with, I need you to let him know the league is serious."

"You bet."

"We're gonna need a cashier's check for $1 million."

"Great! Outstanding! Good job! I'll call you back right after this aortic dissection."

Within a week, Dr. Dietrich and I were chatting in my luxury hotel suite, staring out a window at the New Orleans skyline, where the white Superdome seemed to have landed like a giant sloping spaceship right in the middle of downtown.

The door opened, and Gene arrived with Walker in tow, less than twenty-four hours before Georgia would battle Penn State for the national title. I stood up and greeted Herschel with a big hug.

"Herschel, this is Dr. Ted Dietrich, the owner of the Chicago Blitz," I said. They shook hands, and Ted's hand disappeared entirely, as if it had been swallowed whole by a Burmese python. "Herschel, Ted's coach is George Allen, one of the most famous coaches in the history of the NFL."

I explained that Dr. Dietrich was there specifically to express his interest in his future.

"Obviously, Herschel, you can make no decisions until after the game, and with someone to represent you," I said. "I just wanted you to know the league is dead serious about signing you. In fact, Ted, don't you have something to show Herschel?"

Ted reached inside his jacket pocket, pulled out a white envelope, and handed it to Herschel, who opened it and removed a cashier's check for $1 million, made payable to Herschel Walker. Gene and I looked at each other like disbelieving spies; we thoroughly understood the historical significance and ramifications of that moment.

To hell with the NCAA, I thought.

"It's tax-free," I told Herschel.

He methodically stared at the check for about five seconds, and made not a single facial expression. Herschel just as easily could've been playing Texas hold'em with a million dollars at stake and seemed to enjoy the seconds of silent thunder.

With poker eyes, he looked at me and handed back the check.

"Doc, I can't accept this right now," he said softly.

Right to the grand finale, Herschel was controlling the entire situation. He politely thanked everyone, hugged me, and left as quietly as he had arrived.

Gene turned to Ted and me, incredulous.

"The kid just walked away from $1 million," Gene said, "but I swear, on the way over here, he asked me to loan him $20! Unbelievable."

On February 23, 1983, two weeks prior to the USFL's inaugural game, Herschel and his attorney Jack Manton accepted a $3.9 million personal-services contract with New Jersey Generals' owner J. Walter Duncan in what was the biggest collegiate football signing since George Halas landed Red Grange.

Manton had called the NFL's offices hours before Walker signed and offered the older league one last chance. He spoke directly with NFL attorney Jay Moyer, who put him on hold while he interrupted Pete Rozelle. Jack later would recount that when Moyer came back on the line, he said, "The NFL isn't changing its rules for Herschel Walker, or anyone else." Manton thanked him, and moments later, Herschel rewrote football history with a single swipe of his pen, and Moyer's comment now lives in infamy.

The NFL had played right into the hands of the USFL. In the months leading up to the new league's first season, a jury ruled the NFL was guilty of antitrust laws by not allowing the Oakland Raiders to move to Los Angeles. Then, thanks to Ed Garvey, the NFL players had gone on a fifty-seven-day strike, shortening the season to eight games and a special sixteen-game playoff tournament.

The NFL as a whole was a mess, and the USFL had drawn first blood. You never ask a barber if you need a haircut. The NFL, sorely in need of a trim, was about to get a little taken off the top.

36

THE CURIOUS CASE
OF GARY WAYNE
ANDERSON

I CELEBRATED NEW YEAR'S in 1983 at the Houston Astrodome at the Blue Bonnet Bowl, where I witnessed one of the most electrifying college running backs not named Herschel Walker rush for 161 yards, score 2 touchdowns, and lead Arkansas to a 28-24 upset victory over Florida.

Gary Wayne Anderson was a slashing and dashing tailback, despite standing barely six-feet and weighing hardly 170 pounds. He wasn't huge like Herschel, flamboyant like Sims, or a world-class sprinter like Dickey. But give him a football, and he was a magician, finding slivers of space and running at impossible angles. He made his mark at Columbia, Missouri's, Hickman High School, but played so large that he caught the eye of legendary University of Arkansas head coach Lou Holtz, who was just a five-hour, 312-mile drive away in Fayetteville.

Anderson played running back and wide receiver, but also returned punts and kickoffs. He was a threat to score every single time he touched the football. Routine screen passes turned into breathtaking sixty-yard touchdowns. He could catch a punt in a crowd and emerge from the pack, eyes wide, like a scared rabbit chased by barking hounds. Near the goal-line, he would leap into the night, soaring like a superhero toward the end zone. "He is," Lou Holtz would repeatedly say, "the most versatile player I've ever coached."

Gary was shy, introverted, and quieter than a church mouse leaning in a corner. He had grown up in a small mid-Southern town that was whiter than a saltine cracker. He liked girls and football, but not necessarily in that order. Football was his language, and he spoke it fluently. Tucked away safely inside the warm confines of a Riddell helmet, however, Gary was capable of anything and everything, performing athletic feats that defied both logic and kinesiology.

Off the field, however, not so much: Gary Anderson couldn't read.

Now, before we all saddle up and get on our high horses, pump the brakes for just a second.

The Herschel Walker saga had exposed the NCAA's rules of eligibility as nothing more than a sham of limiting competition for athletic talent between two competing industries—the NCAA and the NFL. By collaborating on artificial "eligibility" criteria, the two organizations successfully had lowered the cost of competing for that talent by sharing it. The NCAA had virtually eliminated the cost of its work force; players "worked" for scholarships.

The NFL—without a minor-league feeder system—denied players the right to pursue their livelihood unless they lived up to the NCAA's ever-changing rules of amateurism and eligibility, which led former NCAA director Walter Byars to eventually say himself that "collegiate amateurism is not a moral issue—it's an economic camouflage for monopoly practices."

In 1926, when the NFL declared underclassmen off-limits, colleges embraced the idea. In fact, in later years—first by Halas in 1957, and later by Rozelle—the NFL would often remind reporters and politicians that the underclassman rule was instigated on the behest of colleges, not pro football.

Professional football owners agreed not to compete for underclassmen until their college eligibility, as defined by the NCAA itself, had expired. No mention was ever made of the athletes graduating. Athletes were confined to amateur status until the NCAA and NFL "declared" them fit to turn professionals.

So how did the NFL defend its position of delaying eligibility throughout the Herschel Walker saga?

The league claimed it was protecting the academic interests of the "student-athlete."

Are you kidding me?

By the time Anderson was recruited at Arkansas, the NCAA was firmly entrenched in decades of lies and deception that exist to this very day: What is amateurism? What constitutes a professional? Is a scholarship a contract? Is a grant-in-aid payment? Are the value of scholarships artificially suppressed by the NCAA and its members, thus making players university employees? Are scholarships really just a money-laundering scheme? Who defines eligibility? Draft status? Maturity? Why does the NCAA have one set of rules for revenue-producing, tier-one schools, and another set of separate rules for non-revenue-producing, tier-two schools? Who is in charge? Who is on first? Who is making these rules? Is this antitrust, or not antitrust?

Then, when all else begins to fail miserably, as it was with Herschel, the NCAA just lobs out a grenade called "education," and ducks? Let's get this straight: When challenged, the NCAA is seriously, and purposefully, going to use its amateur mythology to mask the reality of its employer-employee relationships and hide behind the façade of education? The NCAA's radical and manipulative policies to deny workman's compensation to their football players (employees) are, frankly, disgusting.

Of course, the NFL stood around with its hands in its pockets, whistling Dixie, and why not? ·

Why should the NFL screw up its own farm system?

You should never do card tricks in the same place you play poker. The NFL and NCAA had tried and failed with Walker, which is why I worked so tirelessly to deliver him to the USFL. But the NFL and NCAA were playing hot potato with hand grenades, and once again, my involvement with the USFL was going to make the curious case of Gary Wayne Anderson explode in their faces.

There were a million things Gary could do well; it's just that none of us knew that reading wasn't one of them.

On a football field, the only thing he was asked to read were defenses, and he could find holes like a mouse finds cheese. How a young man can get through high school, pass a college entrance exam, and enroll at a major university with a severe reading deficiency remains a mystery, but apparently, it happens. Really?

By the time Anderson was selected in the first round of the 1983 USFL draft by the New Jersey Generals, the University of Arkansas had extracted its pound of flesh. On the surface, everything appeared normal. Gary had maintained a C average and earned 82 of the required 124 credits to graduate during his nearly four years at Arkansas. He was a single credit short of being on schedule to graduate in five years.

More than 100 agents had pursued Gary, and I, too, had sent him my standard two-page letter inviting him to join the Argovitz family. *Sports Illustrated* would later excerpt the following:

> We of the Argovitz family desire to share with you the philosophy which has
> enabled me to build my business empire. A smart man is not the man who
> has all the answers, but is the man who realizes what he doesn't know and
> surrounds himself with the best people to give him the best answers. Gary, I
> look forward to our meeting and to introducing you to the right people with
> the right answers for you and your future.

I met Gary and his wife, Ollie, in Houston, right after the New Year's Eve Bluebonnet Bowl, in which Anderson became the game's Most Valuable Player. On January 3, Gary signed our standard 630-word contract (which is about the same number of words you're reading on this page).

As with all of our clients, Gary would also hire us as his exclusive business manager.

On January 4, Gary was picked by the New Jersey Generals in the first round of the USFL draft. The Generals would subsequently trade his rights to the Tampa Bay Bandits. That same day, I guaranteed a bank loan of $10,000 to carry him over to the NFL draft in April.

On January 5, Gary and I flew to a press conference in New Jersey, but obviously the focus there had shifted to the pursuit of Herschel, not Gary. When the Generals started talking second- and third-round money, I told them to save their breath. We would wait on the NFL draft, where Gary would most certainly be a first-round pick, too. The benefit of the USFL was now working in both directions.

Then, in February, I received a call from David Dixon.

"Hey David, what's up?"

"Jerry, you know that as founder of the USFL, I was automatically grandfathered a franchise," he said.

"Of course," I said. "You deserve it. You've done a helluva job. I can't wait for the league to kick off next month. Are you thinking about exercising your option?"

David was quiet for a second. "Not really," he said. "I'm curious if you'd like to buy my franchise."

I almost dropped the phone.

Owning a team had definitely crossed my mind. I think it's a natural reaction when you work with or for people you don't respect that you imagine yourself in their role, and often question how they came to power in the first place.

Without a doubt, in negotiations with the Lions, Bills, Bucs, Colts, and Oilers, I felt I could do a better job as an owner and a general manager. The NFL and the NCAA were running monopolies that were based on outdated rules, antitrust violations, predatory practices, and unfair scales of economy. Everyone was suffering, including football fans.

I had nurtured Dixon's ideas and his new league because I saw the immediate, enormous benefit of fair-market value for all players, not just those whom I represented. When David made his offer, I also understood that the backlash could be swift and severe: No question the media and the public—not privy to the years of effort I had given the new league—would view such a move as selfish, and most certainly, a conflict of interest.

Nevertheless, when opportunity arises, you have to weigh all of the pros and cons. Where could I have the greater impact? I'd now spent years bitching about the NFL; now was a chance to literally turn the tables, become an owner myself, and "put up or shut up." What man worth his salt doesn't relish the chance to prove himself, fair and square?

My first responsibility was to every player I currently represented. While our 1982 draft included a windfall of talent, 1983 had been increasingly difficult, because NFL personnel were telling college players that if I represented them, they may not be picked because I was too difficult to work with. Gene had made numerous trips into my office decrying this fact.

We sat down together and laid all of our cards on the table.

"Let's be honest with each other, Jerry," Gene said. "We're being blackballed. I'm running into brick walls out there trying to recruit new players. NFL teams are tired of us. You beat them up with guaranteed contracts. You made them pay out Lloyd's of London insurance, and now everybody's doing it. You took two first-round picks to Canada. You embarrassed them with Herschel Walker. You've been beating them like a dog, but now the dog is biting back."

"You are right, Gene," I replied. "Fighting the NFL is like gambling at a casino. They never run out of time or money. I think we need to evaluate all of our options. In fact, I'm seriously considering buying Dixon's franchise for Houston.

"What are your thoughts, Gene?"

"Do you believe in your own five-year plan that you presented the USFL?" Gene asked.

"Of course I do," I said. "There's so much corruption and unfairness in the NFL that I really believe if the owners of the USFL teams follow my plan, the USFL will become a huge success."

"Well, then," Gene replied, "you've answered your own question. We need to tell all of our players your decision, and we need to take care of Gary Anderson."

On March 23, 1983, I formed a partnership with Houston businessmen Bernard Lerner, Alvin Lubetkin, and Fred Gerson to purchase David Dixon's USFL expansion franchise for that city, which would begin play in 1984, the league's second year. I accepted the position as president and managing general partner.

My first move was to make Gene the first African American general manager in professional football. My second move was to call each of my players, tell them I was selling my sports agency, and explain that I no longer could represent them. All of them understood, and wished me well, except for three: Billy Sims, Joe Cribbs, and Gary Anderson. Those three players insisted I continued to represent them, in spite of any perceived conflict of interest.

This was going to be dicey, for sure. I called Chet Simmons, the USFL commissioner, in New York, and gave him a thorough update. I trusted Chet, and he was one of the most genuine, warm, all-around great guys you'd ever want to meet. This was obvious when he resigned as the first president of ESPN to come to the USFL—nobody at the network wanted to see him leave. The man was full of life, ideas and energy, and best of all, he had the knowledge and contacts to lead a new league made for television.

Simmons had been an excellent choice for the USFL's first commissioner. Accustomed to working in tight spaces with flamboyant personalities and sports celebrities, Simmons was no puppet for USFL owners who were new at their trade, but accustomed to getting their way.

To name a few, Chet had influenced or launched the commentating careers of Jim Simpson, Merlin Olsen, Greg and Bryant Gumbel, Dick Enberg, Curt Gowdy, Tony Kubek, Joe Garagiola, Sandy Koufax, Vin Scully, Chris Berman, Bob Ley, Tom Mees, Dick Vitale, Tim Ryan, and Jack Buck. As a founding father of sports television, Simmons started his career with Sports Programs, which became ABC Sports.

While at ABC, from 1957 to 1964, as vice president and general manager of sports programs, Simmons had played a key role in the development of *Wide World of Sports* and helped bring the Olympics to television. He worked at NBC for fifteen years, culminating as the first president of Sports in 1977. At NBC, he was involved in the creation of "instant replay" and securing major sports properties, including the American Football League, National Football League, Major League Baseball, National Hockey League, NCAA basketball, the Rose and Orange Bowls, Wimbledon, and the Olympics.

Simmons joined ESPN as president on July 31, 1979, just prior to the network's launch on September 7 the same year. Along with close friend and fellow NBC Sports alum Scotty Connal, who ran production and operations, he led ESPN through its infancy. Among Chet's most notable achievements were the birth and direction of *SportsCenter*, which would define sports as a TV news genre. In 1980 he had engineered television's first comprehensive coverage of the early rounds of the NCAA Men's Basketball Tournament and the NFL Draft telecast.

Chet and I had a good relationship, but he wasn't about to stake his professional reputation on me.

"Jerry, you know it's not personal, but our bylaws prohibit anyone who has an interest in a member club from acting as agent or representative for any player," he said. "We did this on purpose. Steve Ehrhart, our own league counsel and a personal friend of yours, had to quit representing players, too. We're friends, but you know the rules."

"I realize that," I answered. "I'm not asking to keep my agency business. I'm only asking for a special waiver in regard to just three players who understand the conflict but still want me to represent them."

"Who are the players?"

"Billy Sims, Joe Cribbs, and Gary Anderson," I said. "Billy and Joe are coming into option years in the NFL and are adamant that they don't want to change representation midstream. I already was representing Gary before the opportunity arose. In the meantime, I'm selling my business to Steve Zucker, the Chicago attorney. Trust me, Chet, I'm playing by the rules and I promise you that once I get these three players signed, I will not represent another player."

"Let me talk to the other owners and our counsel," he said, "and I'll see if we can waive those three guys. But if I get this approved, it's those three guys, and that's it. No more."

"I understand, Chet," I said. "And thanks."

The next day, I received a fax from the USFL informing me I had been both approved as an owner, and that all my activity as an agent would cease after ongoing negotiations with Sims, Cribbs, and Anderson were completed.

Chet called me to make sure I received it.

"I got this approved, Jerry," he said, "but only under the strict condition that each player specifically be told and state that they understood that you are officially, and temporarily, wearing two hats."

What happened next was a crash course in capitalism and free enterprise.

On April 26, 1983, the Chargers selected Anderson as the twentieth pick in the NFL draft, and I opened negotiations with San Diego general manager John R. Saunders.

On April 29, Gary appeared at a San Diego Chargers press conference. He spent the next three days at the team's rookie minicamp. On May 1, back in Houston, I received a call from John Bassett, owner of the Tampa Bay Bandits.

"Is Gary still available?" he inquired. The Bandits, under head coach Steve Spurrier, had been an early USFL surprise, but sorely lacked a running game.

"Yes," I said. "Don't do anything until I can make an offer," Bassett said. "I can be in Houston in two days."

On May 2, I reached Gary at his mother Ethel Mae's home in Columbia, Missouri. "We've got another team who wants you," I told him. "I have a ticket to Houston waiting for you at the airport."

On May 3, at a hotel in Houston, we held a press conference announcing that my application to purchase David Dixon's franchise had been approved and that the Houston team would begin play in the USFL's second season in 1984. Most of my Argovitz family attended, including Hugh Green, Joe Cribbs, Curtis Dickey, Jacob Green, Keith Gary, George Cumby, Robert Brazile, and Billy Sims. The presence of my players sent shudders through NFL front offices, and false rumors spread like wildfire that I had plans to somehow sign them all. Peter Hadhazy called me from the USFL's headquarters. "You have brought the apocalypse on the NFL," he chuckled.

With Gary in Houston, the Chargers hastily offered him a three-year, $830,000 contract. Meanwhile, I furiously worked the phones with the Bandits and John Bassett. On May 4, I introduced Gary and John to each other at the Houston Hobby airport. The following day Bassett offered Anderson a four-year, $1.375 million contract—a deal that included an immediate interest-free loan of up to $275,000, a $500,000 signing bonus ($200,000 up front, the rest deferred until 1987), and annual salaries of $125,000, $175,000, $225,000, and $350,000, the first three years fully guaranteed.

I went back to the phones, and called San Diego, informing John Sanders of Tampa Bay's interest, and my final proposal: A guaranteed $975,000 for three years ($450,000 signing bonus; salaries of $125,000, $175,000, and $225,000).

"Are you crazy?" Sanders said. "Let me talk to my owner, and I'll call you back."

"No, I'm not crazy, John," I said. "We have another offer. Apparently you have a short memory. There is another league now. Either you take it, or you don't. If I don't hear from you in an hour, we're gone!'"

That day, Anderson shook hands with Bassett and agreed to sign with Tampa Bay. Then I sent Gary back to his mother's house in Columbia, where I instructed him to not answer the phone for anybody. "The Chargers are going to try to find you," I told him. "Ignore them, or just tell them to call me. I gave them every chance to step up to the plate and sign you. They refused."

The Chargers, of course, reacted with fury. When they couldn't locate Gary, San Diego owner Gene Klein had his staff call Lou Holtz at Arkansas, Gary's mother—even other Arkansas players on the San Diego roster. Then Sanders called me.

"Where is he, Argovitz?" he yelled.

"It's not my job to find him for you," I said.

"This isn't over!" Sanders roared, before angrily slamming down the phone.

On May 7, we flew to Tampa, and two days later, on May 9, Anderson signed his Bandits contract while appearing at another press conference. Head coach Steve Spurrier declared him the new starting tailback. "Gary's gonna run the ball, and he's gonna catch the ball," said Spurrier, who had the look of a kid on Christmas with a new toy fire engine. "Bottom line is Gary's gonna get the ball."

On May 15, in his first pro game, Anderson rushed for 99 yards on 18 carries, caught 4 passes for 54 yards and scored the Bandits' winning touchdown against the Arizona Wranglers.

"Runners like Gary make us coaches look pretty smart," joked Spurrier, when asked how Anderson had learned the offense in only seven days. "Imagine how good he'll be in another week."

Back in San Diego Klein was seething over the loss of Anderson—and vowed revenge. In 1981, two years earlier, he had suffered a heart attack on the witness stand testifying in the antitrust suit that Al Davis had brought against the NFL. A year later, federal investigators told him that one of his Chargers players had smuggled an entire kilo of cocaine back to San Diego on the team flight returning home from a playoff win over Miami.

Now I had whisked his first-round draft pick from under his nose, and he was ready to brawl.

On the surface, Klein was difficult to dislike. He'd grown up in the Bronx in New York, worked his way through college selling encyclopedias, and spent five years flying in the Army Air Corps. He moved to California and carved out a living for many years hustling used cars. Dressed in cowboy boots and hats, he starred in his own commercials as "Cowboy Gene" and used a fake Texas drawl to lure in customers. Then his investment into National Theatres and Television Corp. turned into National General, a massive insurance and entertainment company. By the time he was fifty, Klein was a billionaire.

He told the media he purchased the San Diego Chargers in 1966 "just for fun." For his players, however, it was anything but. Klein's problem in football was that he wanted the milk from his cows, but he didn't believe in feeding them. Players were little more to Klein than a pain in his ass, and he thought even less of agents. He refused to renegotiate contracts and took public pride in throwing future Hall of Famers out of his office rather than re-do a deal. As long as the NFL could lead its players like sheep to the slaughter, this attitude had served him. Now, with the advent of the USFL, this was no longer the case. Much to Klein's disgust, I had spared Gary Anderson from his clutches, and now the lamb had publicly slain the butcher.

When word leaked to the media—strangely enough, out of San Diego—that Bassett was chairman of the USFL expansion committee and that I had "sold out" Anderson in exchange for a USFL franchise, the shit hit the proverbial fan. There wasn't an ounce of truth to this: I had purchased Dixon's franchise, and therefore it had nothing to do with the expansion committee. "Gary Anderson is going to find out the truth about Jerry Argovitz," Klein said, "and the truth is that Argovitz is a scumbag."

The story was too good to ignore, and it grabbed sports headlines across the nation. Klein was desperate to get even with me and the USFL and to reclaim Gary, who in his shortened rookie season with Tampa Bay combined for nearly 1,000 yards and 4 touchdowns.

Imagine my surprise, however, when just weeks after the USFL's first season, I received a phone call telling me that not only was Gary in San Diego, but he also had just signed another contract with the Chargers; even more, he had filed a lawsuit against me, the Bandits, and John Bassett, and was seeking a temporary injunction that would allow him to play in the NFL.

Barely a season old, the USFL was in court with the NFL, and I was the primary defendant.

As the story unfolded, it would shock the sporting public, college, and professional football alike.

After Gary had been paid by the Bandits, he bought cars for himself and his mother, bought her a new house, filled it with furniture, and also gave her a check for $10,000. He finished the season in Tampa, where he became friends with Lloyd C.A. Wells, a "writer" with the *Forward Times*, a weekly paper serving Houston's African American community.

Wells told Anderson he once had been a member of Muhammad Ali's entourage and was a former pro football scout. He also claimed to be an agent and told Gary he could probably help him break into acting. After earning Gary's trust, and unbeknownst to me, he visited Gary in Florida several times, bought him gifts, and even called to congratulate Gary and his wife, Ollie, on the birth of their first child. After the season ended, Wells visited Gary in Columbia, and offered to be his agent and to get him a better deal with the San Diego Chargers, in spite of the fact he was under contract to the Bandits.

Then Wells called the Chargers and spoke with his longtime friend Paul "Tank" Younger, San Diego's assistant general manager. He informed him that Gary now wanted to play for San Diego. Klein was giddy at the news, and did the unthinkable—gave Wells interest-free "loans" totaling $30,000, with no payback terms. The man who called me a dirtbag and hated agents was now giving them money to interfere with a contract in an effort to undermine me and the USFL.

Younger and Klein recommended several lawyers to Wells. The first was Marvin Demoff, who represented John Elway and Dan Marino. Shocked, Demoff suggested the law firm of Luce, Forward, Hamilton & Scripps in San Diego, who represented the Chargers. No fools themselves, that firm recoiled in horror and suggested Bracewell & Patterson in Houston. Magically, a retainer reached that firm, and attorney Charles G. King took the case.

On August 3, 1983, Anderson, led by Wells and King, filed suit against me, my company, Bandits' owner John F. Bassett, and the Bandits organization. Among other things, the affidavit alleged the following: (a) "Argovitz conspired with Bassett, the chairman of the expansion committee, to deliver Anderson to the Bandits in exchange for the Houston USFL franchise;" (b) Argovitz never told Anderson he was to be awarded a USFL franchise; and (c) Argovitz misrepresented the Chargers' contract offer. Anderson was asking the court to declare his Bandits contract void, award him $289,000 in damages, and allow him to play for the Chargers.

King also sought a temporary restraining order in Houston to enable Anderson to sign and practice with the Chargers "without interference." There's nothing funnier than when people who are guilty of interference seek relief from you interfering with their interference.

The very same day, Wells and Gary flew to San Diego and met, of all places, at Younger's apartment. There, in the apartment of a Chargers employee, Anderson signed a series of four one-year Charger contracts worth $1.5 million, including a $550,000 "signing, reporting, and playing" bonus (whatever that is), and salaries of $150,000, $200,000, $250,000, and $350,000.

However, $800,000 of the total contract was deferred beyond 1986; and the salaries were not guaranteed, against injury or otherwise. The Chargers gave Anderson a $50,000 bonus to sign. Anderson's wife, Ollie, paid Wells $15,000 of that for his services, meaning in less than ninety days, between Anderson and Klein, Wells had received $45,000 for tampering with my client.

The case was set for August 12.

"Gary Anderson is a scapegoat," I told the media, "he's a pawn in the first big battle between the great NFL and those little kids from the USFL."

U.S. District Court Judge Norman W. Black and the rest of his packed courtroom sat in silence as attorney Charles G. King opened his case. Anderson sat at the plaintiff's table, while his mother, Ethel Mae, and wife, Ollie, sat in the gallery behind him. King started down the expected path, explaining that me, Bassett, and the Bandits had misrepresented ourselves and our intentions, and somehow had duped Gary into signing an inferior contract. Then he took a left turn that stunned even the most casual court observer.

"My client," King said, pointing at Gary, "is functionally illiterate. He cannot read."

Functionally illiterate, he explained, means sixth-grade level. Therefore, he told the court, Gary wasn't capable of comprehending things like contracts and was susceptible to anything.

No kidding, I thought, like unscrupulous attorneys and agents.

To prove his point, King asked Gary to take the witness stand, and handed him a copy of his four-year, $1.375 million deal with the Bandits.

"Can you read that for me?" King asked.

"Club . . . Guarantees . . . The . . . Payment . . . Of . . . Salary . . ."

People looked around the courtroom in shock. Like a grade-schooler, Gary kept reading.

"For . . . The . . . First . . . Second . . . And . . . Third . . . Salary . . . Years . . . If . . . In . . . Excess . . . Thereof . . . Then . . . Player . . . Shall . . . Keep . . . All . . . Such . . . Other . . . Salaries."

It was painful, horrible, and embarrassing to watch. Gary's mom bowed her head and his beautiful wife, Ollie, was sobbing out loud.

Frankly, I was furious—and simultaneously amazed.

Indeed, Gary could barely read. That was obvious to anyone in the courtroom. But how could a kid graduate from high school, qualify for college, and attend a major university . . . like this?

And why would his own attorney embarrass his client like this before the world?

My attorneys had no choice, and went to work. At stake for me was my reputation, and in the bigger picture, the Gamblers and the entire USFL. There had been hours of depositions. I had been forthright and cooperative. Our contract had been explained verbally, and in writing, and Gary's wife, Ollie, had read it. There had been no coercion, as they claimed. There had been no side deal with Bassett for a franchise.

Finally, at the crux of the case was Sanders, the Chargers' general manager, who claimed that he had tried to counter-offer, but that I hadn't returned his phone calls—another lie.

By the time Bruce W. Greer, Bassett's attorney, began to question Gary, I just wanted to rescue him. If there was any coercion in this case, it was Klein, Wells, Sanders, and Younger who had convinced Anderson to bring this suit to trial. Sadly, our attorneys had no option but to continue the public basting, and it didn't get any prettier.

"Did you know why [Wells] was giving you presents?" Greer asked.

"No," Gary said. He was scared, nervous, and fidgeting. "We got to be pretty good, you know, friends . . . and he said he didn't have nothin' else to do and he liked to be around friends, and we got to be real close. He said he had done contracts all his life. He said he didn't believe that San Diego was offering that less for me, being my name, and that I can go to San Diego and help out. He believed that they was offering more."

"The contract is for how many years?" Greer asked.

"Four," Gary answered.

"What do you get paid for each of those four years?"

"One-fifteen—the first year, 175—the second, 2—I don't remember," he paused, and stared at his wife. "I don't recall the last two years for sure."

"Are you familiar with what they call a guaranteed contract?"

"Right."

"Now, is this contract guaranteed?"

"Yes."

"What do you mean by that when you say that it would be guaranteed?"

"It would be guaranteed that regardless of what is happening, your contract is guaranteed."

"If you get hurt?"

"Right."

"You get paid throughout the whole four years?"

"Right."

"How about if you get cut from the team for any reason?"

"Everything is guaranteed, you still get paid."

"Did you read the contract at the time?"

"Yes."

"You read the whole thing?"

"I breezed through it."

"So you didn't read it carefully?"

"No."

"Did anyone read it carefully?"

"My wife, she read it."

"Did she read it very carefully or —"

"I don't know how carefully she read it, but she read it."

"Did Lloyd [Wells] read it?"

"I'm not for sure whether he read it."

After five hours of grueling testimony, Judge Black not only denied the injunction, but also admonished the Chargers for "financing" Anderson's cause. He called the entire ordeal "distressing . . . a sad commentary," and described Gary as a "fine young man being put in the middle of a very unpleasant situation, and being treated like a soccer ball."

"I don't find any evidence that Dr. Argovitz, or anyone else, entered into a conspiracy against Gary Anderson," the judge said. "The most telling point is that the initial contract with Tampa Bay has as good or better present value as the one he got from San Diego.

"What makes this entire scheme unconscionable is the fact that the Chargers offered Anderson an inferior contract after reviewing the contract he signed with the Bandits."

Sports Illustrated writer Bill Brubaker covered the hearing, and when it was over, asked my opinion. "The Chargers took a nice young man," I said, "and warped him and turned him against the people who really cared for him."

When the article was published in *SI* a week later, Gary was publicly humiliated before millions of readers. "The Anderson affair is a study in manipulation," wrote Brubaker, "pitting agent against agent, owner against owner and league against league, all in a mad scramble for a twenty-two-year-old athlete who admits that, even after almost four years at the University of Arkansas, he has trouble reading."

In Fayetteville, Arkansas, Holtz strongly denied Charles King's assertion that Anderson is functionally illiterate. Adella Gray, academic counselor for Razorback athletes, also disputed King's contention, but acknowledged that Anderson has a serious reading deficiency. "It's a shame he got this far without being able to read," she said.

When the dust settled, Bassett considered suing Klein, the Chargers, and the NFL. "Gary Anderson and Tampa Bay are the victims," said Bruce Greer, his attorney. "San Diego has hurt Gary Anderson's public image. Tampa Bay had a valid contract with which San Diego interfered."

Klein, Sanders, and Younger sulked back to San Diego defeated. Anderson went back to the Bandits, his reputation forever tarnished. He would be called "functionally illiterate" for the rest of his career.

Certainly, in its first landmark courtroom scrimmage, the USFL had scored a lopsided shutout. John Bassett and I had been exonerated, our credibility and integrity upheld. The validity of the contract had been tested and proven in court.

But nobody, nobody, challenged the NCAA. As fast as possible, it swept Gary Anderson under the rug. The NCAA didn't want to answer the question:

How can a four-year scholarship athlete be unable to read?

37

BUFFALO STEW

THE CAREER EXPECTANCY of an NFL running back is 3.6 years. I had no idea when I crashed the NFL's party and pissed in their punchbowl that my career expectancy as an agent would be about the same. "The only thing worse than Argovitz being an agent," huffed Lions' GM Russ Thomas to the media, "is to imagine him being an owner."

Behind closed doors, however, the NFL wasn't laughing. My dual roles had cracked open their door of ethics, and NFL team owners, as well as GMs, were clamoring for my head on the grounds of perceived "conflict of interest." NFL brass delighted at the thought of the hunter becoming the hunted, and my ass felt very much like it bore a Texas-sized bulls-eye. In the days after the Anderson trial, I got a call from Peter Hadhazy, the USFL's director of operations, and he confirmed as much.

"Congratulations, Jerry," Peter said, "you've succeeded at becoming the most hated man in football." When Peter worked in the NFL, we'd gained a mutual respect in our negotiations from opposite sides of the table. When he joined the USFL front office, it was fun to finally be on the same team. Peter was a trusted confidant whose opinion I valued and took to heart.

"If you've got a skeleton in your closet," he told me, "you might want to bury it in your backyard, because the people you're playing with aren't playing. I'm serious, Jerry. Watch your ass."

Chuckling, I told Peter I wasn't worried. Then I told him my favorite campfire story about the "Texas Three-Kick Rule," where a Texan and a New Yorker are in an argument over who's the toughest. The Texan, of course, challenges him to the "Texas Three-Kick Rule."

"I kick you three times," the Texan says, "then you kick me three times, and we go back and forth, until one of us gives up." So the New Yorker agrees, and the Texan kicks him right in the nuts. The New Yorker falls to his knees, and the Texan rears back and kicks him again, driving the pointed toe of his boot into the New Yorker's ribs. As the New Yorker falls forward, the Texan drills him again, this time in the kidneys.

"Now, you bastard," gasps the New Yorker, as he climbs to his feet, "you're about to discover what New York's all about."

"Nah," laughs the Texan, mounting his horse. "'I quit. You win."

I was now a full-fledged USFL owner. Granted, my agent "career" was about to end in a blaze of glory, but not before I figuratively applied the Three-Kick Rule to a very special New Yorker: Stew Barber, general manager of the Buffalo Bills.

Russ Thomas and Bill Ford had privately tried to humiliate me. Hugh Culverhouse did, too. Bob Irsay might have stayed sober for a whole day if someone had told him that it meant my death. Then Klein took it all public, and in the process of trying to ruin me, had utterly humiliated my youngest and most vulnerable client—Anderson. Klein limped off into the sunset, and so embarrassed, he left football for horse racing, because, he said, "horses don't talk, don't have agents, and don't ask to renegotiate their contracts."

Screw him. I had done my best to provide the best options for my players. Now I felt like an exhausted Muhammad Ali who had grown tired of playing rope-a-dope with a power-punching George Foreman; now, it was time to stop leaning and start punching back and knock somebody out. Yes, I was finally madder than hell. Manners, mothers, niceness, and protocol were out the window. The gloves were off. You don't know who a man is until he has a little blood in his mouth, and I never liked the taste of my own. Somebody was about to pay dearly, and it wasn't going to be me.

Left on my fight card was defending the likes of Joe Cribbs and Billy Sims, and next up immediately was Little Joe. I had done my best to negotiate in good faith with the Bills, and Barber had lied to my face. He had told me and Joe that if he outperformed his contract, he would renegotiate in the option year. When that option year arrived, he—like Russ Thomas before him—suddenly suffered from amnesia. But now I had, as Chet Simmons said, the "green light" to temporarily wear two hats: USFL owner and agent. At this point, my goal now was to publicly expose them and embarrass them all.

I now had physical, emotional, and financial leverage to increase the potential return of Little Joe and Billy, and I planned to use every bit, for their sake. Turnabout is fair play, and paybacks are a bitch. Buffalo and Detroit wanted to pay Joe and Billy like they were two common mutt horses, when the football world knew they were clearly a pair of thoroughbreds.

Barber made the mistake of dropping his left hand, just for a split second, and he never saw me coming.

Lights out.

Ironically, from the beginning, the careers of Jim Kelly and Joe Cribbs had been intertwined in Buffalo history: both had been drafted by the Bills with picks acquired from the trade that sent O. J. Simpson to the San Francisco 49ers in 1979. The number-one pick in 1979 became linebacker Tom Cousineau, who jumped to Canada, wouldn't play for the Bills, and was traded to Cleveland for a first-round pick in 1983, which became Kelly. The second-round pick in 1980 was Cribbs.

After eighteen months of listening to Stew's preposterous bullshit regarding Joe, I was ready to deal the cards, and now it meant more than just Little Joe. Gene had handed me his scouting report on the first-round quarterbacks in the 1983 NFL draft, and we thought the University of Miami's Jim Kelly was the best. Yes, better than Dan Marino, better than John Elway, better than them all, maybe even better than Johnny U when it was all said and done.

Best of all, Buffalo had drafted Kelly, and that narrowed my focus to one. Gene and I sat down in my office and reviewed his file, start to finish.

High school stud in Pennsylvania . . . recruited by Joe Paterno at Penn State as a linebacker . . . went to a losing school at Miami determined to play quarterback and face the challenge of turning around the program . . . father was raised in an orphanage . . . laser arm . . . intelligent and cunning . . . stunning, absolute pinpoint accuracy . . . fearless born leader who will challenge everyone around him . . . confident . . . relentless . . . a sonuvabitch if you cross him . . . needs a little push to be great . . .

"Where do we stand, Gene?" I asked.

"Well, he just had shoulder surgery," Gene answered. " He got dinged against Virginia Tech. His last season at Miami, he only played a couple games before he separated his right shoulder. He was a preseason Heisman guy. This is just enough to make the NFL dumb asses use it against him in negotiations. The Chicago Blitz and Dr. Dietrich own his rights. We can get him, Jerry. If you treat Kelly right, you'll end up the smartest guy in the room."

Don't challenge the soil that feeds you corn; Gene and I knew talent, and that was all I needed to hear. Furthermore, I was relishing the opportunity to piss in the well of the NFL.

"What do you think it will take financially?" I said. Gene replied, "I'm sure Buffalo is trying to sign him cheap, as usual. Jerry, you can out-negotiate Buffalo in your sleep. If Jim is the guy you want, then by all means let's go get him."

Gene was smirking. I wanted an anti-establishment guy, a leader who would make everyone around him a better player; I wanted the Joe Namath of the USFL and Kelly seemed to be the right fit. "Gene, I'm calling Carl Peterson, who I think is one of the best personnel guys in professional football." Carl was the GM of the Philadelphia Eagles and was now the president of the Philadelphia Stars.

"He's the franchise," I said. "From now on, we'll just call him T.F., as in, The Franchise."

But there were minor concerns. "The first thing I'll do is check out his shoulder," I stated. "I want Dr. Matsu to do an MRI and evaluate him to make sure there is no nerve damage or adhesions or any other recurring effects from his injury. We can't afford to buy a pig in a poke."

We both laughed before I continued. "I have an idea that I'll put in his contract: I'll guarantee that he's always among the three highest-paid quarterbacks in the USFL, if he is in the top three statistically in passing efficiency. If any quarterback gets more than him, we'll readjust his contract on the spot."

Gene busted out laughing. "Don't get too high on your own ether, Jerry!" he said. "With your new offense, this guy is going to be the best quarterback in the history of the game, trust me!"

"I'll tell Jim Kelly myself that as long as he throws touchdowns," I said, "we'll not only make him rich, but we'll hire a few guys so damn fast he can't throw that far."

"Gene, my advice is you better stop looking at just football guys, and maybe look at some track guys, too. Speed kills. Start thinking offense, speed, and receivers," I added. "We must commit our resources to the type of players who will be effective in the Run 'N Shoot," a revolutionary new system we were planning to use.

"And don't forget about the big boys up front," I said. "Gene, we're going to build the most entertaining team in the history of football."

Two days later, Gene burst into my office. "Jerry, you've got to do something," he said. "Kelly and his agent Greg Lustig are in Buffalo right now. They're about to sign a $2.1 million, five-year deal. You're the man. Do something about it, Chief."

He handed me a pink message sheet. On it was the phone number for the Buffalo Bills.

I called immediately. "Can I speak to Greg Lustig?"

"He's in a meeting," said the Bill's secretary. "How can I help you?"

"Please put Greg on the phone," I said. "It's a family emergency."

"Please hold," she said.

Seconds later, Lustig picked up. "Hello, this is Greg," he said.

"Greg, this is Dr. Jerry Argovitz. I know you're there with Jim Kelly to sign a contract with the Bills. The 'family emergency' is that if you sign with Buffalo, you're making the biggest mistake of your life, Jim's life, and his family's life. I'm prepared to make you a deal you can't refuse for Jim, and I'm also willing to sign Mark Rush. When you hang up this phone, don't sign anything, walk out of that room right now, get on a plane, come to Houston, and I'll have a limo pick you up."

"Are you serious?" Lustig asked

"I'm as serious as cancer."

"I will guarantee your guy will be one of the three highest-paid players in the USFL, always," I said. "Pack your bags and get your ass to Houston."

"We're on our way," Lustig said. "But if you waste our time, Jerry, I'll take you to the cleaners."

"The only place you're taking me," I promised, "is to the bank."

I was never overly concerned about Jim's healing shoulder or his arm strength, but if you were about to buy a race car for $3.2 million with a first-of-its kind, unprecedented "escalating" contract, would you want to take it for a quick spin? When Jim arrived in Houston, I picked him up the next morning after breakfast, drove straight to Memorial Park, parked the car and pulled a football from the back seat.

I tossed it to Jim. "Go deep," he said, laughing.

I ran fifty yards downfield and, like a heat-seeking missile, I could hear the ball hissing behind me. When I turned, I put my hands up, less for the purpose of catching it and more in self-defense. The velocity of the ball bent my ring finger in half, clearly breaking it.

"That'll do," I said, looking at my distorted hand. "I've seen enough." I spent the rest of the day showing Jim around, like a representative of the Chamber of Commerce, before taking him to see Dr. Matsu. After running his battery of tests on Jim's shoulder, it was evident there was nothing to worry about.

When we got back to my office, it took Lustig, Jim, and myself several hours to come to terms. On Thursday, June 9, 1983, Jim Kelly officially was a Houston Gambler and would lead my team when we started play in 1984. For now, the Buffalo Bills had just lost their first-round pick—again.

It was the second time in a month I'd plundered the first round of the NFL draft.

Meanwhile, back at the ranch in Orchard Park, New York, the Buffalo Bills were seething over the defection of Kelly, and would have to play with aging Joe Ferguson as quarterback. Frustration permeated the organization, and the team was in smoking ruins. In January, head coach Chuck Knox—weary of his own front-office battles with Barber and owner Ralph Wilson's refusal to pay top-dollar for top talent—resigned and went to Seattle.

The loss of Knox and Kelly led safety Bill Simpson, linebacker Isaiah Robertson, and running back Lawrence McCutcheon to all retire. Kay Stephenson took the head coaching job, but not before the Bills turned down former Kansas City head coach Marv Levy.

Now I had my sights set on Cribbs, who sadly had become the poster boy for the outright cheapness of the Bills. In Joe's first season, he had rushed for 1,185 yards, made the Pro Bowl, and was AFC Rookie of the Year. But in his final regular-season game, he was strangely benched late in the fourth quarter, and came up fifteen yards short of 1,200, which would have earned him a $10,000 incentive bonus. When I called Stew Barber to question the suspect benching and play-calling and ask that Joe be paid his bonus, I was told in no uncertain terms that the team simply wouldn't "pay bonuses that weren't earned."

Wow. Then, Joe's second year, he once again led the team in rushing and receiving, and guided the Bills to the playoffs, where he suffered a minor fourth-quarter injury in a loss to Cincinnati. When doctors told Joe the injury would keep him on crutches and prevent him from playing in the Pro Bowl, I called Stew again. "He earned the Pro Bowl," I said. "At least pay to send Joe and his wife to Hawaii as your way of saying thanks."

"We have policies against such things," was Stew's curt reply. "No deal."

After he led the Bills in rushing again during the strike-shortened 1982 season his third year, Joe was calling me constantly to get the Bills to either trade him or cut him before 1983, his fourth and option year. "They don't respect me, Doc," he said. "Now it's the principle. I just want out of Buffalo no matter how much they pay me."

Put yourself in my shoes: You've got the best players in football, you have hand-shake agreements in good faith, your players outperformed their original agreements and now, with the USFL you have a viable option with twice the money, and your job is to protect the kids who put their faith and trust in you.

Are you kidding me?

I knew, of course, that Barber had coyly added a "right-of-first-refusal" clause in Joe's contract, which ideally meant the Bills would be able to match any other team's offer, such as one in Canada. This was a sticking point with Barber, because he had lost Cousineau to the CFL in 1979. Barber was now convinced that same clause would protect him from the USFL. Think again: I had shown my attorneys Joe's contract, which was signed in 1980, two years prior to the announcement of the USFL.

Any person on a sixth-grade reading level could understand that when Little Joe signed his Buffalo contract, there could have been no way for that clause to have included the USFL. I couldn't wait to tell Stew Barber about my policy on this deal and make him rue the day he had denied Little Joe his performance bonus and a trip to Hawaii for the Pro Bowl.

The first USFL season in 1983 was now in full swing, and I made a suggestion to Little Joe: Sign a futures contract with the Birmingham Stallions for the spring of 1984. Joe was ecstatic at the idea to return home to Alabama. His mother was aging, and the idea of her traveling to Buffalo to sit in the snow was ridiculous, but she was delighted to learn the Stallions were less than a two-hour drive from her Sulligent, Alabama, home. I called Joe, and in the words of the great Vince Lombardi, told him the moment is now.

"I love it, Doc," he said. "But what's a 'futures' contract?"

I explained that it would be like any other contract, only he would play out his option year in the fall of 1983 in Buffalo, then report to Birmingham for the spring of 1984.

"Let's do it," Joe said. "For me, the sooner, the better."

So I called Stallions general manager Jerry Sklar. Jerry was a helluva man: A cigar-smoking, riverboat gambler who prior to football had directed Loveman's department stores to the pinnacle of the Southern retail market. Sklar had called me repeatedly to tell me that if, given any player on the board, he would take Little Joe to lead his Birmingham Stallions.

"Jerry, here's the deal," I said. "If you want Little Joe, you got him."

"How much?" Sklar said.

"Two-point-five million for four years, plus a $350,000 signing bonus, totally guaranteed," I said.

Sklar hung up, called his owner, Marvin L. Warner, and called me right back.

"Deal," he said. "When can we do this?"

"Well, you guys have a game this Saturday night at home against Tampa Bay on ESPN," I said. "Why not have Joe come out on the field at halftime and sign in front of the fans?"

"That's brilliant," Sklar chortled. "I love it."

"Me, too," I said. "You have no earthly idea just how much I love it. I'll get Joe and we'll see you this weekend."

Legion Field in Birmingham, Alabama, at 400 Graymont Avenue, had become one of the South's best showcases for college football. Notably it was home to one of college football's best traditions, the "Iron Bowl," which pitted bitter rivals Auburn University and the University of Alabama, each of whom played for bragging rights in the football-crazed state. Bear Bryant, Joe Namath, Kenny Stabler, Pat Sullivan, Bo Jackson, and other legends were among the ghosts who graced its gentle confines, and on July 2, 1983, another Auburn legend named Joe Cribbs made history there once again.

The Stallions led the Bandits 23-10 at halftime when Cribbs, Sklar, and Warner strode to a makeshift table at midfield. The Alabama crowd embraced Little Joe as if he'd never left the state. Viewers on ESPN were treated to something they'd never seen before, and one can only imagine the bedlam that broke out in Buffalo sports bars as Bills fans watched in sheer disbelief.

Warner was handed a microphone. "Joe," he cried, "shall we tell the fans how much it is?"

With the sweep of his pen and to deafening approval from the crowd, Cribbs signed the first "futures" contract in USFL history.

Twenty years earlier, the Reverend Billy Graham had spoken in this same stadium to a packed house at the height of the Civil Rights Movement in Alabama. With the signing of Joe Cribbs, the USFL had triggered quite a movement of its own.

Of course, the Bills reacted as we thought and hoped—with a lawsuit, arguing that the "right-of-first-refusal" clause would quash the Birmingham contract. A few months later, Buffalo U.S. District Court Judge John Elfvin, in a rare oral ruling, summoned reporters to his courtroom and explained that the right of first refusal clause was "ambiguous . . . it cannot have any effect on any teams outside the National Football League. I've decided the Buffalo Bills have not sustained the burden of the language in the 1980 contract, that it was something other than what was said."

Thank you. And Judge Elfvin ruled in our favor even after hearing Bills' head coach Kay Stephenson practically beg him to keep Cribbs, explaining that Little Joe was "irreplaceable" in the Bills lineup. To put salt in the wound, Joe—ever the professional— poured it on during his "lame duck" season with the Bills, rushing for 1,131 yards, and leading the team in receiving, too.

But there was one boot kick left to my Texas Three-Kick: After Stew Barber lost Kelly and then Cribbs, he lost his job, too, when he was fired by Buffalo owner Ralph Wilson.

In Tampa Bay, I wasn't done yet with Bucs owner Hugh Culverhouse, either. Through Hugh Green, I'd come to know Bucs quarterback Doug Williams very well. He was the clubhouse leader and had directed the Bucs' attack since 1978, but Culverhouse had refused to pay his quarterback more than $120,000 a year, which ranked forty-second among NFL quarterbacks and was lower than the salary of running back Terdell Middleton, who had carried the ball only twice his entire Tampa Bay career. This incensed the Tampa Bay fans: Williams was asking for only $600,000 a year and Culverhouse refused to budge, going as far as mocking his quarterback in the local media.

So I called Bill Tatham Sr. and Bill Tatham Jr., the two new owners of the USFL's Oklahoma Outlaws, another expansion team that would also begin play in 1984. I suggested Doug Williams and told them that for $3 million they could be set at the quarterback position for the next five years. In September 1983, Williams signed with Oklahoma, which sparked anarchy within the Bucs organization and the Tampa Bay community. Coupled with the success of the USFL's Tampa Bay Bandits and Spurrier's brand of wide-open "Banditball," the NFL was now reeling in south Florida, too.

I couldn't contain my glee. Chet Simmons had allowed me to tie up loose ends with Anderson, Cribbs, and Sims. I had been vindicated in two courts of law and the court of public opinion with the first two. All that remained now was Billy Sims. My next stop was to watch Sims play his last game for the Lions against Green in Detroit on December 18, 1983.

What could possibly go wrong?

38

START SPREADIN'
THE NEWS

IT WAS THE wee hours of the morning on December 19, 1983, when I finally got back home from Detroit, where—shockingly—I had just been served a lawsuit by my own client Billy Sims and the National Football League's Detroit Lions. I unlocked the bolt, opened the door, dropped my bags, and plopped down on the sofa in the dark, propped up my boots and just stared out the window at the shrouded Houston skyline.

I let out a deep sigh. For four years, I had ripped through the cities, offices, and rosters of the NFL like a Midwestern tornado, upsetting wage scales and free agency and, most recently, plundering players. I had managed and now controlled millions of dollars of football talent, and salaries alone had risen from an average of $69,000 per year in 1979 to $225,000 in the thirty-six months since I'd become an agent. But the NFL was fighting back with furious venom, and had snatched Sims, the cornerstone of my business, from under my nose. No question: This was going to be the biggest fight of my life, and the stress of it all coiled in my back, neck, and shoulders like bedsprings.

Utterly exhausted, I felt numb. Too mentally and physically exhausted to move, I dozed off in my street clothes.

The jangling of the telephone jolted me wide awake, and the morning sun temporarily blinded me as I felt around on the end table for the phone.

My watch read 6:45 AM. Squinting, I rubbed my eyes and answered the phone call. It was Peter Hadhazy, calling from the USFL offices in New York.

"Argo, this is Peter. Wanna tell me what in the hell happened yesterday?"

"One of the worst days of my life," I said. "I can't believe Billy just sued me. Those fuckers in Detroit treated me like a common thief."

"Do you remember me telling you to cover your ass?"

"Nobody likes to hear 'I told you so,'" I said. "How'd you find out? They just served me yesterday at the game."

"My phone rang off the hook last night from friends of mine in the NFL predicting your demise," Peter said. "God almighty, Jerry, don't you realize who's behind this?"

"To be honest, my brain is paralyzed right now, but if I had to take a wild guess, I'd have to go with Russ Thomas. What I don't understand is why Billy just didn't call me and tell me the Lions had stepped up to the plate and given him the $4.5 million I was demanding."

"Jerry, this isn't just about you and Billy," Peter said. "This is the NFL versus the USFL, and Bill Ford and Russ Thomas's opportunity to bury you. This will be front-page news when the NFL media machine gets revved up this morning."

"I've got nothing to be afraid of, Peter—I've done nothing wrong," I said. "I never thought about the ramifications of the Lions signing a contract with Billy Sims, just like the Chargers did with Gary Anderson. But wow—now I've got it."

"Got what?" Peter said. "Those bastards are smart. The Lions realized that if they signed Billy after they knew he signed with the Gamblers, they would've had their ass sued off by the Houston Gamblers, in Houston, Texas, for tortious interference."

"I just don't understand how the frigging Lions got Billy to sue me," I said. "He's like family to me!"

"It's simple, Argo," Peter replied. "Ford paid Billy a million dollars cash. What would most people do for a million dollars cash? Twenty-something-year-old kids have short memories, especially when somebody hands them more than a million reasons to forget. Now Chet is pissed. He wants to see you."

Up to this point, I had nothing but an outstanding relationship with Simmons. But the publicity that would surround this case could threaten the entire league.

"I'll do my best to protect you," Peter continued. "But I can't promise anything. Also, bring a copy of the lawsuit and any supporting documents. Keep your chin up, pal."

"The last thing I want to do is get back on a plane and go to New York," I said.

"You don't have a choice," Peter said, and hung up.

No matter how many times you've been there, the descent into New York City is as heart-stopping and breathtaking as its skyline. From the air, you literally can witness this immense beast, throbbing. It was exactly the elixir I needed to forget why I was flying there. I couldn't believe Sims and the Lions had publicly alleged that I was an unscrupulous agent and dishonest businessman.

On top of that, I was being called on the carpet by the USFL, the very league I helped David Dixon create, and I was flying in without judge or jury to convince them of my word. Pen and paper is a sword, indeed, but now I would have to fight face to face, bayonet to bayonet.

Staring from the oval pane of my Continental flight, I looked at the skyline, which is quintessentially the quality of the city. Look at the pillars of the specific buildings—damn, the World Trade Center towers, the Empire State Building, the Chrysler Building, the Statue of Liberty—and you realize the iconic presence of the lives of the people who live there from all around the world, and why it invokes so much power in its people. Worse, I was guilty of cracking crude jokes about New York, and had stripped one of its best teams, albeit upstate, bare-ass naked.

Now I was about to rely on the faith of a few of its people to believe in me, because my own reputation, career, and ownership of the Houston Gamblers hung in the balance.

Every person who witnesses New York, good, bad, or indifferent, is determined to stay with it, from beginning to end. Like the song goes, if you can make it there, you can make it anywhere. New York is an incredible laboratory of everything we think of and associate with American mass culture. As a Houston developer, where there is no zoning and cities become suburbs and suburbs become cities, I always looked in awe at Manhattan, where the explosion of energy, condensed humanity, and this little island somehow maintained the contrite heartbeat of it all. No matter how many times one flies into New York, there simply is no explanation. Once you see it, taste it, feel it, you never lose contact with its continuous energy, thrill, and excitement.

New York City is an aphrodisiac—like standing on the edge of a tall building and realizing, hey, I might fall off, or maybe I'll just jump. Once you've been there, you can imagine the wafting smell of a street vendor's hotdog, pretzel, or bagel; or remember riding the Number 4 bus and jetting up Fifth Avenue to Central Park. Whether you're the most banal Midwesterner or aspiring actor from Ithaca, you realize that here is where you have to be if you intend to win. This sucks, because there cannot be a tougher place to survive.

A flight attendant grabbed the microphone at the front of first-class and brought me to my senses.

"Please return your seats and tray tables to their upright positions. . . ."

Every time you go to New York, it changes, and so do you. Nothing and nobody is ever the same again. And for me, this was no sightseeing trip. I was on my way to the offices of the United States Football League to meet with Commissioner Chet Simmons and Peter Hadhazy, its director of operations.

The wheels barked as we touched down through the mist. I'd been here many times, but every time I came here, I felt like a fish out of water. Once you land in New York, you enter the fog of war. To people from abroad, New York is thought of as the most American of places. To a boy from Borger, Texas, it's the most foreign of American cities. But the fascination is its gateway as the melting pot of the world, where new things are supposed to happen and new opportunities are supposed to take place.

Exiting the plane, I was concerned and confused, but somehow still OK in my own space, if that makes any sense. Every other businessman was wearing a suit and tie, regardless how wrinkled. Clearly, my cowboy boots, hat, and southern drawl separated me from the others. I was uncomfortable, but my mother had taught me that dirt shows up on the cleanest cotton. I was convinced the truth would set me free, regardless how tough you or your city might be.

The USFL's Manhattan offices at 53 Vanderbilt Avenue were a short walk between Park Avenue and Madison Avenue, just across the way from Grand Central Station. They were nondescript; like walking into just about any attorney's office—wide-open windows, plain waiting room with magazines and plain wooden desks, with black phones and cubicles. The "executive" offices were the exact same thing, except they had doors with locks, books, and small family photos in fake silver frames that identified and stereotyped whoever was momentarily occupying space in the room.

I headed directly into the office of Peter Hadhazy.

Pete jumped up and greeted me with a big hug and closed his door. Chet and I shook hands, and we all sat around an oval table. I really liked Chet. The USFL owners in 1983 had literally offered Pete Rozelle $5 million in cash in a suitcase to be their commissioner, but when he declined, Simmons became their next choice. I'd always thought of him in the same light as Rozelle: A visionary who understood the power of television and football, and not necessarily in that order. Now Chet had a chance to rule over a piece of the action himself and create year-round interest in the sport.

"Jerry, you know we've got some serious issues here," Chet said, opening one of many files atop the desk before him. He wasted no time. "You should know that several USFL owners were on the borderline in approving you as an owner because of your 'media' personality and the controversy you create."

Uh oh, I thought. Chet Simmons is about to toss my ass out of the USFL.

"I agreed to let you represent Sims, Cribbs, and Anderson," he continued. "What I should've done is hire you as the league's public relations director. The Gamblers are getting more press than any team in football, and they haven't played a game. But damn, Jerry, you didn't tell me you were going to war against the NFL."

"I was doing my job to use the USFL as leverage to get my players the best contracts," I said.

Peter stepped in. "Chet, it's a personal vendetta that Russ Thomas has against Jerry," he said. "It's no secret in NFL circles that Jerry embarrassed him. He wants to get even, plain and simple."

I opened my leather saddlebag briefcase. From it, I pulled my own stack of files, which included every detail of my agency business; my ownership with the Gamblers; the Gary Anderson case; the Joe Cribbs case; and now, my contracts and documents that would provide my defense in the Billy Sims case.

I plopped them on their desk.

"They're all yours," I said. "Read it and weep. We will get our $300,000 bonus back that we paid him, and let Sims play where he wants. I'll settle and we'll move on to the next saloon."

"There is no settling, Jerry," said Hadhazy. He already had copies of the files, but he snapped up mine so he could see my notes. Simmons grabbed a copy of the lawsuit and began flipping through its pages.

"You can't settle. You have to fight this, or every Tom, Dick, and Harry are going to fight us when an NFL player decides to sign a 'futures' contract. You fought for free agency. You brought the fight to the NFL. Now you have to fight this lawsuit to the bitter end. Everybody's ass is on the line here."

Chet sighed out loud. "You've been a great asset to us. First as a friend of ours, David Dixon's, and now as a USFL owner and member of our various league committees," he said. "But this lawsuit threatens the efficacy of not just you, but all of your dealings, our league, and everyone in it. Start talking, Jerry, and make it quick, and no nonsense. My opinion is that, win or lose, you have to defend this lawsuit and countersue."

"Well, to begin with, stop talking about me in the past tense," I smiled. "Second, I have not begun to fight. Third, you can't render a verdict until you weigh the truth. And, fourth, if we go to court, I don't plan on losing."

Page by page, I walked Chet and Peter through the entire progression of every detail of Anderson, Cribbs, and Sims, one excruciating piece at a time. I had memos, court documents, timelines, faxes ... even cassette tape recordings. They took their time, and were relieved as they surveyed every item.

Hadhazy read through copies of the Sims contracts with the Lions and Gamblers. "Well, if there's any good news," he said, "it's that I've talked to most of the owners and

GMs, and they've all agreed that it's essential to protect the Gamblers and the USFL's position from the National Football League regarding Sims. Just because you have personal feelings for Billy, you can't let him out of his contract with the Gamblers, because this will set a precedent and hurt the entire league. How can Sims sue you for not knowing you owned the football team, when he was at the press conference? Hell, there was a picture of you, Billy, and Chet in the Houston newspaper."

I shook my head in disbelief. "I have mixed feelings about litigating against Billy, but I understand we have no choice. Suit me up, and we'll take on the Lions. When Chet gave me permission to temporarily wear two hats as an agent and owner, I had no idea I'd wind up in three lawsuits. But so far, I'm undefeated."

"You've been in litigation almost since the day you became an owner," Chet said. "San Diego, Buffalo, now Detroit. But you must protect your rights with Billy, for all of us. I never doubted you, but look at my position for a second, OK?"

"I wouldn't trade places with you if I could," I said. Suddenly, I felt the tide turning. "Running a football league with all these egos has to be a lot tougher than ESPN. There are no egos at ESPN."

Finally, Chet laughed. "ESPN pales in comparison," he said.

Hadhazy interrupted. "Talking about egos, have you spent any time with Donald Trump yet?"

"Guys, prior to this past September when he bought the franchise, I swear, I'd never heard of him," I said.

Chet said, "Donald told me the same thing about the rest of the owners in the league, except for Alfred Taubman and you, because of your agent background. He knows Taubman could buy him five times over, and he doesn't like him, or anyone that disagrees with him, including me."

"If you ask me," Hadhazy said, "Trump only cares about Donald, and anyone who thinks different is fooling himself."

"Can I go home now?" I asked. "I actually have a team to run, and now, apparently, a lawsuit to win."

Both Chet and Peter hugged me on the way out.

"I hear your quarterback looks pretty good," Peter said. "Good job getting Jim Kelly."

Chet echoed his sentiments. "We'll work with you on making Jim our marquee guy. We agree—this kid could be Joe Willie Namath, reincarnated."

"Wait until you meet Mouse Davis, our offensive coordinator," I said. "When you see his deal—it's called the Run 'n' Shoot—wow, what we are about to do to the entire game of football is going to revolutionize offense. We're going to make history, I promise."

Chet put his hand on my shoulder and loosened his necktie.

"You do that, Jerry," he said, "and we'll both be famous. Please start doing it more on the field and TV, though, and less in the courtroom, OK?"

A short time later, I was outside and breathing the strident air of New York. I walked defiantly to Times Square, looked straight up, stared at the glowing radiance of the night lights, and imagined Jim Kelly, the Houston Gamblers, and the Run 'n' Shoot in that frame. I couldn't resist. Like a tourist, I held my hands skyward.

Start spreadin' the news, I thought. Football as you think you know it is about to change.

39

BULLFROGS WITH WINGS DON'T BUMP THEIR OWN ASSES

DONALD J. TRUMP, who had been biding his time considering USFL ownership, had purchased the New Jersey Generals from J. Walter Duncan on September 21, 1983—mere months after the Michigan Panthers edged the Philadelphia Stars in the first USFL championship game—and by the time he showed up for his first real USFL owners meeting held in Houston in October of the same year, he already seemed to have his own clear agenda, and it was not about being a team player.

During that meeting, Trump immediately made the suggestion that the USFL should play in the fall, but it fell on totally deaf ears. "That's where the fans are," he said, "and that's where the money is. We can beat the NFL in court. The fall is when football is supposed to be played." The other owners, who at that time knew very little about Trump, did their best to ignore him as a flannel-mouthed politician. But when he stood up and declared that "what separates winners from losers is how they accept their new twist of fate," I had no earthly idea he was talking about himself, and that I would eventually become a pawn in his future scheme.

Give him the chance to speak, and it immediately became clear he'd speak forever. "Experience has taught me a few things," he told us. "One is to listen to your gut, no matter what it says on paper. The second is that you're better off going with what you know works. And the third is that some of your best investments are the ones you don't make.

"To tell you the truth, I've never liked spring football."

Now, that, we should've listened to. Donald was ignoring everything positive about the spring. He certainly didn't seem to appreciate the years of groundwork David Dixon had done, or the years of experience of the other owners and the millions they'd earned in their own right. Second, I don't think Donald knows football from a hole in the ground. He was signing second-rate NFL defensive backs like Gary Barbaro for millions. "Why is Trump paying the NFL hookers when the college kids are giving it away for free?" bitched San Antonio owner Clinton Manges. Third, the league owners had already invested nearly $100 million when he signed up, and that should've been enough.

In fact, when Trump first spoke about moving to the fall, other owners were literally rifling through their messages and scratching on legal pads or talking to one another when he said it. They all turned collectively as if to say, "What the hell?" Every owner in the league had bought in because they believed in the spring, and frankly, the positive results pouring in were giving us far too much to be happy about to concern ourselves with Trump's idea.

But when we reconvened on January 17, 1984, just after our draft and a week before my trial was set to begin with Sims in Detroit, Trump became increasingly vocal, insisting we take the issue of a fall schedule seriously. To forestall him, we agreed to sidestep the idea by appointing a long-range planning committee to study the idea.

During recesses, Tampa Bay owner John Bassett and Manges approached me privately. Bassett was a close friend, a powerful marketer, and a savvy businessman at every level. Manges was a brand-new owner who wasted no time making us realize that while he might have been rich enough to buy a team, he was as out of place as a gnat in a hailstorm.

"I'm totally shocked," John said. "I can tell you right now, Jerry, he's going to be a major problem.

"I don't give a shit about New York real estate or whatever his goals are," piped Manges, a South Texas rancher and oilman. Manges' jeans always looked a size too small; his face was always red with bluster, and he always had the look of a man who had either just ridden a bull or been kicked by one. "In Texas, if something's working, we don't fix it. Bullfrogs with wings don't bump their own ass."

But we all agreed on one thing. We all bought into the USFL to make spring football work, and we all put up a shitload of money, our lives, our families, and our history to make it successful.

"Except for Trump," Bassett railed. "Nobody joined this league to go head-to-head with the NFL in the fall. We're kicking major ass in Tampa, Philadelphia, Detroit, Denver, and New York. All are major TV markets. We know that if we go to the fall, we lose every market. Look at you, Jerry—Bud Adams is running scared from you in Houston, and Hugh Culverhouse is running from me in Florida.

By now, Philadelphia owner Myles Tanenbaum had joined the fray.

"It's the same situation in every market," Myles said. "If we continue to do our jobs and we just add a strong West Coast team, we're there. We are the real deal. I'm here to gobble up market share in the spring and overachieve with our fans, our television partners, and our players."

When the meeting resumed, it was evident why we all believed in spring football. For starters, David Dixon's original ideas had proven hotter than a whorehouse on nickel night. When one looked at the numbers and the math, every guy in the USFL realized he had a fighting chance to beat the devil around the stump. The 1983 ratings were far better than Dixon predicted or anyone could have ever hoped, and the Michigan Panthers' 24-22 title thriller over the Philadelphia Stars certainly didn't hurt matters. ABC averaged a 6.23 and ESPN 3.8, prompting ESPN founder Stu Evey to write in his own memoirs that "The USFL has fulfilled our greatest expectations. It is generating huge fan interest and its initial season is our highest-rated series ever!"

We were no longer merely an "upstart" league, like many others who had failed before us. The USFL wasn't just knocking on the NFL's door: In every major market, we were pounding it down.

For our owners, they all had cash and liquidity and knew how to spend it and win at business. They were chasing a business model, one that made sense. For players, especially those whom I represented, it was the best of all worlds; they now had leverage. Until the American Football League, the NFL had consisted of only twelve teams with thirty-three-man rosters—a total of about 400 players. With the merger of the AFL and the NFL, as well as expansion, there were about 1,400 pro football players, until the USFL hired nearly 500 more.

It seemed like our league was going to be a breathtaking ride for all of football, and frankly, headed into the 1984 season I was downright giddy with excitement. Ideas that the staid NFL would not or could not consider were all being given a fair shake, and typically met with refreshing consideration. One thing was clear: Any opportunity that could "one-up" or "show-up" the NFL was a possibility in the USFL; and the owners, GMs, coaches, and players were all about making the game more fan-friendly. I'd screamed for NFL reforms, and now, sitting in USFL meetings, I loved that we were blasting away with both barrels.

• The significance of Herschel Walker and the signing of underclassmen were nothing to sneeze at; its impact eventually would overhaul the relationship between the

NCAA and NFL. I was—and still am—staunch in my opposition to any legislation that would immunize professional sports from antitrust law. It was always my opinion that the Division I student-athlete was never an amateur at all, but a professional, and that it was time everyone admitted it as such. The only people who wanted to define players like Walker as amateurs were those—the NCAA, and the NFL—who had their own interests at stake.

- When the league announced it would implement the two-point conversion, it changed entire coaching strategies, possibilities, and point differentials. Coaches didn't like it because it was another way to second-guess them, but it opened the door for thrilling late-game comebacks. The old AFL had allowed the two-point conversion, but when it merged with the NFL, it was cancelled. I had pointed out to Dixon that in 1982, nearly 65 percent of NFL games had been decided by eight points in the fourth quarter. As I predicted, our games had followed suit. And the thrill of such a comeback was brought to life when Arizona quarterback Alan Risher made a miracle throw for a breathtaking, last-second two-point conversion for the win with no time left to beat the heavily favored Chicago Blitz on ESPN.

- My suggested use of instant replay had drawn an immediate negative response from ABC, which argued that networks should cover the game, not be part of the game. I vehemently disagreed, and told Dixon, Simmons, and anyone else who would listen that if technology had a chance to get a call right, they should allow it, and put the power to use it in the hands of the coaches, not the officials. "They [ABC] are partners, not journalists," I told them. "They have a vested interest in bettering the product." The league tabled the idea for 1983, but vowed to use it in the future "if we can make it work."

The destination of pro football would be changed in that January meeting, but when my turn came up to speak to the owners, I wasn't thinking about making history. I just wanted our league to work. I've kept my notes, the speech meant that much to me:

"Entrepreneurship," I said, "is like giving birth to a brand-new baby. An infant entrepreneur tends to bite off more than he can chew, hoping he'll quickly learn how to chew it. Everything takes a little longer, especially the money part."

I stood up in front of the podium. "Within the partnership," I said, "there are other owners who believe that in order to maintain this five-year plan, we must sign top-quality players from the draft and recognizable names from the NFL in order to achieve the long-range success and ultimate profitability.

"Regardless of the team's win-loss record, or attendance figures, there are only seven teams out of the original twelve who signed at least one top-name player, either from the draft or the NFL. Our other five partners—Denver, Boston, Arizona, Oakland, and Los Angeles have elected, for whatever reasons, not to sign at least one or more top players.

"There might be several teams who may show a financial profit this first year, such as Denver or Oakland, but is that what we are really trying to do in the early stages of developing a new football league? My recommendation would be to take our profits and reinvest into our individual franchises whereby in the fifth year we can assure ourselves of the huge dollars which will be available to us at that time.

"Again, I go back to the philosophy that favors short-term losses for long-term profits. I personally don't think it is fair if some of the partners go out and sign top players and create the excitement and credibility necessary for the longevity of the league and other partners sharing equally in this revenue and not reach in their pockets to spend their money on their own franchise.

"For example: The [1983] playoff game between Oakland and Michigan was played in Michigan. The Michigan owners had a substantial payroll and the team had a tremendous record. By the same token, Oakland received 40 percent of the gate with an 8-8 record, minimum payroll, and no major-name players on its team. What would have happened if the teams were to have played this game in Oakland? Attendance might have been only 30,000, which would have meant a significant financial difference to both teams. I don't think it is fair for one team to have to create the gate and the other team share these revenues and make personal financial gains when their partner is taking a financial loss.

"There are several franchises out of the original twelve who might want to relocate after the first year. In all fairness, there may be several of the original twelve owners who might find it in their best interest, or the league's, to sell their franchise after experiencing football ownership following the first full year of operation.

"We are now entering an expansion phase. The league has elected to add six teams to the 1984 schedule. What happens if five of these new teams elect the same philosophy as the five teams who don't want to or think it necessary to spend the money on quality football players for their fans and their coaches? You now have a league made up of 18 teams, out of which 10 have no top-name players or actual drawing capacity. Meanwhile, the other 8 teams are spending the necessary dollars to build their teams to a quality that will bring us to NFL parity by the fourth year.

"The league has sacrificed much control of its product by this early expansion and this is more reason why we must have a five-year game plan for our league. Not only must we have this plan for each team, we must be able to implement it.

"There are creative financial ways a team can sign top football players without spending exorbitant amounts of cash for these players. The league as a whole must be visionary in structuring ways we can add top talent to our league. The draft for our second year has just been completed. The second year is, by far, the most important because we must create credibility; we also need to realize the second year is the final year of our ESPN contract and ABC is in its option year.

"Other problem areas are officiating. We need to have better quality and shorter games. A lot of owners thought that if they just owned a football team, people would knock down the gate. I think we can put that philosophy to rest at this point. Several of the owners felt if we signed a Hershel Walker, it would give our league instant credibility.

"In my opinion, we have created fan awareness. We have introduced spring professional football programming and created spring football fans and advertisers. It will take us at least to the third year to get more fan and media acceptance of our product and our league. You have fan acceptance when a Houston Oilers fan is willing to cancel his Oiler tickets and only go with the Houston Gamblers, and a Detroit Lions fan buys Michigan Panther tickets. I think this type of fan support will not occur until the third year. It will take us this long to create team rivalries and a stable of name-recognized players along with the development of some of our own players.

"I think if we build this league the way it should be built, we will have league parity with the NFL by our fourth year. What I mean by league parity is when the best team in our league can beat the best team in their league. This is what Joe Namath and the AFL did against the Baltimore Colts in the Super Bowl. And I've got Joe Namath—his name is Jim Kelly.

"Although we all come from different areas of the country and from different walks of life, we must do everything humanly possible to make this partnership work. It is one thing to compete on the football field, but quite another to share revenues and build equities through this partnership."

I went to a white board and drew two circles.

"There are two distinctive factors that make the NFL such a huge success," I said, as I wrote in both. "One is revenue sharing, and the other is the draft."

I reminded them not to forget this. "We must adjust our thinking and adapt a sound philosophy for the future drafting and stacking of our teams. The territorial draft is a revolutionary idea. I have heard much criticism of Al Taubman [Michigan Panthers], Myles Tanenbaum [Philadelphia Stars], and Ted Dietrich [Chicago Blitz] for spending money and building a football team.

"I personally think we must all be committed to building a league because we are no stronger than our weakest links. Again, I go back to the initial philosophy that we must all be willing to take short-term losses for long-term benefits. We must all be committed for the eventual profitability of the entire partnership."

Trump seemed totally disinterested. I watched his body language as I spoke, which was to slightly shake his head "no" to everything I was saying. I was being cautious, and flying in tight airspace. He had a scowl on his face. I had learned many years ago that you keep your friends close and your enemies closer. I had always believed that if negative attention comes your way, you can counterpunch and redirect it for a rightful and positive purpose. If I acted agitated about anything he had said, in Trump's view I'd be wrong. If I ignored him completely, I'd look dumb. If I fought him, I'd be defensive.

So I made the decision to do my best to channel this brash, thirty-seven-year-old man in our direction, which meant at the time to just be smart and not move before I was ready. In business, I always believed patience was power. I was not ready to make things more difficult for me and those around me. I didn't want to be someone who deliberately created more obstacles. If we simply remained alert, inventive, and attentive, we could find the path to our goals.

The USFL had to succeed. Judging by the votes and passion in the room—save for one—we had all the horses in the barn.

40

A BETTER MOUSETRAP

"WHAT'S THE DEAL, Jerry Argovitz?"

The rich baritone voice on the other end of the phone was that of Darrel "Mouse" Davis. "I heard you've quit the agent business and decided to get a real job!"

Mouse—all 5-foot-6 of him—thundered again with laughter; and before I could get a word in edgewise, he lowered his voice to a whisper. "I can't say I blame you for changing careers," he said. "It's nice to see you're taking some time off to relax . . . doing something a little easier . . . like buying a pro football team." He exploded again with laughter.

It was late spring 1983, and Mouse—now the "godfather" of the Run 'n' Shoot offense—was anything but at that moment, working in Toronto in near-anonymity on the blustering, icy fields of the Canadian Football League. He had seized the moment to prove his offense could work at the pro level, sometimes against 70-mile-per-hour headwinds and temperatures hovering near zero, and had taken a perennial loser to the Grey Cup in his first season.

Mouse wanted the chance to prove it in the States, and I wanted the best offense in history. I thought together we could revolutionize American professional football, which is why I had placed the call.

"Mouse, what's the temperature up there today?" I asked.

"It's a brisk 12 degrees," he said, belly laughing. "But if you stand in the sun, it's a balmy 15."

"You know the Astrodome is climate-controlled," I said. "How do you feel about playing some offense down here in Houston?"

"Jerry, we don't play offense," Mouse roared, "we inflict it."

I had never forgotten the utter look of amazement on Gene Burrough's face in 1980 the day he returned from a trip to Portland, Oregon, where I had asked him to go check out Portland State, a tiny Division I-AA school, and its record-setting, walk-on quarterback Neil Lomax.

"Wait until you see this, Jerry," Gene had said, popping in a videocassette. "They call their offense the "Run 'n' Shoot." They line up all over the field. The receivers are tiny, faster than hell, and bounce around like pin-balls. There is motion everywhere. This kid Lomax throws it all over every inch of the field. And the best part—I'm not kidding—the head coach is named Mouse."

I looked at the reel, and my jaw dropped. The 1980 Portland State team had won by margins of 93-7, 105-0, and 75-0. They ran out of a four-wide receiver formation, every single play, with never a tight end. They spread the field on every down as wide as you possibly could. The quarterbacks had the ball in the air before you could blink, and defensive backs scrambled to keep up—and keep track—with seemingly endless fleets of wide receivers. They ran up and down the field in Civic Stadium until they wore paths in the shiny turf, and most of the time in the teeth of Portland's famed torrential gully-washers.

In 42 games, Lomax passed for 13,220 yards and 106 touchdowns, en route to 8 NCAA records. The coach was indeed Darrel "Mouse" Davis, who had perfected the system for years as a legendary Portland high school coach, winning four league championships and a state title. When Mouse took the job at Portland State, his first quarterback had been another walk-on named June Jones, who had quit football before Davis talked him back onto the field. Jones threw enough touchdowns to be drafted in the fifth round by the Atlanta Falcons in 1977.

That year, Lomax rejected my offer to represent him, choosing instead my friend Leigh Steinberg, who also represented June Jones. But I was intrigued by the Run 'n' Shoot, and this larger-than-life character named Mouse. I made tons of calls to my compatriots in both the NFL and USFL, and while some called his ideas revolutionary, all the reports weren't flattering.

"He can be difficult," warned Chicago Blitz head coach George Allen. "It's his way, or the highway, and he won't compromise. Great guy, but if you run his deal, don't interfere and be sure to sign the right players."

"Mouse is a one-man band," echoed long-time NFL coach Chuck Fairbanks. "What he does is totally unsound. No tight end? Is he nuts? No goal-line formations?

It's a gimmick. If it really worked, trust me, you'd see it in the NFL every week. Ask any NFL coach."

So I did. I called my friend Bum Phillips, former head coach of the Houston Oilers, who was then coaching the Saints.

"Well, it probably worked in Canada because the field is so damn big you can chase bears with a switch," Bum drawled. "But I wouldn't bet my saddle on it down here."

Still, the more phone calls I made, the more I loved the Mouse. I related well to his devil-be-damned attitude. I loved his energy and excitement. Hell, I'd had enough of the NFL's boring football—if I never saw another 10-7 score again, it'd be too soon. As far back as I could find any research on Mouse Davis, even high school, all his teams scored so many points it always looked like someone had snuck in an extra number.

I had always been a maverick; my team was called the Gamblers, and I was ready to roll the dice: Hire an offensive coordinator before I hired a head coach.

By the time I called Mouse in Canada, the smallest coach in football had me sold that his offense and infectious character was bigger than the entire state of Texas. I thought it would take an elephant to please the egos in my home state, but instead, I was going to deliver a Mouse. I put him on a plane to Houston, where history would be ours for the taking.

Mouse hit the door like a tornado, and from the second he walked into my office I realized instantly why it's impossible not to be overwhelmed by his garrulous personality. Within minutes of his arrival, he had already charmed everyone in the building with his booming voice and barreling laughter. Snapping his gum and cracking jokes in rapid-fire succession, he squeezed my hand like a bear trap. Mouse doesn't look at you; he looks through you, and you sizzle to your core.

"As you know, Mouse, football is a religion in Texas," I drawled. "Our fans know football. Houston is a football market. And since Bud Adams' pathetic Oilers are the only game in town, my goal is to give this city, this state, and the whole country the most wide-open, entertaining, highest-scoring football machine in history. And I think you're the man who can do it."

His eyes glinted like gun barrels. First, he was quick to give original credit for the offense to Glenn "Tiger" Ellison, who had written a book about it called The Offense of the Future, which Mouse had read as a high school coach. "I stole Tiger's ideas for our formations," Mouse said openly, "but most of the similarities end there. Tiger's teams were more of a veer and ran the ball more than we do."

All Mouse did was drastically modify the route conversions of the receivers—the concept of allowing both receivers and quarterbacks to read, or convert, their own routes—on the fly. This decision would change football forever. In other words, instead of calling a "post route" or a "square-in" or another route in the huddle, Mouse allowed his players to make all of their own decisions in the heat of battle with split-second timing.

The result?

"Give me an accurate guy under center with a quick trigger, and four piss-ants who can fly, and we can damn near hang sixty on anybody," Mouse said.

"Piss-ants?"

"Itty-bitty guys," he answered, "who can fly. I'm talking pure speed, like faster than any kids playing pro football today. Trust me—there's a thousand of 'em out there who can run fast but are too small to be an NFL receiver. But they are perfect for us."

Mouse started scribbling X's and O's on his legal pad in my office, explaining the offense in breathless terms.

"If the safety comes out of the hole, we break it across his face for the touch . . . "

"Or we high-low this corner here, and this kid catches a five-yard out and goes eighty-five yards for the touch. . . ."

"Do the formations change?" I asked.

"We're four wides, every play, baby!" he cackled.

I asked about defenses specifically geared to stop him.

"They get to spend the day chasing a 140-pound piss-ant who runs a 4.2—their view never changes! All they see is asses and elbows!"

"What about zone defenses?"

"We LOVE zone defenses! We run where they ain't!"

Mouse was in his element now, and looked happier than a gopher in soft dirt. He was drawing lines forward, backward, in-between, but what I liked most was that the lines that mattered were all landing in the end zone. This went on for hours, and Mouse had me so excited I wanted to suit up myself. I loved the idea of giving "little guys" the opportunity to play a big-man's game.

"What about the running game?"

"Our running game is successful mostly by the element of surprise," he said. "We don't use regular backs. We use really big guys at that position, and we call them an S-back, or super back. The S-back is essentially a tight end or fullback type who mostly blocks playside, but we run the hell out of the ball on traps, draws and screens. You'll see."

The second he accepted the role as offensive coordinator, Mouse made something very clear. "I want June Jones as my receivers coach."

"No problem," I said, and we shook hands.

Weeks later, I had settled on Texas A&M great Jack Pardee to be the Gamblers' head coach. I had interviewed Marv Levy and Leeman Bennett first, and then of course, Mouse was already on board and sorely wanted the job himself.

I felt strongly, however, that we needed a Texas guy who had a great local reputation and the respect of the NFL and who would field a good defense. Bum Phillips suggested Jack Pardee, and he was all of the above: A two-time NFL coach of the year, and if you recall, a favorite of Jim Finks, the Chicago general manager whom I'd battled for Jim McMahon. Finally, Finks and I found something we agreed on.

When Jack came in the day we hired him, I told him we already had an offensive coordinator named Mouse Davis.

"Mouse who?" Jack asked.

I explained Mouse and his ideas and showed Jack the offense. He wasn't happy. In fact, he looked like his heart was about to stop. "Jack, just field a great defense," I said, "and leave the offense alone. You will never lose your job if we don't score enough points—that's Mouse's job. Your main job is quality control. Do you know how McDonald's is run? The burgers are cooked the same way every time, the fries come out the same every time. That's how I want you to run this football team in every area, except the offense."

"Not a single tight end?" Jack asked. He was dumbfounded. "One tight end? Please? Just in case?"

"If it makes you feel better, Jack, we'll sign one, just for you. But don't tell Mouse we have one. We'll call him a backup linebacker."

At the time, none of us realized the historical significance when we added Kelly to play quarterback to execute Davis' revolutionary idea, or that what we were about to do would make the offense a staple of modern professional football. In fact, it almost never got off the ground. First, Mouse was still a relative unknown in pro coaching circles, and his "schemes" were considered sandlot football. Second, Kelly wasn't sold on the idea, at all. Jim was still rehabbing his college shoulder injury, and he immediately resisted hearing the word run in the Run 'n' Shoot.

"Jerry, I'm not a running quarterback," confided The Franchise. "I'm a pure pocket passer."

To the contrary, I had Jim's college film memorized. Actually, we had files on Kelly that were thicker than his ten-inch forearms. For starters, he was a different kid under the lights: He had been the Most Valuable Player in every national TV game in which he played in college. He was also right about his foot speed—his college nickname was Slew Foot. A few scouts were dubious about his shoulder, but the doctors had us convinced he'd be more than ready for prime time.

We also knew he could be sensitive: Jimmy told me he had actually cried the day Buffalo had drafted him, ahead of Tony Eason and Dan Marino, because he couldn't see himself withering away with a bum shoulder on a horrible team on a frozen field in up-state New York.

Former NFL passing craftsman Earl Morrall had tutored Kelly in college under Miami head coach Howard Schnellenberger, and he had told me that his former pupil would do whatever it took to win, and that he was wolverine mean. "Marino might have a slightly quicker release, but nobody reads defenses faster, or is meaner, or is tougher than Jim," Morrall told me. "If you have any problems, bet on his heritage, and challenge his competitive spirit. He'll surprise you."

His heritage was well documented. Kelly had grown up in the tiny blue-collar town of East Brady, Pennsylvania, where his Irish-Catholic father, Ed, worked eighteen-hour days as a machinist, and his mother Alice raised Jimmy and his five brothers. His father, in an effort to motivate his sons to use sports as their springboard to a better life, pushed them brutally hard to succeed. Jimmy and his dad actually earned a trip to the Punt, Pass, and Kick finals in 1970. All of the boys were roughly Kelly's size, and one can only imagine what it took to survive in that household, and the hell they must have rained down on East Brady, which had a population of less than 1,000 people when Kelly was a kid. "The boys were their own army, that's for sure," Ed would later joke.

As a competitor, Kelly made his point when he was recruited by Joe Paterno at Penn State as a linebacker, but went instead to Miami as a quarterback to prove Paterno wrong. Actually Paterno was half right: By Kelly's senior year, at 6-3, 230 pounds, he was a linebacker playing quarterback.

By the time we got him on the field in Houston, after only a few workouts, Mouse and June were telling me that Jim was resisting the footwork of the offense. In their efforts to make him a complete quarterback, Jim was rebelling. He especially didn't like the required half-rollout while reading and throwing on the run, although the "run" was really about three to five yards. Mouse, in those days, still insisted his quarterbacks work from under center, as opposed to the shotgun, which is where his offense would eventually evolve.

"It's not that he can't do it," Mouse told me. "The big kid's not dumb. He's definitely not scared either—he wants to fight. The kid has every possible thing you could want. Good Lord, he's what we call special. But with him, it's mental. He just needs to get comfortable and embrace it."

You can't get lard unless you boil the hog, and we turned up the heat in the form of Todd Dillon, a bright, small, and record-setting rookie quarterback from Cal-State Long Beach. Todd had great feet—he was a ballerina in shoulder pads, with a capable arm. Standing next to Kelly, he looked like Jim's son, but Todd took to the offense immediately, and the local media went nuts. We were paying Kelly a widely reported $3.5 million, and Dillon, about $3.45 million less. And Dillon was outplaying him in practice.

"If you played right now, who would start?" a reporter asked me. I thought about Morrall's advice to challenge Kelly, and dipped into my bag of Psychology 101. "We'll start the best guy," I choked, "no matter what he's making. And you gotta hand it to Todd—he's doing a helluva job."

The next morning, Kelly roared into my office like a yellowjacket in an outhouse. "I don't care if you bring Dan-fucking-Marino in here," he rasped, pounding my desk. "Whoever you bring in here will be holding a fucking clipboard."

"Jim, if you'll learn this offense and pay attention to it," I said, "and let these coaches coach you, you will become the most prolific quarterback in the history of professional football. It's your job if you want it. Whoever is going to give us the best chance to win will play regardless of the money. The real problem, Jim, is that if you don't get with the program, your ass will be sitting on the bench. We'll both look like schmucks. You, for not starting; and me, for being the idiot who paid you $3.5 million."

Amazingly, Kelly's footwork in the Run 'n' Shoot became tighter than Baryshnikov, and he was angrily throwing rifle-shot lasers in practice that were knocking down our receivers from forty-five yards away.

"What in the hell did you say to Jimmy?" Mouse asked me a few days later. "He's a different guy."

"Let's just say I stoked his competitive fire," I laughed.

Mouse and June—along with our Wayne Tedder and Bill Groman in our scouting department—scoured Texas and the rest of the country to find their "itty-bitty piss-ant" wide receivers, and they had me signing so many that I was busier than a cat trying to cover up crap on a marble floor. June's research was incredible. He was finding guys who hadn't played football in years—some who hadn't played football at all—but who all had one common denominator: Speed.

We found guys on the waiver wires. We found guys working at supermarkets, where June would time them in the parking lot in their work shoes. We found guys the whole world had deemed too small to play pro ball. With every player we signed, June would shrug his gangly shoulders, adjust his glasses and flash a crooked grin. Every one of them was shorter than 5-foot-10 and weighed less than 160 pounds. Hell, Mouse was bigger than most of them.

Richard Johnson was out of football when Mouse and June called him and told him to get his ass to Houston. They forgot, however, to tell me. He rode the bus to Houston, found his way to my office, and walked in looking like a lost, disheveled, pudgy, slightly overgrown Gary Coleman. He was carrying a beat-up gym bag. I was on the phone with my boots on my desk, and my immediate reaction was anger—why in the hell did my secretary let some stranger just walk in my office? At the time, we were still hiring front-office and stadium personnel, and our offices were full of strangers every day asking for work.

"Can I help you?" I scowled, covering the phone, motioning him to back out the door. "Tell my secretary to get you an application. Thanks for stopping by."

He set his bag down. "Sir, my name is Richard Johnson, and I'm here to play football," he said. "June Jones sent me up here to sign a contract."

I nearly dropped a load in my pants. He looked like anything but a football player. Are you kidding me?

My God, I thought, reaching in my desk for a standard players contract, I hope June and Mouse know what they're doing.

These kinds of surprises happened every day. Among the flood of receiver signings were Ricky Sanders, our first territorial pick from Southwest Texas State. Vince Courville was a track star from Rice who had beaten both Darrell Green (soon to become the NFL's fastest man) and Herschel Walker in the 100 meters at the Texas Relays. Scott McGhee was an unemployed free agent who had last played in Canada. Greg Moser had been a walk-on at Oregon and had bounced around football. We grabbed another territorial draft pick in Clarence Verdin, a former football and track star at Southwestern Louisiana. Mark Barousse was out of football, but had been a football, pole vault, and track star at McNeese State University.

Our last signing was Gerald McNeil. He had been born in West Germany and became a high school track star in Texas and a college football legend at Baylor. He came with only one drawback: He was 5-foot-7 and weighed 139 pounds. Soaking wet. But he ran a 4.19 in the 40.

We signed him immediately.

Watching Mouse's offense on tape was one thing. Seeing it in real life for the first time was awe-inspiring. The first thing I noticed is they coached without whistles. Mouse and June were speaking an entirely different language, constantly barking at guys to catch "in the noose" and "open your hips" and "run to space." Suddenly, footballs soared like rainbows in every direction, and just as they would arc toward the ground, a blurring object would appear from nowhere, and one of these itty-bitty piss-ant kids would pluck them from the sky in full stride, like bass striking minnows. Then they'd just explode through the defense like shit through a goose.

"Woooooooweeeeee," whistled Jones at one practice, "this could get unbelievable."

At running back, we signed Sam Harrell, a free agent and former Minnesota Viking. Finally, I got Jack Pardee his coveted tight end: Rookie Todd Fowler, from Stephen F. Austin University. Mouse thanked us by immediately converting Fowler to an S-back.

The Houston media, accustomed to seeing slow, tall, stiff wide receivers running predictable routes with the Oilers, were shocked. They clearly didn't have a clue what they were witnessing.

"Jim Kelly and his receiving corps of what could best be described as 'Mousketeers'…" wrote one scribe, "are, if nothing else, thrilling to watch, even in practice…"

The Mouseketeers! Thrilling! Fans were flocking to our practices. The Gamblers, before playing a single game, had shown up to play some spring football in true Texas style: Big, bad, bragging, and larger than life. Off the field, our tickets were hotter than a pistol at an all-night shootout. Kelly's talent and mouth were attracting national publicity. Our creative TV ads had become notoriously popular on ESPN. Locally, we were slamming Bud Adams and the Oilers with a ferocious, city-wide billboard campaign that declared: Gambler Football: Because You've Waited Long Enough.

In another month, our home opener would be against Donald Trump, Herschel Walker, and the New Jersey Generals in front of 40,000 Houstonians.

I had never been so proud in my entire life. By the same token, if this didn't work, I would be ridden out of town, or worse, hung from the highest tree.

"What's this deal going on with Billy Sims?" asked Mouse one afternoon as we all walked out to a minicamp practice. "No hard feelings, but if he doesn't want to be here, who in the shit cares? I don't need him here. He's a distraction. If you win the lawsuit, we'll get creative and find a way to use him, but he doesn't fit into what we do. He's not big enough to play S-back, and he's not fast enough to be a slot."

I reassured Mouse that my intention the entire time had been to give Billy leverage against the Detroit Lions, but now, I had become determined to win the case.

"Well, if you get him, trade him," Mouse suggested. "For that kind of money, you can buy us some more linemen to protect Jimmy." He laughed like only Mouse can. "Both you and Jimmy would be pretty happy about that deal."

As Mouse trotted toward his players, I chuckled. Sims was the best running back in the NFL, and Davis had just told me we don't need him here.

It didn't change my predicament, but it sure as hell made me feel better.

41

DONALD "TRUMPH"

AFTER THE BEATING I took in Detroit at the hands of Sims, the Lions, and Judge Robert Edward DeMascio, there was nothing quite as comforting as returning home in the spring of 1984 to the warm confines of Houston and the glorious euphoria of professional football.

Regardless of the outcome of the Sims trial—in which Billy and the Lions had essentially branded me for life, and tarnished my once-sterling reputation—I still owned the hottest new franchise in sports. The Houston Gamblers were storming the best football market in America, and made the United States Football League the first enterprise in twenty years to challenge the sovereign NFL.

I also signed one of the greatest quarterbacks in the game: Jim Kelly. The Gamblers had the most exciting offense in the history of football, period; one that very soon every team and every league would forever copy. We were ready for some football. And who could disprove these facts?

We opened the 1984 season, and our spring television ratings on ABC and ESPN were crushing the NBA, Major League Baseball, and any other tractor-pull programming ESPN—the World Wide Leader in Sports?—could rummage together. We had an awesome product and legitimate, deep-pocket owners in our major markets—Philadelphia, Tampa Bay, Houston, New York, Detroit, Denver, Tennessee, Arizona, Jacksonville, and Birmingham. We had incredible players in Jim Kelly, Doug Williams, Steve Young, Herschel Walker, Gary Anderson, Bobby Hebert, Reggie White, Mike Rozier, Joe Cribbs, Kelvin Bryant, and Cliff Stoudt.

Our coaches were legendary, too—Pardee, Davis, Spurrier, Jones, Allen, Jim Mora, and Marv Levy. Several of these men alone would take what we did in Houston and—along with personnel guys like John Butler and Bill Polian—later build NFL empires. The NFL Hall of Fame, however, would have to wait, because we had current business at hand: namely, proving David Dixon true that playing the USFL in the spring was, in fact, a correct assumption.

What could possibly go wrong?

The only guy rattling sabers was this guy in New York—Donald Trump, who kept talking about playing in the fall, head-to-head with the NFL, and clamoring that "spring football will never work." Huh? I'm from Texas, and I'm a little slow, but if your team—with Herschel Walker—is leading the league in attendance, television ratings, and opens on the road in Birmingham in front of 60,200 people with the highest TV sports spring rating in history—help me out here—what's not working? If that game drew a 6.2 national rating, ahead of the NBA playoffs, and fans and our network partners are clearly supporting us, why in hell are you talking about moving us to the fall?

In our first owner's meeting together in 1983 he sat next to me. I didn't know him from Adam's housecat. I wrote his name on my legal pad, and I spelled it Trumph. He leaned over, took his pen and marked out the "h." He said, "There is no 'h' in Trump—it's T-R-U-M-P."

"Don't you ever forget that."

Here's what I will never forget: Donald "Trumph" went out and bought the Generals for $10 million, and invested another $8 million in NFL talent, including veteran linebacker Bobby Leopold and safety Gary Barbaro.

On March 18, 1984, in the Houston Astrodome—before 44,212 screaming fans—our itty-bitty piss-ants, track stars, and earning a collective $200,000, did exactly like Mouse and June said: They ran through "The Donald's" vaunted NFL firepower like shit through a goose.

A sweat-soaked Jim Kelly ripped off his helmet and grabbed everybody on the sideline.

"Jerry," said The Franchise. "Everything works! Mouse! June! Tell the defense to just give me the goddam ball back! Lights out! Everybody's wide-ass open! You guys up front just hold your blocks! I got this! Offense, keep your hats on, because every play is going for six! Nobody sit down! Just give me the fucking ball! Time to go to work!

"Let's go, goddammit, let's go."

Oh, and remember Richard Johnson? You know the lost, disheveled, pudgy, slightly overgrown Gary Coleman who looked like anything but a football player? He promptly led all of our receivers, as the NFL looked on with awe.

42

I'D RATHER HAVE A SKUNK INSIDE MY TENT PISSING OUT, THAN A SKUNK OUTSIDE PISSING IN

TRUE TO WHAT Mouse Davis said, we didn't miss a beat losing Billy Sims. I had promised to refund any money for any fan that had purchased a season ticket thinking Billy would join our ball club, and exactly twelve people took me up on the offer. I paid them back out of the cash I had in my pocket.

On March 11, our "no-name" running back, Sam Harrell, set a USFL single-game rushing mark with 200 yards against the Chicago Blitz, who were coached by future NFL Hall of Famer Marv Levy. A few weeks later, on June 3, Todd Fowler—our "tight end" whom Mouse had converted to S-back—promptly broke Sam's rushing record with 208. Our running backs were leading the league in average yards per carry, with a whopping 6.0 every time they touched the ball.

Jim Kelly, as expected, was playing lights out. The big kid was averaging 400 yards passing per game and—get this—on the few occasions he called his own number, the man who didn't want to "run" was rushing for 5 yards a carry. Our itty-bitty guys were leading all receivers at every level of football in every category. Richard Johnson—double deuce—was seemingly scoring at will.

"Nobody can stop our offense," Jim told the Houston press, "except God."

Trouble was brewing, however, back at the ranch. Bernard Lerner, one of my partners in buying the Gamblers, was telling me he wanted out. Bernard had failed to raise the $12 million he promised when his plan to find forty people to buy $300,000 shares each didn't happen. The first $4 million was to reimburse Bernard, Alvin, and me for the monies we had invested to that point, with the balance of $8 million to be used as future operating capital.

We had invested $2.5 million to finance the Gamblers, and were responsible for a $1.5 million letter of credit.

So I called my friend Jay C. Roulier, a real estate developer in Denver, and uttered the most profound words in the human language: "Jay," I said, "I need your help."

His answer: "You got it pardner! How much money do you need?"

Jay showed up to replace Bernard, and we made his introduction at the next owner's meeting in New York at the Grand Hyatt Hotel. Jay was totally sold on ESPN, the spring, and our football team. When he stood up to address the other owners, he instantly proved he was an ace in the hole.

"There is no question that spring football and this league will work," Jay said. "And I'm here to help the Gamblers run the table."

Sit down! Nobody cares what you think," Trump blurted out.

Jay is not a small man, standing 6-foot-2 and weighing upwards of 270. He remembers, "I had to control myself. My normal instincts would be to retaliate." Instead, he calmly went ahead and shared his thoughts with the other owners.

At some point, Trump dropped a bombshell on all of us: "I have no interest in playing in the spring," he said.

Trump pointed to the fact that his team was leading the league in attendance, owned Herschel Walker, and was in the middle of a great season. The other owners countered that the league as a whole was pulling record television ratings in the spring.

On June 10, the Gamblers became the USFL Central Division Champions with a win over Marv Levy's Chicago Blitz in the Astrodome. On June 19, Roulier officially became the newest partner in my Gamblers' ownership.

Then Donald went public and told the New York media that the USFL would officially be moving to a fall schedule.

Clearly, he had a hidden agenda that didn't involve the rest of us.

"Jerry," said Roulier, "I'd rather have a skunk inside my tent pissing out than outside my tent pissing in."

Simmons, our league commissioner, called me.

"Jerry," he said, "if you guys decide to go to the fall and take on the NFL head-to-head, I quit. That's a death sentence."

And he hung up.

43

HIDDEN AGENDAS

I DON'T BUY INTO conspiracy theories. For instance, I'm not sure who killed JFK, I'm puzzled over the Lincoln assassination, and I am still gravely concerned over who really shot J.R. Ewing.

However, let me give you the facts about this deal, and you can be the judge.

Clandestinely, and unbeknownst to the other partners, on March 11, 1984, Donald Trump had met alone with NFL Commissioner Pete Rozelle at the Hotel Pierre in New York. I don't know if he spoke on behalf of the entire league; however, he had no permission to do so. The focus of the discussion was to somehow "merge" the USFL with the NFL.[*]

In our next owners' meeting on August 22, 1984, we got the results of the "long-range study" regarding Trump's idea to move our league to the fall. The study cost all of us a collective $600,000. Sharon Patrick, an executive with McKinsey and Company Consultants, stood before the room to say, and I quote, "The league's best hope is to continue playing in the spring and move to the fall later on." She also showed us the results of a poll taken by several thousand USFL fans.

"The fans," she said emphatically, "want the USFL to remain in the spring."

I got up in front of the room and delivered a passionate speech.

"Gentlemen," I began, "we just spent $600,000 to have McKinsey and Company tell us something that every one of us already knew. The only two people that want to

---

* *Rozelle: Czar of the NFL*—Davis (McGraw-Hill, 2008).

move to the fall are Eddie Einhorn, who owns a baseball team, and Donald Trump, who wants to own an NFL team.

"I can only speak for myself and my partners, but this is suicidal."

Donald raised his voice. "Staying in the spring is suicidal and a slow death—a move to the fall makes the NFL have to deal with us."

"The NFL already has to deal with us," I replied. "We have driven the cost of players up substantially, and we have created a form of free agency for the players. We have an exciting product and a good fan base. Besides, the NFL will strike in 1987, so it's imperative that we follow our original five-year plan and play in the spring for the 1986 and 1987 seasons."

"If the NFL strikes," I continued, "we will have the only game in town, and I'm sure the networks will want to work with us."

Again, I reiterated what we had been talking about since the outset of the USFL. "I am convinced if we stay in the spring for two more years our league will have parity with the NFL and we can control our own destiny . . . to either merge or keep our own league.

"I didn't buy into the NFL," I roared, "I bought into the USFL, a spring league. We're idiots if we move to the fall and compete directly with the NFL. This is instant death."

Trump stood up. "I will not fund another spring season in New York. The fall is where football is supposed to be played. The NFL knows that they cannot legally control and monopolize all the networks for the fall. They are scared that we will move to the fall and sue them. I own the New York market and I want a vote to at least announce that we are moving to the fall and see what they do."

Clinton Manges leaned over to me. "I swear I'm going to kill this sumbitch before this is over," I recall him saying.

Meanwhile, unbeknownst to us, there had been a study commissioned by the NFL. It was a forty-seven-page document created by Michael Porter, and delivered to sixty-five members of the NFL executive committee on "how to kill the USFL."

In perfect detail, it said that to destroy our league would require us to challenge the NFL head-to-head, remove ourselves from our successful markets, and engage in a bidding war for players.

Ironically, Trump was following the Porter plan to the most minute detail.

The Giants and Jets were playing at the Meadowlands in New Jersey; there was no football team in New York City. More ironically, Trump was negotiating with the mayor of New York to renovate Shea Stadium—or build a new stadium—and if there was going to be a merger, it was going to be one team for sure. Hmm.

Remember that prior to buying the New Jersey Generals, Trump was a New York real-estate developer. Owning a USFL team, meeting with Rozelle, and clamoring about the Generals had made him front-page news around the nation, and he was basking in the notoriety.

Case in point, Donald told me he gave several million dollars to help build a library and the only press he got was some small print in the back of the New York newspapers; but when he signed football players and coaches they played it up big on the front page.

Donald believed that our league could win an antitrust suit against the mighty National Football League, and that the only way to prove it would be to declare we move our season to the fall. He said "this will force a merger." Now, keep in mind, I knew from my agent days the NFL was, and still is, guilty of antitrust. But I also know that you don't bring a knife to a gunfight.

The other owners at this point were exhausted and willing to listen. Trump's plan would require that we make radical changes—Detroit would merge with Oakland, Philadelphia would move to Baltimore. Chicago would be owned by Eddie Einhorn, a friend of Trump's. The Gamblers and the Generals would merge, and I would run the team from New York.

Essentially, we would have to vacate all of our successful markets.

I was stunned. This would mean I would have to leave Houston. My team was on fire. Kelly was putting up astronomical numbers, and the Houston fans loved him like guys love a Playboy centerfold. Our season-ticket holder numbers were rising by the minute. I knew an announcement of this kind would doom us.

Donald J. Trump continued his relentless march to the fall. On October 17, 1984, our league followed Trump's advice and filed an anti-trust suit against the NFL, specifically stating that the NFL be limited in dealing with two of the three networks, and award the USFL $1.32 billion dollars in damages, and announced its intentions to begin play in the fall 1986.

Chet Simmons, our incredible commissioner, resigned on January 15, 1985. "Good luck guys, I quit. Show me the fucking door," and told me personally that he virtually danced on his way out to get away.

We hired Harry Usher to replace Chet. A prominent attorney, Harry had been Peter Ueberroth's right-hand guy at the Los Angeles Olympics, and he became another Donald "yes-man."

The lawsuit had been Harry's main focus. I had argued with Donald, Harry Usher, and every owner that if we were actually going to sue the NFL, then Donald Trump could not be the face of the USFL. We couldn't beat the Giants, Jets, and Pete Rozelle in a New York City courtroom.

However, Trump was now dictating the future of our league. His first choice of attorneys was Roy Marcus Cohn, who had gained prominence in the 1950s at Senator Joseph McCarthy's investigations into Communist activity in the United States during the Army-McCarthy hearings. But by this point Cohn was so sick with AIDS that he couldn't even function, and in the end we didn't hire him.

I had no confidence in Roy Cohn or in Donald for making such a choice. I begged Donald to meet with Joe Jamail in Houston. I knew Joe personally. He won the Penzoil Texaco lawsuit, which was the largest anti-trust victory in the United States. I had met with Joe for a couple of hours to discuss the merit of the USFL's anti-trust claims against the NFL. He agreed that the litigation should be filed in Houston and we would kick ass and take names. To win this lawsuit against the NFL—which I testified under oath and proved to be a monopoly—we still had to prove damages.

When my plan failed, Trump picked Harvey Myerson. His press clippings called him "Heavy Hitter Harvey"; a gravelly voiced "pit bull" litigator Trump called him the "master of disaster" for rescuing troubled companies from their legal problems (in 1992 Myerson was convicted of defrauding clients and sentenced to six years in Federal prison).

I was as scared as a sinner in a cyclone.

On November 23, 1984, Doug Flutie of Boston College threw the now famous "Hail Mary Pass" against the University of Miami that not only helped win him the Heisman Trophy, but is a play now considered among the greatest moments in college football and American sports history.

Trump courted him, called him to New York, and signed him to the richest pro football contract in history. Yet, he was too short for a USFL or NFL quarterback—and one play does not a career make. Kelly was putting up numbers like a pinball machine.

Here's the funny part: I had signed Kelly to an "escalating contract," guaranteeing him that he would be among the three highest-paid quarterbacks in the league. The second Trump signed Flutie to his outrageous contract, I was in line to take a major hit for Jim. And if the Generals and Gamblers ever merge, what were we going to do with two high-priced quarterbacks?

And now, with the announcement that our league was moving to the fall, our spring fans had decided to stay away in droves. Attendance fell off everywhere; we were bleeding from every orifice, exactly like the Michael Porter dossier had predicted.

But wait, there's more. Donald proceeded to circulate a memorandum to all of the owners saying he had signed Flutie "in the best interest of the league," and that we should all absorb the cost of his contract.

Here's how the owners were informed of Trump's proposal by Harry Usher:

J. Argovitz

USFL
United States Football League
52 Vanderbilt Avenue
New York, New York 10017
212 682-6363

MAR 2 6 1985

DATE: MARCH 21, 1985

TO: ALL OWNERS

FROM: COMMISSIONER USHER

As we discussed at the owners' meeting on March 20,
I am enclosing Donald Trump's letter of March 11, 1985
to me requesting an allocation of Doug Flutie's cost to
each team. As you know, because of the crowded agenda,
we did not have time to discuss the enclosed. It will
be on the agenda for the succeeding owners' meeting.

/SE

Enclosure

«
»
(2/3)

March 11, 1985

Mr. Harry Usher
Commissioner
United States Football League
52 Vanderbilt Avenue
New York, N. Y. 10017

Dear Harry:

As you are aware, and as I announced at our Owners' meeting prior to signing Doug Flutie, I would come back and ask the Owners to bear some of the costs of Doug's contract. I did not need Doug as a player, but felt the League desperately needed someone — or something fast.

At that point in time, if you can remember, the perception of the League was at an all time low. Doug Flutie's signing has given us a new and vital life, causes excellent television ratings when he is on and opened up an additional 21 per cent of the affiliates to ABC (affiliates which were not going to broadcast the USFL). As an example, all of New England now telecasts the USFL when, in fact, they had previously cancelled.

This was a move calculated for the League and not for the Generals. As it turns out, it was more successful that even our wildest expectations. Everyone is now benefitting from Doug Flutie.

I would appreciate your putting on the next agenda the allocation of Doug Flutie's costs to each team. The money will be returned when he plays at away games and fills additional seats.

Thank you for your attention to this matter.

With best wishes,

Sincerely,

Donald J. Trump

THE TRUMP ORGANIZATION
725 FIFTH AVENUE · NEW YORK, N. Y. 10022   212·832·2000   TELEX·427715

44

DONALD, YOU'RE FIRED

WHEN TRUMP PULLED his stunt, I wondered how he could be so naïve to believe the rest of his partners would pay for his signing of Doug Flutie? Then I thought: How could anyone sign a player for millions of dollars for five years—to a personally guaranteed contract, no less—when he knew in two years he wanted to move to the fall with no television contract and no assurances the USFL would even suit up for games in the fall of 1986? Hell, it's no wonder Donald wanted his partners to pay for Flutie's contract. Maybe he is smarter than I gave him credit for.

Donald Trump is the best self-promoter on selling his brand—his name, his likeness in the world and a renowned real estate developer of some magnificent buildings—but he had a lot to learn about football and how to be a good partner.

I sincerely believe if Donald had the same enthusiasm for our spring season, the USFL would still be playing football today or merged with the NFL. We had signed some great players and coaches. In three years, we already had several of our teams that could have competed in the NFL. In 1984, the Houston Gamblers became the first franchise in professional football history to win their division and make the playoffs as an expansion team. Because of Donald and his plans to start the USFL fall schedule in 1986, we were being forced to vacate the Houston market, and he was coveting Jim Kelly and my team the way a sailor looks at a prostitute after a six-month deployment.

Kelly achieved everything we told him he would: He became one of the most prolific passers in the history of professional football. Kelly broke records almost every time he stepped on the field, including passing for the most yards, with the most completions, and most touchdowns in a single game against the Chicago Blitz coached by—get this—his future coach in Buffalo, Marv Levy. Our run and shoot offense worked well for Jim and my friend Marv—four Superbowl appearances and both of these great men got enshrined in the NFL Hall of Fame. Meanwhile, in New York, Herschel Walker, behind Maurice Carthon, set the all-time professional football rushing record.

Donald and I merged our teams—we owned the most exciting team in professional football, and would play in the Big Apple, and Donald wants to go head-to-head with the NFL in the fall—Donald, you're fired.

45

CUSTER'S
LAST STAND

WHAT DID DONALD Trump and General Custer have in common? Custer was a general who led his troops into battle with the Indians at the Little Big Horn. Trump owned the Generals and led his fellow owners into the battle against the NFL at the courthouse in New York. Both achieved the same results.

On March 16, 2004, Random House released *America's Game*, by renowned author Michael MacCambridge. On the cover was a picture of Johnny Unitas, and MacCambrdge did a pretty great job of telling the rest of the epic story of how pro football captured a nation.

In the book's Epilogue, he had a quote from my buddy Ernie Accorsi, who said, "To me, the fans are the purists, because they have nothing to gain. They have no winning share, they get no break, they pay their way in; they put up with their discomfort; they have to live with the detachment. They're all-the-time selfless people. That's why I give the fans the benefit of the doubt."

We felt the same way about our fans in Houston, and we rewarded them with a brand of football the likes of which had never been seen. And it's been copied ever since, right down to the high-school levels all across the nation.

I challenged Bud Adams, the owner of The Houston Oilers, to a $1 million charity game with The Gamblers; the money was to be donated to charity. If the Oilers won, I would pay $1 million to his favorite charity and if The Gamblers won, Bud would donate a million to my favorite charity. He never took the bait.

But now we were being forced to rob those fans who loved us—in Detroit, with crowds of 32,457 people; in Birmingham, with crowds of 36,850 people; in Tampa Bay, with crowds of 45,220 people; in New York, with crowds of 61,000 people; in Houston, with crowds of 28,152 people—and follow a man to the fall who had a plan that was going to take all of us to our knees hovered over the porcelain throne.

And, don't forget, our spring television ratings were beating the living hell out of anything else.

Truthfully, I liked Harry Usher and thought he could be his own man and make decisions independently from Donald and in the best interest of our league.

The first thing Harry did in office was to approve a loan to my team for $1 million that we needed immediately when we lost 15,000 season-ticket holders by our announcement to move to the fall.

Next thing I knew, we were merging teams left and right—Oakland and Michigan? Washington and Orlando? And now, Houston and New York? Moving out of our successful markets and actually following the Michael Porter plan to a "T." I'm not accusing anybody of anything, but I'm just saying if it walks like a duck, looks like a duck, and quacks like a duck, it might be a duck.

Are you kidding me?

All to appease Donald, who was promising that if we followed him—me, Myles Tanenbaum and his new partner Steve Ross, Fred Bullard, Tad Taube, Alfred Taubman, some of the most affluent men in America—we might somehow benefit when we win a lawsuit against the mighty NFL.

I certainly had my doubts. It was crystal clear to me that Donald's plan to engage a lawsuit with the NFL had several major flaws, and I pointed them out to him and Usher.

I felt the lawsuit should be filed in Houston, Texas—not New York—and Donald should not be the face representing our league. Donald had always pontificated in the New York media about his great wealth, and a person on the jury in New York would say "so what if Trump lost $25 million dollars?" It was no big deal; but a jury in Houston, Texas, would connect with me and my partners when it found out we lost most of our money and provided them with the most exciting football and won our division two years in a row. As well, many Houston fans did not like Bud Adams. Besides, I didn't believe Donald would be a credible witness to benefit this litigation.

I also advised Donald and Harry to bifurcate the lawsuit, that we sue the NFL for anti-trust violation first and then, in a separate trial, try them on the damage amounts. Obviously, when the jury announced the NFL was guilty of violating the Sherman Anti-Trust Laws, it was checkmate. The penalties for the damage suit that followed would be trebled. Under this scenario, we would have achieved Trump's goal to merge several of our teams into the NFL.

Courage is being scared to death, but saddling up anyway. I was scared shitless that Donald J. Trump was now in complete control.

ACT SIX

The return from the killing field is more than a debriefing. It is a slow ascent from hell.
—Renowned author and psychologist James Hillman,
from his New York Times bestseller, *A Terrible Love of War*.

46

IF YOU SHOOT STRAIGHT, YOU ONLY NEED ONE STONE

WE SIMPLE JEWISH folks from Borger, Texas, always remember from where the source of our strength arises. I cherish the epic story of David and Goliath, because David was one Jewish leader who is not likely to ever be forgotten. Still too young to fight in the army, David became Israel's champion because he took on the greatest giant in the land, defended the entire nation of Israel, and became more than a superhero.

Not long before his historic battle, he calmly walked down to a brook and carefully selected five smooth stones. When he returned to the camp of Israel, he was prepared to battle the most feared man in all the land with nothing more than his slingshot and that sack of stones.

He may have picked five, but knew all along in his mind: If you shoot straight, you only need one.

The only thing Donald and David have in common is that their first name starts with *D*. Trump had led us into a colossal nightmare. Our league would live or die depending on Donald's plan to own an NFL franchise. I recall my quiet times alone in the nights leading up to the ultimate confrontation with Goliath (NFL). I remember my doubts and frustrations in trying to get Donald focused on winning this major litigation. I thought about my partners and all of the money they lost, about Dave Dixon, the players, the fans—the league. I was dying inside.

We won our lawsuit. The courts found that the NFL had indeed violated anti-monopoly laws, as I had been fighting for all along. But it was a Pyrrhic victory. The

280

USFL was awarded a judgment of $1—$1! Under anti-trust laws the judgment was tripled—so the total result of our struggles and Trump's insistence on a fall season won us $3.

We had come so far in such a short period of time. Sure, as a young professional sports league, we made some correctable mistakes; but overall, we did a lot of positive things that made football better for the fans. At this point, the partners in the USFL had invested approximately $160 million, and Donald Trump was willing to risk it all on the roll of the dice. Unfortunately, he was the shooter, and he was gambling with his partners' money.

In 1985, after our spring season was over, I was living in the St. Moritz Hotel, which Trump owned. My total net worth was at stake and my cash was fading fast. I realized Donald had undermined—and sacrificed—all of the other owners and myself for his own selfish greed. How in the world can you go to battle with the NFL—the most powerful monopoly in America—and underestimate its strength and fire power? Donald was over-matched in his battle against Rozelle and the NFL.

Our league was hardly a failure as entertainment, however. Despite a decline in the USFL's television ratings to 5.7 on ABC and 2.8 on ESPN, ABC exercised its option to carry the USFL in the spring of 1985 at $14 million, and offered a new contract worth $175 million for four years in the spring of 1986. And ESPN, where the USFL was the highest rated program, offered a contract worth $70 million over three years.

In today's dollars, I estimate our teams would now be worth hundreds of millions of dollars apiece had we continued to play in the spring; I'm sure, too, that by now a merger would have been completed with the NFL on favorable terms. This is not small potatoes.

But thanks to Trump, and his move to the fall in the ensuing months, the USFL was forced to withdraw from Chicago, Detroit, Philadelphia, Pittsburg, Washington, D.C., and, eventually, Houston, each of which provided large television markets, and each of which already possessed an NFL team. Through internal mergers, our league bolstered franchises in Baltimore, Jacksonville, Memphis, Oakland, and Phoenix, which had been discussed as possible NFL expansion cities.

To me, the viability of Trump's strategy was destined for failure. Tad Taube, Bobby and Alfred Taubman, John Bassett, Carl Peterson, Fred Bullard, Donald Dizney, Jerry Sklar, Bill Tatum Sr. and Jr., and others knew that a move to the fall was suicidal. We also knew that the NFLPA was going to strike in 1987. The USFL would be the only professional football league, and in two more years our product would be competitive with the NFL.

We had several teams in the USFL that could have competed in the NFL. I would bet and give you odds that our merged team of the New Jersey Generals and Houston

Gamblers would light up the scoreboard; we could have easily hung forty points on the Bears the year they won the Super Bowl, led by the one-and-only Jim McMahon. The Gamblers/Generals featured Jim Kelly at quarterback and Herschel Walker at super back in the Run 'n' Shoot Offense. We had the four fastest men who ever played on the same professional football team: Herschel Walker, Vince Courville, Gerald McNeil, and Clarence Verdin. All were world-class sprinters. They would have been the core of a football team that was probably the most exciting offense, on paper, that never played a down.

Our brand of football was exciting. In two short years, we developed loyal fans. Television ratings were good. We had a five-year plan; every owner knew he would likely lose money in the early years. Short-term losses would eventually turn into long-term profits. Ask the AFL owners how much they lost before they merged with the National Football League.

Even today, it remains unclear to me whether the other partners really believed Donald's plan had a chance for success. How did Trump convince other owners to believe he could force a future merger with the NFL through litigation? Everything else told us to stay in the spring; don't forget about the $600,000 McKinsey Study (which advised us to stay in the spring). What about the $245 million television contracts to stay in the spring? What people don't know is that Trump refused to play another spring season after 1985; he knew that without a team in New York City the league was doomed.

The message was clear: Don't ever underestimate Donald J. Trump. Any opposition to Donald was ruthlessly eradicated. In one meeting, I argued against him so heatedly that I stormed out of the room, and slammed the door as I left. All the while I was wearing a jockstrap with a stainless steel cup to protect my balls.

Because of our stated intentions to file a suit against the NFL and begin a fall season in 1986, our 1985 spring season was a "lame duck" season, the last for our fans in Houston.

Donald did everything I warned him not to do.

In one instance, he signs a high-profile player for springtime football (Trump and his team, the Generals, were on national television for four of the first five weeks). Approximately five weeks later he kills the league by announcing a move to the fall.

One thing for sure that I learned from Donald in this charade: If one thinks logically, one is in a heap of trouble.

I had been the most deposed witness prior to the trial, but would never be called to the stand. Obviously, I was able to provide very damaging facts and testimony against the NFL because of my agent days and negotiations with most of the teams. I exposed their monopolistic tendencies.

I had openly fought with Donald about the way he was managing the litigation. I was fairly certain we would win the anti-trust portion of the lawsuit, but I was concerned about the damage issues.

The lawsuit should never have been tried in New York, with Trump as the face of the USFL and Myerson as our attorney. In my opinion, this was a huge mistake.

I didn't feel that Donald would be believable before a jury of his peers. He refused to listen.

Ultimately, he had a master plan of which none of us knew—his team would be absorbed into the NFL.

Executives from all three major networks also testified that by 1986, after the USFL had left several large television markets and was encountering financial and other difficulties, it was no longer an attractive entertainment product.

Trump actually testified under oath that in his private meeting with Rozelle, the Commissioner offered him an NFL franchise in exchange for his blocking the USFL's proposed move to the fall and his preventing the league from filing the anti-trust litigation against the NFL.[*] Rozelle absolutely denied that he made such an offer to Trump.

"Trump got up there and lied and contradicted Pete," Joe Browne, a major executive with the NFL, said. "It was on the front page of the New York Post."

Trump called Pete, and Pete took notes which were used in the trial.[**]

"Listen," Trump told Rozelle over the phone, "I'll get these USFL owners to drop this litigation if I get an NFL team in New York City."

"What are you going to do about the Generals?" Pete asked.

"I'll get some stiff to buy it," Trump said, as Rozelle recorded in his notes.

"That expression really resonated with the jury," Browne said.

I had a friendly relationship with Commissioner Rozelle over the years. After Donald's testimony and during a break in the proceedings, I was in the men's room washing my hands, and Rozelle was at the next sink. "Commissioner, did you really offer Trump an NFL franchise?" He answered, "What do you think?" I walked away because I knew the answer.

I felt sorry for Donald on the witness stand. The NFL attorneys were brutal. Whatever he was trying to sell, the jurors were not buying. The jurors would quickly see through his facade. And because of Donald being Donald, they frankly felt no mercy toward him. Those of us who had risked our financial resources, and lived and died for

*   "Rozelle: Czar of the NFL"—Davis (McGraw-Hill, 2008)
** "Rozelle: Czar of the NFL"—Davis (McGraw-Hill, 2008)

the birth and growth of the United States Football League, were shown no consideration by the New York jury.

My worst dreams were coming true: that Donald was a great witness for the NFL. Myerson was like a pit bull. He marched around the courtroom, putting on a show for the judge and jury; he was pugilistic and argumentative. In my opinion, he was totally ineffective; the jury didn't buy into his courtroom demeanor and drama. To prove damages, he had a woman economist as an expert witness, and she didn't know if a football was stuffed or pumped. He totally failed by his legal presentation to convince a jury to pay us damages in excess of $1.3 billion.

I couldn't believe what was happening right before my eyes. Here we were: representative owners of a league with loyal fans, T.V. contracts, some great players, and many others who would never have a chance to play professional football without the USFL. In my opinion, we had created a market for football in the spring, and we were about to lose everything because of the greed and deceitful wishes of a single man.

I urged, begged, and pleaded with Donald to play two more years in the spring, but to no avail. He said, "There is no money in spring football, it is minor league crap. Football should be played in the fall."

The NFL, on the other hand, would continue to find enormous success with billions of dollars in revenue pouring in from its television contracts and the NFL Network, as I predicted many years earlier. The television rights to broadcast NFL games are the most lucrative and expensive rights of any sport, hauling in in excess of $30 billion. ESPN recently paid $1.1 billion per year for eight years, a total of $8.8 billion to televise Monday Night Football.

ESPN, which partnered with us, has now become the largest sports network in the world. The folks at the network were shocked and disappointed the USFL did not stay in the spring, and they were willing to pay us $70 million to stay put where we could grow together. ESPN as our TV partners. Are you kidding me? Who knows what our franchise might be worth today?

Clearly, we had drilled and defeated the NFL. We proved them guilty of anti-trust and we had laid the foundation for two future strikes that would follow. We opened the markets for football in Jacksonville, Arizona, and, ultimately, for the Raiders' move back to Oakland as well. We implemented the two-point conversion, created the red flag challenge for instant replay, and installed the Run 'n' Shoot spread offense, effectively changing the way the game is played today.

Most of all, we changed free agency, the salary structure of the NFL, and how it treats its players.

More than 150 players from the USFL went on to NFL careers, and some ultimately became enshrined in the Pro Football Hall of Fame.

We won the suit, and I proved the NFL to be a total and complete monopoly. But it was a hollow victory that reminded me of the words of my beloved father, Harry: "We won the battle, but lost the war."

And so I sat in the St. Moritz Hotel, stuck in New York with Donald Trump.

Sadly, I now had lost nearly everything. But I was going to stay and help get Donald out of his personal service contracts and dismantle the team.

47

TURN OUT THE LIGHTS ... THE PARTY'S OVER

THE LAST PERSON I wanted to hear from, and the first who called at the crack of dawn, was Donald Trump. I picked up the receiver and didn't even have time to say "Hello."

"We got screwed, Jerry," Trump said. "The judge was terrible. We'll win on appeal. Can you believe the fucking judge said it was all right just to award the USFL a dollar—a dollar!—if you can't decide on a damage award?"

I replied, "He also should have said, 'It's okay to award them $200 million dollars.'" It was his duty to instruct the jury accordingly, and not to bias them.

Donald, skipping foreplay, moved right to his point with a measured cadence, "Jerry ... can you go over a few ... contracts with me?"

"Sure, Donald, what contracts?" I bit.

"Just Doug Flutie, Herschel Walker ..." I thought, He must be negotiating now.

He goes on, "The idiots who drafted this crap ought to be shot."

I inquired reluctantly, "What's the problem?"

"My attorney says the agreements are ironclad and I'm stuck."

I rolled my eyes.

"Donald, if your lawyers drafted the agreements, they should be banished from your kingdom. If Flutie's and Herschel's lawyers drafted them, they must have done a good job—you signed them. And no loopholes."

"I'll see you at 11:00," he answered. The conversation was over.

As Donald's secretary led me into his office, he got out of his chair and came over to me, put his hand on my shoulder, looked me straight in the eye, and said, "This is not over yet." He then offered me a chair with a wave of an arm. "Sit down, I'm having lunch brought in.

"If we don't win an appeal, Jerry, I might try to buy the Jets; and you know you're my man. I'd want you to run the team for me." I was not surprised by this, because I knew Donald needed me, so I was all ears. "One of the reasons I wanted to merge with you and your team was to have you run the operation," he continued. Donald's eyes focused on me like a hawk sizing up his prey.

I, too, put on my poker face.

He continued. "You know, Jerry, most of the time I don't do too well with partners. Something usually happens and I wind up in a lawsuit and make another lawyer rich."

"Donald, does this include the USFL lawsuit, the one we just lost?"

"No! This wasn't my lawsuit. This was the USFL suing the NFL."

I could only stare at the man in disbelief as he ate his sandwich. I couldn't even speak, for in that moment I realized that Donald J. Trump really believed this hadn't been his lawsuit at all.

"What are you staring at?" he asked, really not understanding.

"You," I reply.

We were locked into a shared cadence now, like two Bighorn sheep on a mountainside, one about to fall off the cliff.

I stood up, moved around. and made the room more of my own. And proceeded to measure my breath and my words evenly to speak plainly.

"Donald, what is wrong with you? You are in total denial." Donald started shaking his head slowly side to side. "I don't agree with you. I breathed life into the USFL. I signed Flutie. The league was dying; it was shit football in the spring. I tried to save it."

Just then the phone on his big desk lit up and Donald said, "I have to take this call."

As I walked out of his office, my mind was racing. When Trump was being a spinmeister, there is never any blame to take. Everything he did was bigger, better, more fabulous than anyone else.

Sometimes, trying to do business with Trump was like trying to nail spit to the wall. While he is an intelligent and shrewd businessman, he was a terrible partner.

"If you're telling the truth, you're not bragging," he once told me, and Donald actually believes whatever he says.

But, I have to admit it, he can get things done. He told the New York print media that the city had been working on the outdoor Wolman Rink in Central Park for seven or eight years and was millions of dollars over budget. He said he could bring it in under budget in nine months, and he did.

Working with Donald was like being exposed to a hurricane, earthquake, tornado, volcano, and a rainbow, depending on his moods, and they can change rapidly. He could be difficult, but he could also be the most charming, engaging, and interesting man you have ever met, and he was only thirty-seven years old when I met him. Donald loved the media attention, and he knew how to work the press and television cameras.

The secretary brought me out of my self-hypnotic state. "Jerry, Mr. Trump is off the phone." Donald's mood had changed; he was all business now.

Crisply, he peppered questions my way: "How long do you think it will take to get rid of all of the players and expenses?"

"Probably two to three weeks," I replied.

"My attorney informed me that Walker and Flutie's contracts are personally guaranteed and I will have to pay them. Hell, Jerry, you've forgotten more about football contracts than he even knows." He handed me the contracts. "Read them and let me know tomorrow." For the first time since I reentered his office he looked up at me. "Jerry, I know you can find a way to get me out. I need answers right away."

Rose and Harry Argovitz did not raise a quitter. Although, in my opinion, Donald's actions helped kill the league, and most of my fortunes, I was loyal to my moral obligation to close the show in the most efficient and effective way possible.

There were two personal-service contracts, Flutie's and Walker's, and then there was Kelly's for a Gambler bank loan guarantee that Trump was liable for as part of his purchase of the Gamblers. The Generals also had a guarantee with the Meadowlands to play in the stadium.

The next morning I walked into his panoramic office and told Trump that I could get him out of these contracts with Flutie and Herschel only if he followed my advice: Tell Flutie's agent, Bob Woolf, that Jerry Argovitz is taking care of all contract issues. I demanded that there would be no more dialogue. Ditto for when IMG would call to discuss Herschel Walker.

"They will not want to deal with me, and they will keep calling you. Do not take their calls. No dialogue whatsoever." It felt good to exercise so much control over Donald Trump, but I kept the thought to myself.

I told him I would meet with the Meadowlands on the stadium lease and reminded him that he owed the bank in Houston $300,000 for the loan to Jim Kelly, which he assumed when he bought the Gamblers in August 1985. "This is a debt you have to pay."

"Jerry, I'll take care of the Kelly note, but I really need you to handle the press. You know, keep it positive. We're going to win the appeal. You know what to say; just keep me out of it."

Little did he ever know that I didn't know what to say or do. I was still shell-shocked; the league was dead, and I was buried financially by it and crying in my heart outside of Donald's line of sight.

Walking into the Generals' office was like walking into a mortuary. The secretaries were crying; Larry Sherman, our public relations director, was in tears; all of the players, cheerleaders, the coaches . . . everyone was saddened by the death of our team and league.

Sudden death had arrived without overtime—just a five-day jury review of the facts, and it was over. Disassembling the team in a professional and efficient manner was the last task.

Over a period of the next few weeks, I met with all the employees personally; I thanked them, told them that Donald also thanked them, and handed them their severance checks . . . all the while working out my plan to get Donald over the major hurdles of his so-called ironclad contracts.

The National Football League was licking its chops to sweep in and sign players from the now-defunct USFL, but it needed written releases from each USFL team for each player. We still filed an appeal against the verdict, and the players remained obligated to their respective USFL teams until released.

Flutie's contract was negotiated and represented by my old nemesis Bob Woolf. You'll remember this is the same Bob Woolf who threw me under the bus in the Billy Sims lawsuit; what goes around comes around. Flutie's contract balance was approximately $2.5 million, was well-prepared, and was guaranteed personally by Donald J. Trump, with only two exit clauses: The agreement could be terminated and made null and void if Flutie ever committed any criminal acts or actions detrimental to the organization or league, which would never happen. The other splinter I hung my hat on was the second clause, which stated, "if Doug Flutie ever retires or threatens to retire as a professional football player, the contract would become null and void."

In a newspaper article based on an interview with Flutie and Woolf, statements were made that if Flutie didn't get a substantial offer from an NFL team, he had a personal-services contract with Mr. Trump and would retire from professional football.

Checkmate!

I had my out. I could deliver what Donald wanted.

The Dallas Cowboys took Herschel—represented by IMG—in a supplemental draft. You talk about destiny changing the future and fortune of a team. The Cowboys were hell-bent on signing a deal with Hershel's agent and set up an artificial deadline to obtain his release from the Generals to sign with the Cowboys for millions. Walker and Kelly would now become the highest-paid players in the NFL, thank you very much.

But after several phone calls with Herschel's agent, I told him the only way I would sign the release from the Generals was if we terminated the personal-services contract that was guaranteed by Donald J. Trump. His agent refused to budge and wanted to get full compensation from Donald and to enrich Herschel's future with his new Dallas Cowboy contract. I didn't blame his agent; after all, I would have wanted the same.

In the meantime, Donald was doing a great job. Woolf and IMG kept calling him and he refused to talk.

Silence cannot be quoted.

I called Herschel's agent and told him that I visited with Donald and we were going to honor his personal-services contract . . . but he won't be playing football.

"He will be employed by the Trump Organization," I told him.

"I don't get it," his agent replied in disbelief.

"Have you ever seen the doorman at Trump Tower—his uniform and 3-foot-tall green hat? Donald thought it would be a great attraction to have Herschel as a marquee doorman signing autographs on photos for his shoppers."

The thought of Walker not playing for the Dallas Cowboys loosened their resolve, if not their bowels.

Lastly, the Meadowlands agreed to terminate the Generals' contract without penalty.

I saved Trump millions of dollars, backed his media coverage into a neutral corner, and turned off the lights. I did everything but sweep the floors. Although I was grieving, hurt, and a bit depressed, I refused to show these emotions to the outside world.

Donald seemed pleased by the effective way I dismissed the employees and handled the press. He loved the way I worked out his personal-services contracts with both Flutie and Walker.

He promised to pay the $300,000 owed to the Houston bank for Kelly's contract.

I helped Dave Dixon give life to the USFL and I helped Trump bury its remains. To be sure, it was a sad, sad time.

Funny—or maybe typical—I don't remember Donald ever saying, "Thank you."

FORTY-EIGHT HOURS

ON WHAT TURNED out to be one of the worst days of my life, the weather of the morning mirrored my mood. An ominously dark gray sky was punctuated by a torrential downpour of cold rain, and people walking down the sidewalks of New York tried to shelter themselves from the storm under the cover of umbrellas.

I wish life provided such protection from its storms.

Standing on the balcony, high above the hustle and bustle and splashes of humanity far below, I watched from the top of Trump's hotel.

I ached all over. I was tired. I had taken a beating mentally and felt the effects physically. All I wanted at this point was to be able to relax and simply step back, get some perspective, and somehow get my head on straight. Stress sure is a tough opponent sometimes. If truth be told, the best way to describe where I was mentally at that tumultuous point in my life was that I had been tip-toeing through a mine field for months, trying not to make one wrong step and get blown up.

I was loyal to Donald, had given him good, sound advice, and protected him. But in the end, after all my efforts to do the right thing and help people, I had nonetheless taken one bad step and blown everything to smithereens anyway. I felt like I had failed; that I didn't do enough to save the United States Football League. My friend John Bassett, owner of the Tampa Bay Bandits, said, "Jerry, it's up to you to save the league. You are Donald's partner; he'll listen to you. I'm depending on you to convince Trump to stay in spring or we're dead."

I couldn't convince Donald in that regard, and not long after Bassett died of cancer. I failed! I know now that most of the depression I was experiencing was directly related to the amount of personal guilt I was feeling.

Maybe a shower would wash away some of the gloom and mental anguish. As the
hot water hit my body, sure enough, I finally began to feel better and more relaxed. I had
been so depressed the last several days, I didn't even leave my hotel room. As I shaved
and saw my face in the mirror, I remembered my favorite poem:

> When you get what you want in your struggle for self
> And the world makes you king for a day,
> Just go to a mirror and look at yourself,
> And see what that man has to say.
>
> For it isn't your father or mother or wife,
> Whose judgment upon you must pass;
> The fellow whose verdict counts most in your life
> Is the one starring back from the glass.
>
> He's the fellow to please, never mind all the rest.
> For he's with you clear up to the end,
> And you've passed the most dangerous, difficult test
> If the man in the glass is your friend.
>
> You may be like Jack Horner and "chisel" a plum,
> And think you're a wonderful guy,
> But the man in the glass says you're only a bum
> If you can't look him straight in the eye.
>
> You may fool the whole world down the pathway of years.
> And get pats on the back as you pass,
> But your final reward will be the heartaches and tears
> If you've cheated the man in the glass.
>
> Dale Wimbrow, 1934
> *reprinted with permission*

I've always tried to do the right things, and I can honestly say as I stood there and
examined my life, the man I saw in the mirror that day is my friend.

The bottom line comes down to this: If you don't believe in yourself, the vote is unanimous. So, as I finished shaving and wrapped a towel around my waist, I found myself sitting on the edge of the bed lost in deep thought.

I had lost most of my fortune. It reminded me of the old story I had heard before: The way to make a small fortune is to start with a large fortune . . . and then go and buy a football team. Well, at least I still had a sense of humor, a roof over my head, and food to eat.

In the grand scheme of things, I guess things could be worse.

I was startled back to reality by the sharp ringing of the phone. "Hello?"

It was Donald. "Are you still there," he asked.

"Yes."

"I thought you were going back to Texas."

"I haven't decided yet what to do. I'd like to come over and talk to you about . . . "

Donald interrupted me before I could finish. "I need you to vacate the apartment in forty-eight hours because I've got someone else moving in. Why don't you go back to Texas and find me some real estate deals like we discussed. Take the letter I gave you and meet with the banks. I need that apartment empty in forty-eight hours."

Click.

Still wet and mostly naked, save for a towel loosely fitted around my waist, I sat on the edge of the bed with the weight of reality slapping me in the face.

Things, indeed, could be worse.

49

STARTING OVER

EVERY END HAS a new beginning

I had started with nothing, and I still had most of it left. I wasn't exactly sure what I wanted to do, but I damn sure knew the things I didn't want to do. I met with two major head-hunting firms to see what companies would hire me and what they might pay me. I sent a letter to each NFL team; it was pretty obvious I knew how to structure and negotiate contracts on both sides of the table, both as an agent and owner. I definitely knew football talent and put together two professional football operations. Plain and simple, I was blackballed by the NFL . . . for doing my job. One of the biggest compliments I ever received was from the late, great Al Davis. The last time I spoke to Al was when Super Bowl XXXVIII was played in Houston in 2004. Al shook my hand and, to be honest, I was a bit surprised, because Al doesn't like to shake hands.

"Jerry. I want to congratulate you. You were a great agent; you gave the sons of bitches hell and Gene Klein hated your fucking guts. I want you to know if I had a son playing in the NFL I'd want you to represent him."

Up to this point in my life I had made a lot of money for myself and others. I had been rich and poor; and there is nothing wrong with being poor . . . except it is very inconvenient. The greatest thing I had going for me was the love and support of my mom and dad. My good name was now tarnished because of the Sims' case, in which I was convicted of "an egregious conflict of interest."

No one wanted to hire me.

One of my closest friends is Kenny Rogers, and one of my favorite songs is his mega hit, "The Gambler." Some of the words in that song provide tremendous philosophy: Don't count your money while you're sitting at the table. In essence, you have to know when to hold 'em and when to fold 'em.

As always, my plan to succeed is the same plan I always used:

1. Set my goals in writing.
2. Establish a specific plan in writing and a timetable to accomplish those goals.
3. Have a burning desire to succeed set my priorities.
4. Be persistent.
5. Be confident.
6. Be smart.

The first thing I had to do before I could start over was to settle my outstanding debts with everyone to whom I owed money.

To make matters worse, Houston was in a severe financial downturn and extremely depressed. The local economy was at less than a standstill, because people who had built immense wealth through oil and gas, banking, and real estate had been wiped out. The steady migration of new people moving to Houston came to an abrupt halt. There were no jobs and no growth, foreclosures, bankruptcies; my God, what had happened since I left? Once the shock and realization of the sign of the times set in, I immediately recognized the great opportunities that existed in Houston, Texas. To me, real estate is never good or bad; it is either a buyer's market or a seller's market. And in my lifetime, there will never be a greater buyer's market in this dynamic city. There was fantastic opportunity for anyone who had major cash and knew what he was doing. At least I had half of these requirements.

The problem was, Houston was red-lined with the banks and savings institutions, which meant they would not make any new real estate loans. Most of the local rich real estate players were facing drastic financial challenges, and the few people I knew who had a lot of cash were so scared and uncertain that they had no interest in acquiring real estate.

I had an ace up my sleeve: I took the letter Donald gave me, which authorized me to locate selective real estate acquisitions for him, and met with all the top commercial and office building brokers in Houston. I also met with the banks and lending institutions that needed to get off the hook. Obviously, I knew the kind of buildings that would impress Donald, and I was prepared to negotiate my ass off to deliver them for him. I wanted Class A buildings in great locations that would bear the Trump name. I literally spent months putting detailed information packages together for Donald. I was able to negotiate a couple of major, almost brand spanking new office buildings fifty stories high in great locations in downtown Houston.

I negotiated financing (with no personal liability), minimum cash outlay, and a price of 30-40 cents on the dollar with certain moratoriums on the mortgage payments until we reached certain occupancy levels. Donald's name was still magic in real estate circles, especially in Houston, since there were many more sellers than buyers. The saying, "in life and in real estate, timing is everything," rang particularly true in this case.

I had done what Donald had asked me to just before he kicked me out of his hotel in New York. Frankly, I thought he—or at least his brother Robert—would be impressed enough to come to Houston to evaluate the properties I proposed on site.

A few days after sending the pro-formas and complete information package to Donald, I called him to get his response. He said, "I've just bought another casino in Atlantic City and I'm really focused on this right now, and I don't want to spread out."

"Donald, this is a once in a lifetime opportunity."

"I'm not interested." Then he hung up.

Some things never change. Not only did Trump not pay his obligation to the bank, but Kelly's attorneys sued the Gamblers, me, and my partners. I was very disappointed in how Donald treated my partners and me. Another win for Donald. I borrowed money from my dad and paid $100,000 to settle my part with the bank. I wonder what Trump sees when he looks in the mirror.

Foreign capital began to pour into Houston, and, in a heartbeat, they swept up the good deals.

Most all of the debt I owed was associated with the Houston Gambler ownership. Finally, though, I was able to settle with all of my creditors—some by securing them with assets and others by settling with them upon liquidation of certain properties.

It was time to take my show on the road. I needed to locate the next real estate hot spot that would have a more immediate return for me, which I found in Nevada. Las Vegas was getting ready to explode in growth and jobs; 98 percent of the land in the state of Nevada is owned by the federal government, so I did a land exchange with the federal government to acquire approximately 1,000 acres of prime real estate and sold the property for $26 million.

In the meantime, I started 3CI—Complete Compliance Corporation—a medical waste company with my father and took it public. The stock went from 18 cents a share to $12 dollars a share. I was the president for three years, while our family was the second-largest shareholder.

I had been interested in casinos, especially if you were the house. I always like the best odds of success in any business venture. So, when you think about it, almost everything we do is tied to the odds of winning vs. losing, success vs. failure; the higher the risk, the higher the return. So I formed a company, Kean Argovitz Resorts, Inc. (KAR) and I started representing the Indian tribes for casino development and management. It was just like the old days of representing athletes, except I didn't have to deal with the NFL. We eventually partnered up with Lakes Entertainment (a public company), and Lyle Berman was the chairman of the board. We sold one of our casino ownerships to Lakes in 2010 for $14 million.

I started three mobile home subdivisions—Tealbrook, San Jacinto Plantation, and Timberbrook with my father—and developed the properties for cash (no debt), and carried the notes at 11.5 percent interest. As the lots sold, this generated tremendous cash flow.

I bought and sold more land in different states, which in turn quickly sold for huge profits. I joint-ventured shopping centers with my cousin Herb Weitzman, who has forgotten more than most people will ever know about shopping-center development. Rags to riches to rags and back.

I have followed the advice from The Gambler: "I have picked up my chips and left the table."

Thank you, Kenny Rogers.

50

THE DONALD, MARLA, AND ME

APPROXIMATELY THREE-AND-A-HALF YEARS after I moved back to Houston, I was the president of 3CI, a public company that I started with my father that deals with major hospitals, doctors, and medical waste. I was happily married to Paddy Boyd, a former Mrs. America, and I had settled with all my creditors.

The past is the past and time cures everything. So I thought.

Eddie Chwatt, a friend who lived in New York City, called me in Houston with news that would, once again, drop "the past" in my lap. "Your partner and ex-girlfriend are an item."

"You're kidding. This relationship has two chances—slim and none . . . and slim just left town."

"There's more. The newspapers also implicate you."

"How so?"

"You are being accused of being a beard, a pimp, for Donald. You are the go-between. One article said it would be your fault if the marriage between Donald and Ivana ended in divorce.

I was mortified.

Vicious rumors began to spread on a national level in the *National Enquirer* and big time in the New York media. As always, to Donald, all publicity is good publicity as long as they spell your name right.

I met Marla Maples in Daytona Beach, Florida, when I was asked to be a judge at the Miss Hawaiian Tropic Beauty Pageant. She was one of fifty-two contestants— among some of the most gorgeous, personable, competitive, and determined young women in America.

Ron Rice, the owner of Hawaiian Tropic Sun products and a friend, had asked me to be a judge at the pageant for a number of years, including 1985, the year Marla finished runner-up. I had just merged the Gamblers with the Generals and was on my way to New York to set up shop. The night before I was leaving, the pageant hosted a big party. Marla and I were dancing to a very slow song when she whispered in my ear. "Will you take me to New York with you?" I thought to myself, "Wow, are you kidding?"

"Let me think about it."

I called her the next morning. "I will only take you to New York on one condition."

"What is the condition?"

"I want to meet your mother in person and see if she approves."

Upon meeting Ann Maples, it was easy to see where her daughter got her beauty, smile, and congeniality. Ann was great and gave us her blessings, so off we went to New York.

Once Donald's marriage to Ivana dissolved into more of a business partnership, he got caught up by the youth, beauty, and charm of Marla. When she spoke, it was like dripping honey from a spoon. I'm sure Donald thought he had died and gone to heaven when Marla approached him in a New York church and said, "Hi, Mr. Trump. My name is Marla Maples, and Jerry Argovitz is a good friend of mine." I'm sure she didn't tell him how she had first met him on his helicopter when she was travelling with me to Trump's casino in Atlantic City for a USFL meeting. At that moment, that very second, Donald was hooked, and Marla was slowly—but surely—reeling him in.

So, I can see why Donald would flip out over Marla. It gave him an opportunity to run away in search of another life. After all, he was literally struggling for his financial survival; the banks, the creditors, the bond holders were all attacking him from every side. There were few in the business world who thought he could escape such a financial free fall.

Never underestimate Donald J. Trump.

Shortly after the call from Eddie, I got the strangest call from Donald, with whom I had not spoken since the day he evicted me from his hotel three-plus years before.

After some small talk, Trump finally blurted, "I met the most beautiful woman, and she thinks you are the greatest thing since sliced bread."

"Who is it, Donald?"

"Mar, Ma, Mar . . . " It was very odd, because he does not stutter.

"Marla Maples?" I asked.

"Yes, she's some hot chick. Was she your girlfriend?"

"No, Donald. We're just good friends."

"That's what she said," Trump said, then, "I'm thinking about buying the Jets; and if I do, I want you to manage the team. Stay in touch, Jerry."

Click.

Just like the last time we talked, my conversation with Donald ended as quickly and as surprisingly as it had started.

I was disturbed and concerned about two people I know very well. I knew Donald was emotionally vulnerable, and Marla's beauty, southern charm, personality, and drive were too much for him to handle. Marla was ambitious, and it seemed that she wanted to make a name for herself; how about Mrs. Marla Maples-Trump?

Not bad for a little girl from Dalton, Georgia.

Both my conscience and my relationship with both caused me enough anxiety that I deliberated over and over about the possibilities of this new "merger." I felt responsible as a friend to call both Donald and Marla. When Donald called me he seemed to be searching for information. My first call was to Marla. Her agent, Chuck Jones, (probably on Donald's payroll) would not let me talk to her. "Could I give her a message?" he asked. "Yes. Tell her I said to hire a good lawyer."

Then I called Donald.

"Do you remember when you called me last week and asked about Marla?"

"Yes."

"Donald, if you had a friend who was driving a sports car 110 miles an hour in the pitch dark, the bridge ahead was out, and beyond the bridge was a 300-foot drop, would you call your friend and warn him the bridge was out?"

There was complete silence on the other end; ten seconds of silence in a phone conversation is a long damn time.

Donald finally said, "I guess so."

"Donald, the bridge is out. If you and Marla are just good friends, we can hang up."

"Keep talking, Jerry."

"Marla is a beautiful woman. But I've spent a lot of time with both of you and, in my opinion, together you are like water and oil. Make sure you get a good lawyer." I laughed and hung up.

I wondered if Donald would heed my advice this time.

Some things never change. I was watching this young Georgia peach—whom I had brought to New York and introduced to one of the most powerful, successful, and recognized men in the world—bring him to his knees.

My friend Norma Fedorer, Donald's assistant, who was his right and left hand while I was with him, made no bones about informing me that she always was angry with me because I introduced Marla and Donald. Marla came up to visit me one day, and Norma still remembers what she was wearing, twenty-five years later.

I couldn't believe it. "My God Norma, that was twenty-five years ago. What was she wearing?"

"She had on a black leather mini skirt, cowboy boots, white western shirt with silver collar tips, and a cowboy hat."

I'd remembered the silver collar tips; I gave them to her. I'd say Marla made a big impression on a lot of people. If you ask me, she definitely knew how to close a deal. She must have read Donald's bestselling book, *The Art of The Deal*.

Sometimes, truth is stranger than fiction. In my mind, Donald's arrogance and insensitivity were painful.

There is no greater proof than in his sharing his Christmas holiday in Aspen with both his wife and his mistress. Here he is, one of the most recognizable faces—and hair—in America, and he takes his wife with him, and sneaks Marla on a ski trip, during the busiest time of the year.

This public encounter with Ivana, Marla, and Donald on the Aspen slopes made front-page headlines, probably all over the world.

This was just before the *New York Post* proclaimed that Marla said that sex with Donald was the best she ever had.

Maury Povich, on his nationally syndicated show, exposed Marla and me kissing on the dance floor at a party for the pageant in Daytona Beach. The British tabloids, and our own rags, like the *National Enquirer*, started all kinds of bullshit rumors that I was sleeping with Marla and her mother, Ann. A nice compliment to me, but totally false. The *National Enquirer* offered me $50,000 dollars for some pictures and my story. Silence cannot be quoted.

51

SMALL POTATOES, MY ASS . . .

TWO WORDS I have never heard Donald Trump say: "I'm Sorry."

Have you ever held anything inside for many years when, and all of a sudden, the last straw is placed on your back and it just pushes you over the edge?

For twenty-five years I had pretty much blocked out all of the negative factors regarding the USFL and everyone involved. I forgave, but never forgot, especially when I remembered what could have been. Inside me I have carried this guilt and anger for a lot of years.

So, when I saw Donald Trump's interview on ESPN's *30 For 30* episode, "Small Potatoes: Who Killed the USFL?" The bottled up anger just poured out. I was pissed off! I was embarrassed for you, Donald. You were out of sorts. You were mean-spirited and you obviously are still in denial of your "Art of the Kill" of the USFL.

No one knows Donald's strengths and flaws better than I do, so his comments and actions were a huge disappointment. It hurt me personally and everyone else to whom I had spoken.

There were so many people who had a financial and emotional attachment to the league and, frankly, I felt like he pissed on the grave of the USFL.

If there were two words I would be tempted to pay money to hear come out of Trump's mouth, they would be: I'm sorry. In all the years I have known him, those seem to be two words he is incapable of saying.

Through the power of his influence, Donald was able to make President Barack Obama show his birth certificate to prove that he was, indeed, born on American soil. I still don't believe Donald is convinced.

This is not a kiss-and-tell story about Donald. This book is about my life, and Donald was and is a chapter in it. We were partners, and at the time I was the only one who co-signed checks for him. I introduced him to his beautiful ex-wife Marla. I had total access to him, and we spoke almost every day. The truth is, Donald is an amazing man in many respects.

I guess because I saw so much greatness and potential in Donald, I also saw his shortcomings. The truth is Donald and I agreed we always have the right to disagree.

So now, through my efforts, I'd like to hear an apology for something Trump did that was far-reaching when it came to an interview he did regarding the USFL.

Mike Tollin produced the *Small Potatoes* documentary in which he interviewed Donald. In my view, Trump was insensitive and disrespectful to all of his partners (who lost $160 million), every player who wore a USFL uniform, every coach, every team employee, and certainly to every fan who paid his money to watch a great product developing on the field. And, he seemed to me to be every bit as disrespectful to Mr. Tollin, who had been the film editor of the USFL and a friend of Trump's during the early days.

"If God wanted football in the spring, he wouldn't have created baseball," Trump told Tollin in the documentary. He obviously was chafed by having to even be in front of the camera talking about the USFL—so Trump was, well, Trump.

Among other quotes, some of the ones I remember most were: "It was such a long time ago I don't even think about the USFL anymore. It was a nice experience. It was fun. We had a great lawsuit."

When Tollin reminded him of a quote from noted sportscaster Charlie Steiner about Trump's buying a USFL team only because he couldn't have an NFL franchise, Trump quipped, "Charlie Steiner was nobody. Charlie Steiner couldn't get a job, and we put him on the USFL so I hope that he said that in a friendly way because if he didn't I'd love to take him on just as I love to take anyone on; so I hope he remains loyal. Because if he doesn't, let me know and I'll attack him."

Finally, this gem: "I never liked the idea of spring football. Everything I do is at the highest level. Frankly, I would have been better off if I just went in and bought an NFL team. It would have been a lot easier. Without me, this league would have folded a lot sooner." When Tollin told him he thought the league might have survived if it stayed the course, Trump huffed as he walked out the door. "It would have been small potatoes."

The "small potatoes" league sent 157 former USFL players to the NFL the year after it folded, and 15 of those played in the Pro Bowl that first year. Donald's own team—the merged teams of the Houston Gamblers and New Jersey Generals with Kelly and

Walker—could have competed immediately in the NFL . . . and our coach's and player's salaries for the year were under $5 million.

Donald, you're fired! Again!

I wish Donald would review the segment of that interview, because I believe he owes an apology to anyone he offended, and can damn sure put me at the head of the list. All I want from him is, "I'm sorry." The league didn't make it, but it was anything but small potatoes, and we should have played two more years in the spring.

52

THE PRODIGAL SON RETURNS: VINDICATION

IT HAD BEEN seventeen years since the last time I had seen or spoken to Billy Sims. I had erased him from my memories; still, truthfully, the pain never went away.

I was totally unprepared for what was about to happen. My son, Rick, and I were comfortably seated in our seats on the 50-yard line watching the Houston Texans play against the Dallas Cowboys in 2002. During the halftime festivities, the announcer introduced some of the Heisman-award winners on the field. The crowd's excitement flourished and became more electric when the great, great All-America running back and Oklahoma University Heisman winner—and Detroit Lion All-Pro—Billy Sims was introduced. I must have gone into a trance.

"Dad, are you all right?" Rick noticed my glazed eyes.

"Wow, that's a name out of my past."

"Billy really looks good," Rick said.

"Rick, go down to the field level and tell Billy I want to see him."

As Billy and Ricky were walking up the aisle approaching me, my mind was spinning and my heart was pounding. I shook Billy's hand and said, "It's been a long time, Simbo."

"It's been too long, Doc."

Billy had really aged and had a certain sadness about him. But, I saw him like the day he cut his hair and flashed that infectious million-dollar smile over twenty years ago.

"Can I get your phone numbers? I'd like to talk to you," Billy said.

My emotions were so tangled at that moment. I didn't know if I should laugh with joy or cry with the pain of the red-hot branding iron burning "Egregious Conflict of Interest" across my forehead forever. We exchanged business cards. I replied, "Give me a call and we'll set up a meeting."

About a week later, my secretary buzzed me and said, "Mr. Sims is here for his appointment."

"Please show him in and hold my calls."

It was so strange—awkward, really—as we both stood staring at each other. The silence was deafening, and the emotions intensified. Soon, tears welled up in both of our eyes, and we grabbed each other in a huge bear hug.

"Doc, I owe you a big apology."

"Billy, before you say anything, let me share my feelings. Have I ever lied to you or taken advantage of you?"

"No."

"Did I ever cheat you or treat you unfairly?"

"Hell, no."

"Billy, for seventeen years I have lived my life as an embarrassment to my family's name. I have been branded as someone who screwed and cheated his client and friend because of an egregious conflict of interest. Russ told me you never had a chance in the lawsuit."

"Doc, you did nothing wrong. You told me everything; the Lions bought me for a million dollars more, just like you said they would."

"Why didn't you just pick up the phone and call me and say, 'Doc, you were right; the Lions offered me $4.5 million. What should I do?'"

"Doc, seriously, that is what I wanted to do. My advisor and Russ Thomas told me this is the only way they can pay me the extra million. The lawsuit was really between the NFL and the USFL. I told Russ I never had a problem with you. The craziest thing though, was that Russ' own lawyer was advising him not to sign me because the Lions would be risking a big lawsuit for some kind of contract interference."

"That was good advice," I said. "Billy, to make the Lions pay you $4.5 million, I would have had a ticker tape parade in downtown Houston for Bill Ford and Russ Thomas. One phone call and you were a Lion 'no lawsuit necessary.'"

"This was the biggest mistake of my life, and if there were any way to take it back, I would," Billy replied. "Doc, this was not about you; it was about me, and I have regretted what I did to you, and my life has never been the same since. The Lions misled me."

"What happened, Billy?"

"To tell you the truth, Doc, there were so many times I wanted to talk to you—I just didn't know what to say."

"Billy," I replied, "I know the Lions deceived you, and used you to destroy me. Truthfully, for the last seventeen years I never talked about you or kept up with you. How is Brenda?"

"Brenda and I got divorced, I blew my knee out in the 1984 season, and eventually had to file for bankruptcy."

"I'm sorry, I had no idea."

"Doc, do you remember that insurance policy you bought for me?"

"Of course, it was a $2.2 million tax-free career-ending insurance."

"Yes. I blew that, too. Doc, I did it to myself, I trusted the wrong people."

"Billy, when I was with you, do you think this could have happened to you? What about all of the things we used to talk about?"

"Hell, no! Doc, you always protected me. You gave me good advice; you were the businessman and father I never had. Coach Switzer and you have been like fathers to me. Doc, you told me three things to watch out for, because they can destroy the success of a man."

"What were they, Billy?"

Billy was animated and pointing his fingers at my chest as he spoke. "Greed, ego, and women; and you said, 'not necessarily in that order.'" And Billy, with that contagious laughter, added, "You were right about that, too!"

"Doc, I remember your five-second rule, too. If I ever have to think about something for five seconds, it is wrong."

"Did you ever use it?"

"Sure, many times. When I got desperate and started thinking about various avenues or opportunities to follow I used it."

"What do you mean desperate?"

"We were both branded by the Lions," Billy said. "Doc, I lost everything—my wife, kids, home, money . . . they even put me in jail for not paying child support. I lost everything except my name, Billy Sims—Heisman Award winner from Oklahoma University. I even had to sell my Heisman Trophy."

As I sat there and watched the young man who was once my son with his head bowed in shame and broad shoulders heaving, I started to rain big tears. This was one of the most poignant moments of my life.

"Billy, why didn't you call me when you needed help?"

"Doc, I figured you would be the last person in the world that would help me."

"Just because you turned on me, doesn't mean I'd turn on you. I was always there! But Billy, that is history and tomorrow is a mystery. Let's go get some bar-b-que. I know my mother is smiling in heaven now, because she wanted us to get back together."

About a month later, Billy called me. "Doc, can you loan me $2,500? I can pay you back in sixty days." (Which he did). Now, I know how proud he is, so Billy must truly have been in a financial bind to call me and ask for money.

"Give me your mailing address and I'll send you a check. Billy, what kind of job do you have?"

"Right now, I'm kind of in-between. I don't have anything permanent."

"Let me make a few phone calls and see if I can help you."

My cousin and partner is Herb Weitzman. I call him Mr. Dallas, because everyone knows Herb; he was on the board of America Can Academy, a private school that offers second chances to minority and problem kids. This was a match made in heaven for Billy and all the young students whose lives he touched. Billy worked for the academy for four years, and he became a mentor and friend to so many young kids who grew up without a father figure and in poverty. I was so proud of him. He'd call just to say hello and would come in often just to visit and stay with me.

Billy called me one morning to tell me that some people wanted to open up a bar-becue restaurant in Oklahoma and wanted to use his name and likeness. He asked if I would represent him, and he would pay me. "I will negotiate the deal for you," I told Billy, "but you do not owe me anything."

Today, Billy owns an interest in twenty-one Billy Sims Bar-B-Que restaurants in three states, and is a successful businessman. He remains an avid Sooners supporter and has a line of Billy Sims football memorabilia; the greatest work he does, though, is what he does with underprivileged children.

Sometime in the spring of 2011, Billy surprised me and came to our vacation home in Rancho Mirage, California, to spend a few days with Loni and me. He said, "Doc, I love you and thank you for all you have done for me, and if you ever need me, I'll always be there."

That is the same thing I always told my father.

53

REFLECTIONS OF MY LIFE

EVER SINCE I can remember as a young Jewish kid growing up in the rough and tumble streets of Borger, Texas, I had the realization that all one truly has is his name—good or bad depends on the life you have lived. "Be a good boy," my grandmother Dora used to say in Yiddish and broken English.

My dad taught me that the two most important things in life are a good name and that one's word is one's bond. He told me on my thirteenth birthday that the only thing I was given when I entered this world as a baby was my name—Jerry Allen Argovitz; and the only thing I would take out of this world was the same. "What you accomplish with your life in between is how you will be remembered," he said. These things my father taught me, and my mother made damn sure I tried to follow them.

On the other hand were the not-so-fond memories of the teasing, taunting, name-calling, embarrassment, humiliation, and fist-fights I endured. I don't know if I was born with anger and hate or if it came with the environment and times of my youth. If it weren't for boxing and athletics—which provided for me a means of redirecting my anger—I would have been in a lot of trouble.

My parents always instilled confidence in me—and my dad used to repeat to me the quote made famous by W. Clement Stone, who said, "Anything the mind can conceive and believe it can achieve." I've always remembered that, and I guess that it's true; I am a living, breathing example that an average kid could be successful.

Still, nothing I ever did came easy for me, but I set my goals, devised a plan, and persevered until the mission was complete.

Unfortunately, I really believe that the focus and determination I had to be successful and achieve financial independence put a stress on my marriages. Admittedly, although sometimes I would be visible to my family, my mind and focus was a million miles away.

I have three children whom I love very much, each of whom is approximately two years apart. Brent is the oldest, followed by Ricky and Kari Lynn, and all three were adopted from three different sets of biological parents. Elaine and I got them as babies when they were one week old. I also have a goddaughter, named Kathy Griffin Townsend, whom I am very proud of.

Raising children is one of the toughest jobs I ever had, and I'm sure there are some things I could have done differently. I tried to instill in my kids the valuable lessons my parents taught me: do the right thing; always do the right thing; and, repeat rules 1 and 2.

Brent, my oldest son, was precocious and advanced as a young child. When he was older, we tested his IQ, and his score was off of the charts. Brent was a musician and traveled the world with his band, The Real McCoy. He now resides in Hawaii.

Rick is a big man, 6-2 and about 240 pounds. Ricky was a good athlete growing up and loved sports. Today, he is happily married to Mindy, and they have three children: Jake, Rylie, and Grayson. Rick has his own successful business in Scottsdale, Arizona, called Glacier Pool.

Kari ("Kari Bears," as I call her) is an exact look-alike of Ann Coulter. It is almost scary. People stop her all of the time and ask her if she is Ann Coulter. I wonder if Ann Coulter ever gets asked if she is Kari Argovitz? What they say is true: A daughter captures her father's heart. Kari is a medical assistant and has one child, Jacob, who is nine years old and a good little athlete.

To all of my children and grandchildren, I love you; and if I make you upset sometimes, that's okay, too. Just remember I'm always going to be your father and you're always going to be the child regardless of your age.

If you measure life as a football game, I'm in the fourth quarter. I have been so blessed to have such close friends whom I love and respect. I was able to practice dentistry, a profession I loved. I was a damn good dentist, and dentistry provided me with the initial money for my real estate investments. Dentistry gave me the magnificent feeling of utmost accomplishment when I could treat a patient who was in great pain—and immediately provide relief from their pain.

When I retired from dentistry I missed the relationship I had with my patients. They trusted me to care for them, and do so in a professional manner. I believe that is one of the reasons I was able to have success as a sports agent; I truly cared about all of those men who I represented. They were not merely clients to me; they were family. To this very day, any of my players can call me—day or night—and know with confidence that if I can help them, I will.

I was already financially stable before I became an agent, so I didn't have the urgency to quickly sign a contract to get some money. I was an astute businessman and managed millions of dollars for others.

I believe Gene Burrough and I were a great team, and I was willing to fight the system for my players. I believe that is what set me apart in a business where, sadly, greed sometimes takes precedence over relationships. I realized the responsibility I had to these young men: to make sure they were totally prepared to deal with the journey and business side of professional sports and life after football.

The only difference between then and now? The amount of money and the instant worldwide exposure by the social media—Facebook, blogs, tweets: Do something wrong and the entire world knows about it in fifteen seconds.

But the same problems exist. A twenty-, twenty-one-, or twenty-two-year-old young professional athlete who just signed a multi-million dollar contract to play professional football or basketball, many of whom did not have a father or came from poverty, needed a mentor to teach them and prepare them for the future. I was blessed to be that man for them, who could help them navigate the business side of their profession while they performed on the field without worrying whether or not their futures were well taken care of. Otherwise, five years after playing their last season, most would have been broke.

As an agent, I believe my legacy speaks for itself. I never paid a player illegally to sign with me. I never lost a client to another agent. None of my players ever got into any trouble off the field. They were solid citizens, and they did not have any financial problems under my management.

Hugh Green, who is like another son to me, told me once, "You were the father figure we never had. Jerry, you were our moral compass." Joe Cribbs said, "You were the successful businessman mentor I always wanted." Curtis Dickey said, "You gave me faith and hope." Jim McMahon said, "The NFL always hated you because you fought for your players." Jim Kelly said, "Jerry always put his players first."

I loved my players, but that did not exempt them from carrying themselves in a professional manner. I also had tough love, as well. There was no gray area: if you were one of mine, I expected you to act professional and realize you are a role model for kids, and parents also. My players heard me say more than once: One torpedo can sink your ship, so make good choices. Be smart, don't be stupid. My players were well educated on how sex, drugs, and alcohol could bring them down and ruin not only their careers, but their reputations. They were prepared. On the practical side, I taught them about taxes, investments, public speaking, and how to dress appropriately.

Too many players are getting in trouble; DUI's, drugs, rape, assault and battery, etc., are rampant in professional sports. If you are a good agent, this can be controlled. To be sure, being a great agent is a lot of responsibility. One thing the NFL teams did recognize about me was while I was a tough negotiator, my players came to camp in shape and the league never had any non football related problems from my players.

I saved the best for last. On November 11, 2011, I married Loni Bader, the love of my life. We have been together for eight years. Loni owned and operated a hotel in New York and converted it into a retirement community before selling it in 2001, and is one of the smartest women I have ever been around. I trust her judgment and have come to learn she has an amazing instinct when it comes to people. I think she is a much better judge of people and their character than I am.

One thing about Loni, she is brutally honest. If she is your friend, you can damn sure count on her. She is a strong woman and a cancer survivor; she lost her wonderful son, Steven, to cancer when he was only nineteen years old. Her other son, Richard, is a high school guidance counselor in Virginia. He has two daughters, Sarah and Alexis. Loni donated and raised money for the Steven and Richard Bader Immunological Institute Building at Hackensack University Medical Center in New Jersey. We have a wonderful life together.

EPILOGUE

IN THE WORLD of sports, legacy is a tricky thing. One day you're an owner, a player, an agent, a headline, then—*poof*—you're gone. Your moment in the spotlight is fleeting. I hadn't given much thought to it until my friend Darryl Burman approached me in 2007 at my Houston home.

"Jerry, when you're long gone what will be your legacy? How will you be remembered?"

That's a great question for all of us, I thought. Unfortunately, I felt I would be remembered in the law books for having an "egregious conflict of interest" in the Billy Sims case. I am convinced that one of the worst things that can happen to a person is being convicted of an act he didn't commit.

I have been locked in my own brain for many years, and I refuse to be the victim any more—thanks to Alfred Nobel, my father, Harry, and my wife, Loni. This book is based on my life, my opinions, and actual events and conversations as best as I can recall. It will clear my name and continue my unfinished business with the National Collegiate Athletic Association.

I discovered I had friends and family members who had no idea the impact I'd had on the modern game of professional and college football. But more important, I didn't want to be remembered by anyone, especially my own loved ones—grandkids and great-grand kids yet to be born—as nothing more than a side show in sports-law journals, someone who had been branded for having committed an "egregious conflict of interest."

I knew I had to erase the stigma from the Argovitz name before I died and let my legacy be judged on the truth.

How do you start? Each year, a new class of law students is introduced to the *Sims vs. Argovitz* case and my historical courtroom loss. Would you do business with a man who has been convicted of an egregious act?

I sat down with my dad two years before he died and discussed my dilemma regarding my legacy and how I had cast a dark shadow over the Argovitz name. "Billy has apologized to both of us," he told me, "and I hope your conscience is clear."

"Dad, my conscience was always clear—I knew I did nothing wrong, and Billy has attested to that. I just want to clear my name—I mean—our name," I replied.

"Son, have you ever heard of the Nobel Peace Prize?"

"Sure dad—everybody has," I said.

"Do you know who Alfred Nobel was?"

"No," I admitted.

Dad continued, "Alfred Nobel invented dynamite— and when his brother died, the obituary in the paper made a mistake and said, 'Alfred Nobel, the father of dynamite died yesterday.' When Alfred read this, he realized that this would be his legacy—dynamite, explosion, destruction, death—so he founded the Nobel Prize."

"Dad, that man was brilliant. What a creative concept to actually change the perception of one's past into a more acceptable legacy to be remembered by," I told him.

"The story about you and Billy has never been told," he reminded me.

"No—it hasn't," I said.

"Son, my suggestion is that you and Billy should unite in a common cause that is bigger than both of you—that will become your legacies. You need to tell your story— write a book," he told me.

This sage advice from the wisdom of my father, Harry, was a defining moment for me, and I set out to tell my story, correct untruths and misperceptions, and to use the rest of my life and whatever influence I have to follow my passion and advocate for the young collegiate football and basketball players who have no representation in a broken system.

The next thing I did was call Billy and discuss my writing a book that would be a truthful replay of my life—and obviously he was a major chapter in my life—and I wanted to set the record straight.

"Doc, you write your book," he told me. "You singlehandedly, by representing me and others, and your involvement with the USFL, did more to boost all players salaries than anybody—and you have always been there for me. I encourage you to write a book."

The elegance of honest truth needs no adornment, and reuniting with Billy in 2002 was powerful—and cathartic for both of us. Billy always said, "Doc, together we can make things happen."

I have always believed there is no greater freedom than what you achieve when you call upon your own conscience to give you a brutally honest answer. It is one thing to lie to others—but it is insanity to lie to yourself.

The older we get, the more we are tempted to become simple incumbents— waiting for retirement, or sitting around like a bump on a log—while the real challenge is to reinvent yourself, use your knowledge and experience to assist others or make changes for a better future.

This book was just one leg of a three-legged stool. The second leg was to pass legislation in the State of Texas. Don't Mess with Texas Football (House bill 1123—which I drafted and Governor Rick Perry signed into law). The third leg is to modernize the National Collegiate Athletic Association.

Billy, myself, and many of our friends have agreed to lend our names and support to the modernization of the NCAA.

Stories in real life rarely end where you want them to. They simply end. But I'm proud Billy and I didn't just ride off into the sunset. We've left behind a solid thirty-year body of work: We took on racism, discrimination, corruption, and hypocrisy. We fought the wrongful treatment of athletes, and we created reforms to address the atrocities of the current corrupt culture of the NCAA. We helped reshape the great traditions of college and professional football, and I sleep well now knowing that every day, we are not only working to make the game better, but also blazing a trail that serves as the framework for a new generation of players and fans.

Today, Billy Sims and I share an unshakeable bond. Our reconnection is evidence that forgiveness might be life's greatest currency, and that honor, truth, and integrity are the true agents of a man's character. The next time you pray for a miracle, when you ask for all that is broken to again be made whole, ask yourself, "What is my legacy?"

It's amazing. Once you find it, you stop thinking about it, because you realize you're living it.

APPENDIX

October 20, 1986

Dr. Jerry Argovitz
15 Greenway Place
Suite 23-G
Houston, Texas 77046

Dear Jerry:

Please contact the banks and lending institutions in Houston and Dallas for available properties that would fit the guidelines we have discussed.

Sincerely,

Donald J. Trump

THE TRUMP ORGANIZATION
725 FIFTH AVENUE · NEW YORK, N. Y. 10022   212·832·2000   TELEX·427715

Athletic Scholarship Agreement
For:

_____

This is to certify that the above named student-athlete will be awarded athletically-related financial aid at _____ for the following time period:_____.

Date

The term of the Agreement, as required under NCAA rules, is for a single academic year (fall and spring semesters) unless the specified student-athlete meets specific exceptions within NCAA rules to be awarded for a lesser time period (semester by semester) or the award is for summer school. An award for summer financial aid requires a separate agreement issued on a summer term-by-term basis.

The single academic year award is subject to renewal at the conclusion of the above time period. Renewal of the single academic year award is not automatic for subsequent academic years or semesters.

Eligibility for Award

This award is based on the student-athlete's desire to participate in the athletics program of _____ and is contingent upon the student-athlete qualifying for this financial aid award according to the following criteria:

a. Fulfilling the admissions requirements and meeting academic requirements for participation in athletics competition and receipt of financial aid at _____;

b. Meeting and maintaining eligibility requirements for athletics participation and financial aid established by the NCAA, the Big 12 Conference and _____; and

c. Fulfilling the terms of a contract entered into with _____ that specifies any non-athletic-related requirements (e.g., academic benchmarks, behavior standards) for the student-athlete during the period of the award.

Note: A student-athlete who signs a professional sports contract, accepts money for playing in an athletic contest, or agrees to be represented by a sports agent or other individual marketing the student-athlete's athletics ability, may jeopardize the student-athlete's eligibility to receive athletically-related financial aid under NCAA amateurism regulations.

Bases for Termination of Award

This financial aid award may be terminated during the period of the award at the discretion of the athletics director if the student-athlete:

a. Fails to meet the above "Eligibility for Award" criteria;

b. Renders himself or herself ineligible for intercollegiate competition;

c. Fraudulently misrepresents information on an application, letter of intent or financial aid agreement;

d. Voluntarily withdraws from the athletics program;

e. Refuses to participate in the NCAA, Big 12 Conference, or _____ drug testing programs; or

f. Is found to have engaged in serious misconduct by the Student Judicial Services.

The circumstances listed above also may result in a non-renewal of financial aid at _____ for future academic years. A decision to non-renew athletics aid following the period of this award may also be based on the student-athlete's failure to exhibit a commitment to the achievement of athletics or academic excellence. This financial aid award will not be canceled or reduced during the period of the award on the basis of the student-athlete's athletics ability or because of an injury sustained while participating in practice or competition while under the supervision of a coaching staff member, and if the injury prevents the student-athlete from participating in athletics.

Note: If the financial aid is canceled, reduced or non-renewed for any reason, the student-athlete will be informed of his or her right to pursue an appeal process and campus review. (For incoming student-athletes signing a National Letter of Intent during the designated National Letter of Intent signing periods, it is further understood that this Agreement is null and void if the terms of the National Letter of Intent are not fulfilled.)

Outside Financial Aid

Student-athletes are required to disclose to the Office of Student Financial Services all outside scholarships or aid. The amount of the athletics financial aid award described above may be reduced if the student-athlete applies for and is granted financial aid from other sources which, under NCAA rules, must count in the calculation of athletics scholarship limitations or in circumstances that such reduction is to the benefit of the student-athlete. The athletics financial aid amount may be reduced in order for_____ to maintain NCAA athletics scholarship limits, even if NCAA rules deem it permissible for the student-athlete to receive such outside financial aid. NCAA or federal regulations may prohibit a student-athlete from accepting certain outside aid. In any case, prior to receipt of any outside financial aid, the student-athlete should ensure such financial aid is disbursed to the university and not directly to the student-athlete for verification of permissibility of use.

Note: The Internal Revenue Service requires that scholarship awards are reported as income, other than those applied toward tuition, required fees, and books.

_____   _____

Director of Student Financial Services   Athletics Director

I accept this financial aid award under the conditions listed above and certify that I have not received financial aid or promises of financial aid in excess of that allowed under the regulations of the National Collegiate Athletic Association (NCAA). Both my parents [or legal guardian(s)] and I understand that my failure to meet the specified requirements in this Agreement or my involvement in NCAA rules violations may render this Agreement null or void.

_____   _____

Student Athletes Signature   Date

Copy of a Grant in Aid contract. Read it carefully and see if you can understand it, because most 17- and 18-year-olds can't. Me neither.

DR. JERRY A. ARGOVITZ

730 N. Post Oak Rd., Suite 340 ♦ Houston, Texas 77024 ♦ (713) 682-6822 ♦ Fax (713) 682-6824 ♦ jerryargovitz@comcast.net

August 12, 2011

Dear Jim,

Speaking with you on Tuesday brought me back to those special days we spent together. Having just celebrated my 73rd birthday on July 31, 2011, I realized I am in the 4th quarter of my life. My book is giving me the opportunity to reach out and tell those who have meant so much to me "thanks for the memories."

I knew you were someone very special at the time that I signed you and made you the highest paid player in the game and worth every dime you received. I especially respected your love of family, sharing everything with your mom, dad and brothers. I recognized your great leadership ability, drive and commitment to winning...not just in football but in life as well. I watched you as a young "stud" sow your wild oats to become a dedicated husband and father.

Jim we worked, played and prayed together and I would never compromise our relationship. We always had a line of open communication and at this stage in my life, it saddened me to hear from J. David that you felt you were short-changed with The Gamblers...I personally paid to your attorney $100,000.00 to settle my portion of the claim against The Gamblers (even though The Gamblers legally owed you nothing). I received a release signed by you and your attorney. I was one-third owner and did not leave you out to dry. I never knew what the outcome was regarding Lubetkin and Rouille.

Donald Trump bought out The Gamblers and was responsible for all their past and future obligations. Donald refused to pay you when the league folded and you sued The Gamblers owners for $25 million. The actual amount owed the bank was $250,000...my share—33 1/3 plus Fred Garson's 7%= $100,000...I hope this clarifies any misunderstanding between us...when you signed with the NFL, after playing for the Houston Gamblers for two years and mastering the run and shoot offense—you became the most prolific passer in professional football, you became the highest paid player..again, we should have good memories.

Life has dealt us many tragic hands...my wife Loni lost her son to cancer, you lost Hunter. I will never forget your talk about Hunter at the Gambler reunion. You and Jill are doing God's work in your "Hunters Hope Foundation" which we have supported. I would love to attend one of your motivational sessions, if you let me know where they are being held. You are a natural for this.

I hope you find the right people to get you relief with your back and neck pain. Thank you for sharing with J. David. I truly appreciate the time you gave him. I am looking forward to seeing you and Jill at our home in Rancho Mirage. Please accept our invitation and just let us know what's good for you. We'll have a great time.

Sincerely,

Your friend Jerry

My personal letter to Jim Kelly.